CAMBRIDGE
UNIVERSITY PRESS

Chemistry

for Cambridge International AS & A Level

WORKBOOK

Roger Norris

CAMBRIDGE
UNIVERSITY PRESS

Shaftesbury Road, Cambridge CB2 8EA, United Kingdom

One Liberty Plaza, 20th Floor, New York, NY 10006, USA

477 Williamstown Road, Port Melbourne, VIC 3207, Australia

314–321, 3rd Floor, Plot 3, Splendor Forum, Jasola District Centre, New Delhi – 110025, India

103 Penang Road, #05–06/07, Visioncrest Commercial, Singapore 238467

Cambridge University Press is part of the University of Cambridge.

It furthers the University's mission by disseminating knowledge in the pursuit of
education, learning and research at the highest international levels of excellence.

www.cambridge.org
Information on this title: www.cambridge.org/9781108859059

© Cambridge University Press & Assessment 2020

First published in 2016

20 19 18 17 16 15 14 13 12 11 10 9 8 7

Printed in the Netherlands by Wilco BV

A catalogue record for this publication is available from the British Library

ISBN 978-1-108-85905-9 Workbook with Digital Access

....

....

DEDICATED TEACHER AWARDS

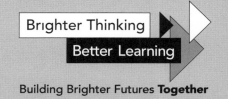

⟩ Contents

> How to use this series

This suite of resources supports learners and teachers following the Cambridge International AS & A Level Chemistry syllabus (9701). All of the books in the series work together to help students develop the necessary knowledge and scientific skills required for this subject.

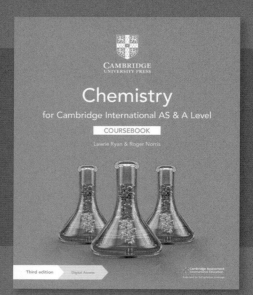

The coursebook provides comprehensive support for the full Cambridge International AS & A Level Chemistry syllabus (9701). It clearly explains facts, concepts and practical techniques, and uses real world examples of scientific principles. Two chapters provide full guidance to help learners develop investigative skills. Questions within each chapter help them to develop their understanding, while exam-style questions provide essential practice.

The workbook contains over 100 exercises and exam-style questions, carefully constructed to help learners develop the skills that they need as they progress through their Chemistry course.
The exercises also help learners develop understanding of the meaning of various command words used in questions, and provide practice in responding appropriately to these.

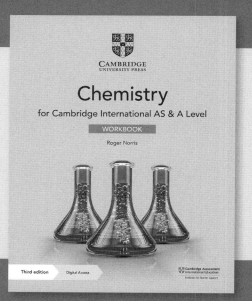

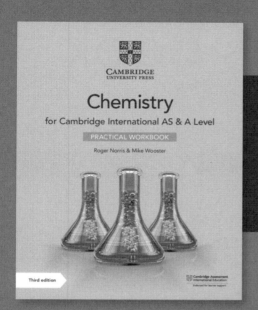

This write-in book provides learners with a wealth of hands-on practical work, giving them full guidance and support that will help them to develop all of the essential investigative skills. These skills include planning investigations, selecting and handling apparatus, creating hypotheses, recording and displaying results, and analysing and evaluating data.

The teacher's resource supports and enhances the materials in the coursebook, workbook and practical workbook. It includes answers for every question and exercise in these three books. It also includes detailed lesson ideas, teaching notes for each topic area including a suggested teaching plan, ideas for active learning and formative assessment, links to resources, ideas for lesson starters and plenaries, differentiation, lists of common misconceptions and ideas for homework activities. The practical teacher's guide, included with this resource, contains detailed support for preparing and carrying out all of the investigations in the practical workbook, including tips for getting things to work well, and a set of sample results that can be used if students cannot do the experiment or fail to collect results.

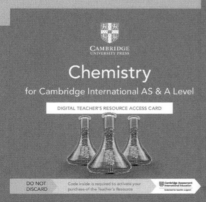

> How to use this book

Throughout this book, you will notice lots of different features that will help your learning. These are explained here.

CHAPTER OUTLINE

A chapter outline appears at the start of every chapter to introduce the learning aims and help you navigate the content.

Exercises

Exercises help you to practice skills that are important for studying AS and A Level Chemistry.

TIP

Tip boxes will help you complete the exercises, and give you support in areas that you might find difficult.

EXAM-STYLE QUESTIONS

Questions at the end of each chapter are more demanding exam-style questions, some of which may require use of knowledge from previous chapters. Answers to these questions can be found in the digital version of the Workbook.

KEY WORDS

Key vocabulary is highlighted in the text when it is first introduced. Definitions are then given in the margin, which explain the meanings of these words and phrases.

You will also find definitions of these words in the Glossary at the back of this book.

COMMAND WORD

Command words that appear in the syllabus and might be used in exams are highlighted in the exam-style questions when they are first introduced. In the margin, you will find the Cambridge International definition.

You will also find the same definitions in the Glossary at the back of this book. *

* The information in this section is taken from the Cambridge International syllabus for examination from 2022. You should always refer to the appropriate syllabus document for the year of your examination to confirm the details and for more information. The syllabus document is available on the Cambridge International website at www.cambridgeinternational.org.

⟩ Introduction

This Workbook has been written to help you develop the skills you need to succeed in your Cambridge International AS & A Level Chemistry course (9701). The exercises in this Workbook will provide opportunities for you to practise the following skills:

- understand the scientific phenomena and theories that you are studying

- solve numerical and other problems

- think critically about experimental techniques and data

- make predictions and use scientific reasons to support your predictions.

This book is in four parts:

- Chapters 1 –18 (AS Level content, covered in the first year of the course).

- Chapters 19 –30 (A Level content)

- Chapter P1 and P2 dedicated to the development of practical skills and developing your ability to plan, analyse and evaluate practical investigations

- Appendices including a Periodic Table and selected standard electrode potentials.

The exercises are designed to help you develop your knowledge, skills and understanding and topics covered in the Coursebook. (The Workbook does not cover all topics in the Cambridge International AS & A Level Chemistry syllabus (9701)). An introduction at the start of each exercise tells you which skills you will be working with as you answer the questions. The exercises are arranged in the same order as the chapters in your Coursebook. At the end of each chapter a set of exam-style questions are provided to further support the skills you have practised in that chapter. They also provide a valuable opportunity to become familiar with the type of assessment you are likely to meet in your exams.

We hope that this book not only supports you to succeed in your future studies and career, but will also stimulate your interest and your curiosity in chemistry.

> Chapter 1
Atomic structure

CHAPTER OUTLINE

In this chapter you will learn how to:

- describe the structure of the atom and the relative charges and masses of protons, neutrons and electrons

- describe how protons, neutrons and electrons behave in electric fields

- deduce the number of protons, neutrons and electrons in atoms and ions

- define proton (atomic) number, mass (nucleon) number and isotopes

- explain why isotopes have the same chemical properties but some of their physical properties are different

- use the symbolism $_y^x$A for isotopes.

Exercise 1.1 Atomic structure

This exercise will familiarise you with the properties of the three types of subatomic particle.

TIP

Remember to read the stem of the question carefully. Here it states that some words can be used more than once.

Copy and complete these sentences using words from this list. Some words may be used more than once.

electron	negative	neutrons	positively	protons
	relative	shells		

An atom contains a dense **nucleus** surrounded by _____ of **electrons**. The

nucleus contains the nucleons (_____ and _____). **Protons** are

_____ charged, electrons have a _____ charge and _____

are uncharged. The _____ and **neutrons** have the same _____ mass.

The mass of an _____ is negligible (hardly anything).

KEY WORDS

nucleus: the dense core at the centre of an atom containing neutrons (except the ^{1}H isotope) and protons.

electron: negatively charged particle found in orbitals outside the nucleus of an atom. It has negligible mass compared with a proton.

proton: positively charged particle in the nucleus of an atom.

neutron: uncharged particle in the nucleus of an atom, with the same relative mass as a proton.

Exercise 1.2 Terms used in atomic structure

This exercise will familiarise you with some terms related to atomic structure.

Match the boxes 1 to 4 on the left with the descriptions A to D on the right.

1	**Atomic number**	**A**	The tiny central core of the atom
2	**Mass number**	**B**	The number of protons plus neutrons in the nucleus
3	**Neutrons**	**C**	The number of protons in the nucleus of an atom
4	**Nucleus**	**D**	Uncharged particles in the nucleus

> **TIP**
>
> It is important that you learn the exact meanings of scientific words such as *mass number* and key definitions such as *isotopes*.
>
> When defining terms, you must be precise.

Exercise 1.3 Isotopes

This exercise will familiarise you with the concept of **isotopes** and help you deduce the number of particular subatomic particles in an atom.

> **TIP**
>
> Number of neutrons = mass number − atomic number

a Deduce the number of protons and electrons or neutrons represented by the letters A to F.

Isotope	Number of protons	Number of electrons	Number of neutrons
$^{86}_{36}$Kr	36	A	50
$^{115}_{49}$In	B	49	C
$^{50}_{24}$Cr	D	E	F

Table 1.1: Isotopes.

> **KEY WORD**
>
> **isotope:** atoms of the same element with different mass numbers. They have the same number of protons but a different number of neutrons. Note that the word 'atom' is essential in this definition.

> **TIP**
>
> The top number in an isotopic formula is the number of protons + neutrons and the bottom number is the proton number.

b Here is a 'cell' of the Periodic Table:

38
Sr
87.6

i   Explain why the relative atomic mass is not a whole number.

ii An isotope of strontium has a nucleon number of 90. How many neutrons are there in this isotope?

iii Explain in terms of the charge on the subatomic particles why the strontium ion has a 2+ charge.

c   How many protons, neutrons and electrons do the following species have?

i $^{27}_{13}\text{Al}$

ii $^{133}_{55}\text{Cs}^{+}$

iii $^{17}_{8}\text{O}^{2-}$

Exercise 1.4 The discovery of the nucleus

This exercise explores how the nucleus was discovered and will familiarise you with the behaviour of charged particles.

TIP
When answering questions about unfamiliar material, always: • Read the information carefully, noting down the key points.   • Take note of the command words such as explain and suggest. The definitions are given in the glossary if you're not sure what these mean.

In 1910, researchers in Manchester, UK, fired alpha-particles (α-particles) at thin sheets of gold foil. Some of the α-particles passed straight through the foil (course A in Figure 1.1). Others were deflected slightly (course B). About 1 in every 20 000 was deflected backwards (course C).

a   Alpha-particles are helium nuclei. Helium atoms have 2 protons and 2 neutrons. Write the isotopic symbol for a helium nucleus.

b   Suggest, in terms of the structure of the atoms, why most α-particles passed straight through the foil.

c   Explain why some α-particles were deflected slightly.

d   Suggest, in terms of the structure of the atoms, why so few α-particles were deflected backwards.

e   Suggest what would happen in this experiment if a beam of neutrons were fired at the gold foil. Explain your answer.

f   Explain why two different isotopes of helium have different densities.

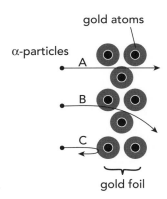

Figure 1.1: Alpha-particles are fired at gold foil.

EXAM-STYLE QUESTIONS

1 This question is about isotopes and subatomic particles. The diagram in Figure 1.2 shows the structure of an isotope of lithium.

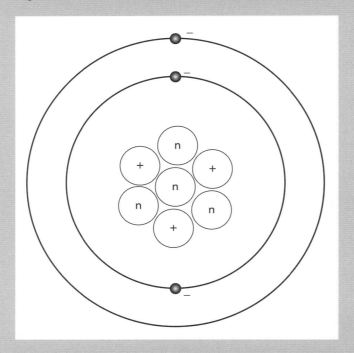

Figure 1.2

a **Describe** the number, charge and relative mass of each subatomic particle present. [5]

b Explain why two different isotopes of lithium have the same chemical properties. [1]

c Write the isotopic symbol for the lithium atom shown. [2]

d Explain why a lithium ion is positively charged. [1]

[Total: 9]

2 Cobalt and nickel are next to each other in the Periodic Table.

27	28
Co	Ni
58.9	58.7

a Which one of these elements has the higher atomic number? Explain your answer. [1]

b **Suggest** why nickel has a lower relative atomic mass than cobalt. [3]

CONTINUED

Explain: set out purposes or reasons / make the relationships between things evident / provide why and/or how and support with relevant evidence.

c The isotopic symbols of two isotopes are:

$^{59}_{27}\text{Co}$ $^{58}_{28}\text{Ni}$

  i Which one of these isotopes has a greater number of neutrons? **Explain** your answer. [1]

  ii Which one of these isotopes has fewer electrons? Explain your answer. [1]

  iii An ion of cobalt has 27 protons and 24 electrons. Give the symbol for this ion. [1]

d A beam of electrons is fired through an electric field between two charged plates.

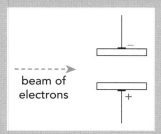

Figure 1.3

Describe how the electron beam behaves when it passes through the plates. Explain your answer. [3]

[Total: 10]

> Chapter 2
Electrons in atoms

In this chapter you will learn how to:

- use and understand the terms shells, sub-shells, orbitals, principal quantum number, *n*.

- describe the number and relative energies of s, p and d orbitals for quantum shells 1, 2 and 3 and the 4s and 4p orbitals

- explain the electron configuration in terms of energy of the electrons and inter-electron repulsion

- describe the shapes of s and 2p orbitals

- describe the electronic configuration of atoms and ions, e.g. $1s^2 2s^2 2p^6$

- use and understand the 'electrons in boxes' notation, e.g.

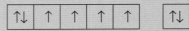

- use and define the term first ionisation energy (IE_1) and understand the factors which influence its value (nuclear charge, atomic / ionic radius, shielding, spin-pair repulsion)

- construct equations to represent first, second and subsequent ionisation energies

- use ionisation energy data to explain trends in periods and groups in the Periodic Table

- describe and explain the variations in atomic radius and ionic radius across a period and down a group

- interpret successive ionisation energy data

- describe free radicals as a species with one or more unpaired electrons.

Exercise 2.1 Electron shells and sub-shells

This exercise is designed to support your understanding of electron shells and **sub-shells**. It also gives practice at deducing and interpreting **electron configurations**.

Make sure that you learn the order of the filling of the electrons in quantum shells, especially from the 3rd energy level onwards.

For groups 1 and 2, the number of electrons in the outer **principal quantum shell** of an uncharged atom is equal to the group number. For groups 13–18, it is the sum (group number − 10).

a The table gives information about electron shells and atomic orbitals. Deduce the numbers and types of **atomic orbitals** represented by the letters **A** to **F**.

Principal quantum shell	Maximum number of electrons in principal quantum shell	Number of sub-shells in principal quantum shell	Types of orbital present
1	**A**	1	**B**
2	8	**C**	2s, 2p
3	**D**	**E**	**F**

Table 2.1: Electron shells and atomic orbitals.

b The table shows the electron configuration of some atoms and ions. Deduce the missing information represented by the numerals **i** to **vii**.

Proton number	Symbol	Electronic configuration
9	F	**i**
14	**ii**	$1s^22s^22p^63s^23p^2$
24	Cr	**iii**
11	Na^+	**iv**
v	K	$1s^22s^22p^63s^23p^64s^1$
35	**vi**	$[Ar]3d^{10}4s^24p^6$
22	Ti^{2+}	**vii**

Table 2.2: Electronic configurations.

c To which group do the atoms with these electron configurations belong?

i $1s^22s^22p^63s^2$

ii $1s^22s^22p^3$

iii $1s^22s^22p^63s^23p^5$

iv $1s^22s^22p^63s^23p^6$

KEY WORDS

electronic configuration: a way of representing the arrangement of the electrons in atoms showing the principal quantum shells, the sub-shells and the number of electrons present, e.g. $1s^22s^22p^3$. The electrons may also be shown in boxes.

principal quantum shells: the main energy levels in the atoms where electrons have particular amounts of energy. The first quantum shell can hold a maximum of 2 electrons, the second 8 and the third 18.

atomic orbitals: regions of space outside the nucleus that can be occupied by a maximum of two electrons. Orbitals are named s, p, d and f. They have different shapes.

Exercise 2.2 Ionisation energies and the Periodic Table

This exercise will familiarise you with the factors that influence the values of the **first ionisation energy** (IE_1). It will also provide practice in interpreting graphs.

KEY WORDS

first ionisation energy, IE_1: the energy needed to remove 1 mole of electrons from 1 mole of atoms of an element in the gaseous state to form 1 mole of gaseous ions.

The graph shows the first ionisation energies, IE_1, of successive elements A to M in the Periodic Table.

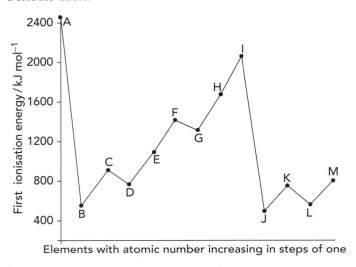

Figure 2.1: First ionisation energies of successive elements.

a   Copy and complete these sentences using words from this list.

attractive	charge	electrons	increase	inner	ionisation
		nucleus	principal		

Across a period, there is a general _____ in the value of IE_1. This is because of the increase in nuclear _____. Across a period the electrons are added to the same _____ quantum shell so the _____ forces between the _____ and the outer electrons increase gradually. So the first _____ energy increases gradually. Across a period, there is not much difference in shielding because there are the same number of _____ shell _____.

b   Which two elements A to M are noble gases?

c   Between which two consecutive elements do these statements apply?

  i   When a new period starts, there is a sharp decrease in IE_1. This is because the next electron added is in a principal quantum shell further from the nucleus.

ii   When the atomic number increases by one, there is a decrease in IE_1 due to **spin-pair repulsion**.

iii   When the atomic number increases by one there is a decrease in IE_1 because the next electron goes into a p sub-shell.

d   Which two elements are in Group 2?

e   Which element is in the same group as element M?

f   Which element is in Group 17?

g   What evidence is there from the graph that the value of IE_1 decreases down a group?

Exercise 2.3 Successive ionisation energies

This exercise will familiarise you with concept of **successive ionisation energies**, IE_1, IE_2, etc. and electron configurations. It will give you further practice in interpreting graphs.

> **TIP**
>
> When plotting ionisation energy against number of electrons removed, there is a large increase in ionisation energy when an electron is removed from the next energy level towards the nucleus.

The graph shows the successive ionisation energies of sodium plotted against the number of electrons removed.

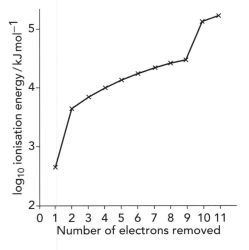

Figure 2.2: Successive ionisation energies of sodium.

a   State how this graph shows that a sodium atom has:

i   one electron which is easily removed

ii   two electrons in the first principal quantum shell

iii   eight electrons in the second principal quantum shell.

TIP

For part **g**, look for the repeating pattern.

KEY WORDS

spin-pair repulsion: a pair of electrons in the same orbital repel each other because they have the same charge. Pairing the spinning electrons so they spin in opposite directions reduces the repulsion. The repulsion is more than that of single electrons in separate orbitals. That is why the electrons in the p and d orbitals go into separate orbitals before being paired up.

successive ionisation energies: the energy required in each step to remove the first electron, then the second, then the third, and so on from a gaseous atom or ion, e.g. IE_1, IE_2, IE_3. Note: you should be able to write equations for each of these steps.

TIPS

In successive ionisation energies, the electrons are removed one at a time.

Don't worry about the $\log_{10}$ scale in the graph. It just helps make the values fit on the graph.

TIPS

When writing equations showing successive ionisation energies remember that:

- they are shown by the charge on the ion formed, e.g. $Na^{4+}(g) \rightarrow Na^{5+}(g) + e^-$ represents the fifth ionisation energy.
- the ions formed are always positive and gaseous.

b The equation below represents the first ionisation energy of sodium.

$$Na(g) \rightarrow Na^+(g) + e^-$$

Write equations for:

i The fourth ionisation energy of calcium

ii The second ionisation energy of phosphorus.

KEY WORDS

electrons in boxes notation: shows each orbital s, p_x, p_y, p_z, etc. as a box. The boxes are arranged vertically in sets of increasing energy levels, e.g., 1s = 1 box, 2p = 3 boxes higher up.

Exercise 2.4 Electrons in orbitals

This exercise gives you further practice in deducing electron configurations and interpreting diagrams showing the direction of electron spin.

TIP

When adding electrons to sub-shells:

- electrons are put one by one into separate orbitals and spin in the same direction
- electrons are only paired when no more empty orbitals in the sub-shell are available.

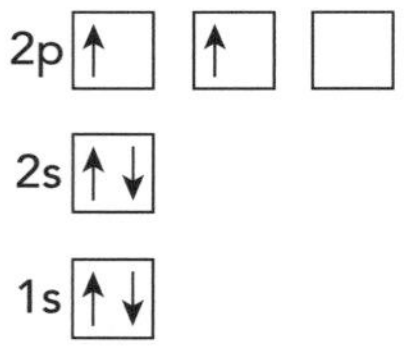

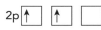

Figure 2.3: The arrangement of electrons in atomic orbitals in a carbon atom.

Figure 2.3 shows the arrangement of electrons in atomic orbitals and the direction of their spin as **electrons in boxes notation**.

a How does this diagram show that:

i in the second quantum shell, the electrons in p orbitals have more energy than the electrons in an s orbital

ii the electrons in an orbital spin in an opposite direction?

b Draw similar diagrams to show the arrangement and spin of electrons in atoms of:

i oxygen

ii chlorine

iii phosphorus.

c Sulfur has one more proton in its nucleus than phosphorus but the value of its first ionisation energy is lower than that of phosphorus. Explain why in terms of repulsions between electrons.

TIP

Remember, electrons repel each other because they have the same charge.

Exercise 2.5 Interpreting line emission spectra

This exercise introduces you to how line emission spectra are used to find information about **energy levels** in atoms. It also provides practice in interpreting information.

Electrons are arranged in energy levels a certain distance from the nucleus of an atom. An electron can jump from a lower to a higher energy level when given a specific amount of energy (quantum of energy). When the electrons fall from higher to lower energy levels, they give off radiation of particular frequencies. The radiation can be recorded as lines in a line emission spectrum. Each line represents a particular **frequency** of radiation. The higher the frequency, the greater the energy associated with the radiation.

Part of a line emission spectrum is shown here, together with the electron energy levels.

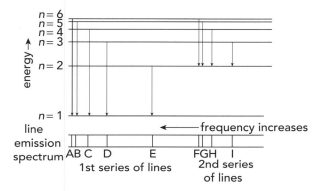

Figure 2.4: Part of a line emission spectrum and the corresponding electron energy levels.

a In the diagram, what do the letters n represent?

b Describe how the spacing of each series of lines changes as the frequency increases.

c What do the vertical arrows represent?

d Which line in the spectrum represents the greatest energy change?

e Which line in the spectrum represents the smallest energy change?

f What happens to the distance between the energy levels as they get further from the nucleus?

g Which line represents an electron falling from the fourth energy level to the second energy level?

h Suggest, using information in the diagram, why the first ionisation energy of lithium is much lower than the first ionisation energy of hydrogen.

EXAM-STYLE QUESTIONS

1 Boron (atomic number 5) and gallium (atomic number 31) are in the same group in the Periodic Table.

   a Write the electronic configuration using $1s^2$ notation for:

      i a boron atom **[1]**

      ii a gallium atom **[1]**

      iii a gallium ion. **[1]**

   b Is a gallium ion larger or smaller than a gallium atom? Explain your answer. **[1]**

   c Which atom, boron or gallium, has the lower first ionisation energy? Explain your answer. **[3]**

   d **i** **Compare** the first ionisation energies of beryllium, boron and carbon and explain why boron has the lowest first ionisation energy of these three atoms. **[6]**

      ii Write an equation to represent the first ionisation energy of boron. **[2]**

   e Gallium has both s and p-type orbitals. Draw the shape of each of these orbitals. **[2]**

[Total: 17]

2 Chromium(III) chloride contains Cr^{3+} and Cl^- ions.

   a Write the electronic configuration using $1s^2$ notation for:

      i a chloride ion **[1]**

      ii a chromium atom **[1]**

      iii a chromium(III) ion. **[1]**

   b **Identify** the element whose atoms have the same electronic configuration as a chloride ion. **[1]**

   c Fluorine is in the same group as chlorine.

     Figure 2.5 shows the $\log_{10}$ ionisation energy against the number of electrons removed from the fluorine atom.

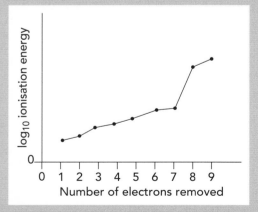

Figure 2.5: The change in ionisation energies as electrons are removed from a fluorine atom.

TIP

In parts **1 c** and **d**, you need to think about what governs ionisation energy and the type of sub-shell.

COMMAND WORD

Compare: identify/comment on similarities and/or differences.

COMMAND WORD

Identify: name/select/recognise.

TIP

For these questions, think about the electronic configuration when you remove the electrons one by one and what governs ionisation energy.

CONTINUED

    i Explain why there is a gradual rise in the successive ionisation energies during the removal of the first 7 electrons. [3]

    ii Explain why there is a sharp rise in ionisation energy when the eighth electron is removed. [3]

    iii Write the equation which represents the third ionisation energy of fluorine. [2]

                        [Total: 12]

3 The table shows the first five successive ionisation energies of four metallic elements, A to D.

Element	IE_1 / kJ mol^{-1}	IE_2 / kJ mol^{-1}	IE_3 / kJ mol^{-1}	IE_4 / kJ mol^{-1}	IE_5 / kJ mol^{-1}
A	578	1817	2745	11 578	14 831
B	496	4563	6913	9544	13 352
C	419	3051	4412	5877	7975
D	590	1145	4912	6474	8144

Table 2.3

a **Define** the term *first ionisation energy*. [2]

b Which two elements are in the same group of the Periodic Table? Explain your answer. [2]

c Which element requires most energy to convert one mole of its atoms to one mole of ions with a charge of 2+? [1]

d Which element, when it reacts, forms an ion with a charge of 3+? Explain your answer. [4]

e Suggest a value for the sixth ionisation energy of element C. Give a reason for your answer. [3]

f Vanadium is a transition metal.

    i Write the electronic configuration of vanadium using $1s^2$ notation. [1]

    ii Write the equation which represents the second ionisation energy of vanadium. [2]

g An atom has the atomic number 16. Draw a diagram of electrons in their orbitals at different energy levels (electrons in boxes notation) to show the electron arrangement in this atom. **Show** the spins of the electrons. [3]

                        [Total: 18]

4 The atomic and ionic radii show a periodic variation.

a Describe how the **atomic radius** varies across a period. Explain your answer. [3]

b Describe how the ionic radius varies across a period. [3]

TIP

Think about electron spin when answering part **3 g**.

COMMAND WORDS

Define: give precise meaning.

Show: provide structural evidence that leads to a given result.

KEY WORDS

atomic radius: the covalent atomic radius is half the distance between the nuclei of two covalently bonded atoms of the same type. This is not the only type of atomic radius but it gives us the best data when comparing the elements across a period.

TIPS

When answering questions about trends, you need to use comparative terms, e.g. greater radius.

Think about factors such as nuclear charge and shielding when answering question **4 a**.

CONTINUED

c   Chlorine, bromine and iodine are halogens. Explain why the atomic radius of the halogen atoms increases down the group.   [3]

d   When a molecule of chlorine is exposed to sunlight, it breaks down to form free radicals.

   i   Explain what is meant by the term **free radical**.   [1]

   ii **Give** the electronic configuration of a chlorine free radical.   [1]

[Total: 11]

KEY WORDS

free radical: a species with one (or sometimes more than one) unpaired electron.

COMMAND WORD

Give: produce an answer from a given source or recall/ memory.

Chapter 3

Atoms, molecules and stoichiometry

In this chapter you will learn how to:

- define and use the terms relative atomic mass, isotopic mass, formula mass and mole based on the Avogadro number

- name and write formulae of ionic compounds (by remembering the formulae NO_3^-, CO_3^{2-}, SO_4^{2-}, OH^-, NH_4^+, Zn^{2+}, Ag^+, HCO_3^- and PO_4^{3-})

- predict ionic charge from the position of an element in the Periodic Table

- analyse mass spectra in terms of isotopic abundances

- find the molecular mass of an organic molecule from the molecular ion peak in a mass spectrum

- suggest the identity of molecules formed by simple fragmentation in a given mass spectrum

- deduce the number of carbon atoms in a compound using the $M + 1$ peak and the relevant formula

- deduce the presence of chlorine and bromine atoms in a compound using the $M + 2$ peak

- write and construct balanced equations, including ionic equations

- use the correct state symbols in equations

- define and deduce empirical and molecular formulae using given data

- understand and use the terms anhydrous, hydrated and water of crystallisation

- perform calculations, including use of the mole concept (reacting masses, percentage yield, use of molar gas volume, volumes and concentrations of solutions, limiting and excess reagent)

- understand the term stoichiometry and deduce stoichiometric relationships from calculations involving reacting masses, volumes of gases and volumes and concentrations of solutions.

Exercise 3.1 Definitions

This exercise will familiarise you with some important definitions about relative masses, moles and the **Avogadro constant**.

KEY WORDS

Avogadro constant, *L*: the number of specified particles (atoms, ions, molecules or electrons) in a mole of those particles. Its numerical value is 6.02×10^{23}.

Copy and complete these sentences using words from the list.

adding	average	Avogadro	atom	carbon	formula	grams	isotope
masses	mole	sample	twelfth	unified	unit	weighted	

We compare the mass of atoms using the _____ atomic mass unit. This is defined as one _____ of the mass of an _____ of _____ -12. Relative atomic mass (A_r) is the _____ average mass of atoms in a given _____ of an element compared to the value of the unified atomic mass unit.

The number of atoms in exactly 12 _____ of the isotope carbon-12 is called the _____ constant. Its value is 6.02×10^{23} mol^{-1}. So there are 6.02×10^{23} atoms of carbon in 12 g of the carbon-12 _____. A _____ is the amount of substance which contains 6.02×10^{23} specified particles (atoms, molecules, ions or electrons).

Relative molecular mass (M_r) is the weighted _____ mass of a molecule compared to the value of the unified atomic mass _____. Relative molecular mass is found by _____ together the relative atomic _____ of all the atoms in the molecule. For ionic compounds we use the term relative _____ mass.

TIP

Learn definitions carefully. You will see an alternative definition of relative atomic mass in some books:

The weighted average mass of a molecule on a scale on which an atom of the ^{12}C isotope has a mass of exactly 12 units.

It is easier to remember the definition based on the unified atomic mass unit.

Exercise 3.2 Compounds and formulae

This exercise will familiarise you with the names and formulae of some **ions** that you have to learn. You will also learn how you can use these ions to deduce the formula of a **compound**. It introduces you to the terms hydrated and anhydrous.

a Write formulae for these ions:
  i hydrogencarbonate **ii** hydroxide **iii** sulfate **iv** silver

b Name these ions:
  i NH_4^+ **ii** PO_4^{3-} **iii** NO_3^- **iv** CO_3^{2-}

c Use ideas about ionic charge and the combining power (**oxidation numbers**) of the elements in the Periodic Table to write formulae for these compounds:
  i carbon dioxide **ii** magnesium oxide
  iii calcium nitride **iv** aluminium sulfide

KEY WORDS

ion: a substance formed when an atom or molecule gains or loses one or more electrons.

compound: a substance containing atoms from two or more different elements which are chemically bonded (joined) together.

d Write the formulae of these compounds by balancing the charge on the positive and negative ions.

   i ammonium sulfate   **ii** zinc nitrate
   iii silver phosphate   **iv** calcium hydroxide

e Here is a reaction:

$$NiSO_4(s) + 7H_2O(l) \rightarrow NiSO_4 \cdot 7H_2O(s)$$

   yellow nickel sulfate   green nickel sulfate

   i Write the formula of the **hydrated salt**.
   ii What is the general name given to salts which are not hydrated?
   iii What is the name given to the water in $NiSO_4 \cdot 7H_2O(s)$?
   iv Suggest how you could change green nickel sulfate to yellow nickel sulfate.

KEY WORDS

oxidation number (oxidation state): a number given to an atom or ion in a compound to show how oxidised or reduced it is.

hydrated salt: a salt which contains water of crystallisation.

TIPS

When naming compounds, change the ending -ine to -ide, e.g. bromine (element) to bromide (in a compound).

Compounds containing oxygen in addition to two other elements end in -ate.

Oxidation numbers for metals are the same as the charge on the ion. For simple non-metals ions, the sum (group number − 18) gives you the oxidation number, e.g. O in compounds is 16 − 18 = −2

Exercise 3.3 Mole calculations

This exercise will familiarise you with some basic calculations using the mole concept.

TIP

$$\text{moles} = \frac{\text{mass (in g)}}{\text{molar mass (in g mol}^{-1})}$$

You may need to rearrange this formula for some questions.

a Lead oxide, Pb_3O_4, is reduced by heating with excess carbon.

   $$Pb_3O_4 + 4C \rightarrow 3Pb + 4CO$$

   Use the following method to calculate the maximum mass of lead formed when 41.12 g of Pb_3O_4 is reduced.

   Calculate:

   i The molar mass of Pb_3O_4 (A_r values: Pb = 207.2, O = 16.0.)
   ii The amount in moles of Pb_3O_4 (to 3 significant figures).
   iii The amount in moles of lead produced.
   iv Mass of lead produced (to 3 significant figures).

TIP

The number of significant figures in your answer should be the same as the least number of significant figures in the data.

Do not round to the correct number of significant figures in the middle of a calculation – only at the end.

b 35.61 g of tin, Sn, reacts with exactly 42.60 g of chlorine, Cl_2, to form 78.21 g of tin(IV) chloride, $SnCl_4$.

    i Calculate the number of moles of tin, chlorine and tin chloride. (A_r values: Sn = 118.7, Cl = 35.5)

    ii Deduce the **stoichiometry** of the reaction.

    iii Write a balanced equation for the reaction.

> **KEY WORD**
>
> **stoichiometry:** the mole ratios of reactants and products shown in a balanced equation.

Exercise 3.4 Deducing formulae and composition by mass

This exercise will help you deduce empirical formulae and molecular formulae as well as percentage composition by mass.

a   **i** Explain why the formula $C_6H_{10}Cl_2$ is *not* an **empirical formula**.

    ii A compound of phosphorus has the empirical formula $PNCl_2$. The relative molecular mass of this compound is 348. Deduce the **molecular formula** of this compound.

b When 14.98 g of arsenic are completely combusted, 19.78 g of an oxide of arsenic are formed. Calculate:

    i The mass of oxygen in this oxide of arsenic.

    ii The amount in moles of atoms of arsenic and oxygen which combine. (A_r values: As = 74.9, O = 16.0)

    iii The empirical formula.

c The molar mass of this oxide of arsenic is 395.6 g. Deduce the molecular formula of this oxide of arsenic.

d The empirical formula of another oxide of arsenic is As_2O_5. Calculate the percentage by mass of arsenic in As_2O_5. Give your answer to 3 significant figures.

> **KEY WORDS**
>
> **empirical formula:** the simplest whole number ratio of the elements present in one molecule or formula unit of the compound.
>
> **molecular formula:** the formula that shows the number and type of each atom in a molecule e.g. the molecular formula for ethanol is C_2H_6O.

> **TIP**
>
> In part **d**, remember that % by mass = atomic mass number of moles of element × molar mass of compound

Exercise 3.5 Using molar gas volume

This exercise helps you use the molar gas volume to deduce the stoichiometry of a reaction.

> **TIP**
>
> The volume of one mole of gas at **r.t.p.** is 24 dm³.
>
> $$\text{Moles of gas} = \frac{\text{volume (in dm}^3)}{24} \quad \text{or} \quad \frac{\text{volume (in cm}^3)}{24\,000}$$

> **KEY WORD**
>
> **r.t.p.:** room temperature and pressure (1 atmosphere / 101 kPa and 20 °C).

a   Calculate the volume, number of moles or mass of gas represented by the letters A to F. (A_r values: P = 31.0, O = 16.0, S = 32.1, H = 1.00)

Gas	Volume of gas	Moles of gas / mol	Mass of gas / g
PH_3	80.0 cm³	**A**	**B**
SO_2	**C** dm³	**D**	8.00 g
O_2	**E** cm³	0.150 mol	**F**

Table 3.1: Using molar gas volume.

b   Two syringes are set up as shown.

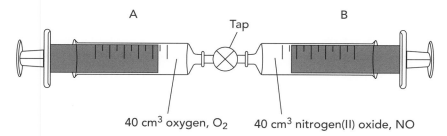

Figure 3.1: A gas syringe experiment.

Small measured volumes of oxygen were pushed from syringe A into syringe B. The product is another gaseous oxide of nitrogen, NO_y. After each addition of oxygen, the tap was closed and the total volume of gases measured. The results are shown here.

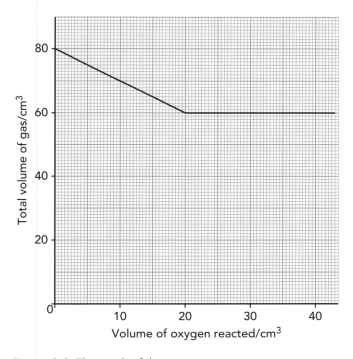

Figure 3.2: The result of the syringe experiment.

i   What volume of oxygen reacts with 40 cm³ of nitrogen(II) oxide?

ii What volume of NO_y is formed?

iii Deduce the formula of NO_y.

iv Write a balanced equation for the reaction.

Exercise 3.6 Solution concentration

This exercise gives you practice in calculating volumes, moles and concentrations. It also revises calculations from **titration** results.

> **TIP**
>
> concentration (in mol dm⁻³) = $\dfrac{\text{number of moles of solute (in mol)}}{\text{volume of solution (in dm}^3\text{)}}$
>
> In some questions you will have to rearrange this equation.

a   Deduce the values represented by the letters **R** to **V**.
    (A_r values: Na = 23.0, O = 16.0, Cl = 35.5, H = 1.0)

Solute	Moles or mass of solute	Volume of solution	Concentration of solution
$CuSO_4$	0.12 mol	200 cm³	**R**
HCl	**S** mol	1.5 dm³	0.4 mol dm⁻³
$ZnCl_2$	0.25 mol	**T** cm³	0.05 mol dm⁻³
NaOH	5.4 g	150 cm³	**U**
NaCl	**V** g	0.20 dm³	2.0 mol dm⁻³

Table 3.2: Solution concentration.

b   20.0 cm³ of a solution of barium hydroxide, $Ba(OH)_2$, is exactly neutralised by 35.4 cm³ of 0.200 mol dm⁻³ hydrochloric acid.

$$Ba(OH)_2 + 2HCl \rightarrow BaCl_2 + 2H_2O$$

Calculate

i   The amount in moles of HCl.

ii The amount in moles of $Ba(OH)_2$.

iii The concentration of $Ba(OH)_2$. Express your answers to 3 significant figures.

c   A sample of 0.9 g of iron powder is added to 20 cm³ of 1.50 mol dm⁻³ hydrochloric acid.

$$Fe(s) + 2HCl(aq) \rightarrow FeCl_2(aq) + H_2(g)$$

i   Demonstrate by calculation that iron is in **excess**.

ii What is the general name given to the reactant that is not in excess?

> **KEY WORD**
>
> **titration:** a method for finding the amount of substance in a solution by reaction with a known amount of another substance. An indicator is used to show when the substances have reacted exactly (in the correct stoichiometric amounts).

> **KEY WORDS**
>
> **excess (reactant):** a reactant that has more moles than needed to react with a given amount of another reactant. There will be some left unused when the reaction is complete.

> **TIP**
>
> Remember to take into account the stoichiometry in part **c** (1 mol Fe to 2 mol HCl).

Exercise 3.7 Writing equations

This exercise provides practice in balancing equations, including **ionic equations**, as well as the use of **state symbols**.

TIPS

Remember that when writing equations:

- You must not alter the formula of a compound.
- The number of atoms of each type must be the same on each side of the equation.
- Balance only by changing the numbers in front of particular compounds.
- In an ionic equation you do **not** include the spectator ions.

---

a Aqueous barium nitrate, $Ba(NO_3)_2$, reacts with dilute sodium sulfate, Na_2SO_4. A precipitate of barium sulfate is formed as well as one other aqueous compound.

    i Write a balanced equation for this reaction. Include state symbols.

    ii Convert the equation in part **i** into an ionic equation.

    iii Name the **spectator ions** in this reaction.

b 2.50×10^{-2} mol of dilute hydrochloric acid reacts exactly with 1.25×10^{-2} mol of an insoluble oxide of iron. The products are aqueous iron(II) chloride and water.

    Deduce the balanced equation for this reaction. Include state symbols.

c Convert the word equation below into a balanced ionic equation. Include state symbols for the substances at r.t.p. (calcium chloride is soluble in water).

    calcium carbonate + hydrochloric acid $\rightarrow$ calcium chloride + carbon dioxide + water

Exercise 3.8 Accurate relative molecular masses

The **mass spectrometer** gives information about the **isotopic abundance** and the mass of each of the isotopes present in a sample of an element. In this exercise, you will be analysing **mass spectra** and using **relative isotopic masses** to calculate an accurate value for the relative atomic mass of strontium. The latter may not be tested in your exam but it is a simple exercise to show how accurate relative atomic masses are calculated.

KEY WORDS

mass spectrum: the chart obtained from the mass spectrometer showing the isotopic abundance on the *y*-axis and the mass / charge ratio of the particle on the *x*-axis.

relative isotopic mass: the ratio of the mass of a particular isotope of an element to the unified atomic mass unit.

KEY WORDS

ionic equation: a balanced equation showing only those ions, atoms or molecules taking part in the reaction. Spectator ions are not shown. Ionic equations are often written for reactions involving a change in oxidation state.

state symbol: a symbol (sign) placed after each reactant and product in a chemical equation to indicate whether they are solid (s), liquid (l), gas (g) or in aqueous solution (aq).

spectator ions: ions present in a reaction mixture which do not take part in the reaction.

KEY WORDS

mass spectrometer: an instrument for finding the relative abundance of isotopes in an element or to help to identify organic compounds.

isotopic abundance: the proportion of each isotope contained in a sample of the element.

The mass spectrum shows the relative abundance of the isotopes present in a sample of strontium.

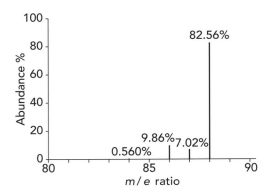

Figure 3.3: The relative abundance of the isotopes in a sample of strontium.

a   Explain the meaning of *m/e* (on the *x*-axis).

b   How many different isotopes are shown in this spectrum?

c   Which is the most abundant isotope?

d   Write the isotopic symbol for the lightest isotope present.

e   Use the following method and the data in the mass spectrum to calculate the relative atomic mass of strontium. Express your answer to 3 significant figures.

   • Multiply each isotopic mass by its % abundance (for the one on the left $84 \times 0.56 = 47.04$)

   • Add these figures together

   • Divide by 100

TIPS

Remember that in part **e** only round to 3 significant figures after you have divided by 100 to get the answer.

The answer is only to 3 significant figures because the data is to 3 significant figures for two of the isotopes.

Exercise 3.9 Mass spectroscopy

This exercise familiarises you with the use of mass spectroscopy in identifying organic compounds and deducing their relative molecular mass. It also revises the use of the **[*M*+1] peak** for determining the number of carbon atoms in a molecule and the **[*M*+2] peak** for determining the isotopes of halogens present in the sample.

KEY WORDS

***M*+1 peak:** the peak seen 1 unit to the right of the molecular ion peak due to the presence of the C-13 isotope.

***M*+2 peak:** the peak seen 2 units to the right of the molecular ion peak due to the presence of the Cl-37 or Br-81 isotope.

> **TIP**
>
> Remember that the [$M+1$] peak is caused by the presence of 1.1% of the ^{13}C isotope in a compound. We can use this to work out the number of C atoms in a molecule using:
>
> $$n = \frac{100}{1.1} \times \frac{\text{abundance } of [M + 1]^+ \text{ ion}}{\text{abundance } of [M]^+ \text{ ion}}$$

Identification of the ions in the **fragmentation** pattern from their mass/charge ratio helps us deduce the structure of the compound. Remember that the ions are *always* positively charged.

a   Deduce the mass/charge ratio of these ions:

   i $[C_3H_7]^+$ **ii** $[C_6H_5]^+$ **iii** $[C_2H_5Cl]^+$ **iv** $[OH]^+$ **v** $[COOH]^+$

b   Suggest which ions have these mass/charge ratios:

   i   43   **ii**   14   **iii**   31   **iv**   29   **v**   91   **vi**   28

c   This diagram shows the mass spectrum of an organic compound.

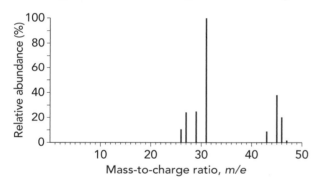

Figure 3.4: The mass spectrum of an organic compound.

   i   Identify the structure of the five ions with the highest abundance.

   ii   Describe how this mass spectrum is consistent with the structure of ethanol.

   iii   The peak at *m/e* 46 is the **molecular ion** peak [M]. What information does this give about the molecule?

d   The molecular ion peak in a mass spectrum has an abundance of 49.3%. The [$M+1$] peak has an abundance of 3.8%. How many carbon atoms are there in the molecule?

e   Naturally occurring chlorine exists as two isotopes with percentage abundance of $^{35}Cl = 75\%$ and $^{37}Cl = 25\%$.

   i   Deduce the *m/e* ratio of the chloroethane molecules, $C_2H_5{}^{35}Cl$ and $C_2H_5{}^{37}Cl$.

   ii   What are the relative heights of these two peaks? Explain your answer.

   iii   How many peaks will be observed above the molecular ion peak for the compound $C_2H_4Cl_2$?

> **KEY WORDS**
>
> **fragmentation:** the breaking up of a covalent compound during mass spectrometry into smaller positively charged species, e.g. $CH_3{}^+$.
>
> **molecular ion:** the ion that is formed by the loss of an electron from the original complete molecule during mass spectrometry. This gives us the relative molecular mass of an unknown compound.

EXAM-STYLE QUESTIONS

1 A sample of 3.60 g of malic acid, $C_2H_4O(CO_2H)_2$, was dissolved in 20.0 cm^3 of distilled water. The solution was titrated with 0.125 mol dm^{-3} aqueous sodium hydroxide.

   a Describe how you would carry out this titration. [4]

   b The equation for the reaction is:

$$C_2H_4O(COOH)_2 + 2NaOH \rightarrow C_2H_4O(COONa)_2 + 2H_2O$$

     Calculate the volume of aqueous sodium hydroxide used. Express your answer to 3 significant figures. [4]

   c 25 cm^3 of a 0.0125 mol dm^{-3} solution of a metal hydroxide, $X(OH)_y$, was titrated with 0.05 mol dm^{-3} hydrochloric acid. It required 12.5 cm^3 of acid to neutralise the hydroxide.

     Deduce the value of y and write a balanced equation for the reaction. [4]

[Total: 12]

2 a What is meant by the term *Avogadro constant*? [1]

   b How many oxygen atoms are there in 0.0011 g of carbon dioxide? ($L = 6.02 \times 10^{23}$, A_r values: C = 12.0, O = 16.0) [3]

   c 14 cm^3 of butene gas, C_xH_y, reacts with exactly 84 cm^3 of oxygen. 56 cm^3 of carbon dioxide is formed. Deduce the formula of butene. Show all working. [4]

   d i A compound has the following percentage composition by mass: C 37.25%, H 7.75%, Cl 55%. Deduce the empirical formula. [3]

      ii What further information is needed to deduce the molecular formula of this compound? [1]

   e State the meaning of the term *molecular formula*. [1]

[Total: 13]

3 The table shows the relative abundances of the four naturally occurring isotopes of iron.

Isotopic mass	Relative abundance
54	5.840
56	91.680
57	2.170
58	0.310

Table 3.3

   a Calculate the relative atomic mass of iron to 3 significant figures. [3]

   b Limonite is a mineral with the formula $Fe_2O_3 \cdot H_2O$. Calculate the percentage by mass of iron in limonite. [3]

TIP

When doing calculations, make sure you show all your working. Remember not to round to the correct number of significant figures until the end of the calculation.

TIPS

For part **2 b**, you need to calculate the number of atoms not molecules.

Equal volumes of gases have equal numbers of moles of molecules.

TIP

Make sure you show all your working clearly.

CONTINUED

   c i Calculate the maximum mass of iron formed when 798 g of iron(III) oxide, Fe_2O_3, is reduced by excess carbon monoxide.

$$Fe_2O_3 + 3CO \rightarrow 2Fe + 3CO_2$$

Express your answer to 3 significant figures.
(A_r values Fe = 55.8, O = 16.0)   **[3]**

     ii Calculate the volume of carbon dioxide formed at r.t.p.   **[2]**

   d A sample of 26.6 g of iron(III) oxide is produced when 60.0 g of iron(II) sulfide is heated strongly in excess air.

$$4FeS_2(s) + 11O_2(g) \rightarrow 2Fe_2O_3(s) + 8SO_2(g)$$

Calculate the **percentage yield** of iron(III) oxide.
(A_r values Fe = 55.8, O = 16.0, S = 32.1)   **[4]**

   e Red hot iron reacts with steam to form Fe_3O_4 and hydrogen. Write a balanced equation for this reaction.   **[2]**

   f Iron reacts with aqueous copper(II) sulfate. The products are copper and aqueous iron(II) sulfate. Construct the ionic equation for this reaction, including state symbols.   **[2]**

                                                          [Total: 19]

KEY WORDS

percentage yield $= \dfrac{\text{actual yield}}{\text{predicted yield}} \times 100$.

> Chapter 4
Chemical bonding

CHAPTER OUTLINE

In this chapter you will learn how to:

- define and describe ionic and covalent bonding (including co-ordinate bonding) in a variety of compounds

- describe how some atoms in Period 3 can expand their octet of electrons

- use dot-and-cross diagrams to show the arrangement of electrons in compounds with ionic, covalent and co-ordinate bonding

- describe, explain and predict the shapes and bond angles in simple molecules using 'valence shell electron pair repulsion' theory (VSEPR)

- describe covalent bonding in terms of orbital overlap giving sigma (σ) and pi (π) bonds

- describe hybridisation of atomic orbitals to form sp, sp^2 and sp^3 orbitals

- define electronegativity and explain the factors influencing the electronegativity values of the elements across a period and down a group

- use differences in the Pauling electronegativity values to predict if a compound has ionic or covalent bonds and to explain bond polarity and dipole moments in molecules

- define the terms bond energy and bond length and use these to compare the reactions of covalent molecules

- describe hydrogen bonding and explain why some physical properties of water are unusual for a molecular compound

- describe and understand the different types of intermolecular forces (van der Waals' forces) as either instantaneous dipoles or permanent dipoles

- describe metallic bonding

- describe the relative bond strengths of ionic, covalent and metallic bonds compared with intermolecular forces.

Exercise 4.1 Ionic bonding and metallic bonding

This exercise will help you develop your understanding of ionic and metallic bonding.

a   i   Copy and complete the **dot-and-cross diagram** for magnesium fluoride. Show electrons originating from the metal atom as a cross (×) and those originating from the non-metal atom as a dot (•).

> **TIP**
>
> In metallic structures:
> - the particles present are metal ions and **delocalised electrons**
> - there are forces of attraction between these particles.

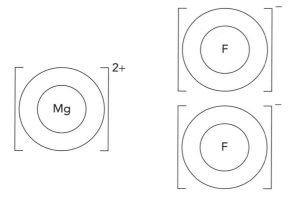

Figure 4.1: Dot-and-cross electron diagram for magnesium fluoride.

ii   Draw dot-and-cross diagrams for:

• lithium chloride

• sodium oxide.

In each case, show all the electrons and their shells.

b   Copy and complete these sentences about bonding, using words from the list.

| atoms   attraction   charge   covalent   directions   ions |

An **ionic bond** is the strong force of electrostatic _____ between positive

and negative _____ in a crystal lattice. The _____ on the ions

is spread out in all _____. It is not like a _____ bond where the

bonding is in one direction between two particular _____.

c   Copy and complete these sentences which relate the properties of metals to their bonding.

| move   ions   electrostatic   delocalised   electrons |

Metals conduct electricity because the delocalised electrons are able to

_____ throughout the structure between the positive metal _____.

Many metals are strong, and hard because the metal ions are held together by the

strong _____ forces of attraction between the ions and the _____

_____.

Exercise 4.2 Covalent bonding

This exercise will help you develop your understanding of covalent structures and how to draw dot-and-cross diagrams.

a Copy and complete these dot-and-cross diagrams for three covalent compounds. Show only the outer shell electrons.

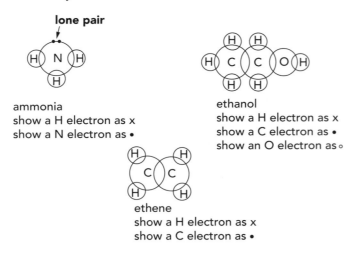

ammonia
show a H electron as x
show a N electron as •

ethanol
show a H electron as x
show a C electron as •
show an O electron as ○

ethene
show a H electron as x
show a C electron as •

Figure 4.2: Structure diagrams for ammonia, ethanol and ethene.

b Draw dot-and-cross diagrams for the molecules in Figure 4.3. Show only the outer shell electrons. Note that the diagrams do not all show the exact shapes of the molecules.

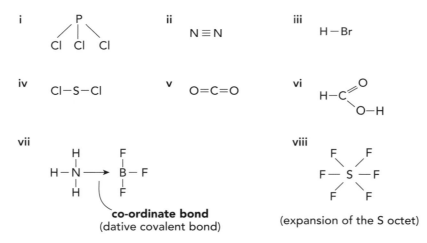

Figure 4.3: Structure diagrams for eight substances.

KEY WORDS

covalent bond: the electrostatic attraction between the nuclei of two atoms and a shared pair of electrons.

lone pairs (of electrons): pairs of electrons in the outer shell of an atom not involved in bonding.

TIP

When drawing more complex molecules such as ethanol, start with the carbon and oxygen.

KEY WORDS

co-ordinate bond: the sharing of a pair of electrons between two atoms where both the electrons in the bond come from the same atom. Also called a dative covalent bond.

TIP

When drawing a dative covalent bond, the arrow points away from the atom which donates (gives) both electrons

Exercise 4.3 Shapes of molecules

This exercise will help you deduce the shapes of molecules using the **valence shell electron pair repulsion (VSEPR) theory**.

Use this information to help you with the questions that follow:

lone pair of electrons repelling lone pair of electrons

lone pair of electrons repelling bonding pair of electrons

bonding pair of electrons repelling bonding pair of electrons

↑ stronger repulsion

Figure 4.4: Repulsions of pairs of electrons.

a   Deduce the bond angles R to V in Figure 4.5.

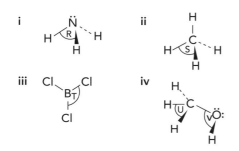

Figure 4.5: Bond angles.

b   Figure 4.6 shows the arrangement of the bonds in various molecules and ions. Draw and describe the shapes of these molecules or ions. On your diagrams, give the values of the bond angle. Note that the diagrams do not show the exact shapes of the molecules and do not show lone pairs of electrons.

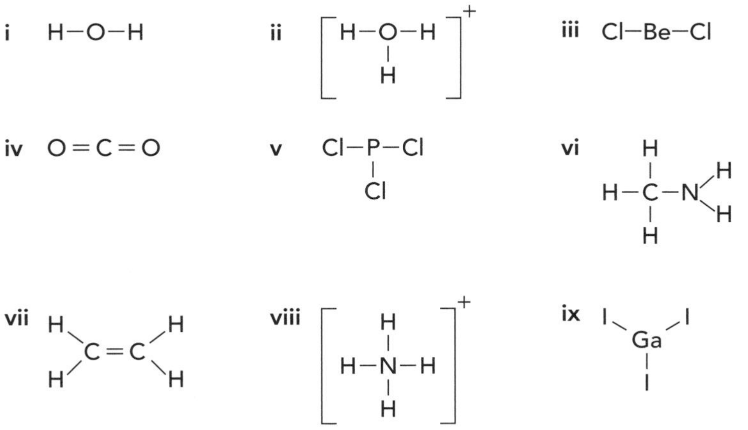

i   H—O—H

ii $\left[\begin{array}{c} H-O-H \\ | \\ H \end{array} \right]^+$

iii   Cl—Be—Cl

iv   O=C=O

v   Cl—P—Cl
　　　　　 |
　　　　　Cl

vi $H-\overset{\overset{\displaystyle H}{|}}{\underset{\underset{\displaystyle H}{|}}{C}}-N\overset{\displaystyle H}{\underset{\displaystyle H}{\diagdown}}$

vii $\overset{H}{\underset{H}{\diagup\!\!\!\diagdown}}C=C\overset{H}{\underset{H}{\diagdown\!\!\!\diagup}}$

viii $\left[\begin{array}{c} H \\ | \\ H-N-H \\ | \\ H \end{array} \right]^+$

ix $I\diagdown_{Ga}\diagup I$
　　　　　 |
　　　　　 I

Figure 4.6: Shapes of molecules.

Exercise 4.4 Intermolecular forces

This exercise will help you distinguish the relative strength of these forces based on molecular structure. It will also help you understand the relationship between these forces and the physical properties of simple molecules.

> **TIPS**
>
> Electronegativity increases from Group 1 to 17.
>
> Electronegativity increases going up a group.
>
> The strength of intermolecular forces is in the increasing order:
>
> **id-id forces < pd-pd forces < hydrogen bonding**.

a Put these atoms in order of their **electronegativity**. Put the most electronegative first.

| chlorine | hydrogen | fluorine | nitrogen | oxygen |

b **i** Figure 4.7 shows the electron clouds of hydrogen and hydrogen fluoride.

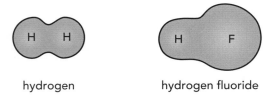

hydrogen   hydrogen fluoride

Figure 4.7: Electron cloud diagrams.

Copy these diagrams and put a + to show the centre of positive charge in each molecule and a − to show the centre of negative charge.

ii Explain why hydrogen fluoride is a **polar molecule**.

c Name the strongest type of attractive force between each of these pairs of molecules. Use the list above to help you.

 i CH_3Cl and CH_3Br

 ii CH_3NH_2 and CH_3OH

 iii $CH_3CH_2CH_2CH_2CH_2CH_3$ and $CH_3CH_2CH_2CH_2CH_3$

 iv CH_3COCH_3 and $CH_3COCH_2CH_3$

 v CH_3Br and CH_3NH_2

d Draw diagrams of each of these molecules to show how the atoms are arranged. On each diagram, show the direction of the dipoles as $\delta^+ \longrightarrow \delta^-$. If no net dipole is present, write 'none'.

 i CH_2Cl_2

 ii CBr_4

 iii NH_3

 iv $ClBr$

e Suggest in terms of intermolecular forces why:

 i Water has a higher boiling point than pentane, C_5H_{12}, even though pentane has a higher molar mass.

 ii Pentane is a liquid at r.t.p. but butane C_4H_{10} is a gas at r.t.p.

 iii CH_3NH_2 has a higher boiling point than CH_3Cl.

Exercise 4.5 Different types of bonds

This exercise will help you revise the types of bonding present in a variety of structures and compare their strengths. It also helps you to revise aspects of electronegativity.

a Describe what is meant by the terms:

 i co-ordinate bond

 ii electronegativity.

b **i** Describe how electronegativity varies across a period. Explain your answer.

 ii The compound bromine monochloride has the structure Br–Cl.
 Explain why this is a polar molecule.

 iii Suggest why Br–Cl is more reactive than Cl–Cl in some reactions.

c Some Pauling electronegativity values are given.

 $C = 2.5 \;\; Cl = 3.0 \;\; Mg = 1.2$

 Use these values to explain how you know that magnesium chloride is an ionic compound but carbon tetrachloride is a molecular compound.

d The **bond lengths** of the hydrogen halides are given.

 H–Cl = 0.127 nm; H–Br = 0.141 nm; H–I = 0.16 nm

 i Define what is meant by the term bond length.

 ii Describe and explain the differences in the bond lengths of the hydrogen halides.

e **i** Put these attractive forces in the correct order starting from the weakest.

 A hydrogen bonding

 B instantaneous dipole-induced dipole forces

 C ionic bond

 D permanent dipole forces

 ii Suggest why it is difficult to compare the strength of covalent and metallic bonds.

> **TIP**
>
> In **b ii**, you should use the words polar and electronegativity in your answer

> **KEY WORDS**
>
> **bond length:** the distance between the nuclei of two covalently bonded atoms.

> **TIP**
>
> In **e ii**, think about the properties of sodium and iron.

Exercise 4.6 Bonding and orbitals

This exercise focuses on covalent bonding, the **hybridisation** of atomic orbitals and how these affect the properties of simple molecules.

a Atomic orbitals overlap in various ways. Three types of hybrid orbital are sp, sp^2 and sp^3.

   i Figure 4.8 shows the hybridised orbitals in ethane and ethene. What words best represent the letters A to D?

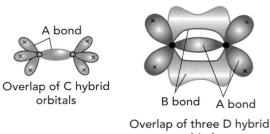

Figure 4.8: Hybridised orbitals in molecules.

   ii Refer to the hybridised structure of ethane to explain why the H–C–H bond angles are 109.5°.

b Figure 4.9 shows the p orbitals in benzene, C$_6$H$_6$.

   i Predict the shape of the electron clouds arising from the p electrons when the p electrons are brought closer to each other.

   ii Suggest why some of the electrons in benzene are delocalised.

   iii Benzene does not conduct electricity even though it has delocalised electrons. Explain why it does not conduct.

   iv Use ideas of overlap of p orbitals to suggest why graphite conducts electricity.

c When molecules react, bonds are broken and new bonds are formed. Suggest why oxygen is more reactive than nitrogen.

d The type of bond, **sigma** or **pi**, influences chemical reactivity. Suggest why ethene is more reactive than ethane.

e The polarity of a bond can influence chemical reactivity. Suggest why CH$_3$CH$_2$CH$_2$Cl is more reactive than CH$_3$CH$_2$CH$_3$.

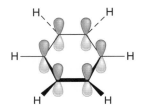

Figure 4.9: p orbitals in benzene.

EXAM-STYLE QUESTIONS

1 This question is about the structure of simple molecules and the relative strength of the forces between these molecules.

The table shows the boiling points of some hydrides.

Hydride	CH_4	SiH_4	GeH_4	SnH_4	NH_3	H_2O	HF
Boiling point / K	112	161	185	221	241	373	293

Table 4.1

a Describe and explain the trend in the boiling points of the Group 14 hydrides CH_4, SiH_4, GeH_4 and SnH_4 [4]

b Explain the differences in the Period 2 hydrides CH_4, NH_3, H_2O and HF in terms of attractive forces between the molecules. [6]

c Draw a dot-and-cross diagram for water. [2]

d i Water is a V-shaped molecule. Explain why. [2]

ii Suggest a value for the H−O−H bond angle in water. [1]

iii The molecules of water are hydrogen-bonded. Explain the meaning of the term *hydrogen bonding*, including the essential features needed for hydrogen bonding. [4]

e CH_3Cl is a polar molecule. Draw a diagram to show the three-dimensional structure of this molecule. On your diagram show the direction of the dipole as $\delta^+ \longrightarrow \delta^-$. [2]

f Suggest why CCl_4 is not a polar molecule. [1]

[Total: 22]

2 Polymers consist of long chains of molecules. When heated, the chains begin to move over each other. The temperature at which this happens is called the glass point, T_g.
The structures of a section of the chains of three polymers are shown in Figure 4.10 together with their T_g values.

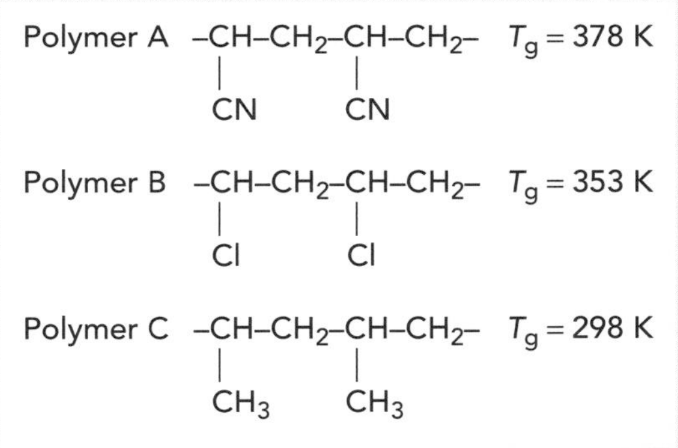

Polymer A   –CH–CH₂–CH–CH₂– $T_g = 378$ K
                      | |
                     CN   CN

Polymer B   –CH–CH₂–CH–CH₂– $T_g = 353$ K
                      | |
                     Cl   Cl

Polymer C   –CH–CH₂–CH–CH₂– $T_g = 298$ K
                      | |
                    CH₃   CH₃

Figure 4.10

TIPS

In part b, think about the number of hydrogen bonds per molecule as well as other factors.

There are 6 marks so you will need to write at least 6 points.

TIP

This question introduces the concept of the glass point, which may be unfamiliar to you. If you think about the glass point in a similar way to the melting point then you will be able to answer this question.

CONTINUED

a Explain these differences in the values of T_g by referring to the relative strengths of permanent dipole-permanent dipole forces and **London dispersion forces**. [5]

b The CN group is called a nitrile group. This group has a triple bond. Draw a dot-and-cross diagram of the nitrile ion CN^-. Show only the outer shell electrons. [2]

c Liquid ammonia contains molecules, NH_3, which are extensively hydrogen bonded. Draw a diagram to show two hydrogen-bonded molecules of ammonia. Show the lone pairs of electrons and the correct orientation of the hydrogen bond. [3]

d i Aqueous ammonia reacts with dilute sulfuric acid to form a salt. Write the balanced equation for this reaction including state symbols. [3]

ii The salt formed in this reaction boils (under pressure) at 513 °C. Ammonia boils at –33 °C. Explain the difference between these boiling points in terms of bonding. [4]

e Magnesium oxide is also a salt. Draw a dot-and-cross diagram of the ions in magnesium oxide. Draw only the outer shell electrons. [2]

[Total: 19]

3 This question is about the structure and bonding in some halogens and halogen compounds.

a The structure of iodic acid is shown in Figure 4.11.

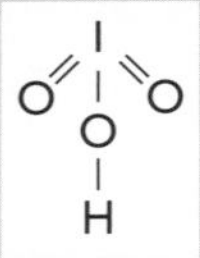

Figure 4.11

i Draw a dot-and-cross diagram for iodic acid. [3]

ii Explain why iodic acid has this pyramidal structure. [2]

iii Suggest a value for the O–I–O bond angle. [1]

b Iodine is a solid at r.t.p. but hydrogen iodide is a gas at r.t.p. Explain this difference in terms of intermolecular bonding. [2]

c Hydrogen iodide has a much lower boiling point than hydrogen fluoride. Explain why in terms of different types of **van der Waals' forces**. [3]

d The structural formulae of 1-iodopropane and 2-iodopropane are shown below.

CH_3–CH_2–CH_2–I CH_3–CHI–CH_3

1-iodopropane   2-iodopropane

Suggest why 2-iodopropane has a lower boiling point than 1-iodopropane. [3]

KEY WORDS

London dispersion forces: another name for instantaneous dipole-induced dipole forces.

TIPS

Questions often contain material from other parts of the course. In **2 d i** you have to write a balanced equation.

In parts **3 a ii** and **iii** you will need to use electron pair repulsion theory (VSEPR theory).

In part **2 b** remember that I is not very electronegative.

KEY WORDS

van der Waals' forces: weak forces of attraction between molecules involving either instantaneous (id-id) or permanent dipole-permanent dipole (pd-pd) forces (including hydrogen bonding). The expression covers all types of intermolecular forces.

CONTINUED

e At low temperatures, aluminium chloride, $AlCl_3$, forms a molecule with the structure shown in Figure 4.12.

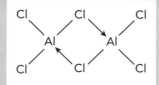

Figure 4.12

Give the name of the type of bond shown by the arrows and suggest why $AlCl_3$ molecules join together in this way. **[2]**

[Total: 16]

4 a The **average bond energies** of single and double carbon-carbon bonds are shown.

C—C 347 kJ mol^{-1}; C=C 612 kJ mol^{-1}

  i Define the term *average bond energy*. **[2]**

  ii Suggest why the bond energy of the C=C bond is not double that of the C—C bond. **[2]**

  iii Suggest a value for the C≡C bond energy. **[1]**

 b i Draw a dot-and-cross diagram of ethyne, H—C≡C—H. **[1]**

  ii Describe the shape of the ethyne molecule and suggest a value for the bond angle H—C≡C. **[2]**

 c i Describe the bonding of ethyne in terms of sigma bonds and pi bonds and their arrangement in space. **[5]**

  ii State the type of hybridisation between the hydrogen atom and the carbon atom next to it in ethyne. **[1]**

[Total: 14]

TIP

The type of hybridisation depends on the number of p orbitals which combine with an s orbital.

> Chapter 5

States of matter

CHAPTER OUTLINE

In this chapter you will learn how to:

- explain the origin of pressure in a gas in terms of collisions between gas molecules and the walls of the container

- describe an ideal gas as having zero particle volume and no intermolecular forces of attraction

- use the ideal gas equation, $pV = nRT$ in calculations, including the determination of relative molecular mass

- describe and use the term lattice

- describe the different types of structures as giant ionic, simple molecular, giant molecular and giant metallic

- describe, interpret and predict the effect of different types of structure and bonding on the physical properties of substances, e.g. effect on melting point, boiling point, electrical conductivity and solubility

- deduce the type of structure and bonding present in a substance from given information.

Exercise 5.1 Properties of the three states of matter

This exercise will familiarise you with the properties of the three **states of matter**. You will also learn about the structure of a simple covalent molecule and a **giant molecular (giant covalent) structure**. It will also help you relate the properties of these substances to their structures.

a   Carbon dioxide, bromine and sulfur have **simple molecular structures**. Copy and complete the table to show the proximity (closeness), arrangement and motion of the molecules in these three substances. Three of the answers have been done for you.

Substance	State at 25 °C and 1 atm pressure	Proximity	Arrangement	Motion
bromine	liquid		irregular / random	
carbon dioxide	gas			moving rapidly from place to place
sulfur	solid	close together		

Table 5.1: Proximity, arrangement and motion of molecules.

KEY WORDS

states of matter: the three states of matter are solids, liquids and gases.

giant molecular structure / giant covalent structure: structures having a three-dimensional network of covalent bonds throughout the whole structure.

simple molecular structure: molecules which are composed of atoms covalently bonded within the molecule but have weak intermolecular forces of attraction between the molecules. Crystalline solids can form lattices.

b The structure of solid carbon dioxide and part of the structure of one form of boron nitride are shown in Figure 5.1.

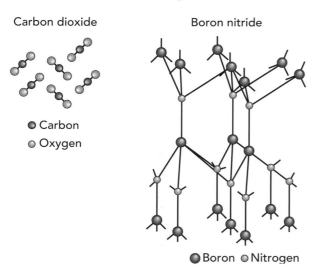

Carbon dioxide

- Carbon
- Oxygen

Boron nitride

- Boron - Nitrogen

Figure 5.1: The structures of carbon dioxide and boron nitride.

TIPS

Make sure that you can interpret diagrams of these structures.

Remember that a line between atoms represents a covalent bond.

i Copy the following passage, selecting the correct statements about the structure and properties of boron nitride.

Boron nitride has a <u>giant</u> / <u>simple</u> molecular structure. It has <u>covalent</u> / <u>ionic</u> bonds. Its structure is similar to the structure of <u>diamond</u> / <u>graphite</u>. Each boron atom is bonded to <u>three</u> / <u>four</u> nitrogen atoms. The nitrogen atoms are arranged <u>hexagonally</u> / <u>tetrahedrally</u> around each boron atom. Boron nitride has a <u>high</u> / <u>low</u> melting point because all the <u>atoms</u> / <u>molecules</u> are joined by <u>strong</u> / <u>weak</u> bonds. Boron nitride <u>conducts</u> / <u>does not conduct</u> electricity because all the outer electrons in the boron and nitrogen atoms are used in bonding.

ii Copy and complete these statements by writing suitable words or phrases in the spaces.

Carbon dioxide has a _____ _____ structure. It has

_____ _____ bonding between each carbon and oxygen atom.

Carbon dioxide is a gas at room temperature because the forces _____ .

Exercise 5.2 Giant structures

This exercise will help you distinguish between the three types of giant structure: **ionic**, giant molecular (giant covalent structures) and **giant metallic**. It will also help you relate the properties of these substances to their structures.

KEY WORDS

giant ionic structure: structures having a three-dimensional network (lattice) of ionic bonds.

giant metallic structure: structures having a three-dimensional network of positive ions attracted to a sea of delocalised electrons between the ions (metallic bond).

The diagram shows three different types of giant structure, **A**, **B** and **C**.

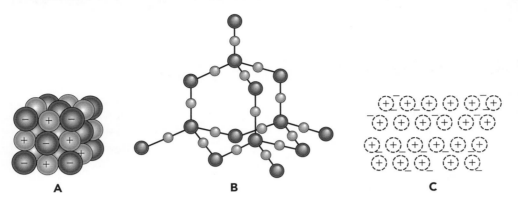

Figure 5.2: Structures A, B and C.

a   Name each of the three types of giant structure represented by the letters **A**, **B** and **C**.

b   Copy and complete the table to compare the structures and properties of **A**, **B** and **C**.

	Structure **A**	Structure **B**	Structure **C**
Type of particles present in the diagram		atoms of Si and O	
Melting point	high		(generally) high
Electrical conductivity of solid		does not conduct	
Electrical conductivity when molten	conducts		

Table 5.2: Comparing structures and properties.

c   Match the properties 1 to 5 of compounds A and B on the left to the correct explanations A to E on the right.

Property

1	Compound A has crystals with a regular shape

2	Compound B does not conduct electricity when molten

3	Compound A is hard

4	Compound B does not dissolve in water

5	Compound A conducts electricity when molten

Explanation

A	because the ions are free to move from place to place

B	because there are strong attractive forces between the large number of positive and negative ions

C	because there are neither ions nor electrons free to move throughout the structure

D	because the particles are arranged in a **lattice**

E	because the forces of attraction between the atoms of B are greater than the forces of attraction between the atoms of B and the water molecules

d   Describe the structure of metals and explain why they conduct electricity and are malleable. In your answer include the following words and phrases:

> **outer shell electrons   delocalised electrons
> metal ions   layers of metal ions
> attractive forces between the metal ions and delocalised electrons**

Exercise 5.3 The ideal gas equation and molar mass of gases

This exercise gives you practice in using the **ideal gas** equation, $pV = nRT$ to calculate relative molecular mass. It also develops your skills in processing data from the results of an experiment.

a   A 0.2 mol sample of a gas is placed in a closed container of volume 250 cm³. The temperature of the container is raised to 100 °C. Calculate the pressure of the gas inside the container in kPa. ($R = 8.31 \, \text{J K}^{-1} \text{mol}^{-1}$)

b   The relative molecular mass of a volatile liquid, L, can be found experimentally using the apparatus in Figure 5.3.

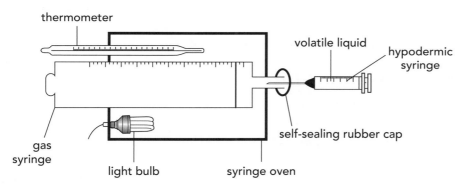

Figure 5.3: A syringe oven.

TIPS

When using the ideal gas equation make sure that the units are the correct ones, e.g. temperature in K.

If the volume inserted into the equation is in dm³, the pressure is in kPa. If the volume is in m³ the pressure is in Pa.

Make sure that you can rearrange the ideal gas equation to make any of p, V, n or T the subject,

e.g. $n = \dfrac{pV}{RT}$

The results are given here:

Temperature in the syringe oven = 120 °C

Mass of hypodermic syringe at the start of the experiment = 10.71 g

Mass of hypodermic syringe after injection of L into gas syringe = 10.54 g

Volume of air in the gas syringe at the start of the experiment (at 120 °C) = 4.0 cm^3

Volume of vapour in the gas syringe after vaporisation of the liquid = 69.0 cm^3

Atmospheric pressure = 1.00×10^5 Pa

i   Use the information to determine the following values:

The temperature of the vapour = _____ K

The mass of L vaporised = _____ g

The volume of vapour in the gas syringe = _____ m^3

ii   Rearrange the gas equation $pV = nRT$ to make n (number of moles of vapour) the subject.

iii   Calculate the value of n ($R = 8.31 \text{ J K}^{-1} \text{mol}^{-1}$). Express your answer to 2 significant figures.

iv   Use the value from part **iii** and the mass of L injected into the gas syringe to calculate the relative molecular mass of L. Express your answer to 2 significant figures.

v   What effect, if any, would the following errors make on the measured value of the relative molecular mass? In each case, explain your answer.

- Having 4 cm^3 of air (at 120 °C) in the syringe at the start of the experiment.

- Losing some of liquid L from the syringe into the atmosphere during its injection.

- Reading the temperature inside the syringe oven as 130 °C instead of the correct 120 °C.

Exercise 5.4 Different forms of carbon

This exercise will help you investigate some different forms of carbon including graphite, fullerenes and graphene.

Diamond, graphite, fullerenes and graphene are all **allotropes** of carbon.

a   Copy the following passage about graphite selecting the correct statements.

Graphite is an <u>allotrope</u> / <u>isotope</u> of carbon. The carbon atoms in graphite are arranged in <u>layers</u> / <u>pyramids</u>. The carbon <u>atoms</u> / <u>ions</u> are arranged in <u>hexagons</u> / <u>pentagons</u>. Graphite has a <u>high</u> / <u>low</u> electrical conductivity. This is because some of the <u>atoms</u> / <u>electrons</u> are delocalised and are able to move when a voltage is applied. Graphite has <u>weak van der Waals' forces</u> / <u>strong covalent bonding</u> between the <u>layers</u> / <u>pyramids</u>.

> **TIP**
>
> When given questions on structures which are new to you, think of the properties of a similar structure that you know about.

> **KEY WORD**
>
> **allotrope:** different crystalline or molecular forms of the same element.

b The diagram shows the structure of diamond, **buckminsterfullerene** (C_{60}) and graphene.

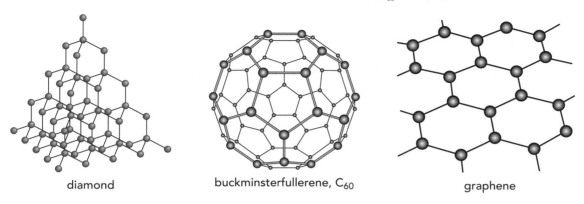

diamond   buckminsterfullerene, C_{60} graphene

Figure 5.4: The structures of diamond, buckminsterfullerene (C_{60}) and graphene.

i Explain in terms of structure and bonding, why C_{60} has a lower melting point than diamond.

ii Suggest why C_{60} dissolves in organic solvents such as benzene (C_6H_6), but not in water.

iii Graphene and graphite both contain carbon atoms. Give one other similarity and one difference in the structures of graphene and graphite.

Exercise 5.5 Kinetic theory of gases

This exercise will familiarise you with ideas related to the kinetic theory of gases. It will help you revise the concept of an ideal gas and the kinetic theory.

Remember that:

- The volume of an ideal gas is inversely proportional to pressure and directly proportional to the temperature in K at all temperatures and pressures.
- At high pressures and low temperatures, when the molecules are very close, a gas no longer behaves as an ideal gas.

a Explain gas pressure in terms of the kinetic particle theory.

b A student fills a gas syringe with oxygen. The tip of the syringe is sealed off but the syringe plunger can still move. The pressure remains constant. Explain, using the kinetic theory, why the volume of the gas in the syringe increases when the temperature increases.

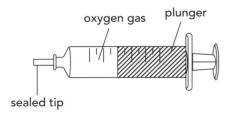

oxygen gas   plunger

sealed tip

Figure 5.5: A gas syringe.

> **TIP**
>
> In your answer to part **b ii** use ideas of polar / non-polar.

> **KEY WORD**
>
> **buckminster-fullerene:** a simple molecular structure of carbon, with formula C_{60}. The molecule has the shape of a football (soccer ball). The carbon atoms are arranged at the corners of 20 hexagons and 12 pentagons. The bonds where two hexagons join are shorter than the bonds between the hexagons and the pentagons.

> **TIP**
>
> For parts **a** and **b** you need to think about what the moving particles do.

c   Complete this sentence about an ideal gas using words from the list. Not all the
    words are used.

| attractive | large | no | particle | zero |
| repulsive | solution | stoichiometric |

In an ideal gas the _____ volume is _____ and there are

_____ intermolecular _____ forces.

d   Which one of the graphs in Figure 5.6 shows the relationship between the volume
    of a gas (in m³) and its pressure (in pascals)? Explain why the graph is this shape.

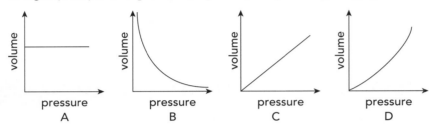

Figure 5.6: Volume-pressure relationship in gases.

e   An ideal gas is a gas which obeys the gas laws over a wide range of temperature
    and pressure. The kinetic theory of gases makes several assumptions about an
    ideal gas. Describe these assumptions.

f   The ideal gas laws do not always obey the kinetic theory of gases at high pressures
    or low temperatures. Explain how and why in terms of the proximity (closeness)
    of the molecules and the forces of attraction between the molecules.

EXAM-STYLE QUESTIONS

1   Titanium and aluminium are metals with high melting points. Diamond is an
    allotrope of carbon with a high melting point. Titanium carbide has an ionic
    structure similar to sodium chloride. All four structures form crystal lattices.

    a   What is the meaning of the term:

        i   allotrope   [1]

        ii lattice?   [1]

    b   Explain, using ideas of structure and bonding, why both titanium
        and diamond have high melting points.   [5]

    c   i   Describe the lattice structure of titanium carbide.   [2]

        ii Explain why titanium carbide conducts electricity when molten
            but does not conduct when solid.   [2]

    d   The table shows data on some physical properties of four substances
        A, B, C and D.

TIPS

In parts **1 b**, **c** and **d**
you need to make
sure that you have
identified:

*   The type of
    structure, e.g.
    giant or simple
    molecular, as
    well as the type
    of bonding,
    e.g. covalent,
    metallic.

*   The correct
    particles which
    are moving (ions
    or electrons).

CONTINUED

Substance	Melting point / K	Electrical conductivity of solid	Electrical conductivity of liquid
A	1274	poor	good
B	1145	good	good
C	317	poor	poor
D	1903	poor	poor

Table 5.3

Describe the type of structure and bonding present in these four substances. [7]

[Total: 18]

2   Chemists have recently been able to make single sheets of boron nitride, BN. A sheet of boron nitride has a similar structure to a single layer of graphite.

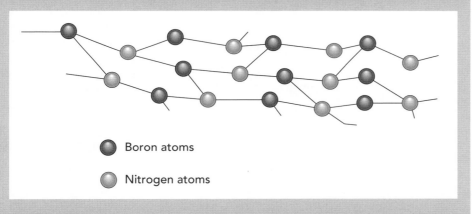

Boron atoms

Nitrogen atoms

Figure 5.7

a   Apart from the types of atom present, describe one difference between a sheet of boron nitride and a layer of graphite. [1]

b   Suggest why a sheet of boron nitride:

   i   is very strong [1]

   ii   conducts electricity. [1]

c   Another form of boron nitride has a structure similar to graphite. This form of boron nitride is a good lubricant. Explain why. [2]

CONTINUED

d Buckminsterfullerene (C_{60}) is a form of carbon. Buckminsterfullerene **monomers** can be polymerised. The structure of the polymer is shown below.

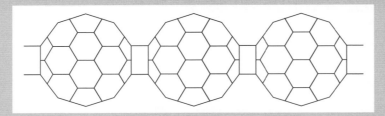

Figure 5.8

Explain why the melting point of the polymer of buckminsterfullerene is higher than that of the buckminsterfullerene monomer.　　　　**[5]**

[Total: 10]

3 a Iodine has a simple molecular structure with a crystalline lattice.

　i Describe the arrangement of the molecules of iodine.　　**[2]**

　ii **Predict** the solubility in water and the **relative electrical conductivity** of iodine.　　**[2]**

b When a crystal of iodine is heated in a closed container, it turns to a liquid and then to a vapour. When the temperature of the vapour increases, the pressure increases. Explain why.　　**[2]**

c When 0.22 g of liquid P was vaporised at 90 °C, 85 cm³ of vapour was formed. The atmospheric pressure was 1.1×10^5 Pa.

　i Calculate the number of moles of P vaporised. Express your answer to two significant figures. ($R = 8.31 \ JK^{-1} mol^{-1}$)　**[3]**

　ii Calculate the relative molecular mass of P. Express your answer to 2 significant figures.　　**[2]**

d Calculate the volume in dm³ occupied by 0.400 moles of ethane gas at a pressure of 2.00×10^5 Pa and 40.0 °C ($R = 8.31 \ JK^{-1} mol^{-1}$). Express your answer to 3 significant figures.　　**[3]**

[Total: 14]

KEY WORD

monomers: small molecules that react together to make long chain molecules (polymers).

COMMAND WORD

Predict: suggest what may happen based on available information.

KEY WORDS

relative electrical conductivity: the electrical conductivity of a substance compared with other substances, e.g. good, poor, fairly good.

TIP

Remember to set out your calculations clearly, showing all relevant working, and only round at the end of the calculation.

Note the number of significant figures required.

Chapter 6

Enthalpy changes

CHAPTER OUTLINE

In this chapter you will learn how to:

- explain and use the terms standard conditions, exothermic, endothermic and enthalpy change

- construct and interpret a reaction pathway diagram in terms of enthalpy changes and activation energy

- define and use the terms enthalpy change of reaction, formation, combustion and neutralisation

- calculate enthalpy changes from experimental results

- use Hess's Law to construct simple energy cycles and carry out calculations using energy cycles

- explain energy transfers during chemical reactions in terms of breaking and making chemical bonds

- use bond energies to calculate enthalpy change of reaction

- carry out calculations using bond energy data.

Exercise 6.1 Enthalpy changes and reaction pathway diagrams

Reaction pathway diagrams (enthalpy profile diagrams) show the enthalpy of the reactants and products in the reaction pathway. This exercise gives you practice in constructing reaction pathway diagrams for **exothermic** and **endothermic reactions** including the **activation energy**. It will also remind you of **standard conditions**.

a Copy and complete these sentences about **enthalpy changes** using words from this list.

absorbed	chemical	exothermic	ΔH	heat
kelvin	pascals	physical	products	surroundings

An enthalpy change is the exchange of _____ energy between a

_____ reaction mixture and its _____ at constant pressure. The

symbol for enthalpy change is _____. If heat is _____ from the

_____ the reaction is endothermic. If heat is released to the surroundings

the reaction is _____. In comparing enthalpy changes we use standard

conditions. These are a pressure of 10^5 _____ , a temperature of 298

_____ with the reactants and _____ in their normal _____

state under these conditions.

KEY WORDS

reaction pathway diagram: a diagram showing the relative enthalpies of the reactants (on the left) and the products (on the right) and the enthalpy change as an arrow. It may also include the activation energy.

exothermic: heat energy is released during a reaction. The value of ΔH is negative.

endothermic: heat energy is absorbed during a reaction. The value of ΔH is positive.

activation energy, E_A: the minimum energy that colliding particles must possess to break bonds to start a chemical reaction.

b **i** Draw a reaction pathway diagram, including activation energy, for the reaction:

$$Mg(s) + CuSO_4(aq) \rightarrow MgSO_4(aq) + Cu(s) \qquad \Delta H = -531 \text{ kJ mol}^{-1}$$

   ii Is the reaction endothermic or exothermic? Explain your answer.

c Draw a reaction pathway diagram, including activation energy, for the reaction:

$$2NaNO_3(s) \rightarrow 2NaNO_2(s) + O_2(g) \qquad \Delta H_r^{\ominus} = +218 \text{ kJ mol}^{-1}$$

Exercise 6.2 Enthalpy changes

This exercise will familiarise you with the different types of enthalpy changes and how to define them.

TIP

It is important that you learn definitions of enthalpy changes precisely. Make sure that you refer to:

- moles (usually one mole) of the relevant product or reactant

- the correct state of reactants and products

- standard conditions.

---

a Copy and complete these definitions.

   i **Standard enthalpy change of neutralisation** is the enthalpy change when one

   mole of _____ is formed by the reaction of an _____ with a

   _____ under standard conditions.

   ii **Standard enthalpy change of combustion** is the enthalpy change when

   _____ mole of a substance is burnt in excess _____ under
   standard conditions.

   iii Standard enthalpy change of reaction is the enthalpy change when the

   amounts shown in the _____ react to give _____ under

   _____.

KEY WORDS

standard enthalpy change of neutralisation, $\Delta H_{neut}^{\ominus}$: the enthalpy change when one mole of water is formed by the reaction of an acid with an alkali under standard conditions.

standard enthalpy change of combustion, $\Delta H_c^{\ominus}$: the enthalpy change when one mole of substance is burnt in excess oxygen under standard conditions.

KEY WORDS

standard conditions: a pressure of 101 kPa and temperature of 298 K, shown by $^{\ominus}$.

enthalpy change, ΔH: the heat energy transferred during a chemical reaction.

TIPS

The enthalpy change of a exothermic reaction is negative. It is shown as $-\Delta H$.

The enthalpy change of a endothermic reaction is positive. It is shown as $+\Delta H$.

The arrow showing ΔH is downward for an exothermic reaction and upward for an endothermic reaction.

b   Link the enthalpy changes 1 to 5 with the equations A to E which represent them.

Enthalpy change	**Equation**
1 Bond energy	**A** $H^+(aq) + OH^-(aq) \rightarrow H_2O(l)$
2 Standard enthalpy change of combustion of methane, $\Delta H_c^{\ominus}[CH_4(g)]$	**B** $C(graphite) + 2H_2(g) \rightarrow CH_4(g)$
3 Standard enthalpy change of formation of methane, $\Delta H_f^{\ominus}[CH_4(g)]$	**C** $CaCO_3(s) \rightarrow CaO(s) + CO_2(g)$
4 Standard enthalpy change of neutralisation, $\Delta H_{neut}^{\ominus}$	**D** $\frac{1}{2} I_2(g) \rightarrow 2I(g)$
5 Standard enthalpy change of decomposition, $\Delta H_r^{\ominus}$	**E** $CH_4(g) + 2O_2(g) \rightarrow$ $CO_2(g) + 2H_2O(l)$

c   Write balanced equations to represent:

i   the enthalpy change of combustion of propane

ii   the enthalpy change of neutralisation of sodium hydroxide with sulfuric acid.

iii   the enthalpy change of reaction for the decomposition of magnesium carbonate

iv   the enthalpy change of formation of sodium oxide.

d   Which reaction in part **c** is definitely endothermic reactions?

e   Complete this sentence using numbers and symbols from the list.

10.1   101   273   298   atm   °C   K   Pa   kPa

Standard conditions are a temperature of _____ _____ and a

pressure of _____ _____.

Exercise 6.3 Enthalpy changes from experiment

This exercise provides practice in revising the concept of enthalpy change of combustion. It also develops your skills in processing results.

Figure 6.1 shows the apparatus used to calculate the enthalpy change of combustion of hexanol.

> **KEY WORDS**
>
> **bond energy:** the energy required to break one mole of a particular covalent bond in the gaseous state. The units of bond energy are kilojoules per mole, $kJ\,mol^{-1}$.
>
> **standard enthalpy change of formation, $\Delta H_f^{\ominus}$:** the enthalpy change when one mole of compound is formed from its elements under standard conditions.
>
> **standard enthalpy change of decomposition, $\Delta H_r^{\ominus}$:** the enthalpy change when one mole of a substance is decomposed into products under standard conditions.

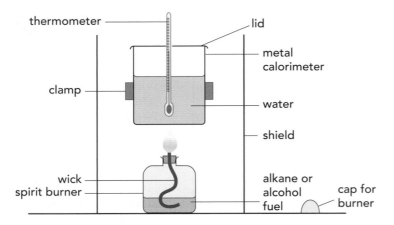

Figure 6.1: Measuring an enthalpy change of combustion.

a   Describe how to carry out this experiment.

b   The results from the experiment are given below.

Mass of water in calorimeter = 80 g

Mass of burner and hexanol at start = 92.33 g

Mass of burner and hexanol at end = 92.19 g

Initial temperature of water = 20.5 °C

Final temperature of water = 35.2 °C

Calculate:

i   the mass of fuel burned

ii   the change in temperature of the water

iii   the energy released by burning the hexanol, using the relationship:
      $q = -mc\Delta T$, where the value of c is 4.18 J g^{-1} °C^{-1}

iv   the relative molecular mass of hexanol, $C_6H_{13}OH$

v   the energy released per mole of hexanol burned, in kJ mol^{-1}.

c   The data book value for $\Delta H_c^{\ominus}$ [$C_6H_{13}OH(l)$] is −3984 kJ mol^{-1}.

Explain why this value is more exothermic than the answer obtained in part **b**.

d   Write a balanced equation for the complete combustion of hexanol. Give
the value of the enthalpy change using the correct symbol and sign for the
enthalpy change.

Exercise 6.4 Bond energy

This exercise will familiarise you with the concept of bond energy and gives you
practice with calculations involving bond energies.

The equation for the complete combustion of methane is:

$$CH_4(g) + 2O_2(g) \rightarrow CO_2(g) + 2H_2O(l)$$

a   The combustion of methane is exothermic. Explain, in terms of bond breaking
and bond making, why it is exothermic.

b   i   Copy and complete the table to calculate the energy needed to break the bonds in methane and oxygen and the energy released when new bonds are formed.

Bond energy values (in $kJ\,mol^{-1}$): $E(C–H)+410$, $E(O=O)+496$, $E(C=O)+805$, $E(O–H)+465$.

Bonds broken / $kJ\,mol^{-1}$	Bonds formed / $kJ\,mol^{-1}$
$4 \times (C–H) =$	$2 \times (C=O) =$
$2 \times (O=O) =$	$4 \times (O–H) =$
total =	total =

Table 6.1: Calculate energy needed to break the bonds.

ii   Calculate the enthalpy change of the reaction.

c   Use bond energies to calculate the enthalpy change of the reaction.

$$CH_2=CH_2(g) + 3O_2 \rightarrow 2CO_2(g) + 2H_2O(g)$$

Bond energy values in $kJ\,mol^{-1}$: $E(C=C) +612$, $E(C–H) +410$, $E(O=O) +496$, $E(C=O) +805$, $E(O–H) +465$

Exercise 6.5 Using Hess's Law

We can calculate enthalpy changes using **Hess's Law** and an **energy cycle** (enthalpy cycle). This exercise provides practice in drawing and interpreting energy cycles to calculate enthalpy change of reaction.

TIPS

When drawing energy cycles (enthalpy cycles) remember that:

- The reaction you want goes across the top.
- The cycle is completed by putting elements, combustion products or aqueous solutions at the bottom.
- The arrows should go in the correct direction so that Hess's Law can be applied.

a   Iron(III) oxide can be reduced by carbon monoxide:

$$Fe_2O_3(s) + 3CO(g) \rightarrow 2Fe(s) + 3CO_2(g)$$

i   Copy and complete the enthalpy cycle for this reaction.

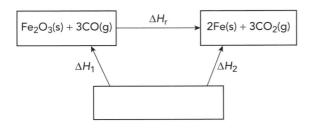

Figure 6.2: An enthalpy cycle for a reaction.

    ii Calculate the enthalpy change, ΔH_r

        $\Delta H_f^{\ominus}$ values in kJ mol^{-1}: Fe$_2$O$_3$(s) = –824.2, CO(g) = –110.5, CO$_2$(g) = –393.5

b Calculate the enthalpy change of combustion of propane using an enthalpy cycle similar to the one you completed in part **a**.

    $C_3H_8(g) + 5O_2(g) \rightarrow 3CO_2(g) + 4H_2O(l)$

    $\Delta H_f^{\ominus}$ values in kJ mol^{-1}: C$_3$H$_8$(g) = –104.5, CO$_2$(g) = –393.5, H$_2$O(g) = –285.8

c We can use enthalpy changes of combustion to find the enthalpy change of formation of butane.

    i Draw the enthalpy cycle for this reaction.

    ii Calculate the enthalpy change of formation of butane using Hess's Law.

        $\Delta H_c^{\ominus}$ values in kJ mol^{-1}: C(graphite) = –393.5, H$_2$(g) = –285.8, C$_4$H$_{10}$(g) = –2876.5

    iii The enthalpy change of combustion of carbon is the same as the enthalpy change of formation of carbon dioxide. Explain why.

Exercise 6.6 Further enthalpy change calculations

This exercise provides you with further practice in experimental methods and processing data.

a Aqueous magnesium nitrate reacts with aqueous sodium carbonate. A precipitate of magnesium carbonate is formed.

    Write a balanced equation for this reaction.

b 20.0 cm^3 of 1.0 mol dm^{-3} aqueous magnesium nitrate was added to 20 cm^3 of 1.0 mol dm^{-3} aqueous sodium carbonate in a beaker. The temperature of both solutions before mixing was 18.9 °C. After mixing, the maximum temperature reached was 23.2 °C.

    i Describe the precautions you would take to prevent heat losses in this experiment.

    ii Calculate the energy released to the **surroundings**. Use the information in Exercise 6.3 if you are unsure how to do this.

        Specific heat capacity of water = 4.18 J g^{-1} °C^{-1}.

    iii What assumptions did you make about the use of the equation you used in part **ii**?

    iv Calculate the enthalpy change of the reaction per mole of magnesium nitrate.

TIP

For the simple experiment which follows you should consider:

- how to reduce heat losses (details of insulation, materials used for the container, etc.)

- use of the equation $q = mc\Delta T$.

KEY WORDS

surroundings: anything other than the reactants and products in a chemical reaction, e.g. solvent, reaction vessel.

specific heat capacity, c: the energy needed to raise the temperature of 1 g of a substance by 1°C (by 1 K).

EXAM-STYLE QUESTIONS

1   Figure 6.3 shows a can which can heat up soup without an external source of heat.

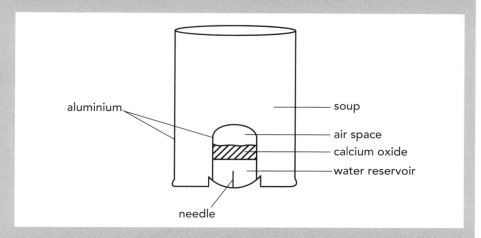

Figure 6.3

When water in excess is mixed with calcium oxide, an exothermic reaction takes place.

   Equation 1: $CaO(s) + H_2O(l) \rightarrow Ca(OH)_2(aq)$

a   Explain why the soup heats up when the calcium oxide reacts with water.   [2]

b   When the calcium oxide reacts, the volume of the solid expands.
   i   Why might this be a problem?   [1]
   ii   Use the information in the diagram to explain how this problem is overcome.   [1]

c   **Calculate** the enthalpy change of the reaction:

   Equation 2: $CaO(s) + H_2O(l) \rightarrow Ca(OH)_2(s)$

   $\Delta H_f^\ominus [CaO(s)] = -635.1 \text{ kJ mol}^{-1}$

   $\Delta H_f^\ominus [Ca(OH)_2(s)] = -986.1 \text{ kJ mol}^{-1}$

   $\Delta H_f^\ominus [H_2O(l)] = -285.8 \text{ kJ mol}^{-1}$ [3]

d   The energy released by the reaction in equation 2 does not heat the can sufficiently. By comparing equations 1 and 2 describe one other enthalpy change involved in heating the can.   [1]

e   Calcium oxide is a product of the reaction:
   $$3Ca(s) + Fe_2O_3(s) \rightarrow 2Fe(s) + 3CaO(s)$$
   i   Draw an energy cycle to calculate the enthalpy change of reaction.   [2]
   ii   The enthalpy change of this reaction is $-1081.1 \text{ kJ mol}^{-1}$. Draw a fully labelled reaction pathway diagram for this reaction.   [5]

   [Total: 15]

CONTINUED

2 Bond energies can be used to find the enthalpy change of a reaction.

   a i   What is meant by the term *exact bond energy*? **[2]**

      ii The enthalpy change of formation, $\Delta H_f^{\ominus}$, of ethanol, C_2H_5OH, can be calculated using bond energies. Explain why the use of exact bond energies leads to a more accurate value for $\Delta H_f^{\ominus}[C_2H_5OH]$ than the use of average bond energies. **[2]**

     iii Write an equation which represents the bond energy value for bromine. Include state symbols. **[2]**

   b Calculate the enthalpy change of the reaction:

$$H_2(g) + Cl_2(g) \rightarrow 2HCl(g)$$

     Use the following bond energies in $kJ\,mol^{-1}$:

$$E(H{-}H) +435.9, \ E(Cl{-}Cl) +243.4, \ E(H{-}Cl) +432.0 \qquad \textbf{[3]}$$

   c **Sketch** the reaction pathway (energy level) diagram for this reaction to show the breaking of bonds in hydrogen and chlorine and the formation of bonds in hydrogen chloride. Do not show the activation energy. **[3]**

   d Is energy absorbed or released when hydrogen chloride decomposes to hydrogen and chlorine? Explain your answer. **[1]**

   e Use the enthalpy cycle in Figure 6.4 to calculate the bond energy of the C—Cl bond in carbon tetrachloride, CCl_4.

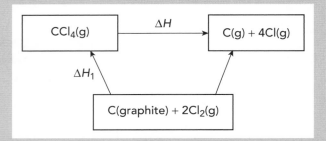

Figure 6.4

$$\Delta H_1^{\ominus} = -129.6 \ kJ\,mol^{-1}$$

$$\Delta H_{at}^{\ominus}\left[\tfrac{1}{2}Cl_2(g)\right] = +121.7 \ kJ\,mol^{-1}$$

$$\Delta H_{at}^{\ominus}[C(graphite)] = +716.7 \ kJ\,mol^{-1} \qquad \textbf{[4]}$$

[Total: 17]

3 a Define standard enthalpy change of neutralisation. **[2]**

   b Describe how you would carry out an experiment to find the enthalpy change of neutralisation of hydrochloric acid with sodium hydroxide. **[5]**

   c $50 \ cm^3$ of $1.0 \ mol\,dm^{-3}$ aqueous sodium hydroxide is mixed with $25 \ cm^3$ of $1.0 \ mol\,dm^{-3}$ sulfuric acid.

$$2NaOH(aq) + H_2SO_4(aq) \rightarrow Na_2SO_4(aq) + 2H_2O(l)$$

COMMAND WORD

Sketch: make a simple drawing showing the key features.

TIP

You should label the axes of a sketch graph. In part **2 c** make sure that you include the arrows for the activation energy and enthalpy change and label them appropriately.

TIPS

The process for working out the unknown value in part **2 e** is the same as with other enthalpy cycles but you will need to read the question carefully.

ΔH_{at} is the energy needed to form 1 mol of gaseous atoms from an element in its normal state.

TIP

Remember to write definitions carefully.

The maximum temperature increase was 8.9 °C.

Calculate the enthalpy change of neutralisation.

Specific heat capacity of water = 4.18 J g^{-1} °C^{-1}. [4]

d The enthalpy change of the reaction shown as equation A cannot be measured directly.

Equation A: $Ca(s) + CuO(s) \rightarrow CaO(s) + Cu(s)$

i Explain why the enthalpy change cannot be measured directly. [1]

ii You are given the enthalpy change $Ca(s) + \frac{1}{2}O_2(g) \rightarrow CaO(s)$.

What other enthalpy change is needed to calculate the enthalpy change in equation A? Write the equation which represents this enthalpy change. [2]

[Total: 14]

TIP

Think about a suitable enthalpy cycle that could be constructed when answering part d.

> Chapter 7
Redox reactions

CHAPTER OUTLINE

In this chapter you will learn how to:

- calculate oxidation numbers of elements in compounds and ions

- explain and use the terms redox, oxidation, reduction and disproportionation in terms of electron transfer and changes in oxidation number

- explain and use the terms oxidising agent and reducing agent

- use changes in oxidation numbers to help balance chemical equations

- use Roman numerals to indicate the degree of oxidation or reduction of an element in a compound.

Exercise 7.1 Oxidation numbers

This exercise will familiarise you with the use of **oxidation number** rules to deduce the oxidation state of atoms or ions in compounds.

a   Copy and complete the following sentences.

   i   The sum of the oxidation numbers in a compound is _____.

   ii   The sum of the oxidation numbers in an ion is equal to _____.

   iii   The oxidation number of fluorine in compounds is _____.

   iv   The oxidation number of oxygen in compounds is _____, except in peroxides where it is _____.

   v   The total oxidation number of the sulfur and the four oxygen atoms in SO_4^{2-} is _____.

b   Fill in the gaps in the procedure given below to find the oxidation number of Fe in Fe_2O_3.

   The sum of the oxidation numbers of all the atoms in Fe_2O_3 is _____.

   Each O atom has an oxidation number of _____.

   The oxidation number for three O atoms is _____.

   The oxidation number for two Fe atoms is _____.

   So each Fe atom has an oxidation number of _____.

> **TIP**
>
> Check that you know the fixed oxidation numbers of particular atoms or ions before starting this exercise.

c   Fill in the gaps in the procedure given below to find the oxidation number of N in the NO_3^- ion.

The sum of the oxidation numbers of all the atoms in the NO_3^- ion is _____.

Each O atom has an oxidation number of _____.

The oxidation number for three O atoms is _____.

The oxidation number for the N atom is _____.

d   Deduce the oxidation numbers of the atoms that are underlined.

i $\underline{Cr}_2O_3$

ii $Sr\underline{Br}_2$

iii $\underline{S}O_3$

iv $\underline{As}_2O_5$

v $HC\underline{l}O_4$

vi $\underline{P}O_4^{3-}$

vii $\underline{S}O_3^{2-}$

Exercise 7.2 Oxidation and reduction

This exercise will help familiarise you with **oxidation** and **reduction**. It also gives you practice in writing half-equations.

TIPS
The more positive (or less negative) an oxidation number, the more oxidised an atom is.
The more negative (or less positive) an oxidation number, the more reduced an atom is.
Remember OIL RIG as Oxidation Is Loss (of electrons) and Reduction Is Gain (of electrons).

KEY WORDS
oxidation: the loss of electrons from an atom, ion or molecule.
reduction: the gain of electrons by an atom, ion or molecule.

a   Deduce the change in oxidation number for the atoms that are underlined. In each case, state whether the change is oxidation or reduction.

i $2\underline{Fe}_2O_3 + 3C \rightarrow 4\underline{Fe} + 3CO_2$

ii $Cl_2 + 2\underline{Br}^- \rightarrow 2Cl^- + \underline{Br}_2$

iii $4\underline{P}H_3 + 8O_2 \rightarrow \underline{P}_4O_{10} + 6H_2O$

iv $\underline{S}_2Cl_2 + Cl_2 \rightarrow 2\underline{S}Cl_2$

v $IO^- + \underline{N}O_2^- \rightarrow I^- + \underline{N}O_3^-$

vi $Ca\underline{S}O_4 + 4C \rightarrow Ca\underline{S} + 4CO$

b State whether oxidation or reduction is occurring in each of these half-equations.

  i $Fe^{3+} + e^- \rightarrow Fe^{2+}$

  ii $Cu \rightarrow Cu^{2+} + 2e^-$

  iii $2Cl^- \rightarrow Cl_2 + 2e^-$

  iv $IO^- + H_2O + 2e^- \rightarrow I^- + 2OH^-$

  v $VO^{2+} + 2H^+ + e^- \rightarrow V^{3+} + H_2O$

c Balance these half-equations by copying them and adding electrons to either the reactant or product side.

  i $Ni \rightarrow Ni^{2+}$

  ii $HNO_2 + H_2O \rightarrow NO_3^- + 3H^+$

  iii $Te + 2H_2O \rightarrow TeO_2 + 4H^+$

  iv $Fe^{3+} \rightarrow Fe^{2+}$

  v $MnO_4^- + 8H^+ \rightarrow Mn^{2+} + 4H_2O$

Exercise 7.3 Oxidising agents and reducing agents

This exercise will help familiarise you with **oxidising agents** and **reducing agents** as well as giving you further practice in using oxidation numbers.

a Define an oxidising agent in terms of **electron transfer**.

b Describe a reducing agent in terms of both change in oxidation number and electron transfer.

c Name the oxidising agent in each of these equations. In each case give a reason in terms of change in oxidation number of the relevant atoms.

  i $2I^- + Br_2 \rightarrow I_2 + 2Br^-$

  ii $3CuO + 2NH_3 \rightarrow 3Cu + N_2 + 3H_2O$

  iii $H_2SO_4 + 2HI \rightarrow S + I_2 + 4H_2O$

d Name the reducing agent in each of these equations. In each case give a reason in terms of change in oxidation number of the relevant atoms.

  i $H_2O_2 + 2I^- + 2H^+ \rightarrow 2H_2O + I_2$

  ii $Cl_2 + 2Br^- \rightarrow 2Cl^- + Br_2$

  iii $H_2S + I_2 \rightarrow 2H^+ + 2I^- + S$

Exercise 7.4 Redox equations

Oxidation and reduction usually occur together. These reactions are called redox reactions. This exercise gives you practice in combining **half-equations** and using oxidation numbers to balance chemical equations.

KEY WORDS

oxidising agent: a substance which brings about oxidation by removing electrons from another atom or ion.

reducing agent: a substance which brings about reduction by donating (giving) electrons to another atom or ion.

electron transfer: in terms of redox reactions – loss of electrons by one species (oxidation) and gain of electrons by another species (reduction).

KEY WORD

half-equation: an equation which shows either oxidation or reduction only. These are sometimes called ion–electron equations, because you need to balance the equation by including the correct number of electrons.

a Define the term *redox reaction*. Include these words in your answer.

chemical reaction	oxidation	reduction	simultaneous

b Zinc reacts with silver ions to form zinc ions and silver.
One of the half-equations is:

Equation A: $Zn \rightarrow Zn^{2+} + 2e^-$

i Copy and complete the other half-equation:

$Ag^+ + \rightarrow Ag$

ii How many electrons are needed to balance the number of electrons in Equation A?

iii Write the equation for the reaction of zinc with silver ions by combining the two half-equations.

> **TIP**
>
> Half-equations can be combined by making sure the numbers of electrons lost and gained are the same in each half-equation.

c Combine each pair of half-equations.

i $Cl_2 + 2e^- \rightarrow 2Cl^-$
$Fe^{2+} \rightarrow Fe^{3+} + e^-$

ii $2H^+ + 2e^- \rightarrow H_2$
$Al \rightarrow Al^{3+} + 3e^-$

iii $IO_3^- + 6H^+ + 5e^- \rightarrow \frac{1}{2}I_2 + 3H_2O$
$2I^- \rightarrow I_2 + 2e^-$

iv $2Hg^{2+} + 2e^- \rightarrow Hg_2^{2+}$
$Cr^{2+} \rightarrow Cr^{3+} + e^-$

d Balance this equation using oxidation numbers by following the steps shown.

$MnO_4^- + Cr^{2+} + H^+ \rightarrow Mn^{2+} + Cr^{3+} + H_2O$

i Copy the equation and write the oxidation numbers of the Mn and Cr atoms or ions below each relevant species.

ii Deduce the oxidation number changes:

Mn from _____ to _____ = _____

Cr from _____ to _____ = _____

iii Balance the oxidation number changes by writing large numbers in front of the relative species.

iv Balance the charges by putting the correct number in front of H^+.

v Balance the water.

> **TIP**
>
> When balancing equations using the oxidation number method, remember that the oxidation number is per atom.

e Use the oxidation number method to balance these unbalanced equations.

i $Cu^+ \rightarrow Cu + Cu^{2+}$

ii $I^- + Fe^{3+} \rightarrow I_2 + Fe^{2+}$

iii $Fe_2O_3 + CO \rightarrow Fe + CO_2$

iv $IO_3^- + Fe^{2+} + H^+ \rightarrow \frac{1}{2}I_2 + Fe^{3+} + 3H_2O$

v $CuO + NH_3 \rightarrow Cu + N_2 + H_2O$

vi $Fe^{3+} + H_2S \rightarrow Fe^{2+} + 2H^+ + S$

vii $MnO_4^{2-} + Cl_2 \rightarrow MnO_4^- + 2Cl^-$

viii $MnO_4^{2-} + H^+ \rightarrow MnO_4^- + MnO_2 + H_2O$

f   i   Explain the meaning of the term **disproportionation**.

   ii Which two of the equations in part **e** are disproportionation reactions?

Exercise 7.5 Naming compounds

This exercise revises how **Roman numerals** (numbers) are used to describe the oxidation number of particular elements in a compound. You are going to use Roman numerals to name compounds and deduce the formula of a compound from its name.

> ### TIPS
>
> Compounds containing oxygen and another element in their negative ions are –ates
>
> The oxidation number which appears in the name of a compound is usually the oxidation number of the least electronegative element. So ClO_2 is chlorine(IV) oxide.

a   Give the **systematic name** of these compounds to include the oxidation number as Roman numerals:

   i Fe_2CO_3 ii MnO_2 iii I_2O_5 iv $NaBrO_3$ v $Cr(OH)_3$ vi K_2MnO_4

b   Deduce the formula for these compounds.

i potassium chlorate(VII)	iv tin(IV) chloride
ii gold(III) chloride-2 water	v potassium chlorate(I)
iii sodium iodate(V)	vi ammonium vanadate(V)

KEY WORDS

disproportionation: a simultaneous oxidation and reduction of the same species in a chemical reaction.

Roman numerals: numbers (I, II, III, IV etc) used to indicate the oxidation state of the least electronegative element in a compound.

systematic names: the names given by the International Union of Pure and Applied Chemistry to name chemical compounds.

EXAM-STYLE QUESTIONS

1   Barium reacts with cold water to form barium hydroxide and hydrogen.

   a   **State** the oxidation numbers of barium in:

     i   barium metal [1]

     ii   barium hydroxide. [1]

   b   Write a balanced equation for this reaction. [2]

   c   Construct two half-equations for this reaction to show:

     i   the change from barium to barium ions [1]

     ii   the change from water to hydrogen and hydroxide ions. [1]

     iii   In which of these half-equations is reduction occurring? Explain your answer. [1]

   d   Iron(**II**) ions react with hydrogen peroxide.

$$2Fe^{2+} + 2H^+ + H_2O_2 \rightarrow 2Fe^{3+} + 2H_2O$$

     i   Which species is acting as a reducing agent in this reaction? Explain your answer. [1]

     ii   Write the half-equation for the reaction involving reduction. [2]

   e   Hydrogen peroxide reacts with Mn^{2+} ions in the presence of OH^- ions to form MnO_2 and water.

     i   **Deduce** the **oxidation number change** of the manganese. [1]

     ii   Deduce the oxidation number change of the hydrogen peroxide. [1]

     iii   Construct a balanced equation for this reaction. [2]

                                 [Total: 14]

2   Sodium nitrate, $NaNO_3$, decomposes to sodium nitrite, $NaNO_2$, when heated.

$$2NaNO_3 \rightarrow 2NaNO_2 + O_2$$

   a   Give the oxidation numbers of:

     i   nitrogen in $NaNO_3$ [1]

     ii   nitrogen in $NaNO_2$. [1]

     iii   Explain in term of electrons and oxidation numbers how you know this is a redox reaction. [3]

     iv   Give the systematic name of $NaNO_2$. [1]

   b   In acidic conditions, iodide ions react with nitrite ions.

$$2I^- + 2NO_2^- + 4H^+ \rightarrow I_2 + 2NO + 2H_2O$$

     i   Deduce the oxidation number change when one iodide ion is converted to one iodine atom. [1]

     ii   Deduce the oxidation number change when one nitrogen atom in NO_2^- is converted to one nitrogen atom in NO. [1]

     iii   Use your answers to parts **i** and **ii** to explain why one mole of iodide ions reacts with one mole of nitrite ions. [1]

     iv   Which species is an oxidising agent? Explain your answer. [1]

COMMAND WORDS

State: express in clear terms.

Deduce: conclude from available information.

TIPS

In parts **d** and **e** don't forget to balance the H^+ or OH^- ions last.

Construct is sometimes used instead of the word *write* when you have to work out a balanced equation from first principles.

KEY WORDS

oxidation number change: the increase or decrease in the oxidation number of a given atom in an equation, e.g. in $Fe + 2HCl \rightarrow FeCl_2 + H_2$ the oxidation number change of the Fe is $0 \rightarrow +2 = +2$.

CONTINUED

TIP

In part **c** don't forget to balance the H$^+$ last.

c The nitrite ion can react with manganate(VII) ions, MnO_4^-, under acidic conditions, H$^+$, to form manganese(II) ions, nitrate ions and water.

   i Deduce the oxidation number change when one manganese ion is formed from one manganese atom in MnO_4^-. [1]

   ii Deduce the oxidation number change of one nitrogen atom. [1]

   iii Write a balanced equation for this reaction. [2]

[Total: 14]

3 This question is about oxidation numbers and their use in balancing equations.

The unbalanced equation for the reaction of iodine(V) oxide with hydrogen sulfide is shown here:

$$I_2O_5 + H_2S \rightarrow I_2 + S + H_2O$$

a Deduce the oxidation number of sulfur in:

   i H_2S [1]

   ii S [1]

   iii Which species has been oxidised in this reaction? Explain your answer. [1]

b Identify the reducing agent in this reaction. Explain your answer. [1]

c i What oxidation number change is needed in sulfur to balance the oxidation number change of two iodine atoms? [1]

   ii Construct the balanced equation for this reaction. [1]

d Hydrogen peroxide reacts with iodide ions:

$$H_2O_2 + 2I^- + 2H^+ \rightarrow 2H_2O + I_2$$

Construct two half-equations for this reaction. For each equation, explain which species has been oxidised or reduced. [4]

[Total: 10]

TIP

Include changes in oxidation number in your answer to part **d**.

Chapter 8

Equilibria

CHAPTER OUTLINE

In this chapter you will learn how to:

- explain what is meant by the terms reversible reaction, dynamic equilibrium and closed system

- define and use le Chatelier's principle to deduce the effects of changes in temperature, concentration, pressure or presence of a catalyst on a reaction at equilibrium

- carry out equilibrium calculations using equilibrium expressions involving concentrations, K_c and partial pressures, K_p

- understand which factors affect the value of the equilibrium constant

- describe and explain the conditions used in the Haber process and the Contact process

- name and write the formula of some common acids and alkalis, and describe salt formation

- describe acidity, alkalinity and a neutral solution in terms of the pH scale

- describe the Brønsted–Lowry theory of acids and bases

- describe strong acids and strong bases and weak acids and weak bases in terms of degree of dissociation

- explain the differences in physical and chemical behaviour of strong and weak acids

- describe neutralisation reactions in terms of $H^+ + OH^- \rightarrow H_2O$

- sketch pH titration curves using combinations of strong and weak acids with strong and weak alkalis

- select suitable indicators for acid / alkali titrations using data provided.

Exercise 8.1 Equilibrium

This exercise will familiarise you with some terms associated with equilibrium and gives you practice in deducing the effect of different **conditions** on the **position of equilibrium**.

KEY WORDS

conditions: when referring to chemical reactions, things other than specific chemicals used in the reaction, e.g. temperature, pressure, pH.

position of equilibrium: the relative amounts of products and reactants present in an equilibrium mixture.

a Match the words or phrases 1 to 6 on the left to the descriptions A to F on the right.

1 surroundings	**A** products are continually forming reactants and reactants forming products
2 dynamic equilibrium	**B** examples are the air, the solvent and the container in which the reaction takes place
3 reversible reaction	**C** no matter is gained from or lost to the surroundings
4 equilibrium	**D** this describes how far the reaction is towards the products or reactants
5 closed system	**E** reaction in which both reactants and products are present and their concentrations are fixed under given conditions
6 position of equilibrium	**F** reaction in which the products can be changed back to the reactants by changing the conditions

> **KEY WORDS**
>
> **dynamic equilibrium:** reactants are being converted to products at the same rate as products are being converted back to reactants.
>
> **reversible reaction:** a reaction in which products can be changed back to reactants by reversing the conditions.
>
> **closed system:** a system in which matter is not lost or gained, e.g. gases in a closed jar.

b The equation for the synthesis of ammonia is:

$$N_2(g) + 3H_2(g) \rightleftharpoons 2NH_3 \qquad \Delta H_r = -92.4 \text{ kJ mol}^{-1}$$

Describe and explain the effect of the following on the position of equilibrium.

i Increasing the concentration of hydrogen

ii Increasing the concentration of ammonia

iii Decreasing the pressure

iv Increasing the temperature

v Liquefying the ammonia (ammonia has a much higher melting point than nitrogen or hydrogen).

c At 300 °C hydrogen iodide decomposes to form hydrogen and iodine.

$$2HI(g) \rightleftharpoons H_2(g) + I_2(g) \qquad \Delta H_r = +9.6 \text{ kJ mol}^{-1}$$

Describe and explain the effect of the following on the position of equilibrium.

i Increasing the pressure

ii Adding a catalyst

iii Increasing the concentration of hydrogen

iv Decreasing the concentration of hydrogen iodide.

d Chlorine is a green gas, iodine monochloride (ICl) is a brown liquid and iodine trichloride, (ICl$_3$) is a yellow solid. When chlorine gas is passed through a tube containing iodine monochloride, iodine trichloride is formed as shown in **a**.

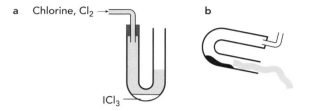

Figure 8.1: A reaction of chlorine.

There is an equilibrium between the reactants (chlorine and iodine monochloride) and the product.

i Write a chemical equation to show this reaction.

ii The U-tube is tipped to one side as shown in **b**. Describe what you would observe.

iii Explain these **observations**.

iv What would you observe when more chlorine is passed through the U-tube?

e Copy and complete this sentence which describes **le Chatelier's principle**.

When any of the conditions affecting the _____ of _____

are changed, e.g. pressure, _____ or _____, the position of

equilibrium moves to _____ the change.

KEY WORDS

observations: what you see happening (also includes what you hear, feel and smell).

le Chatelier's principle: if one or more factors that affect a dynamic equilibrium is changed, the position of equilibrium moves to minimise this change.

Exercise 8.2 Equilibrium expressions

This exercise will give you practice in writing **equilibrium expressions** including those using partial pressure.

TIPS

When writing equilibrium expressions:

- The concentration terms for the products go at the top.
- Square brackets indicate the concentration of the substance within the brackets.
- The concentration terms are to the power of the number of moles in the balanced equation, e.g. 3H$_2$ in an equation is written as [H$_2$]^3 in the equilibrium expression.
- For partial pressures, the equilibrium expression is written without square brackets, e.g. $p_{H_2}^3$

KEY WORDS

equilibrium expression: a simple relationship that links K_c to the equilibrium concentrations, or K_p to the equilibrium partial pressures, of reactants and products and the stoichiometric equation.

a Copy and complete the following sentences using words from the list:

constant   equilibrium   products   reactants   stoichiometric

An equilibrium expression links the concentration of _____ and

_____ to the _____ equation. Under stated conditions the value

calculated from the equilibrium expression is called the _____ _____.

b Which two of these statements about the effect of different factors on the value of K_c are correct?

A The value of K_c increases with increase in pressure.

B The value of K_c for an exothermic reaction increases with increase in temperature.

C A catalyst does affect the value of K_c.

D The value of K_c for an endothermic reaction decreases with decrease in temperature.

E The value of K_c decreases with decrease in concentration of reactants.

c Copy this table. Complete the equilibrium expressions and fill in the correct units. The first three have been partly done for you.

> **TIPS**
>
> The units for K_c can be worked out by putting $mol\,dm^{-3}$ instead of concentration in each square bracket and then cancelling.
>
> Note that the positive power is written first even if it looks unusual, e.g. $dm^9\,mol^{-3}$.

Chemical equation	Equilibrium expression	Units
$Br_2(g) + H_2(g) \rightleftharpoons 2HBr(g)$	$K_c = \dfrac{[\ \_\ ]^-}{[\ \_\ ][\ \_\ ]}$	none
$N_2(g) + 3H_2(g) \rightleftharpoons 2NH_3(g)$	$K_c = \dfrac{[\ \_\ ]^-}{[\ \_\ ][\ \_\ ]^-}$	$dm^6\,mol^{-2}$
$CaCO_3(s) \rightleftharpoons CaO(s) + CO_2(g)$	$K_c = [\ \_\ ]$	$mol\,dm^{-3}$
$2NO_2(g) \rightleftharpoons 2NO(g) + O_2(g)$	$K_c = \dfrac{[\ \_\ ]^-[\ \_\ ]}{[\ \_\ ]^-}$	
$3Fe(s) + 4H_2O(g) \rightleftharpoons Fe_3O_4(s) + 4H_2(g)$		
$Cu(s) + 2Ag^+(aq) \rightleftharpoons Cu^{2+}(aq) + 2Ag(s)$		
$2CrO_4^{2-}(aq) + 2H^+(aq) \rightleftharpoons Cr_2O_7^{2-}(aq) + H_2O(l)$		

Table 8.1: Equilibrium expressions.

d An **equilibrium constant**, K_p, can be written in terms of partial pressures, p_x.

Copy this table. Complete the equilibrium expressions and fill in the correct units. The first two have been done for you.

Chemical equation	Equilibrium expression	Units
$2NO_2(g) \rightleftharpoons 2NO(g) + O_2(g)$	$K_p = \dfrac{P^2_{NO} \times P_{O_2}}{P^2_{NO_2}}$	Pa (or atm)
$2SO_2(g) + O_2(g) \rightleftharpoons 2SO_3(g)$	$K_p = \dfrac{P^2_{SO_3}}{P^2_{SO_2} \times P_{O_2}}$	Pa^{-1} (or atm^{-1})
$2HI(g) \rightleftharpoons I_2(g) + H_2(g)$		
$PCl_5(g) \rightleftharpoons PCl_3(g) + Cl_2(g)$		
$3Fe(s) + 4H_2O(g) \rightleftharpoons Fe_3O_4(s) + 4H_2(g)$		

Table 8.2: Equilibrium expressions.

KEY WORDS

equilibrium constant: a constant which is calculated from the equilibrium expression for the reaction. It can be in terms of concentrations, K_c or partial pressures, K_p.

Exercise 8.3 Acids, alkalis and neutralisation

This is largely a revision exercise about acids, alkalis and **salt** formation. You will be familiar with most of the material from your previous course.

KEY WORD

salt: a compound formed when an acid reacts with a base or metal.

> **TIP**
>
> acid + alkali → salt + water
> pH values below pH 7 are acidic and above pH 7 are alkaline. pH 7 is neutral. Make sure that you know the colours of universal indicator at different pH values.

a Name these acids and alkalis.

  i HNO_3 **ii** H_2SO_4 **iii** KOH **iv** NH_3

b Give the formulae of these acids and alkalis.

  i ethanoic acid   **ii** hydrochloric acid   **iii** sodium hydroxide.

c Suggest pH values for concentrated aqueous solutions of each of the following:

  i NH_3 **ii** HNO_3 **iii** KOH **iv** ethanoic acid   **v** water

d Complete and balance these equations to show the formation of salts by **neutralisation**.

  i   ___ $NaOH + H_2SO_4 \rightarrow$ _____ + _____

  ii $HNO_3 + NH_3 \rightarrow$ _____

  iii   ___ $KOH + H_3PO_4 \rightarrow$ _____ + _____

  iv $Ba(OH)_2 + $ ___ $HCl \rightarrow$ _____ + _____

e Give the names of the salts formed in part **d**.

f **i** Describe how to use universal indicator solution to determine the pH of a solution.

  ii Give the results for part **f i** for:

  • a very alkaline solution

  • a slightly acidic solution

KEY WORD

neutralisation: the reaction of an acid with an alkali to form a salt and water.

TIP

Make sure you can name and write the formula of the acids and alkalis listed in the syllabus.

Exercise 8.4 Acid–base equilibrium

This exercise will familiarise you with some terms used about **acids** and **bases** and provides further examples of how to write equilibrium expressions.

> **KEY WORDS**
>
> **acid:** a proton (H^+ ion) donor (Brønsted–Lowry definition).
>
> **base:** a proton (H^+ ion) acceptor (Brønsted–Lowry definition).

TIPS

Common laboratory acids are strong acids, e.g. hydrochloric, sulfuric, nitric acids.

Organic acids containing the –COOH group are generally weak acids.

Hydroxides of Group 1 elements are strong bases.

Ammonia and organic bases, e.g. CH_3NH_2, are weak bases.

a Match the beginnings of sentences 1 to 7 with the endings A to G.

1 An acid is …	**A** … a proton acceptor.
2 **Dissociation** of acids and bases refers to …	**B** … it dissociates completely into H^+ ions and X^- ions.
3 A base is **strong** if …	**C** … a proton donor.
4 An acid is **weak** if …	**D** … it dissociates partially into OH^- ions and Y^+ ions.
5 A base is …	**E** … it dissociates completely into OH^- ions and Y^+ ions.
6 A base is weak if…	**F** … it dissociates partially into H^+ ions and X^- ions.
7 An acid is strong if…	**G** … the break-up of molecules into ions.

> **KEY WORDS**
>
> **dissociation:** the break-up of molecules into ions.
>
> **strong acids and bases:** acid and bases which dissociate completely in solution.
>
> **weak acids and bases:** acid and bases which dissociate partially (incompletely) in solution.

b In each of the following equations, identify which reactant is the acid and which reactant is the base.

i $HCl + H_2O \rightleftharpoons H_3O^+ + Cl^-$

ii $CH_3NH_2 + H_2O \rightleftharpoons CH_3NH_3^+ + OH^-$

iii $NH_4^+ + H_2O \rightleftharpoons H_3O^+ + NH_3$

iv $NH_2OH + H_2O \rightleftharpoons NH_3OH^+ + OH^-$

v $H_2SO_4 + H_2O \rightleftharpoons H_3O^+ + HSO_4^-$

vi $H_2SO_4 + HNO_3 \rightleftharpoons HSO_4^- + H_2NO_3^+$

c Which of the acids in part **b** are strong acids in aqueous solution?

d Identify the two pairs of acids and bases which are conjugate in each of these equations.

   i $HSiO_3^- + H_2O \rightleftharpoons SiO_3^{2-} + H_3O^+$

   ii $HCO_2H + H_2O \rightleftharpoons HCO_2^- + H_3O^+$

   iii $CH_3NHCH_2NH_3^+ + H_2O \rightleftharpoons CH_3NHCH_2NH_2 + H_3O^+$

   iv $NH_2OH + H_2O \rightleftharpoons NH_3OH^+ + OH^-$

e An acid of concentration $4\ mol\,dm^{-3}$ reacts slowly with magnesium and has a pH of 4.

Which one of these statements about this acid is correct?

   A   It is a concentrated solution of a strong acid.

   B   It is a dilute solution of a weak acid.

   C   It is a dilute solution of a strong acid.

   D   It is a concentrated solution of a weak acid.

f Copy and complete the equilibrium expressions for the dissociation of these acids or bases. Add the correct units.

Chemical equation	Equilibrium expression	Units
$C_2H_5CO_2H(aq) \rightleftharpoons C_2H_5CO_2^-(aq) + H^+(aq)$	$K = \dfrac{[\ \_\ ]\,[\ \_\ ]}{[\ \_\ ]}$	$mol\,dm^{-3}$
$N_2H_4(aq) + H_2O(l) \rightleftharpoons N_2H_5^+(aq) + OH^-(aq)$	$K =$	
$H_2O_2(aq) \rightleftharpoons HO_2^-(aq) + H^+(aq)$	$K =$	
$Pb(OH)_2(s) \rightleftharpoons PbOH^+(aq) + OH^-(aq)$	$K =$	
$HPO_4^{2-}(aq) \rightleftharpoons PO_4^{3-}(aq) + H^+(aq)$	$K =$	

Table 8.3: Equilibrium expressions.

Exercise 8.5 Calculations using K_c

This exercise gives you practice in calculating values of the **equilibrium constant**, K_c, from the data provided. It also introduces you to more complex calculations.

TIPS

When you do equilibrium calculations:

- Write the balanced equation.
- Put the initial concentrations that you are given below the correct species.
- Work out the equilibrium concentrations by subtracting the concentration of product at equilibrium from the initial concentrations of reactants (taking into account the mole ratios in the equation).
- If the equilibrium expression has the same number of concentration terms at the top and bottom, you can use moles instead of molar concentrations.

TIPS

Part **d** is an extension question. There is enough information given to answer it though.

Acids and bases are said to be *conjugate* if they are related to each other in the chemical equation by the difference of a proton.

KEY WORDS

K_c **(equilibrium constant in terms of concentrations):** constant calculated from the equilibrium expression using concentrations in $mol\,dm^{-3}$.

a When a sealed tube containing hydrogen and iodine is heated, the following equilibrium occurs:

$$H_2(g) + I_2(g) \rightleftharpoons 2HI(g)$$

The equilibrium concentrations in $mol\,dm^{-3}$ are: $[H_2] = 1.14 \times 10^{-2}$, $[I_2] = 0.12 \times 10^{-2}$, $[HI] = 2.52 \times 10^{-2}$

i Write the equilibrium expression for this reaction.

ii Calculate the value of K_c.

iii Explain why there are no units for K_c for this expression.

b Pentene reacts with ethanoic acid. The following equilibrium occurs:

$$\underset{\text{pentene}}{C_5H_{10}} + \underset{\text{ethanoic acid}}{CH_3CO_2H} \rightleftharpoons \underset{\text{pentyl ethanoate}}{CH_3CO_2C_5H_{11}}$$

Volume of solution = 800 cm³

Initial amount of pentene = 6.40×10^{-3} mol

Initial amount of ethanoic acid = 1.00×10^{-3} mol

Equilibrium amount of pentyl ethanoate = 7.84×10^{-4} mol

Work through the following procedure to calculate the value of K_c for this reaction.

i Moles of pentene at equilibrium = _____

ii Moles of ethanoic acid at equilibrium = _____

iii Concentration of pentene at equilibrium in $mol\,dm^{-3}$ = _____

iv Concentration of ethanoic acid at equilibrium in $mol\,dm^{-3}$ = _____

v Write the equilibrium expression for K_c = _____

vi Calculate the value of K_c. Include the units.

Exercise 8.6 Calculations using K_p

This exercise provides practice in calculations involving **partial pressures** and the **equilibrium constant**, K_p.

TIPS

For K_p calculations remember that:

- The partial pressure, p, of a gas is given by

$$p = \frac{\text{number of moles of a particular gas in a mixture}}{\text{total number of moles of gas in the mixture}} \times \text{total pressure}$$

- The partial pressures of each gas in a mixture add together to give the total pressure.

KEY WORDS

partial pressure: pressure that a single gas contributes to the overall pressure in a mixture of gases. It is the proportion of the pressure exerted by a single gas in a mixture.

K_p (equilibrium constant in terms of partial pressures): constant calculated from the equilibrium expression using partial pressures in kPa or atmospheres (atm).

a   Define the term *mole fraction*.

b   A mixture of gases in a closed container contains 1.0 mol nitrogen, 3.5 mol hydrogen and 0.5 mol argon.

    i   What is the total number of moles present?

    ii   Calculate the partial pressure of each gas if the total pressure is 40 atmospheres.

c   0.6 g He, 6.4 g CH_4 and 9.6 g oxygen are placed in a closed container. The total pressure of the gases is 200 atmospheres.

    i   Calculate the mole fraction of methane in the mixture.

    ii   Calculate the partial pressure of methane. Express your answer to 3 significant figures. A_r values: H = 1.0, C = 12.0, He = 4.0, O = 16.0.

d   Nitrogen(II) oxide reacts with oxygen to form nitrogen(IV) oxide:

$$2NO(g) + O_2(g) \rightleftharpoons 2NO_2(g)$$

At equilibrium there are 0.96 mol of NO_2, 0.04 mol of NO and 0.02 mol of O_2 present.

The total pressure was 2×10^4 Pa.

    i   Calculate the partial pressure of each gas.

    ii   Write the equilibrium expression for this reaction in terms of K_p.

    iii Calculate the value of K_p. Include the correct units.

Exercise 8.7 Indicators and titration curves

This exercise will give you practice in describing how pH changes when strong or weak acids are added to strong or weak bases. It will also familiarise you with the use of specific indicators for particular types of acid–base titrations.

a   Copy and complete these sentences about indicators, using words from this list:

conjugate	ionised	left	molecular	narrow	right
strong	violet	weak	wide	yellow	

An **acid–base indicator** changes colour over a _____ pH range. These

indicators are usually _____ acids in which the acid, HIn, and its

_____ base, In⁻, have different colours. For example:

    $HIn \rightleftharpoons H^+ + In^-$
    yellow   violet

Adding excess acid to this indicator shifts the equilibrium to the _____

and the indicator turns _____. The colour of the indicator depends on the

relative concentrations of the _____ and un-ionised forms.

> **KEY WORDS**
>
> **acid–base indicator:** a compound that has two different ranges of colours depending on the pH of the solution in which it is placed. It changes colour over a narrow range of pH values.

b The diagram in Figure 8.2 is a **pH-titration curve**. It shows how the pH changes when a strong acid is added to a weak base.

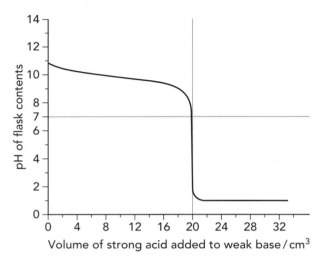

Figure 8.2: Changes in pH during a titration.

i Describe in detail the shape of this curve.

ii What volume of acid has been added when the alkali has been just neutralised?

c The table shows the pH **range** of some indicators.

Indicator	pH range
azolitmin	5.0–8.0
bromocresol green	3.8–5.4
thymol blue	1.2–2.8
thymolphthalein	8.3–10.6

Table 8.4: pH ranges.

i Which of these indicators is the best to use for determining the end-point of the reaction between a strong acid and a weak base? Explain your answer.

ii Methyl violet changes colour over the pH range 0 to 1.6. Explain why this indicator is not suitable for determining the **end-point**.

d Sketch graphs to show how the pH changes in the following titrations. In each case make sure that relevant pH values and volumes are shown.

i $20 \, cm^3$ of $0.1 \, mol \, dm^{-3}$ aqueous potassium hydroxide is titrated with $20 \, cm^3$ of $0.2 \, mol \, dm^{-3}$ ethanoic acid.

ii $20 \, cm^3$ of $0.01 \, mol \, dm^{-3}$ aqueous sodium hydroxide is titrated with $20 \, cm^3$ of $0.01 \, mol \, dm^{-3}$ sulfuric acid.

e Which indicators in the table would be most suitable for each of the titrations in part **d**?

EXAM-STYLE QUESTIONS

1 Hydrogen and carbon monoxide react at high temperature in the presence of a catalyst to form methanol, CH_3OH. The reaction is exothermic.

$$2H_2(g) + CO(g) \rightleftharpoons CH_3OH(g)$$

  a Suggest two ways by which you could increase the yield of methanol in the equilibrium mixture. **[2]**

  b The reaction is a dynamic equilibrium in a closed system. Define the terms:

    i dynamic equilibrium **[2]**

    ii closed system. **[1]**

  c What effect, if any, will the catalyst have on the position of equilibrium? **[1]**

  d The partial pressures in the equilibrium mixture are:

$$p_{CO} = 3.33 \times 10^4 \text{ Pa}$$

$$p_{H_2} = 6.67 \times 10^4 \text{ Pa}$$

$$p_{CH_3OH} = 9.92 \times 10^1 \text{ Pa}$$

    i Write the equilibrium expression in terms of partial pressures for this reaction. **[1]**

    ii Calculate the value of K_p for this reaction. Include the correct units. **[3]**

  e In another experiment, the number of moles of reactants at the start of the reaction was 16.8 mol of H_2 and 7.2 mol of CO. The total pressure was 5.00×10^4 Pa. Calculate the partial pressure of hydrogen in this mixture. **[2]**

[Total: 12]

2 Hydrogen reacts with gaseous sulfur to form hydrogen sulfide. The reaction is exothermic.

$$2H_2(g) + S_2(g) \rightleftharpoons 2H_2S(g)$$

  a Describe and explain the effect of each of the following on the position of equilibrium.

    i Removing some of the sulfur. **[2]**

    ii Decreasing the temperature. **[2]**

    iii Increasing the pressure. **[2]**

  b Write an equilibrium expression for K_c for this reaction. **[1]**

  c The K_c for this reaction is 9.40×10^5 units.

    i What are the units of K_c for this reaction? **[1]**

    ii The equilibrium concentration of H_2S is 0.442 mol dm^{-3}.
      The equilibrium concentration of H_2 is 0.234 mol dm^{-3}.
      Calculate the equilibrium concentration of S_2. **[3]**

  d Sulfur dioxide is oxidised to sulfur trioxide in a reversible reaction.

$$2SO_2(g) + O_2(g) \rightleftharpoons 2SO_3(g)$$

    i Write the equilibrium expression for this reaction in terms of partial pressures. **[1]**

TIPS

In question **1 b**, make sure that you remember all the details of the definitions in the syllabus.

In question **1 c**, you have been given partial pressures, so that you don't have to work out the mole fractions.

In question **1 e**, you need to rearrange the equilibrium expression.

TIPS

Question **2 a** asks you to both describe and explain the effects on the position of equilibrium. This means that you not only have to write what happens (describe) but you also have to use chemical ideas to write about why it happens (explain).

In part **a ii**, read the stem of the question carefully

ii   At equilibrium, the partial pressures of the gases are:

$P_{SO_2} = 10\ 100\ Pa$

$P_{O_2} = 68\ 800\ Pa$

$P_{SO_3} = 80\ 100\ Pa$

Calculate a value for K_p for this reaction.   [3]

e   The equilibrium $2SO_2(g) + O_2(g) \rightleftharpoons 2SO_3(g)$ is the essential part of the **Contact process** for the production of sulfuric acid. The reaction is exothermic.

i   Describe and explain the effect of increasing the pressure on this reaction.   [2]

ii   **Suggest** why the process is carried out at just above atmospheric pressure.   [2]

iii   The reaction is carried out at about 450 °C. Explain why:

• a temperature of 550 °C is not used   [1]

• a temperature of 350 °C is not used.   [1]

f   Ammonia is manufactured by the **Haber process**.

$N_2(g) + 3H_2(g) \rightleftharpoons 2NH_3(g)$

State the conditions required for the Haber process.   [3]

[Total: 24]

3   Ethanoic acid and nitric acid both ionise in water.

Equation 1: $CH_3CO_2H + H_2O \rightleftharpoons CH_3CO_2^- + H_3O^+$

Equation 2: $HNO_3 \rightleftharpoons NO_3^- + H^+$

a   Explain why ethanoic acid is a weak acid but nitric acid is a strong acid.   [2]

b   i   Write an equilibrium expression for K_c for Equation 1.   [1]

ii   The equilibrium expression for Equation 1 often omits the water and H_3O^+ is written as H^+. Explain why the water can be omitted.   [2]

c $0.1\ mol\,dm^{-3}$ nitric acid reacts with zinc ribbon rapidly but $0.1\ mol\,dm^{-3}$ ethanoic acid reacts with zinc ribbon slowly. Explain this difference.   [2]

KEY WORDS

Contact process: the process used to produce sulfuric acid. It specifically refers to the reaction $2SO_2(g) + O_2(g) \rightleftharpoons 2SO_3(g)$, using a V_2O_5 catalyst.

Haber process: the process used to produce ammonia. It specifically refers to the reaction $N_2(g) + 3H_2(g) \rightleftharpoons 2NH_3(g)$, using a catalyst of iron.

TIP

In part **f**, you will need to learn the conditions and why they are used in these processes.

TIPS

Make sure you include the relevant chemical theory when answering questions which use "explain".

Think about the concentration of water when answering part **b ii**.

Read part **d** carefully - you need to work out the change in oxidation number, not just the oxidation numbers themselves.

d Dilute nitric acid reacts with zinc to form zinc nitrate, ammonium nitrate and water:

$$4Zn + 10HNO_3 \rightarrow 4Zn(NO_3)_2 + NH_4NO_3 + 3H_2O$$

Determine the oxidation number change of:

i   the zinc [1]

ii the N in HNO_3 to the N in the NH_4^+ ion. [1]

e Nitric acid is neutralised by sodium hydroxide. Write the simplest ionic equation for this reaction. [1]

[Total: 10]

4 The diagram shows the pH change when $0.20\ mol\,dm^{-3}$ aqueous sodium hydroxide is added to ethanoic acid.

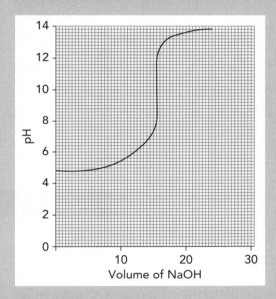

Figure 8.3

a Deduce the ionic equation for this reaction. [1]

b **i** Suggest a suitable indicator that could be used. [1]

   ii Bromophenol blue is yellow at pH 2.8 and blue at pH 4.6. Explain why bromophenol blue would not be used to indicate the end-point of this reaction. [1]

c Sketch a graph to show how the pH changes when a weak base is added to a strong acid. Label the axes fully, to include the pH values. [3]

[Total: 6]

> Chapter 9

Rates of reaction

CHAPTER OUTLINE

In this chapter you will learn how to:

- describe and use the terms rate of reaction, frequency of collisions, effective and non-effective collisions

- use experimental data to calculate the rate of a reaction

- explain, in terms of frequency of effective collisions, the effect of changes of concentration and pressure on the rate of reaction

- define activation energy and explain the importance of activation energy using the Boltzmann distribution curve

- use the Boltzmann distribution curve to explain the effect of temperature change on rate of reaction

- describe and use the term catalyst and explain in general terms how a catalyst works

- use the Boltzmann distribution curve to describe the effect of catalysts

- construct and interpret a reaction pathway diagram in the presence and absence of a catalyst.

Exercise 9.1 Collision theory

This exercise gives you practice in understanding **collision theory** and how changing concentration affects reaction rate.

a   Not all molecules of reactants form products when they collide. Figure 9.1 shows hydrogen and chlorine molecules colliding.

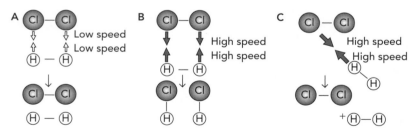

Figure 9.1: Collisions during a chemical reaction.

i   Which of diagrams A, B or C shows molecules with relatively high amounts of kinetic energy?

ii   Explain why the molecules in diagrams A and C are not likely to react when they collide.

iii Explain why the molecules in diagram B react when they collide.

iv   How do we describe collisions which result in a reaction?

b **i** Complete these sentences about activation energy using words from the list.

A_e colliding E_A maximum minimum react separate

Activation energy is the _____ energy that _____ particles

must have in order to _____. The symbol for activation energy is

_____.

ii A reaction is carried out in the absence of a catalyst.

Copy and complete Figure 9.2 to show the **activation energy**, the reactants and products and the enthalpy change, ΔH_r.

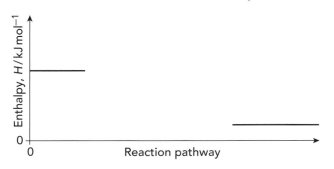

Figure 9.2: A typical reaction/enthalpy diagram.

KEY WORDS

activation energy, E_A: the minimum energy that colliding particles must possess to break bonds to start a chemical reaction.

iii Is the reaction exothermic or endothermic? Explain your answer.

iv How would the reaction pathway diagram differ if a catalyst was used.

c Copy and complete this sentence using words from the list:

activation **effective** **frequency** **greater** **proportion**

A reaction will speed up if the _____ of _____ collisions increases

and the _____ of particles with energy _____ than the _____

energy increases.

KEY WORDS

effective collisions: collisions of particles which lead to bond breaking and a chemical reaction.

frequency of collisions: the number of collisions per unit time, e.g. number of collisions per second.

d When excess magnesium reacts with 0.4 mol dm^{-3} hydrochloric acid, 15 cm^3 of hydrogen is released in the first 20 s of the reaction. When the reaction is repeated under the same conditions but using 0.8 mol dm^{-3} hydrochloric acid, 30 cm^3 of hydrogen is released in the first 20 s of the reaction. Explain this difference using the collision theory.

e Explain why increasing the pressure on a reaction involving gases increases the rate of reaction. The volume and temperature are constant.

Exercise 9.2 Rate of reaction

KEY WORDS

rate of reaction: the change in the amount or concentration of a particular reactant or product per unit time.

This exercise revises the concept of **rate of reaction** through a practical procedure. It also familiarises you with the skills required in presenting data and drawing graphs. You will need a sheet of graph paper for this exercise.

The reaction of excess calcium carbonate with $0.4 \, mol \, dm^{-3}$ hydrochloric acid was investigated using the apparatus shown in Figure 9.3. The calcium carbonate was in excess.

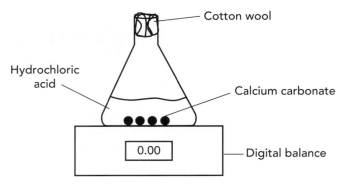

Figure 9.3: Following a reaction using change of mass.

a Write a balanced equation for this reaction including state symbols.

b The flask containing hydrochloric acid was placed on the digital balance. The calcium carbonate was added and the balance immediately set to zero. Readings were taken every 20 seconds. The readings are shown here. Mass is lost during the experiment but, for simplicity, the minus signs are not given.

> Start → 0.00; 0.10; 0.20; 0.28; 0.34; 0.39; 0.425; 0.45; 0.46; 0.49; 0.51; 0.515; 0.525; 0.53; 0.53; 0.53; 0.53; 0.53

i Construct a table to show how the mass of carbon dioxide produced varies with time.

ii Plot a graph of the mass of carbon dioxide released against time. Draw the curve of best fit.

iii Which point is anomalous?

iv For this experiment rate of reaction $= \dfrac{\text{change in mass in grams}}{\text{time taken in seconds}}$

Use the graph to deduce the average rate of reaction:

- over the first 20 s of the reaction

- from 20 to 40 s after the start of the reaction.

v Why is it more difficult to deduce the average rate of reaction between 40 and 100 s after the start of the reaction?

vi Suggest how you could deduce the rate of reaction at 100 s.

vii Calculate the rate of reaction at 100 s using the method you suggested in part **vi**.

c i How many moles of carbon dioxide have been collected when the reaction is complete? A_r values: C = 12.0, O = 16.0

ii Deduce the volume, in cm^3, of hydrochloric acid in the flask.

TIP

When drawing graphs, it is best to mark the points with an x so they can be distinguished from the gridlines.

TIP

When answering part **c ii** you have to use the information in the stem of the question, your answer to part **c i** and the stoichiometric equation (part **a**).

iii   What volume of carbon dioxide measured at r.t.p. would be released if it had been collected in a gas syringe?

iv   Would collecting the carbon dioxide in a gas syringe be a more accurate method than weighing the carbon dioxide? Give a reason for your answer.

d   The experiment was repeated using 0.5 mol dm⁻³ hydrochloric acid. All other conditions were kept the same. On the same grid as you drew the last graph, sketch the curve you would expect.

TIP

Sketch means make a simple drawing showing the key features. In part **d**, you don't need to draw the line showing points.

Exercise 9.3 Temperature and rate of reaction

This exercise revises the **Boltzmann distribution** of energy among particles to explain how change in temperature affects the rate of reaction. It also introduces an equation which may be unfamiliar to you. You will use this to explain why the increase in kinetic energy with increase in temperature has little effect on the increase of rate of reaction.

a   The Boltzmann distribution shows the energy distribution in a sample of molecules.

   i   Explain the shape of this graph in terms of the numbers of molecules having particular amounts of energy.

KEY WORDS

Boltzmann distribution: a graph showing the number of molecules with a particular kinetic energy plotted against the kinetic energy. The exact shape of the curve varies with temperature. The curve shows that only a very small proportion of the molecules have very high energies.

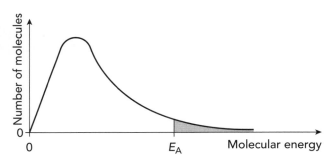

Figure 9.4: A typical Boltzmann distribution graph.

   ii   What does the symbol E_A represent? Explain the meaning of this term.

   iii   What does the shaded area under part of the graph represent?

b   When the temperature of a reaction mixture increases, what happens to the:

   i   average kinetic energy of the molecules

   ii   frequency of collisions

   iii   reaction rate?

c   The relative kinetic energy of molecules is given by the expression $RT = \frac{2}{3} E_k$,

   where $R = 8.31$ J mol⁻¹ K⁻¹, T is the temperature in kelvin and E_k is the relative average kinetic energy.

   i   Calculate the average kinetic energy of molecules:

   •   at 20 °C

   •   at 30 °C.

TIP

Remember that when temperature is increased, the peak of the Boltzmann distribution curve shifts to the right.

TIP

In part **c i**, you will need to rearrange the the expression to make E_k the subject. Read the question carefully and take care the units are correct.

ii Why does the increase in kinetic energy of the molecules not completely explain why the rate of reaction approximately doubles when the temperature increases by 10 °C?

d Figure 9.5 shows how the energy distribution changes when the temperature increases from 20 °C to 30 °C.

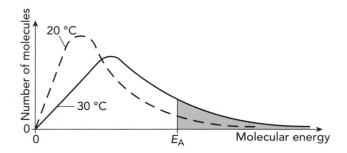

Figure 9.5: How a change in temperature affects a Boltzmann distribution.

Use the information in this graph to explain why there is a large increase in the rate of reaction when the temperature increases.

Exercise 9.4 Catalysis

This exercise familiarises you with how **catalysts** work.

a Figure 9.6 shows the Boltzmann distribution of the energy in molecules of reactants with and without a catalyst.

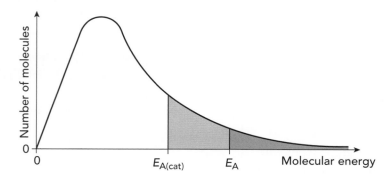

Figure 9.6: The effect of a catalyst on a Boltzmann distribution.

Use this diagram to explain how catalysis increases the rate of reaction.

b i Explain in general terms how a catalyst speeds up a chemical reaction.

ii A reaction is endothermic. Draw a labelled reaction pathway diagram to show the catalysed reaction as well as the uncatalysed reaction. In your diagram include labels for:

- the reactants and products

- the activation energy for the catalysed reaction, $E_{A(cat)}$

- the activation energy for the uncatalysed reaction, E_A

KEY WORD

catalyst: a substance that increases the rate of a chemical reaction but is chemically unchanged at the end of the reaction. It provides a different mechanism of reaction which has a lower activation energy.

KEY WORDS

heterogeneous catalysis: the type of catalysis in which the catalyst is in a different phase to the reactants. For example, iron in the Haber process.

c Catalysis can be homogeneous or heterogeneous.

   i Explain the difference between **homogeneous** and **heterogeneous catalysis**.

   ii Classify the following as either homogeneous or heterogeneous catalysis.

Equation 1: $N_2(g) + 3H_2(g) \underset{}{\overset{Fe(s)}{\rightleftharpoons}} 2NH_3(g)$

Equation 2: $H_2(g) + CH_3COCl(l) \xrightarrow{Pd(s)} CH_3CHO(l) + HCl(g)$

Equation 3: $CH_3CONH_2(aq) + H_2O(l) \xrightarrow{H^+(aq)} CH_3CO_2^-(aq) + NH_4^+(aq)$

> **TIP**
>
> Part **c** is extension work. Look at the definitions of heterogeneous and homogeneous catalysts in the key words boxes before you do this question.

> **KEY WORDS**
>
> **homogeneous catalysis:** the type of catalysis in which the catalyst and reactants are in the same phase. For example, sulfuric acid catalysing the formation of an ester from an alcohol and carboxylic acid.

EXAM-STYLE QUESTIONS

1 Hydrogen peroxide decomposes slowly at r.t.p. The reaction is exothermic.

$$2H_2O_2(aq) \rightarrow 2H_2O(l) + O_2(g)$$

  a How is the rate of reaction affected by each of the following **conditions**? In each case give an explanation in terms of collision theory or activation energy.

    i Decreasing the temperature. [2]

    ii Increasing the pressure. [2]

    iii Adding a catalyst. [2]

  b The apparatus used to investigate the effect of different catalysts on the rate of decomposition of hydrogen peroxide is shown in Figure 9.7. Describe how to carry out this experiment using the apparatus shown. [6]

> **TIP**
>
> You will need to consider dependent and independent variables when answering part **b**.

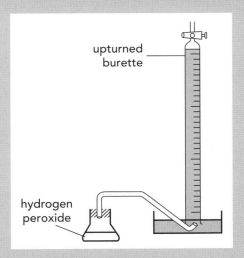

Figure 9.7

CONTINUED

c Draw a labelled reaction pathway diagram to show the catalysed and uncatalysed reactions. **[5]**

[Total: 17]

2 Propene, C_3H_6, is formed when propane, C_3H_8, is passed over a heated catalyst chromium(III) oxide and aluminium oxide. The reaction is endothermic.

$$C_3H_8(g) \xrightarrow{\quad Cr_2O_3(s) + Al_2O_3(s) \quad} C_3H_6(g) + H_2(g)$$

a Is this homogeneous or heterogeneous catalysis? Explain your answer. **[1]**

b Explain why a catalyst increases the rate of reaction by referring to the Boltzmann distribution curve. **[3]**

c Explain, with reference to the collision theory, why a decrease in pressure decreases the rate of this reaction. **[2]**

d Draw a reaction pathway diagram for the uncatalysed reaction to include the activation energy and enthalpy change of reaction. **[5]**

[Total: 11]

3 Magnesium ribbon reacts with hydrochloric acid.

$$Mg(s) + 2HCl(aq) \rightarrow MgCl_2(aq) + H_2(g)$$

a How is the rate of reaction affected by each of the following conditions? In each case give an explanation in terms of collision theory or activation energy.

  i Increasing the concentration of hydrochloric acid. **[2]**

  ii Using magnesium powder instead of magnesium ribbon. Assume that the mass of magnesium is the same. **[2]**

  iii Increasing the temperature. **[2]**

b Figure 9.8 shows the results of three experiments using magnesium ribbon and hydrochloric acid.

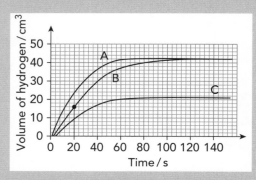

Figure 9.8

TIP

Note the stem of the question for part **1 c**.

TIPS

Refer back to Exercise 9.4 part **c** when answering question **2 a**.

Note the stem of the question in **2 d**.

TIPS

Question **3 b** asks you to interpret graphs. Remember:

- Rate is proportional to

  $$\frac{\text{change in amount of product made (or reactant used up)}}{\text{time}}.$$

- Read the stem of the question carefully to get important pieces of information.

CONTINUED

Line B shows the results when using excess magnesium ribbon and
0.5 mol dm^{-3} hydrochloric acid.

i   Describe how the rate of reaction changes as the reaction proceeds.
    Use the information in the graph to explain your answer.   [2]

ii Calculate the **initial rate of reaction** for line B in cm^3 hydrogen s^{-1}
    during the first 20 seconds of the reaction. Show your working.   [2]

iii A different concentration of hydrochloric acid was used for line C.
    All other conditions remained the same, including the volume of
    hydrochloric acid.

    Deduce the concentration of the hydrochloric acid. Explain your
    answer.   [3]

iv Line A was obtained using the same volume of 0.5 mol dm^{-3}
    hydrochloric acid as for B but at a different temperature. Explain
    why the gradient is initially greater but the final volume of hydrogen
    produced is the same as for B.   [2]

[Total: 15]

KEY WORDS

**initial rate
(of reaction):** the
rate of reaction
at the start of
the experiment
calculated from a
tangent drawn to the
curve at time zero.

Chapter 10

Periodicity

CHAPTER OUTLINE

In this chapter you will learn how to:

- describe the periodicity in the variation of atomic radius, ionic radius, melting point and electrical conductivity of the elements

- describe and write equations for the reactions of the elements in Period 3 with oxygen and with chlorine

- describe and write equations for the reactions of Na and Mg with water

- describe and explain the variation in the oxidation number of the oxides and chlorides in Period 3 in terms of their outer shell electrons

- describe and write equations for the reactions, if any, of Period 3 oxides and chlorides with water, including the likely pH of the solutions obtained

- describe, explain and write equations for the acid / base behaviour of some Period 3 oxides and hydroxides

- explain the variations in the trends in reactivity of the Period 3 oxides and chlorides in terms of bonding and electronegativity

- deduce the types of bonding present in oxides and chlorides of Period 3 from their chemical and physical properties

- predict the properties of an element in a given group using knowledge of periodicity

- deduce the nature, position in the Periodic Table and identity of unknown elements from given information.

Exercise 10.1 Period 3 elements, oxides and chlorides

Periodicity refers to the repeating patterns of properties in the Periodic Table. This exercise revises the structure and properties of some Period 3 oxides and chlorides.

TIP

You will find it useful to refer back to Chapters 4 and 5 to refresh your memory about structure and bonding.

a   Link the description of the oxides 1 to 6 on the left with their properties A to F on the right.

1 An oxide which reacts with water to form an acid of type H_2XO_3	**A** Aluminium oxide
2 The oxide of an element whose atoms have an oxidation number of +5	**B** Silicon(IV) oxide
3 An **amphoteric oxide** with a giant structure	**C** Sulfur dioxide
4 An oxide of type XO which has an ionic giant structure	**D** Magnesium oxide
5 This oxide has a high melting point because of its giant covalent structure	**E** Sodium oxide
6 An ionic oxide which reacts with water to form a strongly alkaline solution	**F** Phosphorus(V) oxide

> **KEY WORDS**
>
> **amphoteric oxide:** an oxide which reacts with both acids and alkalis.

b   Copy and complete these sentences about the reactions of Period 3 chlorides with water using words from the list. Some words may be used more than once.

acidic	chloride	dissolves	hydrogen	hydrolysed
ions	phosphorus	polar	sulfur	

> **KEY WORD**
>
> **hydrolysed:** undergoes hydrolysis. Hydrolysis is the breakdown of a compound by water. Hydrolysis is also used to describe the breakdown of a substance by dilute acids or alkali.

Sodium chloride _____ in water to form a neutral solution because the

_____ water molecules surround the positive and negative _____

and separate them. Aluminium chloride is _____ by water and the solution

becomes _____ . Chlorides of silicon, _____ and _____

react with water. The gas, _____ _____, is released, some of which

_____ in water and reacts to form an _____ solution.

c   Copy and complete these equations:

  i $PCl_5 + \underline{\hspace{2cm}} \rightarrow H_3PO_4 + \underline{\hspace{0.5cm}} HCl$

  ii $SO_3 + H_2O \rightarrow \underline{\hspace{2cm}}$

  iii $Mg(OH)_2 + \underline{\hspace{2cm}} \rightarrow MgCl_2 + \underline{\hspace{2cm}}$

  iv $SiO_2 + \underline{\hspace{0.5cm}} NaOH \rightarrow \underline{\hspace{1.5cm}} + \underline{\hspace{1.5cm}}$

  v $\underline{\hspace{0.5cm}} Na + \underline{\hspace{0.5cm}} H_2O \rightarrow \underline{\hspace{1.5cm}} + \underline{\hspace{1.5cm}}$

  vi $Al_2O_3 + \underline{\hspace{0.5cm}} H_2SO_4 \rightarrow \underline{\hspace{1.5cm}} + \underline{\hspace{0.5cm}} H_2O$

  vii $SiCl_4 + \underline{\hspace{0.5cm}} H_2O \rightarrow \underline{\hspace{1.5cm}} + \underline{\hspace{1.5cm}}$

  viii $\underline{\hspace{0.5cm}} P + \underline{\hspace{0.5cm}} Cl_2 \rightarrow \underline{\hspace{1.5cm}}$

  ix $\underline{\hspace{0.5cm}} Al + \underline{\hspace{0.5cm}} O_2 \rightarrow \underline{\hspace{1.5cm}}$

d   Sodium oxide reacts with water to form a strongly alkaline solution but magnesium oxide reacts to form a weakly alkaline solution.

  i   Suggest the pH of the solutions formed with:

  •   sodium oxide

  •   magnesium oxide.

  ii   Explain why the solution formed when magnesium oxide reacts with water is less alkaline than the solution formed when sodium oxide reacts with water.

  iii   Write the equation for the reaction of magnesium oxide with water.

e   Sulfur has a low melting point and does not conduct electricity. Aluminium has a high melting point and does conduct electricity. Explain these differences in terms of the structures of sulfur and aluminium.

Exercise 10.2 Periodic patterns in physical properties

This exercise will help you revise the **periodicity** of physical properties. It also extends the range of physical properties studied to give practice in answering questions involving handling information.

KEY WORD
periodicity: the repeating patterns in the physical and chemical properties of the elements across the periods of the Periodic Table.

TIP
Before doing this exercise you will find it useful to refer back to Chapter 3 to refresh your memory about the factors affecting the value of first ionisation energy.

a   Figure 10.1 shows a plot of first ionisation energy against atomic number for elements in Period 3.

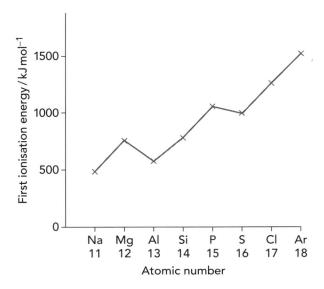

Figure 10.1: First ionisation energy plotted against atomic number in Period 3.

i   Describe and explain the general pattern of first ionisation energies across Period 3.

ii   Explain why aluminium and sulfur break the general pattern.

iii   Predict the values of the first ionisation energy for the first two elements of Period 4.

b   Atomic radius decreases across a period. Copy and complete the following explanation using words from the list

attractive	**electrons**	**increases**	**negative**	**nuclear**
nucleus	**outer**	**protons**	**quantum**	**shell** **shielding**

Across a period, the number of _____ (positive charges) increases. So the

_____ charge also increases. The number of electrons (_____

charges) also _____ across a period. Each electron added to the atom

of successive elements goes into the same principal _____ shell. So the

_____ of outer _____ electrons by inner shell _____ does

not increase significantly. Across a period, the greater _____ force between the

nucleus and the _____ electrons pulls them closer to the _____.

c Figure 10.2 shows a plot of ionic radius of the Period 3 elements against atomic number.

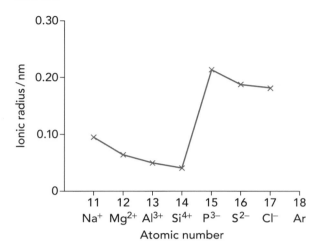

Figure 10.2: Ionic radius plotted against atomic number in Period 3.

Describe and explain how these values change across this period.

d Molar atomic volume is the volume occupied by one mole of atoms of a solid or liquid element.

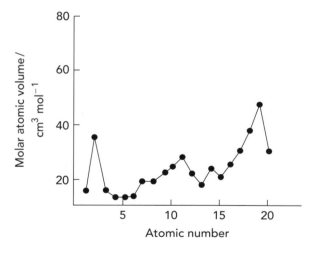

Figure 10.3: Molar atomic volume of the first 20 elements in the Periodic Table.

Figure 10.3 shows the molar atomic volume of the first 20 elements in the Periodic Table.

i Which group of elements are at the peaks of the 2nd and 3rd periods?

ii Describe the general pattern in the molar atomic volume across Periods 2 and 3.

iii In what ways does the trend in molar atomic volume differ from the trend in atomic radius?

iv   Suggest why the trend in molar atomic volume is different from the trend in atomic radius.

v   How does the molar atomic volume of Group 1 elements change going down the group?

TIP

Think about the arrangement of the particles.

Exercise 10.3 Structure, bonding and periodicity

In this exercise, you will examine patterns in periodicity related to the structure of the elements.

Figure 10.4 shows a plot of melting point against atomic number for the elements of Period 3.

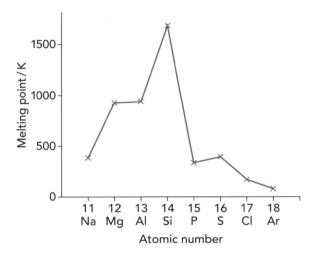

Figure 10.4: Melting point plotted against atomic number in Period 3.

TIPS

Before doing this exercise, you will find it useful to refer to details of structure and bonding in Chapters 4 and 5.

A lot of this exercise is about finding patterns in data. Look carefully at the trends and use them in your predictions.

a   Describe how melting point changes across Period 3.

b   Suggest in terms of structure and bonding why:

i   the elements from phosphorus to argon have low melting points

ii   aluminium has a higher melting point than sodium.

iii   silicon has the highest melting point.

c   Predict the approximate melting points of neon, potassium and calcium.

d   i   Most of the elements in Groups 1 to 13 are good electrical conductors. Explain why.

ii   Explain why aluminium conducts electricity better than sodium.

iii   Why does sulfur not conduct electricity?

e Figure 10.5 shows the number of moles of chlorine which combine with one mole of various elements. Where more than one chloride exists, the one with the highest ratio of chlorine is shown.

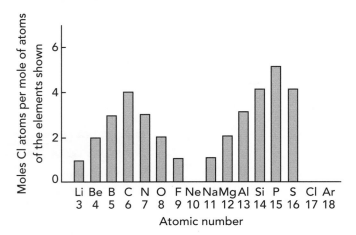

Figure 10.5: The number of moles of chlorine that combine with 1 mole of some elements.

    i Describe the general pattern of the formulae for the chlorides across a period.

    ii Deduce the formulae of the chlorides of carbon, silicon, nitrogen and phosphorus.

    iii Deduce the oxidation numbers of phosphorus and sulfur in the chlorides shown on the chart.

f **i** Explain, using ideas about electronegativity, why magnesium chloride has an ionic structure and phosphorus(V) chloride has a simple covalent structure.

    ii Compare the reactivity of magnesium chloride and phosphorus(V) chloride with water and suggest reasons for any differences.

Exercise 10.4 Making predictions

This exercise will give you practice in predicting the properties of elements from their position in the Periodic Table. It also provides practice in interpreting trends in groups of elements which are less familiar.

a   Figure 10.6 shows the melting points of the elements having atomic numbers between 13 and 54.

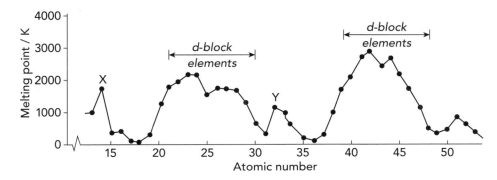

Figure 10.6: Melting point plotted against atomic number.

i   Explain how this graph demonstrates periodicity.

ii   Elements X and Y are in the same group of the Periodic Table. Explain in terms of structure and bonding why these elements have relatively high melting points.

iii Explain why the element with atomic number 15 has a much lower melting point than element X.

iv   Describe how the melting points of the **d-block elements** vary with atomic number.

v   Explain why elements 18 and 36 have the lowest melting points.

b   The table gives some properties of elements in Group 14.

Element	Melting point / °C	Electrical conductivity	Bond energy / kJ mol⁻¹	Electro-negativity	Acid–base character of oxide
carbon (diamond)	3550	hardly any	350	2.5	acidic
silicon	1410	semiconductor	222	1.8	
germanium		semiconductor	188	1.8	amphoteric
tin	232	conductor	–		amphoteric
lead	327		–	1.8	amphoteric

Table 10.1: Properties of elements in Group 14.

i   Predict the melting point of germanium.

ii Predict the **electrical conductivity** of lead.

iii Predict the electronegativity of tin.

iv Suggest the acid–base character of the oxide of silicon.

v   Describe and explain the strength of the covalent bonding down the group.

vi Why are there no bond energies for tin and lead?

c   The electron affinity tells us how easily an atom can attract electrons. The more negative the value, the easier it is for an atom to attract electrons. The electron affinities of the Period 3 elements are shown in the table.

Element	Na	Mg	Al	Si	P	S	Cl	Ar
Electron affinity / $kJ\,mol^{-1}$	−52.9	+230	−42.3	−134	−72	−200	−349	+34

Table 10.2: Electron affinity.

i   Describe the general trend in electron affinity from aluminium to chlorine.

ii Suggest in terms of atomic structure why chlorine has the most negative electron affinity.

iii The electron affinity gets less negative down a group. Suggest why.

d   Element X forms an oxide which has a melting point of 2614 °C. The oxide reacts with water to form an alkaline solution. X forms a chloride, XCl_2, which dissolves in water to form a neutral solution. It has the 3rd highest first ionisation energy in its Group. Identify X, giving your reasons.

EXAM-STYLE QUESTIONS

1   The densities of the Period 3 elements are shown in the table. For Cl and Ar, the densities are those of the liquefied gases.

Element	Na	Mg	Al	Si	P	S	Cl	Ar
Density / $g\,cm^{-3}$	0.97	1.74	2.70	2.32	1.82	2.07	1.56	1.40

Table 10.3

a   i   Suggest three factors apart from temperature or pressure that can affect the value of the density.   [3]

    ii Suggest why there is a general increase in density from sodium to aluminium.   [3]

CONTINUED

b The oxides of the elements of Period 3 get more acidic in nature across the period.

   i Sodium oxide is a **basic oxide**. Construct a balanced equation for the reaction of sodium oxide with water. Include state symbols. [3]

   ii What type of oxide is aluminium oxide? [1]

   iii Write an equation for the reaction of aluminium oxide with hot concentrated sodium hydroxide. [2]

c The melting points of some oxides of the Period 3 elements are shown in the table.

Oxide of	Sodium	Magnesium	Aluminium	Silicon	Phosphorus	Sulfur
Melting point / K	1548	3125	2345	1883	853	290

Table 10.4

Explain, in terms of structure and bonding, the pattern of these melting points across the period. [6]

d Figure 10.7 shows the number of moles of oxygen which combine with one mole of various elements in Periods 2 and 3. Where more than one oxide exists, the one with the highest ratio of oxygen is shown.

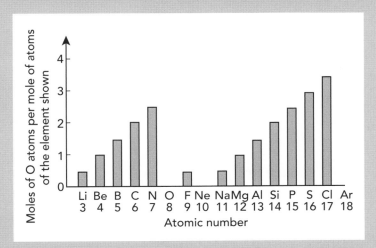

Figure 10.7

   i What pattern is shown by the ratio of moles of oxygen : moles of element in the formulae of these oxides across each period? [2]

   ii Deduce the formulae of the oxides of nitrogen, silicon and chlorine in the chart. [3]

   iii Describe and explain the variation in oxidation number of the Period 3 elements in their oxides in terms of their electronic structure. [3]

[Total: 26]

TIP

Remember:

$$\text{density} = \frac{\text{mass}}{\text{volume}}$$

KEY WORDS

basic oxide: an oxide which reacts only with an acid to form a salt and water. They are generally metal oxides.

CONTINUED

2 a The table shows the electrical conductivity of some Period 3 elements.

Element	Sodium	Magnesium	Aluminium	Silicon	Phosphorus	Sulfur
Electrical conductivity/ $S\,m^{-1}$	0.218	0.224	0.380	2×10^{-10}		1×10^{-23}

Table 10.5

    i Explain the differences in electrical conductivity in terms of the structure of the elements. **[4]**

    ii Suggest a value for the electrical conductivity of phosphorus. **[1]**

  b First ionisation energy shows a periodic trend.

    i Define first ionisation energy. **[2]**

    ii Which Period 3 element has the highest first ionisation energy? Explain your answer. **[5]**

  c Magnesium reacts with oxygen to form magnesium oxide.

    i Write a balanced equation for this reaction. **[1]**

    ii Explain, using ideas about electronegativity, why magnesium oxide has an ionic structure and sulfur dioxide has a simple covalent structure. **[2]**

    iii Magnesium oxide and sulfur trioxide both react with water. Suggest how and why they both react. **[5]**

  d Arsenic is just below phosphorus in Group 15 of the Periodic Table.

    i Predict the type of bonding present in arsenic(V) oxide. **[1]**

    ii Predict the formula of arsenic(V) oxide. **[1]**

    iii Predict the action of water on arsenic(V) oxide. **[1]**

[Total: 23]

3 The elements of Period 3 show trends in some of their properties.

  a i Describe and explain the trend in atomic radius across Period 3. **[4]**

    ii The ionic radius of a sulfide ion, S^{2-}, is much greater than the ionic radius of a magnesium ion, Mg^{2+}, even though sulfur has a greater nuclear charge than magnesium. Explain why. **[3]**

  b The chlorides of Period 3 elements show trends in their properties. One of these trends is the ease of **hydrolysis** of the halides.

    i Describe this trend. **[1]**

    ii Silicon(IV) chloride is a liquid at r.t.p. Construct a balanced equation for the hydrolysis of silicon(IV) chloride. Include state symbols. **[3]**

    iii Aluminium chloride, Al_2Cl_6, is formed when aluminium is heated in chlorine. Construct a balanced equation for this reaction. **[2]**

TIP

If you are asked to define chemical terms, you must be very precise. Standard conditions and states (e.g. gas) are often important parts of the description.

TIP

Refer to Chapter 3 if you need help with ionisation energies.

KEY WORD

hydrolysis: the breakdown of a compound by water. Hydrolysis is also used to describe the breakdown of a substance by dilute acids or alkali.

CONTINUED

c   The melting points of some Period 3 chlorides are shown in the table.

Chloride	Sodium	Magnesium	Aluminium	Silicon	Phosphorus	Sulfur
Melting point / K	1074	987	463 (at 2.5 atm pressure)	203	sublimes at 435	195

Table 10.6

i   Explain the trend in these melting points using ideas about structure and bonding. **[5]**

ii   Use the information in the table to suggest why not all your explanations might be reliable. **[1]**

iii   A solution of sodium chloride in water has a pH of 7. A solution of magnesium chloride in water has a pH of 6.5. Explain these differences. **[4]**

[Total: 23]

TIP

When describing trends, just writing 'increases' or 'decreases' is often not enough. You need to give more precise answers, e.g. 'increases across the period until Group 13'.

Chapter 11

Group 2

CHAPTER OUTLINE

In this chapter you will learn how to:

- describe, and write equations for, the reactions of the Group 2 elements with oxygen, water and dilute acids

- describe, and write equations for, the reactions of the Group 2 oxides, hydroxides and carbonates with water and with dilute acids

- describe, and write equations for, the thermal decomposition of the Group 2 nitrates and carbonates

- describe, and make predictions from, the trends in properties of the Group 2 elements and their compounds that are covered in this chapter

- state the variation in the solubilities of the Group 2 hydroxides and sulfates.

Exercise 11.1 Reactions of some Group 2 elements and carbonates

This exercise focuses on the reactions of Group 2 elements and compounds. It also gives you further practice in constructing balanced equations.

a Copy and complete these equations for the reactions of some Group 2 elements.

　　i　$\underline{\quad} Ca + O_2 \rightarrow \underline{\qquad\qquad}$

　　ii　$Mg + \underline{\quad} HCl \rightarrow \underline{\qquad\qquad} + \underline{\qquad\qquad}$

　　iii　$Mg + H_2SO_4 \rightarrow \underline{\qquad\qquad} + \underline{\qquad\qquad}$

　　iv　$Ba + \underline{\quad} H_2O \rightarrow \underline{\qquad\qquad} + \underline{\qquad\qquad}$

b Copy and complete these equations.

　　i　$CaCO_3 \xrightarrow{\text{heat}} \underline{\qquad\qquad} + \underline{\qquad\qquad}$

　　ii　$CaCO_3 + \underline{\quad} HCl \rightarrow CaCl_2 + \underline{\qquad\qquad} + \underline{\qquad\qquad}$

　　iii　$Ca(OH)_2 + \underline{\qquad\qquad} \rightarrow Ca(NO_3)_2 + \underline{\qquad\qquad}$

　　iv　$CaO + H_2O \rightarrow \underline{\qquad\qquad}$

c Write balanced equations, including state symbols, for:

　　i　The reaction of magnesium oxide with dilute hydrochloric acid.

　　ii　The reaction of aqueous barium hydroxide with dilute sulfuric acid.

Exercise 11.2 Reactions of Group 2 elements and compounds

This exercise focuses on some reactions of the alkaline earth metals and their compounds and gives further practice in constructing balanced equations.

a Link the reactants 1 to 7 with the products A to G.

1 magnesium + water →	**A** magnesium oxide + hydrogen
2 magnesium carbonate $\xrightarrow{\text{heat}}$	**B** magnesium chloride + water
3 magnesium + steam →	**C** magnesium chloride + hydrogen
4 magnesium oxide + water →	**D** magnesium hydroxide + hydrogen
5 magnesium + hydrochloric acid →	**E** magnesium oxide + nitrogen dioxide + oxygen
6 magnesium oxide + hydrochloric acid →	**F** magnesium hydroxide
7 magnesium nitrate $\xrightarrow{\text{heat}}$	**G** magnesium oxide + carbon dioxide

b Copy and complete these symbol equations:

i   ___ $Ca(NO_3)_2 \rightarrow$ ___ $CaO +$ _____ + _____

ii $BaCO_3 +$ ___ $HNO_3 \rightarrow$ _____ + _____ $+ H_2O$

iii   ___ $Sr + O_2 \rightarrow$ _____ + heat

iv $MgCO_3 \xrightarrow{\text{heat}}$ _____ + _____

c Write balanced equations including state symbols for:
  i The **thermal decomposition** of strontium carbonate.
  ii The thermal decomposition of crystalline magnesium nitrate, $Mg(NO_3)_2 \cdot 6H_2O$.
  iii The reaction of strontium carbonate with dilute hydrochloric acid.
  iv The reaction of strontium with water.

KEY WORDS

thermal decomposition: the breakdown of a compound by heat into two or more different substances.

Exercise 11.3 Trends in properties of Group 2 elements

This exercise helps you to learn some trends in Group 2 elements and their compounds. It also gives you practice in interpreting data.

> **TIP**
>
> The Group 2 elements show trends in both physical and chemical properties. Some of these trends are 'general'. This means that there may be an element in the group that breaks the trend. When deducing data from trends in physical properties, look at how the differences between successive values change.

a   The table shows some properties of the Group 2 elements.

Element	Melting point / °C	Metallic radius / nm	Density / g cm^{-3}	Electronegativity
beryllium	1280	0.122	1.85	1.50
magnesium	650	0.160	1.74	1.25
calcium	838		1.55	1.05
strontium	768	0.215	2.6	
barium	714	0.224	3.5	0.95
radium		uncertain		uncertain

Table 11.1: Properties of Group 2 elements.

Use the information in the table to predict:
i   The melting point of radium.
ii   The density of radium.
iii The electronegativity of strontium.
iv   The **metallic radius** of calcium.

b   Describe the trend in density of the Group 2 elements.

c   Which element in Group 2 breaks the trend in melting points?

d   How does the solubility of the Group 2 hydroxides vary with their position in the group?

e   Use your answer to part **d** to explain why a saturated aqueous solution of strontium hydroxide has a higher pH than a saturated aqueous solution of magnesium hydroxide.

f   How does the solubility of the Group 2 sulfates vary with their position in the group?

> **KEY WORDS**
>
> **metallic radius:** half the distance between the nuclei of two adjacent metal ions in a metallic structure.

Exercise 11.4 Heating Group 2 elements and compounds

This exercise mostly provides revision about the thermal decomposition of some Group 2 compounds. It also gives you practice at processing information from other parts of the course and working with information that is new to you.

a   i   What is the trend in reactivity of the Group 2 elements when they are heated in oxygen?

    ii   Write a balanced equation for the reaction of magnesium with oxygen. Include state symbols.

    iii   The product of the reaction in part **a ii** was added to water. A few drops of litmus solution were added. Describe and explain your observations.

b   When heated strongly, magnesium carbonate breaks down to magnesium oxide and carbon dioxide.

    i   Explain why this reaction is likely to be endothermic.

    ii   Draw an **enthalpy cycle diagram** for this reaction.

    iii   Calculate the enthalpy change of the reaction.

$$\Delta H_f^\ominus [MgCO_3(s)] = -1095.8 \text{ kJ mol}^{-1}$$

$$\Delta H_f^\ominus [MgO(s)] = -601.7 \text{ kJ mol}^{-1}$$

$$\Delta H_f^\ominus [CO_2(g)] = -393.5 \text{ kJ mol}^{-1}$$

    iv   Would you expect strontium carbonate to decompose more readily or less readily than magnesium carbonate? Explain your answer by referring to the positions of the metals in the group.

c   Group 2 nitrates decompose when heated.

    i   Construct a balanced equation for the thermal composition of calcium nitrate.

    ii   What would you observe during this reaction?

d   Group 2 hydroxides also decompose when they are heated.

Barium hydroxide decomposes when it is heated at 1500 °C. Calcium hydroxide decomposes when it is heated at 540 °C.

    i   What evidence is there from these values that the ease of decomposition of Group 2 hydroxides is similar to that of the decomposition of Group 2 nitrates?

    ii   Suggest the temperature at which strontium hydroxide decomposes.

    iii   When hydroxides decompose, the oxide is formed as well as a liquid. The liquid turns anhydrous copper(II) sulfate blue. Write an equation for the decomposition of strontium hydroxide.

TIP

The trend in thermal decomposition of Group 2 carbonates and nitrates depends on the size of the metal ion.

KEY WORDS

enthalpy cycle diagram: a diagram showing alternative routes between reactants and products that allows the determination of one enthalpy change from other known enthalpy changes by using Hess's Law.

EXAM-STYLE QUESTIONS

1 a The table shows the sum of the first and second ionisation energies of the Group 2 metals.

Metal	Be	Mg	Ca	Sr	Ba
$IE_1 + IE_2$ / kJ mol^{-1}	2660	2186	1740	1608	1468

Table 11.2

i Write the equation which represents the second ionisation energy of strontium. [2]

ii Use the values of the ionisation energies in the table to explain why the Group 2 elements are more reactive with oxygen going down the group. [5]

iii Write a balanced equation for the reaction of barium with oxygen. [1]

iv Explain why this reaction is a redox reaction in terms of oxidation number changes. [3]

b i Suggest how the values of the ionic radius of the Group 2 elements change going down the group. [1]

ii Write the electronic configuration for a calcium ion using $1s^2$ notation. [1]

[Total: 13]

2 a i Describe how the solubility of the Group 2 hydroxides varies with the position of the metal in the Group. [2]

ii A **saturated solution** of calcium hydroxide has a higher pH than a saturated solution of magnesium hydroxide. Explain why. [3]

b Describe how the solubility of the Group 2 hydroxides varies with their position in the group. [1]

c The solubility of calcium hydroxide in water is 1.50×10^{-3} moles per 100 g of water at 298 K.

Calculate the maximum mass of calcium hydroxide which dissolves in 500 cm^3 of water at 298 K.

Express your answer to 3 significant figures.

A_r values: Ca = 40.1, O = 16.0, H = 1.00 [3]

d The table shows the solubility of the Group 2 sulfates.

Group 2 sulfate	Solubility / mol dm^{-3}
magnesium sulfate	1.83
calcium sulfate	4.66×10^{-2}
strontium sulfate	7.11×10^{-4}
barium sulfate	9.43×10^{-6}

Table 11.3

Describe the trend in solubility down the group. [1]

TIP

In **1 i**, remember that the second ionisation energy starts with the X^+ ion.

KEY WORDS

saturated solution: a solution which can dissolve no more solute at a particular temperature (in the presence of undissolved solute).

TIP

Make sure in part **c** that you write your answer to the correct number of significant figures.

CONTINUED

e   When an aqueous solution of barium chloride is added to an aqueous solution of sodium sulfate, a white precipitate is formed.

   i   Name the white precipitate and explain why it is formed.   [2]

   ii   Write an ionic equation for this reaction. Include state symbols.   [2]

f   Dilute sulfuric acid reacts with pieces of barium carbonate.

   i   Write a balanced equation for this reaction. Include state symbols.   [2]

   ii   Suggest why the reaction stops before all the barium carbonate is used up.   [2]

[Total: 18]

3   a   Strontium oxide reacts with water.

$$SrO(s) + H_2O(l) \rightarrow Sr(OH)_2(aq)$$

Write an ionic equation for this reaction.   [1]

b   Strontium oxide also reacts with dilute nitric acid.

$$SrO(s) + 2HNO_3(aq) \rightarrow Sr(NO_3)_2(aq) + H_2O(l)$$

Calculate the maximum mass of strontium nitrate that can be formed from 41.4 g of strontium oxide. Express your answer to 3 significant figures.

A_r values: Sr = 87.6, N = 14.0, O = 16.0   [3]

c   Strontium nitrate undergoes thermal decomposition to form strontium oxide, nitrogen dioxide and oxygen.

Construct a balanced equation for this reaction. Include state symbols.   [3]

d   Strontium reacts with nitrogen to form strontium nitride.

$$3Sr + N_2 \rightarrow Sr_3N_2$$

Explain why this is a redox reaction in terms of oxidation number changes.   [3]

e   i   Explain why the metallic radius of strontium is larger than the metallic radius of calcium.   [1]

   ii   Deduce the electronic configuration for a strontium atom using $1s^2$ notation.   [1]

   iii   Strontium is a good reducing agent. Construct an ionic half-equation to represent the reducing action of strontium.   [1]

[Total: 13]

TIPS

This question tests your ability to write balanced equations including ionic equations.

You also need to know about electronic structure and redox reactions (Chapters 3 and 9).

In part **b**, don't forget that you only round up only your values at the end of the calculation.

Chapter 12

Group 17

CHAPTER OUTLINE

In this chapter you will learn how to:

- describe the colours of, and explain the trend in volatility of, the Group 17 elements chlorine, bromine and iodine

- describe and explain the relative reactivity of these Group 17 elements as oxidising agents (and the halide ions as reducing agents)

- describe and explain the reactions of the elements with hydrogen

- describe and explain the relative thermal stabilities of the hydrides (in terms of bond energies)

- describe the reactions of halide ions with aqueous silver ions, followed by adding aqueous ammonia

- describe the reaction of halide ions with concentrated sulfuric acid

- describe and interpret the disproportion reactions of chlorine with cold, and with hot, aqueous sodium hydroxide

- explain the use of chlorine in water purification.

Exercise 12.1 Hydrogen halides

This exercise will help you learn about the formation and reactions of the hydrogen **halides**.

a   Match the beginnings of the sentences 1 to 6 with the ends of the sentences A to F.

1 The reaction of hydrogen with chlorine …	**A** … is explosive even in the dark.
2 The reaction of hydrogen with fluorine …	**B** … is not decomposed at 1000 °C.
3 The bond energy of hydrogen fluoride …	**C** … is explosive in sunlight but not in cold, dark conditions.
4 The reaction of hydrogen with iodine …	**D** … is lower than that of hydrogen chloride.
5 The bond energy of hydrogen bromide …	**E** … is greater than that of hydrogen iodide.
6 Hydrogen chloride …	**F** … is slow and forms an equilibrium mixture on heating.

TIPS

The **halogens** become less reactive going down the group as the molecules get larger.

The bond energy of the hydrogen–halogen bond decreases down the group.

KEY WORDS

halogens: the Group 17 elements.

halide: a compound containing an anion with a single negative charge formed by the addition of an electron to a halogen atom.

b   Put the following halides in order of their thermal stability (the one with the lowest stability first):

> **hydrogen bromide**   **hydrogen chloride**   **hydrogen fluoride**   **hydrogen iodide**

c   Write a balanced equation for the thermal decomposition of hydrogen iodide.

Exercise 12.2 Halides

This exercise will help you revise the reactions and specific tests for halide ions. It also revises practical procedures for making hydrogen halides.

Halide ions react with aqueous silver nitrate to give coloured precipitates.

Some of these precipitates dissolve in dilute or concentrated aqueous ammonia.

This gives further confirmation of the type of halide present.

a   Copy and complete these sentences about the test for halide ions.

The suspected halide is dissolved in dilute _____ acid. A few drops of

aqueous _____ _____ are added. If chloride ions are present a

coloured precipitate is formed which goes _____ in the presence of light.

The precipitate dissolves in dilute _____ solution. If a bromide is present

a _____ coloured precipitate is seen which dissolves in _____

ammonia solution.

b   **i**   Copy and complete the equation for the reaction in part **a** but using aqueous potassium iodide in place of the chloride or bromide.

_____ (aq) + _____ (aq) → AgI(s) + KNO$_3$(aq)

   ii   Write the ionic equation for this reaction.

c   Figure 12.1 shows the apparatus used for making hydrogen chloride from solid sodium chloride and concentrated sulfuric acid.

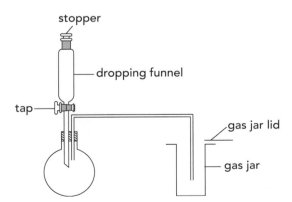

Figure 12.1: Making hydrogen chloride.

TIP

Remember that gases that are less dense than air are collected by downwards displacement of air. Gases that are denser than air are collected by upward displacement of air.

TIP

You should be prepared to answer questions on practical procedures.

    i   Describe how this apparatus is used to carry out the reaction.

    ii   Explain why the hydrogen chloride is **not** collected in an inverted (upside-down) measuring cylinder.

    iii   How do you know when the gas jar is full of hydrogen chloride?

d   Copy and complete these equations:

TIP
Remember hydrogen chloride is acidic.

    i   ___ $HI + H_2SO_4 \rightarrow I_2 + SO_2 +$ _____ H_2O

    ii $6HI + H_2SO_4 \rightarrow$ ___ $I_2 + S +$ ___ H_2O

    iii ___ $HI + H_2SO_4 \rightarrow 4I_2 + H_2S +$ ___ H_2O

e   Deduce the oxidation number changes of the I and S atoms in:

    i   equation **d i**

    ii   equation **d ii**

    iii   equation **d iii**

f   Describe the observations you would make when carrying out reaction **c iii**.

g   The reaction of concentrated sulfuric acid with sodium iodide produces sodium hydrogen sulfate, hydrogen sulfide, sulfur dioxide and sulfur. The reaction of concentrated sulfuric acid with sodium chloride produces only sodium hydrogen sulfate and hydrogen chloride.

    Explain this difference.

Exercise 12.3 Some redox reactions of the halogens

This exercise will familiarise you with the redox reactions between halogens and halide ions. This shows the relative ability of halogens to act as oxidising agents. It also gives you further practice in writing equations.

TIP
A more reactive halogen will displace a less reactive halogen from a solution of its halide ions.

a   Copy and complete the table showing the results when aqueous solutions of halogens are added to aqueous solutions of halide ions. In the last column, give the colour of the hexane layer after the reaction mixture has been shaken with hexane.

Halogen	Halide	Reaction or no reaction	Colour of the aqueous mixture after the addition	Colour of the hexane layer
$Cl_2(aq)$	$NaBr(aq)$	reaction	orange	dark orange
$I_2(aq)$	$KCl(aq)$	no reaction	brown (colour of $I_2(aq)$)	purple
$Br_2(aq)$	$KI(aq)$			
$Cl_2(aq)$	$LiBr(aq)$			
$Br_2(aq)$	$MgCl_2(aq)$			
$Cl_2(aq)$	$NaI(aq)$			

Table 12.1: Redox reactions with halogens.

TIP
You need to know the colours of the halogens in aqueous solution.

b i State which halogen in the table is the best oxidising agent. Explain your answer.

 ii State which halide ion in the table is the best reducing agent. Explain your answer.

c Copy and complete the equations for these reactions.

 i $Cl_2(aq) + \underline{\hspace{1cm}} KI(aq) \rightarrow \underline{\hspace{2cm}} + 2KCl(aq)$

 ii $Br_2(aq) + \underline{\hspace{1cm}} Na\underline{\hspace{0.7cm}}(aq) \rightarrow At_2(aq) + \underline{\hspace{2cm}}$

 iii $Cl_2(aq) + MgBr_2(aq) \rightarrow + \underline{\hspace{2cm}} + \underline{\hspace{2cm}}$

d Write balanced equations with state symbols for:
 i The reaction of aqueous bromine with aqueous potassium iodide.
 ii The reaction of aqueous chlorine with aqueous sodium bromide.

Exercise 12.4 Physical properties of the halogens

This exercise gives you practice in interpreting data about the halogens.

The table shows some properties of the halogens.

Element	Melting point / °C	Boiling point / °C	Density / g cm⁻³	Colour
fluorine	−220	−188		pale yellow
chlorine	−101	−35	1.56	yellow-green
bromine	−7	59	3.12	red-brown
iodine	114	184	4.93	grey-black
astatine	302		uncertain	

Table 12.2: Properties of halogens.

The densities of fluorine, chlorine and bromine are for the liquids at their boiling points.

a Use the information in the table to predict:
 i The boiling point of astatine.
 ii The density of liquid fluorine.
 iii The colour of astatine.
b Describe the trend in colour as you go down the group.
c What is the state of bromine at −4 °C? Explain your answer.
d What is the trend in **volatility** of the halogens down the group? Explain how the information in the table shows this.

TIPS

When interpreting data on melting and boiling points, remember that −20 °C is lower than −10 °C.

Remember that the physical properties of an individual element may not fit the general trend.

KEY WORD

volatility: the ease with which a substance evaporates. A volatile substance will evaporate at a low temperature.

e   The densities of fluorine, chlorine and bromine are for the liquids at their boiling points.

i   Why might it not be fair to compare the densities in this way?

ii   Suggest why comparing the densities in this way could still be useful.

f   Write a balanced equation for the reaction of hydrogen with chlorine.

Exercise 12.5 Some reactions of the halogens

This exercise gives you further practice in using oxidation number changes to identify species which undergo oxidation or reduction.

a   Magnesium burns in chlorine to form magnesium chloride.

i   Write a balanced equation for this reaction. Include state symbols.

ii   Which atom has been oxidised and which has been reduced? Explain your answer in terms of oxidation number changes.

b   Chlorine undergoes disproportionation when it reacts with cold dilute aqueous sodium hydroxide.

$$Cl_2 + 2NaOH \rightarrow NaCl + NaClO + H_2O$$

i   Deduce the oxidation number of chlorine in:

• chlorine

• sodium chloride

• sodium chlorate(I).

ii   Use the changes in the oxidation numbers of chlorine to explain what is meant by the term disproportionation.

iii   Write the ionic equation for this reaction.

iv   Write two half-equations for this reaction, one showing oxidation and the other showing reduction. Explain which is which in terms of electron transfer.

c   Chlorine is added to the water supply.

i   Explain why.

ii   Chlorine undergoes disproportionation in water:

$$Cl_2 + H_2O \rightarrow HCl + HClO$$

Explain why this is a disproportion reaction by referring to relevant oxidation numbers.

d   Write an equation for the reaction of hydrogen with chlorine. Include state symbols.

TIP

We use oxidation numbers to deduce whether a substance has been oxidised or reduced.

TIP

Remember that in disproportion reactions there is simultaneous oxidation and reduction of a species.

EXAM-STYLE QUESTIONS

1 a The table shows the melting and boiling points of chlorine, bromine and iodine.

Group 17 element	Chlorine	Bromine	Iodine
melting point / °C	−101	−7	114
boiling point / °C	−35	59	184

Table 12.3

   i   Deduce the state of chlorine at −32 °C. Explain your answer. **[1]**

   ii Predict the melting point of fluorine. **[1]**

   iii Describe and explain in terms of intermolecular forces the trend in volatility of the halogens. **[4]**

   b Give the electronic configuration of a bromine atom. **[1]**

   c The halogens show a trend in their ability to oxidise other substances. Describe and explain this trend. **[4]**

   d In the presence of excess chlorine, ammonia is oxidised to nitrogen trichloride and hydrogen chloride.

   i   Write a balanced equation for this reaction. **[2]**

   ii Explain why chlorine acts as an oxidising agent in this reaction by referring to oxidation number changes. **[3]**

   e Hydrogen chloride dissolves in water to form chloride ions.

   i   Describe a test for chloride ions. **[2]**

   ii Describe the action of dilute ammonia solution on the precipitate obtained in part **e i**. **[1]**

   [Total: 19]

2 a Explain, including the use of an equation, why chlorine is used in water purification. **[3]**

   b Chlorine reacts with hot concentrated sodium hydroxide:

   $$Cl_2(aq) + 6NaOH(aq) \rightarrow 5NaCl(aq) + NaClO_3(aq) + 3H_2O(l)$$

   i   Deduce the oxidation number of the chlorine in sodium chloride and sodium chlorate(V). **[2]**

   ii Explain why this is a disproportionation reaction by referring to relevant oxidation number changes. **[3]**

   iii Write an ionic equation for this reaction. **[1]**

   c Chlorine is a good oxidising agent. It oxidises aqueous potassium iodide to iodine.

   i   Construct a balanced equation for this reaction. Include state symbols. **[2]**

   ii State the colour change observed in this reaction. Explain your answer. **[2]**

   iii Describe how you would use hexane to confirm the identity of the halogen produced in this reaction. Give the result. **[2]**

TIP

This question starts with a data interpretation question but goes on to use information from other chapters about intermolecular forces and electronic structure. Make sure that you know about these.

TIP

You need to learn the colour changes involved in the reactions between halogens and halide ions.

CONTINUED

TIPS

d i Potassium iodide reacts with concentrated sulfuric acid. Hydrogen iodide is produced but this reacts with the sulfuric acid:

$6HI + H_2SO_4 \rightarrow 3I_2 + S + 4H_2O$

State the name of the reducing agent in this equation. Explain your answer. [2]

ii Further reaction can occur:

$8HI + H_2SO_4 \rightarrow 4I_2 + H_2S + 4H_2O$

State the oxidation number change of the sulfur in this reaction. [1]

iii Describe the observations you would make during reactions **d i** and **ii** above. [3]

[Total: 21]

3 Hydrogen reacts with halogens to form hydrogen halides.

a Describe the differences in the reaction of hydrogen with chlorine and with bromine. [3]

b Hydrogen reacts with iodine in a sealed tube at 500 °C.

$H_2(g) + I_2(g) \rightleftharpoons 2HI(g)$ $\Delta H_r^{\ominus} = -9.6\ kJ\,mol^{-1}$

Predict the effect, if any, on this reaction of increasing the:

i pressure [1]

ii temperature [1]

iii concentration of hydrogen. [1]

c The hydrogen halides are less stable as the atomic number of the halogen increases. Explain why. [3]

d Aqueous chlorine reacts with aqueous potassium bromide.

i Write a balanced equation for this reaction. [1]

ii Describe a test for bromide ions and give the result. [2]

iii Describe the action of concentrated ammonia solution on the precipitate obtained in part **d ii** and give an explanation for the results. [3]

e Iodide ions reacts with manganese(IV) oxide.

$MnO_2 + 2I^- + 4H^+ \rightarrow Mn^{2+} + 2H_2O + I_2$

i Identify the oxidising agent in this reaction. Explain your answer. [2]

ii Write two half-equations for this reaction, one showing oxidation and the other showing reduction. Explain which is which in terms of electron transfer. [4]

[Total: 21]

In **2 d iii** remember that the words *observations / observe* mean what you see. This can be extended in Chemistry questions to what you hear, smell or feel.

Remember that statements such as 'hydrogen sulfide is formed' or 'a gas is formed' are not observations. They are statements of fact. But 'bubbles of gas are seen' *is* an observation.

> Chapter 13

Nitrogen

CHAPTER OUTLINE

In this chapter you will learn how to:

- describe and explain the lack of reactivity of nitrogen gas

- describe and explain the basicity of ammonia and the formation and structure of the ammonium ion

- describe the displacement of ammonia from its ammonium salts

- describe the industrial importance of ammonia and nitrogen compounds derived from ammonia

- describe and explain the natural and artificial occurrences of oxides of nitrogen and their catalytic removal from the exhaust gases of internal combustion engines

- describe and explain why atmospheric oxides of nitrogen are pollutants, including their role in the formation of photochemical smog and in the formation of acid rain, both directly and by the catalytic oxidation of atmospheric sulfur dioxide.

Exercise 13.1 Fertilisers and the environment

This exercise will familiarise you with the effects of nitrate fertilisers on the environment.

Eutrophication is a complex process involving the leaching of fertilisers from fields resulting in the excessive growth of plants in rivers and ponds. The plants eventually die because the algae cover the surface of the water so photosynthesis cannot take place. In the end, the water cannot support life due to the lack of oxygen.

KEY WORD

eutrophication:
an environmental problem caused by fertilisers leaching from fields into rivers and lakes.

a   Copy and complete these sentences about eutrophication using words from this list:

| algae | bacteria | decomposed | die | dissolve | eutrophication |
| growth | leached | light | nitrates | oxygen | surface |

Nitrate fertilisers _____ in rainwater and are then _____ into

lakes and rivers. The _____ promote the excessive _____ of water

plants, especially_____. The algae spread across the _____ of the

water and block out the _____ so that the water plants cannot grow. The

plants are _____ by aerobic _____, which multiply and use up the

dissolved _____ in the water. Fish and other water creatures cannot survive

without oxygen and they _____. This process, which takes place in streams

and rivers, and leads to the death of plants and animals is called _____.

b Farmers add nitrate fertilisers to the soil.

    i Explain why many plants do not grow well in soils which have not had nitrogenous fertilisers added for several years.

    Look for the relative strength of the acids and bases.

    ii Ammonium chloride is hydrolysed by water.

$$NH_4^+ + Cl^- + H_2O \rightleftharpoons NH_3 + H_3O^+ + Cl^-$$

    Use the information in this equation to suggest why ammonium chloride forms a slightly acidic solution.

    iii Explain why ammonia is basic.

    iv Slaked lime can be used to treat acidic soils.

    Copy and complete the equation for the reaction of ammonium chloride with calcium hydroxide.

    _____NH_4Cl + _____ $\rightarrow CaCl_2$ + _____ + _____

    v State the name of another non-alkaline compound of calcium which can be used to treat acidic soil.

Exercise 13.2 Nitrogen and its compounds

This exercise will help you revise some properties of nitrogen, ammonia and ammonium compounds. You will also revise the practical procedure for making ammonia.

When answering questions about inorganic nitrogen compounds, you need to know their structure and bonding (Chapters 4 and 5).

a Nitrogen has a triple bond.

    i Copy and complete the dot-and-cross diagram of a nitrogen molecule (Figure 13.1).

    ii Explain why nitrogen is relatively unreactive.

b The structures of an ammonia molecule and an ammonium ion are shown as Figure 13.2.

    i Describe the electrons labelled A.

    ii Deduce the bond angle B. Explain your answer.

    iii Deduce the bond angle C. Explain your answer.

c Ammonia can be prepared by heating a mixture of ammonium chloride and calcium hydroxide.

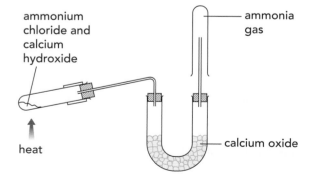

Figure 13.3: Making ammonia.

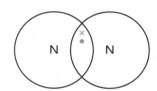

Figure 13.1: Bonding in nitrogen molecules.

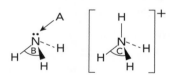

Figure 13.2: An ammonia molecule (left) and an ammonium ion.

> **TIP**
>
> You should be able to distinguish between different types of chemical reaction. Make sure that you know these by reference to specific equations.

i Explain why the ammonia is collected in an inverted test-tube.

ii How can you tell when the test-tube of ammonia is full?

iii What is the purpose of the calcium oxide?

iv Why is sulfuric acid not used instead of calcium oxide?

v What type of reaction is the conversion of ammonium chloride to ammonia?

Choose from:

- Neutralisation of ammonia
- Displacement of ammonia
- Thermal decomposition of ammonium chloride

vi Give a description of each type of reaction in part **c v.**

d Ammonium phosphate is a fertiliser.

i Copy and complete the equation for the formation of ammonium phosphate from ammonia and phosphoric acid.

$$\underline{\hspace{2cm}} + \underline{\hspace{2cm}} \rightarrow (NH_4)_3PO_4$$

ii Describe how an aqueous solution of ammonium phosphate is converted into solid pellets of ammonium phosphate.

iii Explain why fertilisers are important.

e Suggest the name of an acid which is manufactured from ammonia.

Exercise 13.3 Nitrogen oxides and the environment

This exercise gives you practice in revising the origins of nitrogen oxides in the environment. You will also become familiar with their harmful effects and their removal by catalytic converters.

TIPS

Answer parts **a** to **e** of this question using:

- Your knowledge about the oxides of nitrogen, e.g. the colour of nitrogen dioxide.
- The information given in the question. Look out for the formula of ozone.

KEY WORDS

photochemical smog: poisonous fog at low level caused by volatile organic compounds from car exhausts reacting with nitrogen oxides in the presence of sunlight.

During the heat of the day, nitrogen oxides and ozone build up in cities in a layer of hot air which gets trapped near the Earth's surface. At night, the lower temperature allows these pollutants to escape higher into the atmosphere.

Photochemical smog is formed in cities by the interaction of nitrogen oxides, ozone (O_3) and volatile hydrocarbons.

Figure 13.4 shows how the concentration of nitrogen dioxide in a city changes over three days.

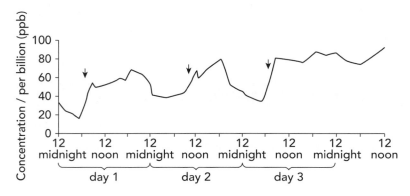

Figure 13.4: Changes in the concentration of nitrogen dioxide in a city over three days.

a Describe how the concentration of nitrogen dioxide changes during these three days.

b Suggest why there is a rapid increase in the concentration of nitrogen dioxide at the times marked by the arrows.

c i In the early morning, nitrogen dioxide is formed by the reaction of nitric oxide (nitrogen(II) oxide) with oxygen.

Write a balanced equation for this reaction.

ii In the presence of sunlight, nitrogen dioxide reacts with oxygen to form ozone and nitric oxide.

Write a balanced equation for this reaction.

iii The reactions in parts **c i** and **ii** are chain reactions. They can carry on and on. Suggest why they can do this.

d Use the information in Figure 13.4 to suggest:

i Why a brown mist builds up in the air from late morning to early evening.

ii How the concentration of ozone in the atmosphere in the city changes during the day.

e If the temperature remains high, nitrogen oxides cannot disperse higher into the atmosphere. Which day in Figure 13.4 is most likely to have a high night-time temperature?

f Nitrogen dioxide can be found naturally in the atmosphere. Describe how it is formed.

g **Catalytic converters** are used to remove nitrogen oxides from the exhausts of petrol engines.

i Explain how nitrogen oxides are formed in the engine.

ii Carbon monoxide and nitrogen dioxide can be removed from car exhausts by catalytic converters.

Copy and complete the equation for one of the reactions which occurs.

$$\_\_ CO + \_\_ NO_2 \rightarrow \_\_ CO_2 + _____$$

h i Explain how nitrogen dioxide is involved in the oxidation of sulfur dioxide in the atmosphere.

ii Explain why nitrogen dioxide is described as a homogenous catalyst in the oxidation of sulfur dioxide.

i State two harmful effects that **acid rain** can have on:

i plants

ii buildings.

KEY WORDS

catalytic converter: a piece of equipment put on the exhaust of cars with petrol engines to remove oxides of nitrogen and carbon monoxide produced in the engine.

acid rain: rain with an acidity of below about pH 5.5 due to the reactions in the atmosphere involving acidic oxides.

EXAM-STYLE QUESTIONS

1 The average concentrations of nitrogen dioxide in a town and in a country area were measured over the same 10-day period.

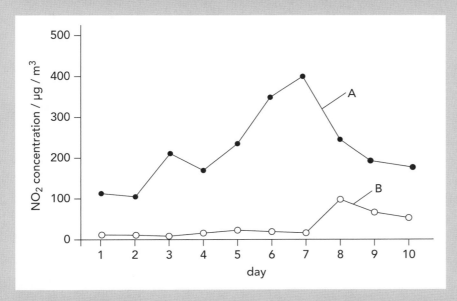

Figure 13.5

a i State which line on the graph is most likely to represent the concentration of nitrogen dioxide in the town. Explain your answer. **[2]**

ii Suggest why there is an increase in nitrogen dioxide in line B, even though there is little traffic or industry in this area. **[1]**

iii Calculate the concentration of nitrogen dioxide in $mol\,dm^{-3}$ for day 7 in line A. $1\,\mu g = 1.0 \times 10^{-6}$ g; A_r values N = 14.0, O = 16.0 **[3]**

b Nitrogen dioxide can be formed during thunderstorms. Explain how this nitrogen dioxide is formed and give one relevant equation. **[4]**

c Nitrogen oxides are removed from petrol engine exhausts using catalytic converters. Nitrogen dioxide reacts with carbon monoxide on the catalyst surface to form two colourless gases, one of which turns limewater milky.

Write a balanced equation for the reaction taking place in the catalytic converter. **[2]**

d Nitric oxide also reacts with carbon monoxide.

$$2NO + 2CO \xrightarrow{\text{Pt/Rh catalyst}} N_2 + 2CO_2$$

i Explain in terms of oxidation number changes why this is a redox reaction. **[3]**

ii State the type of catalysis that is occurring. Explain your answer. **[2]**

e i Nitrogen is relatively unreactive. Explain why. **[2]**

ii Draw a dot-and-cross diagram of a nitrogen molecule. **[2]**

[Total: 21]

TIPS

Make sure you have the correct units when answering question **1 a iii**.

In part **d** remember that homogeneous catalysts are in the same phase as the reactants and heterogeneous catalysts are in a different phase.

CONTINUED

2 a Ammonium sulfate reacts with aqueous sodium hydroxide when warmed. One of the products is ammonia.

   i Construct the chemical equation for this reaction. [2]

   ii State the type of reaction which takes place. [1]

b Ammonia is a *weak* base.

   i State the meaning of the term *weak* when applied to bases. [1]

   ii Explain, using **Brønsted–Lowry theory**, why an aqueous solution of ammonia has an alkaline pH value. [3]

c Nitric acid is produced from ammonia. The first stage in this reaction is the **catalytic oxidation** of ammonia by oxygen to form nitrogen(II) oxide, NO, and water.

   i Write the equation for this reaction. [1]

   ii **Give** one reason why ammonia is industrially important, other than in the production of nitric acid. [1]

   iii NO contributes directly to the formation of acid rain. Describe the reactions that occur during this process. [2]

   iv NO_2 contributes directly to acid rain. It also contributes to acid rain *indirectly*.

      Explain how it does this. [2]

d Nitrogen oxides can be formed naturally in the atmosphere.

   Explain how they are formed. [2]

e Nitrogen oxides are involved in the formation of photochemical smog. One of the reactions involved is:

$$HO_2\bullet + NO \rightarrow HO\bullet + NO_2$$

   Give the general name for the species $HO_2\bullet$ and $HO\bullet$ which have an unpaired electron. [1]

f In the formation of photochemical smog, volatile organic compounds from car engines react with nitrogen oxides.

   i State the essential conditions for this reaction. [1]

   ii One of the substances formed during these reactions has the formula $CH_3CO_3NO_2$.

      State the name of this compound. [1]

[Total: 18]

3 a Some bacteria in the soil convert ammonium ions to nitrate ions. The first stage in this reaction is:

$$2NH_4^+ + 3O_2 \rightarrow 2NO_2^- + 4H^+ + 2H_2O$$

   i Explain why this is a redox reaction by referring to the oxidation number changes of relevant atoms. [3]

   ii Draw a dot-and-cross diagram for the ammonium ion. [1]

TIP

Several parts of this question involve writing equations. Make sure that you look at all the information carefully.

TIP

Make sure that you distinguish between species which have similar atoms, e.g. NO and NO_2. It makes a difference to the answer in part **c**.

KEY WORDS

Brønsted–Lowry theory: acids are defined as hydrogen ion donors and bases as hydrogen ion acceptors.

catalytic oxidation: an oxidation reaction whose rate of reaction is increased by a catalyst.

TIPS

This question is about bacterial actions in the soil.

Do not let this worry you – concentrate on the chemistry and the equations.

CONTINUED

    iii The second stage in the reaction is the conversion of NO_2^- ions to nitrate ions in the presence of oxygen.

       Write a balanced equation for this reaction. **[2]**

    iv Suggest why not all the nitrate ions formed by bacteria in the soil are absorbed by plants. **[1]**

b Other bacteria in the soil convert nitrate ions to nitrogen. Explain why nitrogen does not react with oxygen at r.t.p. **[2]**

c When plants decay, complex molecules are converted to ammonia.

Ammonia reacts with acids present in the soil to form ammonium salts. For example:

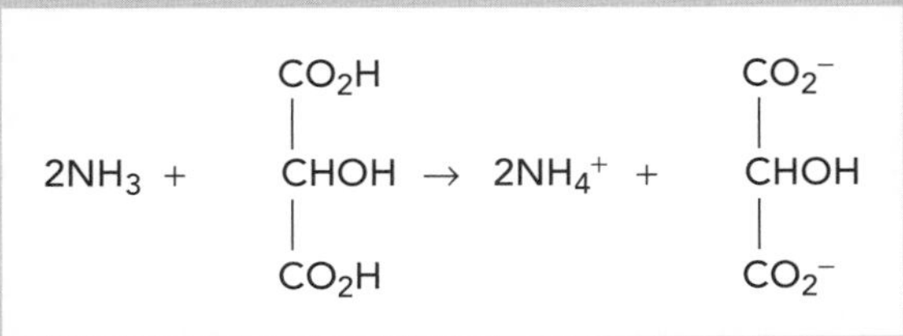

$$2NH_3 + \begin{array}{c} CO_2H \\ | \\ CHOH \\ | \\ CO_2H \end{array} \rightarrow 2NH_4^+ + \begin{array}{c} CO_2^- \\ | \\ CHOH \\ | \\ CO_2^- \end{array}$$

Figure 13.6

Explain why ammonia is acting as a base in this reaction. **[1]**

d Ammonia reacts with nitric acid to form ammonium nitrate, NH_4NO_3.

Calculate the percentage by mass of nitrogen in ammonium nitrate.

A_r values H = 1.0, N = 14.0, O = 16.0. **[2]**

e Most plants are able to absorb nitrate ions but not ammonia or ammonium salts.

The table gives some information about two fertilisers.

Fertiliser	Solubility / mol/100 g water	Density / $g\,cm^{-3}$
ammonium nitrate	2.68	1.72
potassium nitrate	3.75×10^{-1}	2.11

Table 13.1

    i Give one reason why some farmers prefer potassium nitrate rather than ammonium nitrate as a fertiliser. Explain your answer. **[1]**

    ii Give one **other** reason why some farmers prefer ammonium nitrate rather than potassium nitrate as a fertiliser. Explain your answer. **[1]**

f Ammonium chloride reacts with sodium hydroxide when heated.

Write an ionic equation for this reaction. **[1]**

[Total: 15]

Chapter 14
Introduction to organic chemistry

CHAPTER OUTLINE

In this chapter you will learn how to:

- interpret, name and use the general, structural, displayed and skeletal formulae of the alkanes, alkenes, halogenoalkanes, alcohols (including primary, secondary and tertiary), aldehydes, ketones, carboxylic acids, esters, amines (primary only) and nitriles

- explain and use the term functional group

- explain and use the terms homolytic and heterolytic fission

- explain and use the terms free radical, initiation, propagation, termination

- explain and use the terms nucleophile, electrophile, nucleophilic, electrophilic

- explain and use the terms addition, substitution, elimination, hydrolysis, condensation

- explain and use the terms oxidation and reduction in the context of organic reactions

- describe and explain the shape of, and bond angles of, molecules in terms of their sp, sp^2 and sp^3 hybridised atomic orbitals, and their σ bonds and π bonds

- describe and explain the different types of structural isomerism and stereoisomerism

- identify chiral centres in optical isomers.

Exercise 14.1 Naming organic compounds

This exercise will familiarise you with the range of **functional groups** and **alkyl groups** in organic compounds.

TIPS

Functional groups, e.g. —OH, —C≡N, are characteristic of each different **homologous series**. You simply have to learn these!

Organic compounds forming chains have an alkyl group: methyl = 1 C atom, ethyl = 2 C atoms, propyl = 3 C atoms and so on. You simply have to learn these as well!

KEY WORDS

functional group: an atom or group of atoms in an organic molecule that determines its characteristic chemical reactions.

alkyl group: a group having one fewer hydrogen atom than the corresponding **alkane**.

TIPS

Remember that the suffix often tells you the type of homologous series, e.g. -ol is an alcohol, -ene is an alkene

The terms primary, secondary and tertiary indicate that the functional group is attached to a carbon atom which is attached to 1, 2 or 3 other carbon atoms.

a Match the names of the functional groups 1 to 8 with their structures A to H.

1	carboxylic acid

A	$R-C\equiv N$

2	nitrile

B	$\underset{R}{\overset{R}{\diagdown}}C=C\underset{R}{\overset{R}{\diagup}}$

3	aldehyde

C	$R-\underset{O-H}{\overset{O}{\overset{\parallel}{C}}}$

4	alkene

D	$R-Cl$

5	ketone

E	$R-NH_2$

6	chloroalkane

F	$R-OH$

7	amine

G	$R-\underset{H}{\overset{O}{\overset{\parallel}{C}}}$

8	alcohol

H	$\underset{R'}{\overset{R}{\diagdown}}C=O$

KEY WORDS

homologous series: a group of organic compounds having the same functional group, the same general formula and similar chemical properties.

alkanes: saturated hydrocarbons with the general formula C_nH_{2n+2}.

carboxylic acids: organic compounds which have a $-CO_2H$ functional group and a general formula $C_nH_{2n+1}CO_2H$.

aldehydes: organic compounds containing the $-C=O$ group.

alkenes: unsaturated hydrocarbons with $C=C$ double bonds and the general formula C_nH_{2n}.

ketones: organic compounds with a $C=O$ group in the middle of the carbon chain.

chloroalkanes: halogenoalkanes in which chlorine is the halogen.

amines: compounds with an $-NH_2$ functional group.

b Copy and complete the names of these compounds. Assume that there are no side chains.

i C_6H_{14} hex ________

ii C_3H_7OH propan ________

iii $CH_3CH_2CH{=}CH_2$ ________ ene

iv C_4H_9CHO ________ anal

v $C_5H_{11}Br$ 1-bromo ________

vi CH_3COCH_3 propan ________

vii C_2H_5COOH ________ acid

viii C_7H_{16} ________

ix C_4H_9OH ________

x $CH_3CH_2CH_2CH{=}CH_2$ ________

xi HCHO ________

xii C_4H_9CN ________

xiii $C_5H_{11}NH_2$ ________

KEY WORDS

alcohols: organic chain compounds containing the –OH group. (Ring compounds with an OH connected directly to the ring are called phenols).

c Give the correct names of the compounds S to X.

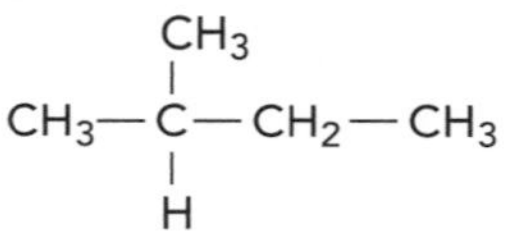

S

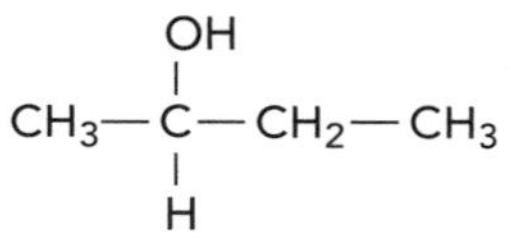

T

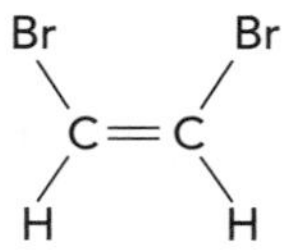

U

$CH_3CH{=}CHCH_2CH_2CH_3$

V

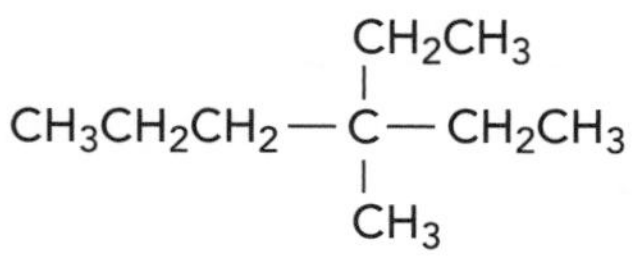

W

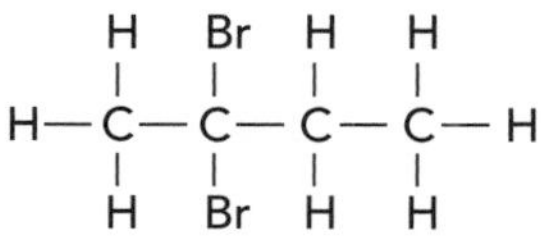

X

d Draw the **displayed formula** for each of these compounds:

i The tertiary alcohol with 4 carbon atoms

ii The ketone with 3 carbon atoms

iii The ester obtained when propan-1-ol reacts with methanoic acid

iv An aldehyde with 4 carbon atoms.

KEY WORDS

displayed formula: a 2D representation of an organic molecule, showing *all* its atoms (by their symbols) and their bonds (by short single, double or triple lines between the symbols).

Exercise 14.2 Classifying organic reactions

This exercise will help you revise the classification of organic reactions and reaction mechanisms.

a Classify the reactions **i** to **viii** as addition, condensation, elimination, hydrolysis, oxidation, reduction or substitution.

   i $CH_3CH=CH_2 + Br_2 \rightarrow CH_3CHBrCH_2Br$

   ii $CH_3CH_2OH + [O] \rightarrow CH_3CHO + H_2O$

   iii $CH_3COOC_2H_5 + H_2O \rightleftharpoons CH_3COOH + C_2H_5OH$

   iv $CH_3CH_2OH + HCl \rightarrow CH_3CH_2Cl + H_2O$

   v $CH_3CH_2CH_2CH_2OH \xrightarrow{H_2SO_4} CH_3CH_2CH=CH_2 + H_2O$

   vi $CH_3COOH + 4[H] \rightarrow CH_3CH_2OH + H_2O$

   vii $C_2H_5Br + H_2O \rightarrow C_2H_5OH + HBr$

   viii $C_7H_{15}NH_2 + C_2H_5COOH \rightarrow C_7H_{15}NHCOC_2H_5 + H_2O$

b Copy and complete the following definitions.

   i   In **heterolytic fission** a covalent bond breaks so that two free _____ are formed.

   ii   In **homolytic** _____ a _____ bond breaks so that one of the atoms in the bond accepts both the bonding _____.

   iii   A **nucleophile** is a species which _____ a pair of electrons to an electron _____ atom.

   iv   An **electrophile** is a species with a positive or partially positive _____ which accepts a _____ of electrons from another species.

KEY WORDS

addition: an organic reaction in which two (or more) molecules combine to give a single product.

elimination: a reaction in which a small molecule is removed from an organic molecule.

substitution: a reaction that involves the replacement of one atom, or group of atoms, by another.

condensation: a reaction in which two organic molecules join together and in the process eliminate a small molecule, such as water or hydrogen chloride.

heterolytic fission: the breaking of a covalent bond in which one atom takes both electrons from the bond, forming a negative ion, and leaving behind a positive ion.

homolytic fission: the breaking of a covalent bond in which each atom takes one electron from the bond to form free radicals.

nucleophile: species that can act as a donor of a pair of electrons.

   v   A **carbocation** is an organic ion which has a _____ atom which is

       _____ charged.

   vi A free _____ is a species which has an _____ electron.

c   Identify each of these steps as **initiation**, **propagation** or **termination**.

   i $CH_3{\bullet} + CH_3{\bullet} \rightarrow CH_3CH_3$

   ii $Cl{-}Cl \xrightarrow{\text{light}} 2Cl{\bullet}$

   iii $Cl{\bullet} + CH_4 \rightarrow CH_3{\bullet} + HCl$

d   Four species are shown in Figure 14.1.

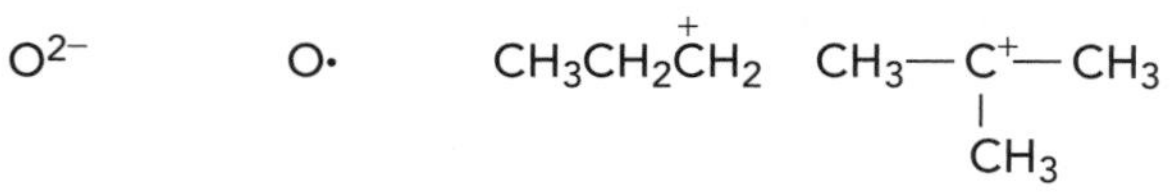

$$O^{2-} \qquad O{\bullet} \qquad CH_3CH_2\overset{+}{C}H_2 \quad CH_3{-}\overset{+}{\underset{\underset{CH_3}{|}}{C}}{-}CH_3$$

A   B   C   D

Figure 14.1: Four species (A-D).

State which one of these species is:

   i   a free radical

   ii   a secondary carbocation.

e   Figure 14.2 shows part of two reaction mechanisms **R** and **S**.

Describe each of these using the words addition, electrophilic, nucleophilic and substitution. Explain your answers.

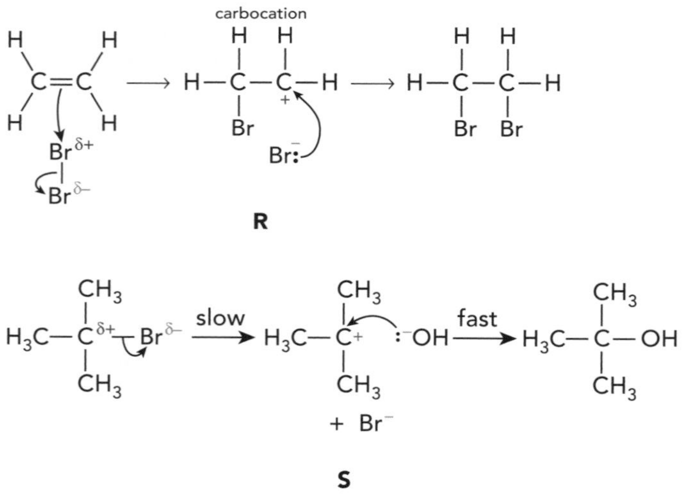

Figure 14.2: Part of two reaction mechanisms R and S.

KEY WORDS

electrophile: a species in organic chemistry that can act as an electron pair acceptor.

carbocation: an alkyl group with a single positive charge on one of its carbon atoms. It is formed in reaction mechanisms.

initiation: the first step in the mechanism of free radical substitution of alkanes by halogens. It involves the breaking of the halogen–halogen bond using energy from ultra-violet light from the Sun.

propagation: the second step in a free-radical mechanism in which the radicals formed can then attack reactant molecules generating more free radicals, and so on.

termination: the final steps in a free-radical mechanism in which two free radicals react together to form a product molecule.

Exercise 14.3 Types of formula

This exercise gives you practice in drawing different types of formulae for organic compounds.

a   Copy and complete the table.

TIP

When writing displayed formulae remember to include the bonds in the functional group as wel, e.g. O—H for alcohol (not OH).

Type of formula	Compound			
	Butane	But-2-ene	Propan-2-ol	Propanone
displayed formula	H—C—C—C—C—H (with H atoms)			
condensed **structural formula**	$CH_3CH_2CH_2CH_3$			
molecular formula	C_4H_{10}			
skeletal formula	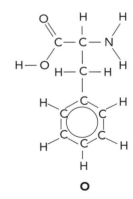			
empirical formula	C_2H_5			

Table 14.1: Types of formula.

KEY WORDS

structural formula: the formula that shows how many, and the symbols of, atoms bonded to each carbon atom in an organic molecule, e.g. $CH_3CH(OH)$, $CH_2=CH_2$.

skeletal formula: a simplified displayed formula with all C and H atoms and C—H bonds removed.

b   The displayed formulae of some organic compounds, L, M, N and O are shown in Figure 14.3.

Figure 14.3: Organic compounds.

For each of these compounds deduce:

i   the molecular formula

ii   the empirical formula.

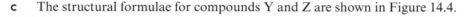

c   The structural formulae for compounds Y and Z are shown in Figure 14.4.

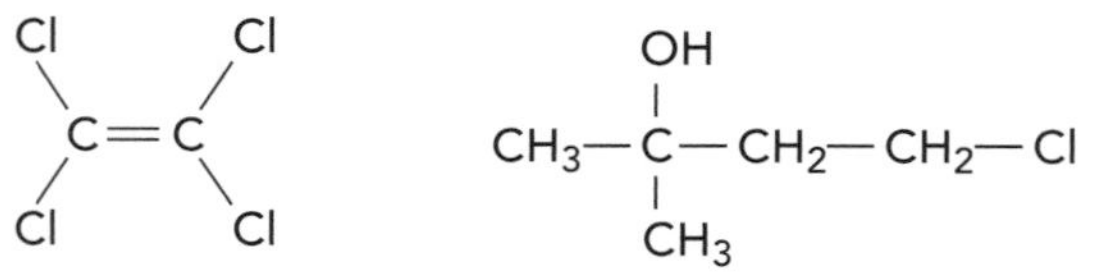

$$Cl\diagdown\atop Cl\diagup C = C \diagup\atop\diagdown {Cl \atop Cl}$$

$$CH_3 - \underset{\underset{CH_3}{|}}{\overset{\overset{OH}{|}}{C}} - CH_2 - CH_2 - Cl$$

Y   Z

Figure 14.4: The structural formulae for compounds Y and Z.

Draw the skeletal formulae for Y and Z.

Exercise 14.4 Isomerism

This exercise revises the different types of isomerism and gives you practice at drawing **stereoisomers** using 3D displayed formulae.

> ## TIPS
>
> In *cis/trans* isomers remember that *cis*- means on the same side (of the double bond) and *trans*- means across (on the opposite side of the double bond).
>
> Stereoisomers are also called optical isomers. When drawing them, imagine looking at the mirror image of the one you are given. The four different groups are attached to a carbon atom.
>
> When drawing stereoisomers, the bond coming out of the page is drawn as a wedge and the bond going away from you is drawn as a dashed line.

a   Copy and complete the definition of **structural isomers**.

Structural isomers are compounds with the same _____ formula but

different _____ formulae.

b   i   Draw the displayed formula for a position isomer of the alcohol $CH_3CH_2CH_2OH$.

ii   Draw a displayed formula for a functional group isomer of the compound with the structure CH_3COCH_3.

iii   Draw displayed formulae for two other isomers of the alkane, $CH_3CH_2CH_2CH_2CH_3$.

c   i   Draw the displayed formulae of two isomers of the compound whose structural formula is $CH_3CBr{=}CBrCH_3$. Give the name of each of these isomers. The double bond should be in the same position.

ii   What type of isomerism is this?

KEY WORDS

stereoisomers: compounds whose molecules have the same atoms bonded to each other in the same way but with a different arrangement of atoms in space so that the molecules cannot be superimposed on each other. (Superimposed means that, however you turn the isomer, the atoms are never in exactly the same place – like your hands.)

structural isomers: compounds with the same molecular formula but different structural formulae.

chiral centre: a carbon atom with the four different atoms or groups of atoms attached. This allows optical isomers to exist.

d i Draw the other optical isomers of compounds P and Q (Figure 14.5).

ii Identify the **chiral centre** in these optical isomers.

e Cyclopropane 1,2-dicarboxylic acid has two optical isomers.

Draw the structure of the *cis-* and *trans-*isomers of cyclopropane 1,2-dicarboxylic acid.

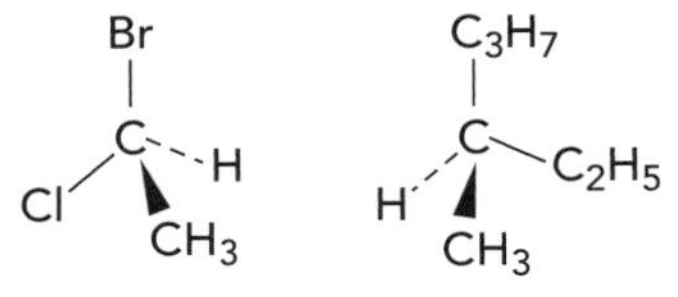

Figure 14.5: For question d i.

Exercise 14.5 Homologous series

This exercise gives practice in extracting information from data provided. It also familiarises you with the concept of a general formula.

> ## TIPS
>
> When predicting the properties of compounds in an homologous series look for:
> - the general trend
> - the difference between the properties of successive members of the series.

The table shows the structural formulae, density and boiling points of some alkanes and alcohols. The density of the alkanes is that of the liquid measured at the boiling point.

Homologous series	Compound	Structural formula	Density / $g\ cm^{-3}$	Boiling point / K
alkanes	methane	CH_4	0.466	109.1
	ethane	CH_3CH_3	0.527	184.5
	propane	$CH_3CH_2CH_3$	0.585	231.0
	butane	$CH_3CH_2CH_2CH_3$	0.601	
	pentane	$CH_3CH_2CH_2CH_2CH_3$		309.2
alcohols	methanol	CH_3OH	0.793	338.1
	ethanol	CH_3CH_2OH	0.789	351.6
	propan-1-ol	$CH_3CH_2CH_2OH$	0.804	370.5
	butan-1-ol	$CH_3CH_2CH_2CH_2OH$	0.810 to 0.815	390.3
	pentan-1-ol	$CH_3CH_2CH_2CH_2CH_2OH$		

Table 14.2: Properties of some alkanes.

a Define the terms:

i homologous series

ii functional group.

b Use the information in the table to deduce:

i the **general formula** of the alkanes

ii the general formula of the alcohols.

KEY WORDS

***cis/trans* isomerism:** a type of geometric isomerism where two different substituent groups joined to the carbon atoms on each side of a double bond are arranged either on the same side of the double bond (*cis*-isomer) or on opposite sides (*trans*-isomer).

KEY WORDS

general formula: a formula that represents a homologous series of compounds using letters and numbers; e.g. the general formula for the alkanes is C_nH_{2n+2}.

c   Write the molecular formula for the next member of the alcohol homologous series.

d   i   Describe the general trend in the density in each homologous series.

ii   Give the name of any compounds which do not fit this trend.

iii   Predict the density of pentane.

iv   Describe the general trend in the boiling points in each homologous series.

v   Predict the boiling points of butane and pentan-1-ol.

vi   Write the formulae and name the alkyl groups present in the compound with the structural formula. $CH_3CH_2C(CH_3)_2CH_2CH_3$

Exercise 14.6 Structure and bonding in organic molecules

This exercise gives further practice in deducing the 3D structure of organic molecules using the electron repulsion theory. It also revises σ and π bonds and hybrid orbitals.

> **TIPS**
>
> This exercise uses previous knowledge about electron repulsion theory and sigma and pi bonds (Chapter 4). Make sure that you have revised this.
>
> Remember that a single sp hybrid orbital has two lobes with one of the lobes much smaller than the other.

KEY WORDS

secondary amine: an amine formed when two of the hydrogen atoms in ammonia have been substituted by two alkyl groups.

a   The structural formula of methane is CH_4. The structural formula of ethane is CH_3CH_3.

i   Draw diagrams to show the stereochemical (3D) formula of methane and ethane.

ii   What is the value of the H—C—H bond angles in these two compounds? Explain your answer.

b   The structure of ethene is shown in Figure 14.6.

Describe the formation of the σ and π bonds in ethene using the terms s orbitals, p orbitals and sp^2 hybridisation.

c   Explain why there is only one form of butane, $CH_3CH_2CH_2CH_3$ but there are *cis/trans* isomers of but-2-ene, $CH_3CH=CHCH_3$.

d   The structure of a **secondary amine** is shown in Figure 14.7.

Explain why the C—N—C bond angle is less than 109.5°.

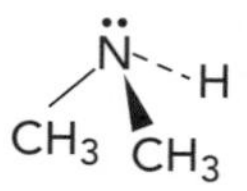

e   Methane has hybridised orbitals with ¼ s character and ¾ p character. Use ideas about these sp^3 hybridised orbitals to state and explain the H—C—H bond angle in methane.

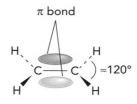

Figure 14.6: The structure of ethene.

Figure 14.7: The structure of a secondary amine.

EXAM-STYLE QUESTIONS

1 a A sample of a compound contains 47.4 g of carbon, 10.5 g of hydrogen and 42.1 g of oxygen only. A_r values C = 12.0, H = 1.00, O = 16.0

   i Deduce the empirical formula of this compound. **[3]**

   ii The relative molecular mass of the compound is 76. Deduce the molecular formula for this compound. Show all your working. **[1]**

  b Butanol, C_4H_9OH, has several isomers.

   Draw the structures of three of these isomers. **[3]**

  c Butan-1-ol reacts with both hydrogen chloride and concentrated sulfuric acid.

     Equation A: $C_4H_9OH + HCl \rightarrow C_4H_9Cl + H_2O$

     Equation B: $C_4H_9OH \xrightarrow{H_2SO_4} C_4H_8 + H_2O$

   State the type of reaction represented by:

   i Equation A **[1]**

   ii Equation B **[1]**

  d Butan-1-ol can be oxidised to butanoic acid by acidified potassium dichromate solution.

   Write a balanced equation for this reaction. Use [O] to represent an oxygen atom added by the oxidising agent. **[2]**

  e The **stereochemical formula** of another alcohol is shown in Figure 14.8.

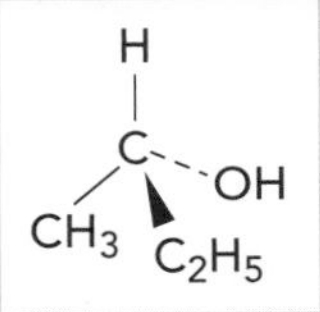

Figure 14.8

   Draw the stereoisomer of this alcohol. **[2]**

  f The structural formula of pentan-2-ol is $CH_3CH(OH)CH_2CH_2CH_3$.

   i Draw the skeletal formula of pentan-2-ol. **[1]**

   ii Identify the chiral centre in pentan-2-ol. Explain your answer. **[2]**

              [Total: 16]

2 1-Chloroalkanes have a –Cl functional group at the end of the carbon chain.

  a Draw the structural formula for 1-chloropropane. **[1]**

  b Chloroalkanes can be made by the reaction of chlorine with alkanes in the presence of light.

   The first step in this reaction is:

     $Cl_2 \rightarrow 2Cl\bullet$

   State the name given to:

   i The species $Cl\bullet$ **[1]**

   ii The type of bond breaking that occurs. **[1]**

TIPS

Make sure that you know how to write the different types of chemical formulae.

When drawing stereochemical formulae for optical isomers, remember to start with the atom that is the chiral centre. This is the one that has four different groups attached to it.

Remember that we can simplify organic equations for oxidation reactions by writing [O] instead of the oxidising agent. This is because the equations are often complex.

KEY WORDS

stereochemical formula: the formula showing the exact arrangement of atoms in space. A bond coming towards you is shown by a wedge of increasing size. A bond going away from you is shown by a dashed line.

CONTINUED

c When 2-chloro-2-methylpropane reacts with aqueous sodium hydroxide, the first step in the mechanism is:

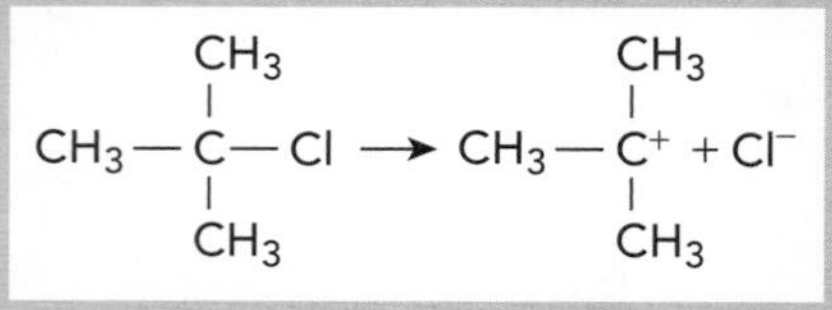

Figure 14.9

State the name given to a species with a positively charged carbon atom. **[1]**

d The second step in the reaction mechanism is:

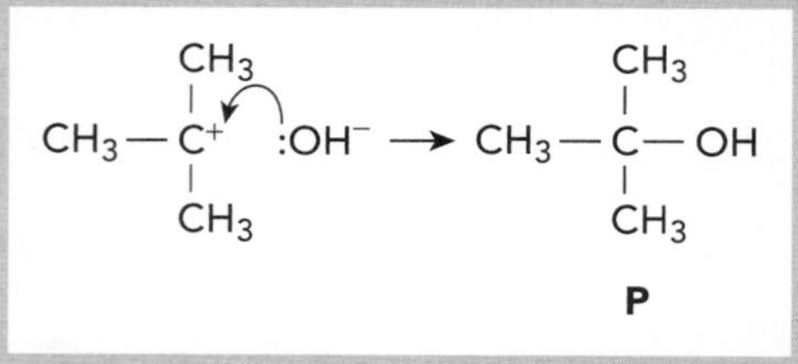

P

Figure 14.10

i State the type of **attacking reagent** the OH⁻ ion acts as. Explain your answer. **[2]**

ii Explain the meaning of the curly arrow. **[1]**

iii To which homologous series (group of compounds) does compound P belong? **[1]**

iv Give the name of compound P. **[1]**

e State the type of reaction occurring when 2-chloro-2-methylpropane is converted to compound P **[1]**

[Total: 10]

3 Aldehydes and ketones both have a carbonyl group, $C=O$.

a Draw the displayed formula of the functional group present in:

i aldehydes **[1]**

ii ketones. **[1]**

b i Give the general formula for aldehydes. **[1]**

ii Draw the displayed formula for an aldehyde having four carbon atoms and no side chains. **[1]**

c Aldehydes can be converted to alcohols using sodium tetrahydridoborate, $NaBH_4$.

$$CH_3CH_2CHO + 2[H] \rightarrow CH_3CH_2CH_2OH$$

i State the name of this type of reaction. Explain your answer. **[2]**

ii Give the name of the alcohol produced. **[1]**

TIPS

When you see an unfamiliar reaction, look carefully at diagrams given, noting any charges and movement of electron pairs.

When drawing reaction mechanisms, remember that the curly arrows go in the direction of the movement of a pair of electrons.

KEY WORDS

attacking reagent: an atom or compound which is an electrophile or a nucleophile.

TIPS

You should be able to deduce the structures of aldehydes and ketones from general principles (Exercises 14.1 and 14.3).

Don't be put off by unfamiliar reactions. There is enough information in the question. Look carefully at the formulae for the reactants and products.

CONTINUED

d The alcohol $CH_3CH(OH)CH_3$ can be made by the reaction:

$$CH_3CH=CH_2 + H_2O \rightarrow CH_3CH(OH)CH_3$$

    i State the name of this of reaction.   **[1]**

    ii Give the name of the compound $CH_3CH=CH_2$.   **[1]**

    iii State the class of compounds $CH_3CH=CH_2$ belongs to.   **[1]**

      [Total: 10]

4 Ethane and ethene are both hydrocarbons.

  a The equations shows two of the steps in the reaction of ethane with chlorine in the presence of sunlight.

    Step 2 $CH_4 + Cl\bullet \rightarrow CH_3\bullet + HCl$

    Step 3 $CH_3\bullet + Cl_2 \rightarrow CH_3Cl + Cl\bullet$

    i Write an equation for the first step in the reaction.   **[1]**

    ii Name the species $CH_3\bullet$.   **[1]**

    iii Give the name of the process shown in both Steps 2 and 3.   **[1]**

    iv Write an equation for a reaction which terminates this mechanism.   **[1]**

  b Ethene, $H_2C=CH_2$, reacts with chlorine.

    i Describe and explain the structure of ethene (including the bond angles) in terms of hybridised orbitals.   **[6]**

    ii State the type and **mechanism of reaction** which occurs when ethene reacts with chlorine.   **[2]**

  c The structures of chloroalkane **F** and chloroalkene **G** are shown.

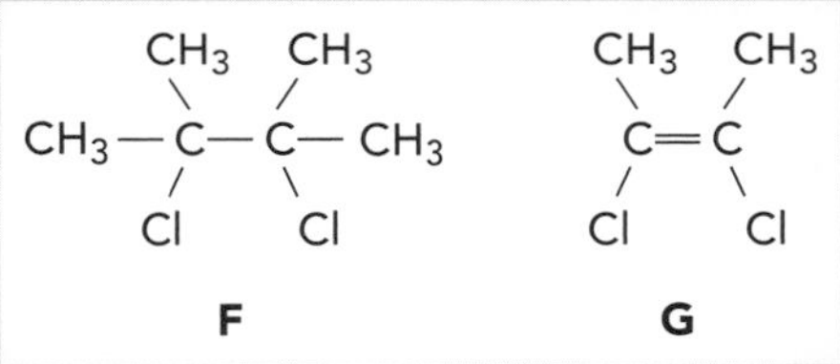

Figure 14.11

    i Draw a **geometric isomer** of structure **G**.   **[1]**

    ii Draw another isomer of structure **G**.   **[1]**

    iii Explain why there is no *cis/trans* isomer of structure **F**.   **[2]**

      [Total: 16]

TIPS

Question 4 is about eth<u>a</u>ne and eth<u>e</u>ne. Make sure that you read the question carefully so that you don't muddle the compounds.

In part **b i** think about the shapes of the orbitals and the electron density of σ and π bonds

KEY WORDS

mechanism of reaction: the individual steps in the reaction, showing the movement of electron pairs or production and movement of free radicals.

geometric isomers: molecules or ions with the same molecular formula and same bonds between their atoms but which cannot be superimposed on each other, due to some lack of rotation around their bonds; these are also known as *cis/trans* isomers.

> Chapter 15

Hydrocarbons

In this chapter you will learn how to:

- explain the general unreactivity of alkanes, and describe their complete and incomplete combustion

- explain the free-radical substitution of alkanes by chlorine and by bromine, as shown by their three-step mechanism

- suggest how cracking can be used to obtain more useful alkanes, and alkenes, of lower relative molecular mass from larger hydrocarbon molecules

- describe the environmental consequences of burning hydrocarbon fuels in vehicles and the removal of pollutants by catalytic converters

- describe the reactions of alkenes as shown by their addition, oxidation and polymerisation

- describe the mechanism of electrophilic addition in alkenes, and explain the inductive effects of alkyl groups on the stability of cations formed

- describe the difficulty of disposing of waste poly(alkene)s.

Exercise 15.1 Distillation and cracking

This exercise will help you revise the properties of alkanes and how cracking long-chain alkanes can be used to obtain alkenes and more useful alkanes.

a   Copy and complete these sentences about the distillation of petroleum (crude oil) using words from the list below:

| alkanes | bottom | condense | fractionating | gaseous | less | liquids |
| lower | molecular | short | temperature | top | volatile |

The top of the _____ column is at a _____ temperature

than the bottom. Petroleum enters the column at the _____ in

both the _____ state and liquid state. The more _____

hydrocarbons with lower relative _____ masses rise up the column further

than the _____ volatile hydrocarbons. The hydrocarbons _____

at different levels in the column as the _____ falls and are collected

as _____. The most volatile hydrocarbons are _____ with very

_____ carbon chains (methane, ethane, propane and butane). These leave

the _____ of the _____ column as gases.

b **Cracking** turns long-chain alkanes, which are in low demand, into shorter chain alkanes, which are in higher demand. Alkenes are also formed.

Read the following paragraph about cracking then answer the questions.

Fractions containing alkane molecules with relatively high molecular mass are fed into a 'cat-cracker' in the absence of oxygen. At high temperature and in the presence of zeolite catalysts they are broken down to alkanes with a lower molecular mass. Alkanes with a lower molecular mass are more in demand for fuels such as petrol and diesel than alkanes with a higher molecular mass. Alkenes are also formed. Alkenes are more reactive than alkanes and are used as a feedstock for synthesising compounds, including plastics.

- i Why is cracking of high molecular mass alkanes to produce low molecular mass alkanes carried out?
- ii Why are alkenes useful?
- iii Why are alkenes more reactive than alkanes?
- iv What conditions are needed for cracking?
- v Why does cracking have to be carried out in the absence of oxygen?
- vi What bonds are broken during cracking?

KEY WORD

cracking: the process in which large, less useful hydrocarbon molecules are broken down into smaller, more useful molecules in an oil refinery.

c Copy and complete these equations for the cracking of alkanes.

- i $C_{12}H_{26} \rightarrow C_7H_{16} +$ __________
- ii $C_{18}H_{38} \rightarrow C_6H_{12} +$ __________ $+ C_4H_8$
- iii __________ $\rightarrow C_3H_6 + C_7H_{16}$
- iv $C_3H_8 \rightarrow C_3H_6 +$ __________

Exercise 15.2 Formulae of hydrocarbons

This exercise will help you revise the different types of formulae for alkanes and alkenes.

TIPS

Displayed formulae show all atoms and all bonds.

Structural formulae do not generally show the bonds although the double bond may be shown for the alkenes.

Skeletal formulae do not show the hydrogen atoms of the C—H bonds. A single line shows the bond between two carbon atoms so $CH_3CH_2CH_2CH_2CH_3$ is shown by

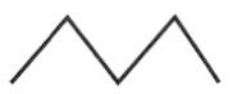

Figure 15.1: A skeletal formula.

Copy and complete the table to show the displayed, structural and skeletal formulae of the five selected **hydrocarbons**. The molecular formula is given.

KEY WORD

hydrocarbon: a compound made up of carbon and hydrogen only.

Hydrocarbon	Displayed formula	Structural formula	Skeletal formula
butane C_4H_{10}			
ethene C_2H_4			
but-2-ene C_4H_8			
cyclopentane C_5H_{10}			
buta-1-3-diene C_4H_6			

Table 15.1: Formulae of hydrocarbons.

Exercise 15.3 Reactions of alkanes

This exercise will familiarise you with the combustion and substitution reactions of alkanes.

> **TIPS**
>
> In combustion equations, first balance the C atoms then the H atoms. Always balance the oxygen last.
>
> The mechanism of light-catalysed substitution of H atoms in alkanes by Cl is:
> - Initiation (breaking the Cl—Cl bond to form free radicals).
> - Propagation (production of more Cl free radicals).
> - Termination (combining free radicals).

a   What would you observe, if anything, during the following reactions? In each case explain your answer.

   i   Addition of sodium hydroxide to a liquid alkane.

   ii   Putting a lighted splint close to the surface of some liquid hexane.

   iii   Mixing ethene with bromine vapour in the dark.

   iv   Adding aqueous iodine to liquid hexane and then shaking the mixture.

   v   Mixing chlorine with ethane in a closed tube in the presence of sunlight.

b   Copy and complete these equations for the complete **combustion** of alkanes.

   i $C_6H_{14} + \underline{\quad} O_2 \rightarrow 6CO_2 + 7H_2O$

   ii $C_3H_8 + \underline{\qquad\qquad} \rightarrow \underline{\qquad\qquad} + \underline{\qquad\qquad}$

   iii $C_{10}H_{22} + \underline{\qquad\qquad} \rightarrow \underline{\qquad\qquad} + \underline{\qquad\qquad}$

c   Copy and complete these equations for the incomplete combustion of alkanes.

   i $C_4H_{10} + \underline{\qquad\qquad} \rightarrow \underline{\quad} CO + \underline{\quad} H_2O$

   ii $C_7H_{16} + \underline{\qquad\qquad} \rightarrow \underline{\qquad\qquad} + \underline{\qquad\qquad}$

   iii $C_{12}H_{26} + \underline{\qquad\qquad} \rightarrow \underline{\qquad\qquad} + \underline{\qquad\qquad}$

d   In the presence of ultraviolet light, alkanes undergo **substitution** reactions. Copy and complete the steps in the reaction of ethane with chlorine in the presence of UV light.

> **KEY WORD**
>
> **combustion:** burning (usually burning a substance in oxygen gas or air).

The first step is _____ fission.

$Cl_2 \rightarrow$ _____

The second step (_____ step) is attack of the chlorine free _____ on ethane.

$C_2H_6 +$ _____ $\rightarrow C_2H_5\bullet +$ _____

In the presence of chlorine, $C_2H_5\bullet$ can react further and regenerate a free radical.

$C_2H_5\bullet + Cl_2 \rightarrow C_2H_5Cl +$ _____

In excess chlorine, this can continue until all the atoms are substituted by chlorine. The reaction can be terminated when free radicals combine. For example:

$C_2H_5\bullet +$ _____ $\rightarrow C_2H_5Cl$

$C_2H_5\bullet + C_2H_5\bullet \rightarrow$ _____

e Copy and complete these sentences about alkanes.

Alkanes such as ethane and propane are generally unreactive except for _____

and the reaction with chlorine in the presence of _____ radiation.

Exercise 15.4 Reactions of alkenes

This exercise revises the reactions of the alkenes including the electrophilic addition mechanism.

a Match the reagents and conditions 1 to 6 on the left with the carbon-containing products A to F on the right.

1 Ethene, hydrogen and nickel catalyst	A CH_2Br-CH_2Br
2 Ethene and hydrogen bromide	B $CO_2 (+ H_2O)$
3 Ethene and cold dilute acidified aqueous $KMnO_4$	C CH_3-CH_3
4 Ethene and liquid bromine	D CH_2OH-CH_2OH
5 Ethene, steam and phosphoric acid at a high temperature	E CH_3CH_2Br
6 Ethene and hot concentrated $KMnO_4$	F CH_3CH_2OH

> **TIP**
>
> Many of the reactions of alkenes are addition reactions. Only one product is formed. So the formula of the product can easily be linked to the formulae of the reactants.

b Name the following compounds:

   i $CH_3CH=CHCH_2CH_3$

   ii $CH_3-C=CH_2$

              |

            CH_3

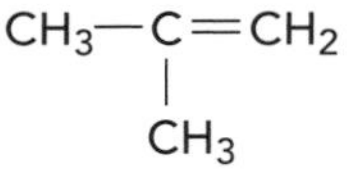

   iii

c When potassium manganate(VII) is used as an oxidising agent, we can write the oxygen added as [O].

When more drastic conditions are used, C—C bonds can be broken.

Copy and complete the equations for some reactions of the alkenes.

   i $CH_3CH_2CH=CH_2 + HBr \rightarrow$ _____

   ii $CH_3CH=CHC_2H_5 + 4[O] \xrightarrow{\text{hot conc. KMnO}_4}$ _____ + _____

   iii $CH_2=CHCH_2CH=CH_2 + \underline{} H_2 \xrightarrow{\text{Ni}}$ _____

   iv _____ $+ H_2O \xrightarrow{\text{conc. H}_3\text{PO}_4} CH_3CH_2OH$

   v $CH_3CH=CHCH_3 + \underline{} H_2O +$ _____ $\xrightarrow{\hspace{2cm}}$

                                   $\underline{} CH_3CH(OH)CH(OH)CH_3$

d Alkenes are **unsaturated hydrocarbons**. Describe how you could distinguish between a **saturated** and an unsaturated hydrocarbon using a chemical test.

Exercise 15.5 Electrophilic addition

This exercise will help you revise the mechanism of **electrophilic** addition to alkenes. You may wish to refer back to Chapter 14 for information on electrophilic addition and the inductive effect.

a The diagram shows species, A, B and C, which are involved in the conversion of ethene to 1,2-dibromoethane.

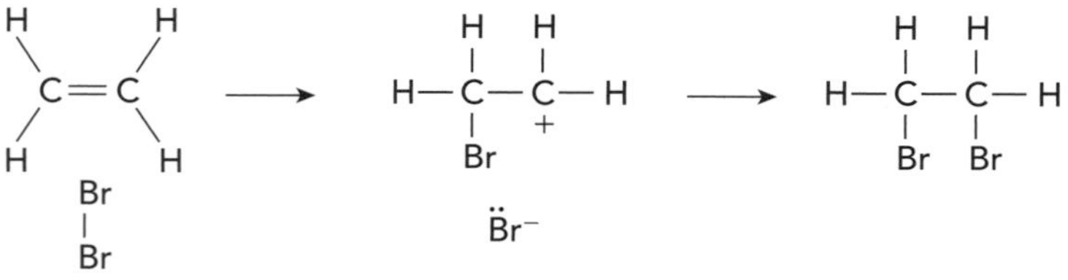

Figure 15.2: Species involved in the conversion of ethene to 1,2-dibromoethane.

KEY WORDS

unsaturated hydrocarbons: compounds of hydrogen and carbon only whose molecules contain carbon-to-carbon double bonds (or triple bonds).

saturated hydrocarbons: compound of hydrogen and carbon only in which the carbon–carbon bonds are all single covalent bonds, resulting in the maximum number of hydrogen atoms in the molecule.

KEY WORD

electrophilic: a reaction where the mechanism involves an electrophile accepting a pair of electrons.

TIPS

Electrophilic addition involves the donation of electron pairs from an 'electron-rich' molecule to part of a molecule which is electron deficient.

Carbocations are an example of an electron deficient species in organic chemistry.

i   When the bromine molecule approaches the ethene molecule it becomes polarised. Explain why.

ii   Copy and complete A to show the movement of electron pairs using curly arrows.

iii Is the breaking of the Br—Br bond homolytic or heterolytic? Explain your answer.

iv   In **species** B, the carbon atom is positively charged. What is the name given to this type of species?

v   Copy and complete B to show the movement of electron pairs using a curly arrow.

vi   Which is the electrophile in step B? Explain your answer.

b   When but-1-ene is bubbled through concentrated hydrochloric acid, two products are formed. The structural formula of the major product is $CH_3CH_2CHClCH_3$.

i   Give the name and draw the structural formula of the minor product.

ii   Draw the formula of the carbocation intermediate which forms the major product.

iii Use ideas about the stability of primary and secondary carbocations to explain why $CH_3CH_2CHClCH_3$ is the major product.

Exercise 15.6 Polymerisation

This exercise will help you revise how to deduce the repeat unit of an addition polymer and to draw the structure of the monomer from which a given addition polymer is made. It will also familiarise you with the problems involved in the disposal of plastics.

The diagram shows how chloroethene polymerises to form poly(chloroethene).

monomer   repeat unit of the polymer

Figure 15.3: How chloroethene polymerises to form poly(chloroethene).

a   Draw a section of the following **polymers**, showing the **repeat unit** in a similar way to that shown in Figure 15.3.

i   poly(propene) from propene, $CH_3CH=CH_2$

ii   poly(phenylethene) from phenylethene, $C_6H_5CH=CH_2$

iii poly(tetrafluoroethene) from tetrafluoroethene, $CF_2=CF_2$

b Deduce the structural formulae of the monomers from the repeat unit of the polymers A and B.

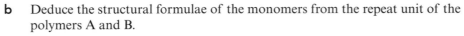

Figure 15.4: Repeat units of two polymers.

c Polyalkenes are non-biodegradable. They are not decomposed in the soil or water.

   i Suggest why they are not easily decomposed.

   ii Describe the problems that arise because polyalkenes are non-biodegradable.

   iii Some plastics contain CN groups or Cl atoms. State two problems associated with the disposal of these plastics by burning.

Exercise 15.7 The combustion of fossil fuels

This exercise will familiarise you with the problems involved in burning hydrocarbon fuels and the use of catalytic converters in reducing emissions of nitrogen oxides and carbon monoxide from car engines.

> **TIP**
>
> Handling information is an important skill. Use the information in the passage together with your own knowledge to answer the questions **a** to **g**.

Read this passage about burning fossil fuels then answer the questions which follow.

Burning fossil fuels releases a small amount of carbon dioxide into the atmosphere compared with that released by the respiration of animals. Carbon dioxide absorbs infrared radiation given off from the Earth's surface. It is a greenhouse gas. Other greenhouse gases include methane and water vapour. The heat absorbed by greenhouse gases raises the temperature of the atmosphere (**enhanced greenhouse effect**). This has been linked to climate change.

The incomplete combustion of fossil fuels results in the release of carbon monoxide, which is poisonous. As well as emitting oxides of carbon and carbon particles, car engines also produce nitrogen oxides and volatile organic compounds (**VOCs**). Particulates and VOCs may be carcinogenic. Cars with petrol engines can be fitted with catalytic converters which oxidise carbon monoxide to carbon dioxide and nitrogen oxides to nitrogen. Fossil fuels also contain sulfur, which when burned forms SO_2 and SO_3, which contribute to acid rain. Scientists can monitor pollutant gases in the air using **infrared spectroscopy**, which measures the characteristic absorption of infrared radiation by particular bonds within a molecule.

KEY WORDS

enhanced greenhouse effect: increase in the average temperature of the atmosphere as a consequence of the increase in greenhouse gases produced by human activity.

VOCs (volatile organic compounds): organic compounds (often hydrocarbons) with low boiling points which are produced in car engines or manufacturing sources. They react with nitrogen oxides and ozone to form photochemical smog.

infrared spectroscopy: a technique for identifying compounds based on the change in vibrations of particular atoms when infrared radiation of specific frequencies is absorbed.

a   Suggest why the increase in carbon dioxide being formed by burning fossil fuels is of global concern even though it is much smaller than the amount produced by respiration.

b   Suggest why scientists are not very concerned by the presence of water vapour in the atmosphere, even though it is a greenhouse gas.

c   Give two effects of climate change.

d   Write a balanced equation for the complete combustion of pentane.

e   What is meant by the term **carcinogenic**? Give two examples of atmospheric pollutants which may be carcinogenic.

f   Construct a balanced equation showing the reaction of nitric oxide, NO, with carbon monoxide in a catalytic converter.

g   Describe how infrared spectroscopy is used to find the concentration of pollutants in the atmosphere.

h   Diesel engines emit nitrogen dioxide as a pollutant.

   i   State one effect of nitrogen dioxide on human health.

   ii   Nitrogen dioxide contributes to acid rain by reacting with rainwater. Explain how nitrogen dioxide contributes *indirectly* to acid rain.

> **KEY WORD**
>
> **carcinogenic:** cancer forming.

EXAM-STYLE QUESTIONS

1   Some reactions of ethene are shown in Figure 15.5.

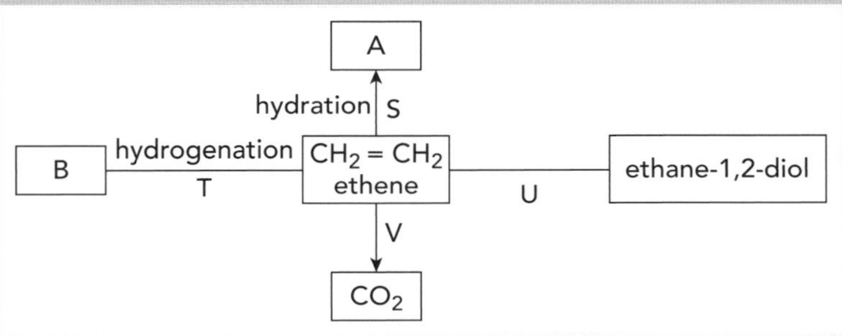

Figure 15.5

a   Write the displayed formulae for A and B.   [2]

b   State the reagents and conditions used for:

   i   Reaction S.   [3]

   ii   Reaction T.   [2]

   iii   Reaction U.   [2]

   iv   Reaction V.   [2]

[Total: 11]

> **TIPS**
>
> You need to learn the additional reagents and conditions used in specific organic reactions.
>
> Ethene can be used to make a variety of other compounds with different functional groups. You should also be able to construct equations for each of these reactions.

CONTINUED

2 An alkene with the structure shown in Figure 15.6 is treated with a hot concentrated solution of $KMnO_4$.

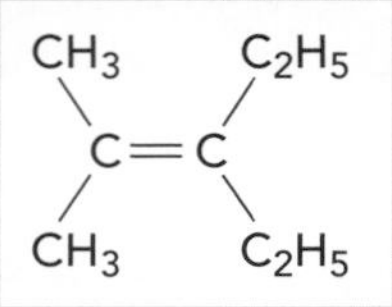

Figure 15.6

a i Write the formulae of the two organic products. **[2]**

 ii State the name of this type of reaction. **[1]**

 iii State the name of the group of organic compounds to which these products belong. **[1]**

b 2-Methylpropene, $(CH_3)_2C=CH_2$, reacts with hydrogen bromide. A **tertiary bromoalkane** is formed.

 i Draw the displayed formula for the organic product of this reaction. **[1]**

 ii Explain why a tertiary bromoalkane is formed and not a **primary bromoalkane**. **[4]**

 iii Draw a section of the polymer, showing the repeat unit, when 2-methylpropene is polymerised. **[2]**

c Poly(2-methylpropene) can be disposed of by burning. This produces carbon dioxide.

 Describe and explain one other problem arising from the disposal of poly(2-methylpropene) **[2]**

[Total: 13]

3 Pentane, C_5H_{12}, is an alkane.

a Draw the displayed formulae for three **position isomers** of C_5H_{12}. **[3]**

b Pentane reacts with chlorine in sunlight to give a mixture of several isomers.

 i Describe the mechanism and type of reaction taking place. **[2]**

 ii Write an equation for the initiation step of this reaction. **[1]**

 iii State the condition needed for all the hydrogen atoms in the pentane to be replaced by chlorine atoms. **[1]**

 iv Write two possible equations for the termination step of this reaction. **[2]**

c When hexadecane, $C_{16}H_{34}$, is cracked, pentane and one other hydrocarbon is formed.

 i Deduce the molecular formula of the other hydrocarbon. **[1]**

 ii State the conditions needed for cracking. **[2]**

[Total: 12]

KEY WORDS

tertiary bromoalkane: a bromoalkane in which the carbon atom bonded to the –Br group is attached to three other carbon atoms.

primary bromoalkane: a bromoalkane in which the carbon atom bonded to the –Br group is attached to only one other carbon atom.

position isomers: isomers where the carbon chain or the functional group(s) are arranged in a different place, e.g. $CH_3CH_2CH_2CH_3$ and $CH_3CH(CH_3)CH_3$.

TIPS

Make sure you distinguish between the type of reaction and mechanism in **2 b i**.

In part **b iii** you should be aware that the word 'condition' is not used in the sense of pressure or catalyst. Conditions can also include limiting or excess (reagent).

CONTINUED

4 a Write an equation for the incomplete combustion of pentane to form carbon monoxide and water. [2]

b Explain why this reaction is carried out in a fume cupboard. [1]

c Carbon monoxide is formed in car engines. It can be removed from the exhaust in a catalytic converter by reacting it with nitrogen oxides.

  i Explain how nitrogen oxides are formed in car engines. [2]

  ii Construct an equation for the reaction of carbon monoxide with nitrogen dioxide. [2]

d Carbon dioxide is released when hydrocarbon fuels burn in excess air.

  i Describe how carbon dioxide contributes to **global warming**. [4]

  ii Give two effects of global warming. [2]

  [Total: 13]

5 Ethane is a saturated hydrocarbon. Ethene is an unsaturated hydrocarbon.

a Describe a chemical test you could carry out to distinguish between ethene and ethane. Give the result of a positive test. [3]

b Draw a dot-and-cross diagram for ethene. [1]

c Describe the structure and bonding in ethene in terms of sigma-bonds and pi-bonds. [4]

d Ethene was bubbled through a solution containing aqueous bromine and aqueous sodium chloride. A mixture of 1,2-dibromoethane and 1-bromo-2-chloroethane, CH_2BrCH_2Cl, was obtained.

  i The first step in the mechanism is the attack of a polarised bromine molecule on the ethene.

  Draw a diagram to represent this step. [3]

  ii The intermediate formed has the structure

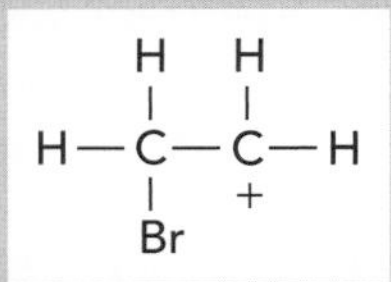

Figure 15.7

Refer to this structure to explain why a mixture of two different halogenoalkanes is formed. [4]

e Propene, $CH_3CH=CH_2$, is an unsaturated hydrocarbon. It reacts with hydrogen chloride to form $CH_3CHCl-CH_3$ not $CH_3CH_2-CH_2Cl$.

Describe and explain why $CH_3CH_2-CH_2Cl$ is not formed. Refer to the mechanism of the reaction including reference to the **inductive effect**. [7]

  [Total: 22]

TIP

Much of this question depends on your previous knowledge of catalytic converters and global warming. Make sure that revise these areas from your previous course and Chapter 12.

KEY WORDS

global warming: the warming of the atmosphere caused by greenhouse gases trapping infrared radiation reflected from the surface of the Earth. Enhanced global warming is the increased global warming due to the increase in greenhouse gases caused by human activity.

KEY WORDS

inductive effect: the uneven sharing of electrons along a covalent bond. Electron-donating species, such as an alkyl group, are said to have a positive inductive effect, whereas electron-withdrawing species, such as an oxygen atom, have a negative inductive effect.

Chapter 16

Halogenoalkanes

CHAPTER OUTLINE

In this chapter you will learn how to:

- classify halogenoalkanes as primary, secondary or tertiary

- write equations for the main reactions that can produce halogenoalkanes, to include the reagents and conditions used

- write equations for the reactions of halogenoalkanes when they undergo nucleophilic substitution (hydrolysis, formation of nitriles, formation of primary amines by reaction with ammonia)

- write equations for the reactions of halogenoalkanes when they eliminate hydrogen bromide (for example, from 2-bromopropane)

- describe and explain the S_N1 and S_N2 mechanisms of nucleophilic substitution in halogenoalkanes and explain the inductive effects of the alkyl groups

- describe and explain the different reactivities of halogenoalkanes with reference to the strength of the C—Hal bond

- describe the use of aqueous silver nitrate in ethanol as a way of identifying halide ions.

Exercise 16.1 Reactions of halogenoalkanes

This exercise will familiarise you with the structure and reactions of the **halogenoalkanes**. It also revises the relative reactivity of the hydrolysis of chloro-, bromo- and iodoalkanes.

a Complete the table to show the displayed and skeletal formulae of some halogenoalkanes.

Halogenoalkane	Structural formula	Displayed formula	Skeletal formula
1-iodobutane	$CH_3CH_2CH_2CH_2I$		
2-chloro-2-methylpropane	$(CH_3)_2CClCH_3$		
3-bromopentane	$CH_3CH_2CHBrCH_2CH_3$		

Table 16.1: Formulae of halogenoalkanes.

b Draw the optical isomers of the chlorofluorocarbon $CH_3CHClCF_3$.

KEY WORD

halogenoalkane: an organic molecule where one or more hydrogen atoms in an alkane has been replaced by one or more halogen atoms.

TIP

When drawing displayed formula, make sure that each carbon atom is connected to four bonds.

c   Match the reagents and conditions 1 to 5 with the products A to E.

1 Reflux 1-bromopropane with aqueous sodium hydroxide

A $CH_3CH{=}CH_2$

2 Treat 1-bromopropane with excess **ethanolic** ammonia under pressure

B $CH_3CH(OH)CH_3$

3 Reflux 1-bromopropane with ethanolic sodium hydroxide

C $CH_3CH_2CH_2NH_2$

4 Treat 1-bromopropane with ethanolic potassium cyanide

D $CH_3CH_2CH_2OH$

5 Reflux 2-bromopropane with aqueous sodium hydroxide

E $CH_3CH_2CH_2CN$

KEY WORD

ethanolic: dissolved in ethanol. This is sometimes written as 'alcoholic' when the alcohol is not specified.

d   Copy and complete this passage about the relative rates of hydrolysis of halogenoalkanes by selecting the appropriate words from the pairs.

When iodoethane is refluxed with aqueous sodium hydroxide, the <u>hydroxide</u> / <u>sodium</u> ion acts as a <u>nucleophile</u> / <u>electrophile</u> and <u>substitutes</u> / <u>eliminates</u> the iodine atom. The reaction is also called a <u>hydrolysis</u> / <u>hydration</u> reaction which means 'breakdown' by water. Hydrolysis with sodium hydroxide is <u>faster</u> / <u>slower</u> than hydrolysis with water because the <u>positively</u> / <u>negatively</u> charged hydroxide ion is a more effective <u>nucleophile</u> / <u>free radical</u>. The hydrolysis of chloroethane is <u>slower</u> / <u>faster</u> than the hydrolysis of iodoethane because the C—Cl bond is <u>stronger</u> / <u>weaker</u> than the C—I bond.

Exercise 16.2 Nucleophilic substitution in halogenoalkanes

This exercise revises the mechanism of **nucleophilic substitution** of halogen atoms in halogenoalkanes by NH_2 groups. It also familiarises you with some of the terms used when discussing reaction mechanisms.

KEY WORDS

nucleophilic substitution: the mechanism of the organic reaction in which a nucleophile attacks a carbon atom carrying a partial positive charge ($\delta+$). This results in the replacement of an atom carrying a partial negative charge ($\delta-$) by the nucleophile.

TIPS

Although the reaction in this exercise is new to you, the mechanism is a typical S_N2 mechanism for a halogenoalkane substitution reaction.

Note that the OH⁻ ion and the ammonia molecule both have lone pairs of electrons.

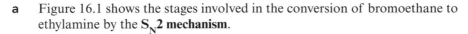
a Figure 16.1 shows the stages involved in the conversion of bromoethane to ethylamine by the **S$_N$2 mechanism**.

$$H_3N: \quad Br-\underset{\underset{H}{|}}{\overset{\overset{H}{|}}{C}}-\underset{\underset{H}{|}}{\overset{\overset{H}{|}}{C}}-H \longrightarrow \left[\begin{array}{c} H_3N \quad H \quad H \\ \diagdown \underset{\diagup}{\overset{|}{C}}-\overset{|}{C}-H \\ Br \quad H \quad H \end{array} \right] \longrightarrow H_3\overset{+}{N}-\underset{\underset{H}{|}}{\overset{\overset{H}{|}}{C}}-\underset{\underset{H}{|}}{\overset{\overset{H}{|}}{C}}-H \longrightarrow H_2N-\underset{\underset{H}{|}}{\overset{\overset{H}{|}}{C}}-\underset{\underset{H}{|}}{\overset{\overset{H}{|}}{C}}-H$$

$$\qquad\qquad\qquad \textbf{A} \qquad\qquad\qquad \textbf{B} \qquad\qquad\qquad +Br^- \qquad\qquad \textbf{D}$$
$$\qquad\qquad\qquad\qquad\qquad\qquad\qquad\qquad\qquad\qquad \textbf{C}$$

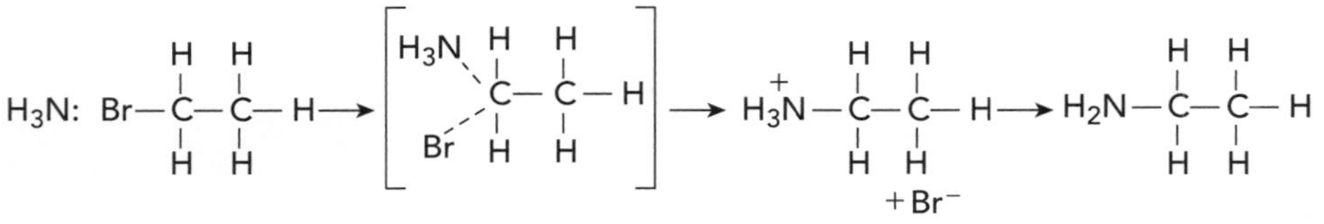

Figure 16.1: The conversion of bromoethane to ethylamine by the S$_N$2 mechanism.

   i   Bromoethane is a polar molecule. Explain why.

   ii   Copy and complete stage A to show:

- The polarisation present in bromoethane using the symbols δ⁺ and δ⁻
- The movement of the electron pair using a curly arrow.

   iii Which is the nucleophile in A? Explain your answer.

   iv How do chemists describe species B?

   v   Describe what happens between stages B and C.

   vi Suggest why the organic molecule in stage C is relatively unstable.

   vii Describe what happens between stages C and D.

   viii There are two molecules involved in the slow step of the reaction. What is the meaning of S$_N$2?

b Figure 16.2 shows the stages when 2-chloro-2-methylpropane is hydrolysed by aqueous sodium hydroxide.

$$H_3C-\underset{\underset{CH_3}{|}}{\overset{\overset{CH_3}{|}}{C}}-Cl \xrightarrow[\text{step}]{\text{slow}} HC_3-\underset{\underset{CH_3}{|}}{\overset{\overset{CH_3}{|}}{\overset{+}{C}}} \quad :OH^- \xrightarrow[\text{step}]{\text{fast}} H_3C-\underset{\underset{CH_3}{|}}{\overset{\overset{CH_3}{|}}{C}}-OH$$

$$\qquad\qquad \textbf{A} \qquad\qquad\qquad +Cl^- \qquad\qquad\qquad\qquad \textbf{C}$$
$$\qquad\qquad\qquad\qquad\qquad\quad \textbf{B}$$

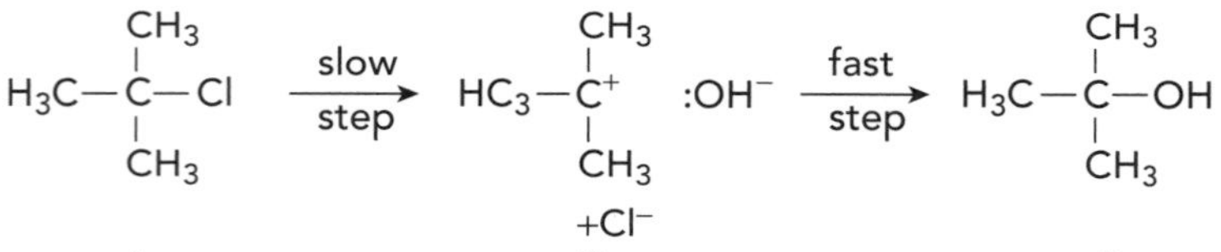

Figure 16.2: The stages when 2-chloro-2-methylpropane is hydrolysed by aqueous sodium hydroxide.

   i   Copy and complete stage A to show:

- The polarisation present in 2-chloro-2-methylpropane using the symbols δ⁺ and δ⁻
- The movement of an electron pair using a curly arrow.

   ii   In stage B, what is the name given to the organic ion with a positively charged carbon atom?

   iii Which species is the nucleophile in stage B? Explain your answer.

   iv The mechanism is called an **S$_N$1 mechanism**. Explain why.

Exercise 16.3 Uses and environmental effects of halogenoalkanes

Extracting and handling information from a passage of writing in order to answer questions related to that passage is an important skill for you to develop. This exercise helps you do this by familiarising you with some specific properties of **fluorohalogenoalkanes** and **CFCs** and their effects on the ozone layer.

Read the passage about the uses of halogenoalkanes and the effect of CFCs on the ozone layer then answer the questions which follow.

Fluorohalogenoalkanes are used as anaesthetics because they have strong F—C bonds which makes them safe to use in the aqueous environment in the body. Chlorofluorocarbons (CFCs) are chemically inert, non-flammable and non-toxic. Volatile CFCs are useful aerosol propellants, solvents and refrigerants. Many countries have banned CFCs because they deplete the ozone layer. CFCs move into the upper atmosphere, where they stay for at least 100 years. They absorb UV radiation and release chlorine free radicals which react with ozone in a series of chain reactions:

Chlorine free radical + ozone → chlorine monoxide free radical + oxygen

Chlorine monoxide free radical + ozone → chlorine free radical + oxygen

a   Why are fluorohalogenoalkanes safe to use as anaesthetics?

b   Give two other uses of CFCs.

c   What is the meaning of the term volatile?

d   What is the source of UV radiation which breaks down halogenoalkanes to form free radicals?

e   Suggest how halogenoalkanes get into the upper atmosphere even though they are large molecules compared with oxygen or carbon dioxide.

f   CFCs are unreactive. So why do they cause the breakdown of ozone?

g   Write equations for:

    i   The reaction of a chlorine free radical with ozone, O_3. The formula of chlorine monoxide is ClO.

    ii   The reaction of a chlorine monoxide free radical with ozone.

h   i   Use the two equations in part **g** to explain why the destruction of ozone is a **chain reaction**.

    ii   How can a chain reaction be stopped?

Exercise 16.4 Equations for reactions of halogenoalkanes

This exercise revises the equations for the reactions of the halogenoalkanes. Remember that you should also know the conditions and nature of the solvent used, e.g. heat, use of alcoholic or aqueous solutions.

When writing equation for organic reactions, don't forget to include any small molecules which are products of the reaction.

KEY WORDS

fluorohalogeno-alkanes: general term for halogenoalkanes containing fluorine and sometimes oxygen (and occasionally chlorine) which are used in anaesthetics. Note that fluoroalkanes contain only fluorine atoms as substituents of hydrogen.

CFCs (chloro-fluorocarbons): halogenoalkanes which have chlorine and fluorine atoms in their structures, e.g. $CH_2FCH_2CCl_3$.

TIP

To answer part **g** you need to revise reactions involving free radicals (see Chapters 14 and 15).

KEY WORDS

chain reaction: a reaction which continues by similar propagation steps. The propagation steps in the free radical substitution of hydrogen atoms in alkanes by chlorine is an example.

a Classify the halogenoalkanes R, S, T and U as **primary**, **secondary** or **tertiary**.

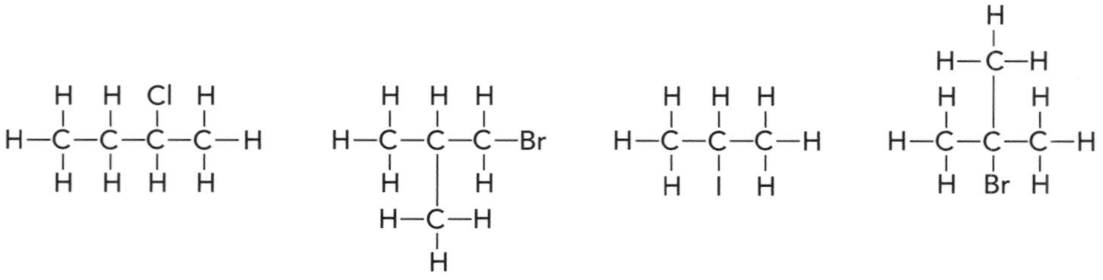

Figure 16.3: Halogenoalkanes.

b Copy and complete these equations for the reactions of halogenoalkanes.

i $CH_3CH_2Br +$ _____ $\rightarrow CH_3CH_2OH +$ _____

ii $CH_3CH_2I + NH_3 \rightarrow$ _____ $+$ _____

iii $CH_3CH_2Cl +$ _____ $\xrightarrow{\text{ethanol}}$ _____ $+ NaCl + H_2O$

iv _____ $+$ _____ $\rightarrow CH_3CH(OH)CH_3 + HCl$

v $CH_3CH_2CH_2Cl + KCN \rightarrow$ _____ $+$ _____

vi _____ $+ KCN \rightarrow C_6H_5CH_2CN +$ _____

vii $CH_3CH_2CH_2Br +$ _____ $\rightarrow$

      $CH_2{=}CHCH_3 +$ _____ $+$ _____

c Describe the type of reaction taking place in reactions **b i** and **b iii**.

d In reaction **b v** chloride ions are formed. Describe how to test for the presence of chloride ions in this reaction.

e Write equations for:

i The reaction of 1-bromobutane with concentrated ethanolic sodium hydroxide.

ii The reaction of 1-bromobutane with ethanolic potassium cyanide.

iii The reaction of 2-chloropropane with dilute aqueous sodium hydroxide.

iv The reaction of 1-chloroethane with ethanolic ammonia under pressure.

KEY WORDS

primary halogenoalkane: a halogenoalkane where the halogen atom is attached directly to a carbon atom which is attached to only one other carbon atom.

secondary halogenoalkane: a halogenoalkane where the halogen atom is attached directly to a carbon atom which is attached to two other carbon atoms.

tertiary halogenoalkane: a halogenoalkane where the halogen atom is attached to a carbon atom which is attached directly to three other carbon atoms.

Exercise 16.5 Making halogenoalkanes

This exercise revises the methods for making halogenoalkanes and gives further revision of equation writing.

a Copy and complete these equations for these reactions that produce halogenoalkanes:

i $CH_3CH_2CH_2OH + SOCl_2 \rightarrow$ _____ + _____ + _____

ii ___ $CH_3CH_2OH + PBr_3 \rightarrow$ ___ $CH_3CH_2Br +$ _____

iii $CH_3CH(OH)CH_3 + HCl \rightarrow$ _____ + _____

iv $CH_3CH_2CH_2OH + PCl_5 \rightarrow$ _____ + _____ $+ HCl$

v _____ $+ Cl_2 \xrightarrow{\text{uv light}} CH_3CH_2CH_2Cl + HCl$

b Which one of the reactions in part **a** is unlikely to produce a single product? Explain your answer.

c In part **a iii** suggest how the hydrogen chloride can be prepared so that it is produced **'in situ'** so that it is immediately released into the reaction mixture.

d A halogenoalkane is formed in the following reaction:

$CH_3CH=CH_2 + HCl \rightarrow CH_3CClCH_3$

i State the type of halogenoalkane formed.

ii Name the type and mechanism of this reaction.

KEY WORDS

'in situ': Latin words meaning 'in that place'. If we make a gas 'in situ', it means that we add the chemicals needed to make the gas to the test tube of reactants. Adding zinc and acid to a reaction mixture gives off hydrogen, which can be used to reduce something else.

TIPS

When writing equations relating to halogenoalkanes, make sure that you are writing the symbol for the correct halogen. It is all too easy to change Br to Cl.

Remember that some equations for organic reactions do need balancing.

EXAM-STYLE QUESTIONS

1 2-Bromo-2-methylpropane is a halogenoalkane.

  a Write the displayed formula for 2-bromo-2-methylpropane. [1]

  b 2-Bromo-2-methylpropane reacts with an aqueous solution containing hydroxide ions.

$$(CH_3)_2CBrCH_3 + OH^- \rightarrow (CH_3)_2C(OH)CH_3 + Br^-$$

   i Explain why this is a substitution reaction. [1]

   ii Explain why an OH^- ion is a nucleophile. [1]

  c Describe how you could test for the bromide ions produced in this reaction. Give the results of the positive test. [3]

  d Describe in terms of the stability of the carbocations why 2-bromo-2-methylpropane reacts by the S_N1 mechanism but 1-bromopropane reacts by the S_N2 mechanism. [5]

[Total: 11]

2 1-Iodobutane reacts with both aqueous and alcoholic solutions of sodium hydroxide.

  a Write an equation for the reaction of 1-iodobutane with aqueous sodium hydroxide. [1]

  b Describe and explain the first step in the reaction mechanism. [5]

  c 1-Chlorobutane reacts more slowly than 1-iodobutane with aqueous sodium hydroxide of the same concentration. Explain why. [2]

  d i Write an equation for the reaction of 1-iodobutane with a hot alcoholic solution containing hydroxide ions. [1]

   ii State the name of this type of reaction. [1]

   iii Explain the role of the hydroxide ions in this reaction. [2]

  e Explain, using ideas about the inductive effect, why primary halogenoalkanes are hydrolysed more rapidly than tertiary halogenoalkanes. [5]

[Total: 17]

TIP

Make sure that you know about reaction mechanisms and the terms carbocation, nucleophile and substitution.

TIP

Part 1 c asks you to test for bromide ions. Look at the ions present in the equation. What should you do before adding the test reagent?

TIP

Make sure that you have revised the inductive effect before attempting part 2 e (Chapters 14 and 15).

CONTINUED

3 A solution of potassium cyanide in ethanol is heated under reflux with iodoethane.

  a **i** Write the ionic equation for this reaction. [1]

    ii Explain the importance of this reaction in organic synthesis. [1]

  b The cyanide ion has a triple bond. Draw a dot-and-cross diagram for the cyanide ion. [1]

  c Explain why the cyanide ion acts as a nucleophile. [1]

  d Copy and complete Figure 16.4 to show the mechanism of nucleophilic substitution by:

    i Predicting the **polarisation** of the C—I bond.

    ii Drawing a curly arrow to show the movement of electron pairs.

    iii Completing the structure of the intermediate. [3]

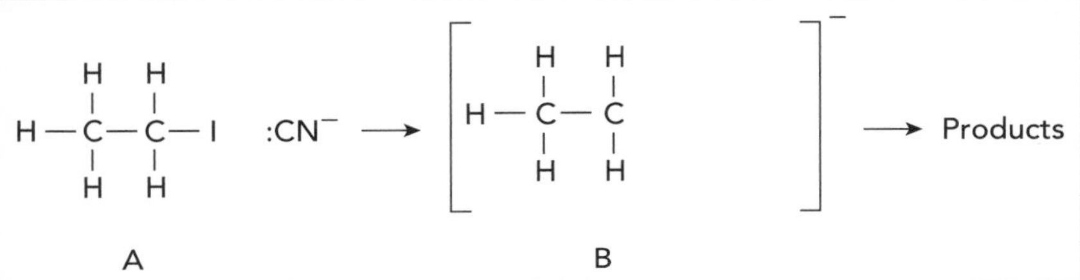

Figure 16.4

  e Suggest why this mechanism is described as S_N2. [3]

[Total: 10]

TIPS

This question is largely about the reaction mechanism of CN^- ions with halogenoalkanes. Make sure that you understand terms such as nucleophile, polarisation and intermediate. In part **b** make sure that you include the electron from the negative ion.

KEY WORDS

bond polarisation: occurs in a covalent bond in which the bonding electrons are attracted more to one atom than the other leading to a dipole in the bond, e.g. $C^{\delta+}-Cl^{\delta-}$.

Alcohols, esters and carboxylic acids

In this chapter you will learn how to:

- explain the acid–base reactions of alcohols compared with water

- recall the reactions (reagents and conditions) by which alcohols can be produced

- recall the reactions of alcohols in combustion, substitution to give halogenoalkanes, reaction with sodium, oxidation to carbonyl compounds and carboxylic acids, and dehydration to alkenes

- classify hydroxy compounds into primary, secondary and tertiary alcohols

- describe the characteristic distinguishing reactions of alcohols and carboxylic acids, e.g. mild oxidation with acidified $K_2Cr_2O_7$ or acidified $KMnO_4$

- describe the acid and base hydrolysis of esters

- describe the formation of carboxylic acids from alcohols, aldehydes and nitriles

- describe the reactions of carboxylic acids in the formation of salts, by the use of reactive metals, alkalis or carbonates

- describe the reactions of carboxylic acids to form alkyl esters, by reaction with alcohols

- describe the reactions of carboxylic acids to form primary alcohols, by reduction using $LiAlH_4$

- deduce the presence of a $CH_3CH(OH)$- group in an alcohol from its reaction with alkaline iodine.

Exercise 17.1 What type of alcohol?

This exercise will help you to distinguish between **primary**, **secondary** and **tertiary alcohols** by their structure and by using acidified potassium dichromate(VI). Practice is also given in writing equations for oxidation reactions of alcohols and aldehydes.

TIP
Make sure that you know the difference between primary, secondary and tertiary alcohols in terms of their structure and reaction with acidified potassium dichromate(VI).

KEY WORDS
primary alcohol: an alcohol in which the carbon atom bonded to the –OH group is attached to one other carbon atom (or alkyl group).

a Classify each of these alcohols as either primary, secondary or tertiary.

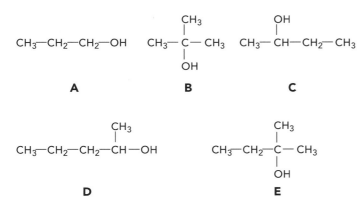

Figure 17.1: Examples of alcohols.

b Give the names of each of the alcohols shown in part **a**.

c Complete the following sentences to describe what happens, if anything, when different alcohols are heated with acidified potassium dichromate(VI).

Primary alcohols: Potassium dichromate(VI) turns from _____ to

_____. The product distilled off is an _____. On further oxidation

a _____ is formed. Secondary alcohols: Potassium dichromate(VI) turns

from _____ to _____. The product is a _____ . On further

oxidation _____ is formed. Tertiary alcohols: Potassium dichromate(VI)

_____. No reaction takes place.

d When balancing organic equations using potassium manganate(VII) or potassium dichromate(VI) as oxidising agents, we use [O] to represent the oxygen arising from an oxidising agent. For example:

$$CH_3OH + [O] \rightarrow HCHO + H_2O$$

  i Name an oxidising agent other than acidified potassium dichromate that oxidises primary alcohols.

  ii State the colour change in this oxidising agent when it reacts with excess primary alcohol.

e Copy and complete these equations for the oxidation of alcohols and aldehydes.

  i $CH_3CH_2CH_2OH +$_____ $\rightarrow CH_3CH_2CHO + H_2O$

  ii $CH_3CH(OH)CH_3 +$_____ $\rightarrow$ _____ $+$_____

  iii $CH_3CH_2CHO +$ _____ $\rightarrow$ _____

  iv $CH_3CH(OH)CH_2CH(OH)CH_2CH_3 +$ _____ $\rightarrow$ _____ $+$

    _____

Exercise 17.2 Some reactions of alcohols

This exercise will familiarise you with some reactions of the alcohols (combustion, substitution, reaction with sodium, oxidation and **dehydration**) and the conditions used. It also revises the writing of equations for the reactions of alcohols.

a Match the reagents and conditions 1 to 6 with the products A to F.

1 Burning ethanol in excess air	**A** ethyl ethanoate
2 Refluxing ethanol with acidified potassium dichromate(VI)	**B** ethene
3 Refluxing ethanol with ethanoic acid and an acid catalyst	**C** chloroethene
4 Passing ethanol vapour over hot aluminium oxide	**D** ethanoic acid
5 Refluxing ethanol with sodium chloride and concentrated sulfuric acid	**E** sodium ethoxide
6 Adding sodium to ethanol	**F** carbon dioxide and water

b Copy and complete these equations.

     i   ___ C_3H_7OH + ___ Li → _____ + _____

     ii   ___ CH_3OH + Ca → _____ + _____

     iii $CH_3CH(OH)CH_3 \xrightarrow{Al_2O_3,\ heat}$ _____ + _____

     iv $CH_3CH_2CH_2CH_2CH_2OH \xrightarrow{Al_2O_3,\ heat}$ _____ + _____

c Write balanced equations for:

     i   The complete combustion of propanol (forming carbon dioxide and water).

     ii   The incomplete combustion of butanol (forming carbon monoxide and water).

     iii   The complete combustion of cyclohexanol.

d Which one of these alcohols, A, B, C or D, will react with an alkaline solution of iodine? Explain your answer.

     A $CH_3CH_2CH(OH)CH_2CH_3$

     B $CH_3CH_2CH_2CH_2OH$

     C $CH_3CH_2CH(OH)CH_3$

     D $CH_3C(CH_3)_2CH_2CH_2OH$

KEY WORDS

dehydration: a reaction in which water is removed from a larger molecule.

refluxing: heating a flask connected to a condenser in the vertical position to minimise the loss of volatile chemical from the flask.

TIP

When writing equations for the combustion of alcohols, don't forget the oxygen in the alcohol!

TIP

In a simplified structural formula such as $CH_3C(CH_3)_2CH_2OH$, note that the $C(CH_3)_2$ shows that there are two methyl groups attached to the second carbon atom from the left.

Exercise 17.3 Halogenoalkanes from alcohols

This exercise will help you revise the halogenation of alcohols and remind you of the different reagents that can be used. It also familiarises you with some practical procedures for making halogenoalkanes.

a   1-Bromopropane can be prepared by heating propan-1-ol with sodium bromide and concentrated sulfuric acid in a flask. The 1-bromopropane is distilled off and collects as oily drops under water.

   i   The hydrogen bromide for the reaction is made in the flask. Explain how.

   ii   What does the description indicate about the density and solubility in water of 1-bromopropane?

   iii Explain why propan-1-ol is a polar molecule.

   iv   Draw a molecule of hydrogen bromide to show its bond polarisation.

   v   Use your answers to parts **iii** and **iv** to suggest the first step in the reaction mechanism.

   vi   Write the equation for this reaction, showing the structural formulae of both the reactants and products.

b   Phosphorus pentachloride can be used to **halogenate** alcohols. The products are $POCl_3$ and an acidic gas.

   Write a balanced equation for the reaction of phosphorus(V) chloride with butan-1-ol.

c   Phosphorus trihalides can also be used to make halogenoalkanes from alcohols. The acid H_3PO_3 is one of the products. Copy and complete these reactions.

   i   ___ $C_2H_5OH + PI_3 \rightarrow$ _____ + _____

   ii   ___ $C_4H_9OH + PBr_3 \rightarrow$ _____ + _____

d   Sulfur dichloride oxide is another compound that can be used to halogenate alcohols. Two acidic gases are produced as well as the halogenoalkane.

   Copy and complete the equation for this reaction.

   $CH_3CH_2CH_2OH + SOCl_2 \rightarrow$ _____ + _____ + _____

> **KEY WORD**
>
> **halogenate:** to substitute one or more halogen atoms in a compound or add one or more halogen atoms to a compound.

Exercise 17.4 Carboxylic acids and their synthesis

This exercise will help you revise the formulae of carboxylic acids. It also familiarises you with their synthesis from alcohols and from **nitriles**.

> **KEY WORD**
>
> **nitriles:** organic compounds containing the CN functional group, e.g. C_2H_5CN (propanenitrile).

a Write the structural formulae for:

   i   hexanoic acid

   ii methanoic acid

   iii ethanedioic acid.

b Carboxylic acids can be made by oxidation of primary alcohols.

   i   Give the name of the oxidising agent and the conditions used.

   ii Write an equation, showing structural formulae, for the synthesis of butanoic acid from an alcohol.

   iii Explain why secondary alcohols cannot be oxidised to carboxylic acids.

c Carboxylic acid can also be made by refluxing nitriles such as CH_3CH_2CN with dilute hydrochloric acid. The reaction is a hydrolysis.

   i   Give the general formula for a nitrile.

   ii What is meant by the term hydrolysis?

   The acid hydrolysis of propanenitrile is shown by the equation:

   $$CH_3CH_2CN + HCl + 2H_2O \rightarrow CH_3CH_2COOH + NH_4Cl$$

d Copy and complete these equations showing the hydrolysis of nitriles.

   i $CH_3CN + $ _____ $ + $ _____ $ \rightarrow $ _____ $ + $_____

   ii _____ $ + $_____ $ + $ _____ $ \rightarrow$

        $CH_3CH_2CH_2CH_2COOH + $ _____

   iii $CH_3CH_2CN + H^+ + 2H_2O \rightarrow$ _____ $ + $ _____

e Give the names of the nitriles in parts **d i** and **ii.**

Exercise 17.5 Reactions of the carboxylic acids

This exercise will familiarise you with the reactions of the carboxylic acids with reactive metals, alkalis, carbonates and their reduction by **LiAlH$_4$**.

a Propanoic acid is a weak acid.

   i   Explain why it is a weak acid.

   ii Write an equation showing the reaction of propanoic acid with water.

b Copy and complete these equations for the typical acidic reactions of carboxylic acids.

   i $CH_3COOH + KOH \rightarrow$ _____ $ + $ _____

   ii ___ $CH_3CH_2CH_2COOH + Mg \rightarrow$ _____ $ + $ _____

   iii ___ $C_6H_5COOH + Na_2CO_3 \rightarrow$ _____ $ + $ _____ $ + $ _____

TIPS

Remember, when naming carboxylic acids, the COOH carbon is also included in the prefix, e.g. CH_3CH_2COOH is propanoic acid not ethanoic acid.

The suffix -dioic acid means that there are two carboxylic acid groups.

Take care in naming nitriles: include the C in the CN group, e.g. CH_3CN is ethanenitrile.

KEY WORDS

lithium tetrahydrido-aluminate: the full chemical name for lithium aluminium tetrahydride, $LiAlH_4$. It is usually acceptable just to write $LiAlH_4$ if you cannot remember the name.

c   Name the salts formed in **b i** and **ii.**

d   Carboxylic acids are reduced to alcohols by lithium tetrahydridoaluminate, $LiAlH_4$, in dry ether.

Copy and complete the following equations. Use [H] to represent the hydrogen from the reducing agent. The first one has been partly done for you.

i $CH_3COOH + \underline{\hspace{3cm}} \rightarrow CH_3CH_2OH + H_2O$

ii $CH_3CH_2COOH + \underline{\hspace{2.5cm}} \rightarrow \underline{\hspace{2.5cm}} + \underline{\hspace{2cm}}$

iii $HOOCCH_2CH_2COOH + \underline{\hspace{2.5cm}} \rightarrow \underline{\hspace{2.5cm}} + \underline{\hspace{2cm}}$

Exercise 17.6 Esters

This exercise will familiarise you with the formulae of esters, **esterification** from carboxylic acids and alcohols, and their acid- and base-catalysed hydrolysis.

> **TIP**
>
> Esters are formed when a carboxylic acid is refluxed with an alcohol in the presence of concentrated sulfuric acid catalyst.
>
> The first part of the ester name comes from the alcohol. The second part comes from the carboxylic acid. So $CH_3COOC_3H_7$ is propyl ethanoate.

a   Name the esters formed when:

   i   ethanol reacts with butanoic acid

   ii   propanol reacts with hexanoic acid

   iii   methanol reacts with pentanoic acid.

b   Now name these esters:

   i $HCOOC_4H_9$

   ii $CH_3COOC_5H_{11}$

   iii $C_3H_7COOC_3H_7$

c   Here are two equations for the hydrolysis of ethyl ethanoate.

   $CH_3COOC_2H_5 + H_2O \rightleftharpoons CH_3COOH + C_2H_5OH$

   $CH_3COOC_2H_5 + NaOH \rightleftharpoons CH_3COO^-Na^+ + C_2H_5OH$

   Esters can be hydrolysed by refluxing with sulfuric acid.

   i   What is the function of the sulfuric acid?

   ii   Write an equation for the acid hydrolysis of propyl ethanoate.

d   Esters can also be hydrolysed by refluxing with concentrated aqueous sodium hydroxide. Write equations for the alkaline hydrolysis of these esters:

   i   propyl methanoate

   ii   methyl ethanoate

   iii   butyl propanoate

Exercise 17.7 Alcohols as products of chemical reactions

This exercise revises the variety of reactions leading to the formation of alcohols. Remember that you should also know the conditions and nature of the solvent used, e.g. heat, use of catalysts.

a Copy and complete these equations about the formation of alcohols.

  i $CH_2{=}CH_2(g) + H_2O(g) \rightarrow$ _____

  ii $CH_3CH_2CH_2COOCH_3 + NaOH \rightarrow$ _____ $+$ _____

  iii $CH_3CH_2Cl +$ _____ $\rightarrow CH_3CH_2OH + NaCl$

  iv $CH_3CH_2COOH +$ _____ $\xrightarrow{\text{LiAlH}_4}$ _____ $+$ _____

  v $CH_3COCH_3 +$ _____ $\rightarrow CH_3CH(OH)CH_3$

  vi $CH_3CH_2COOCH_2CH_3 + H_2O \rightarrow$ _____ $+ CH_3OH$

b Describe the type of reaction taking place in each of the reactions in part **a**.

c Write equations for:

  i the reaction of cold dilute potassium manganate(VII) with ethene

  ii the reaction of **propanal** with sodium borohydride

  iii the reaction of propyl ethanoate with aqueous sodium hydroxide

  iv the reaction of propanoic acid with lithium aluminium hydride to form an alcohol.

TIP

In organic reactions, we can make equation writing simpler by using the symbol [H] to show that the hydrogen from a reducing agent such as sodium borohydride has been transferred during the reaction when no hydrogen gas is used.

KEY WORD

propanal: an aldehyde with three carbon atoms.

EXAM-STYLE QUESTIONS

1 Propan-1-ol is a primary alcohol. Propanoic acid is a carboxylic acid.

   a Describe how you could distinguish between propan-1-ol and
      2-methylpropan-2-ol by a chemical test.   [3]

   b Propan-1-ol can be oxidised to propanoic acid. State the reagents and
      conditions used in this oxidation.   [3]

   c Draw the displayed formula for propanoic acid.   [1]

   d Propanoic acid reacts with methanol to form an ester.

      i   Describe how you would carry out this reaction to form a
          pure sample of the ester.   [4]

      ii Construct the equation for the reaction.   [1]

      iii Give the name of the ester formed.   [1]

   e Ethanol reacts with sodamide, $NaNH_2$.

      $$C_2H_5OH + NaNH_2 \rightarrow C_2H_5O^-Na^+ + NH_3$$

      i   State whether ethanol is reacting as an acid or a base in this reaction.
          Give a reason for your answer.   [1]

      ii The relative ability of water and two alcohols to donate a proton to
          other molecules in aqueous solution are shown:

          $CH_3CH(OH)CH_3$ $CH_3CH_2CH_2OH$ HOH

          least likely to donate H^+ $\longrightarrow$ most likely to donate H^+

          Explain this order using ideas about the inductive effect.   [5]

                                                                    [Total: 19]

2 Ethanol and ethanoic acid both have two carbon atoms.

   a i   Describe and explain the difference in acidity of these two
          compounds.   [3]

      ii Describe the differences in the reaction, if any, of sodium hydroxide
          with ethanol and with ethanoic acid.   [3]

   b i   Write equations to represent the reaction of sodium with ethanol
          and the reaction of sodium with ethanoic acid.   [4]

      ii Describe the observations made during the reaction in each case.   [1]

   c Ethanol reacts with phosphorus pentachloride.

      i   Write a balanced equation for this reaction.   [1]

      ii Describe how observations of this reaction show that an OH group
          is present in ethanol.   [1]

      iii Ethanoic acid also reacts with phosphorus pentachloride. The organic
          product has the formula CH_3COCl. Construct a balanced equation
          for this reaction.   [1]

   d Carboxylic acids are reduced to alcohols by $LiAlH_4$. Deduce the equation
      for the reaction of ethanoic acid with $LiAlH_4$. Use [H] to represent the
      hydrogen from the $LiAlH_4$.   [1]

                                                                    [Total: 15]

TIPS

Remember to state all reagents and all conditions when answering these questions.

Make sure that you know how to name esters (see Tips in Exercise 17.6).

TIP

Before answering this question, make sure that you know about the reasons for the difference in acidity between ethanol and ethanoic acid.

TIP

Make sure in parts 2 b ii and c ii that you write down your observations only.

CONTINUED

3 Ethanoic acid may be synthesised from ethene.

ethene $\xrightarrow{\text{step 1}}$ chloroethane $\xrightarrow{\text{step 2}}$ ethanol $\xrightarrow{\text{step 3}}$ ethanoic acid

a Suggest suitable reagents and conditions for each step of the reaction. [6]

b Alcohols react with hydrogen halides to form halogenoalkanes.

  i Write an equation for the reaction of propan-1-ol with hydrogen chloride. [1]

  ii The mechanism for the first step in this reaction is shown in Figure 17.2.

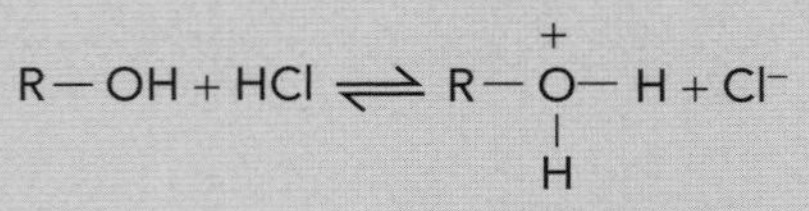

$$R-OH + HCl \rightleftharpoons R-\overset{+}{\underset{H}{O}}-H + Cl^-$$

Figure 17.2

Explain how the alcohol is acting as a base. [1]

  iii The hydrogen chloride is usually generated in the reaction flask by mixing a salt with an acid. Name the salt and acid used. [2]

c Name a reagent that is solid at r.t.p. and can be used to brominate propan-1-ol. [1]

d Butan-1-ol can be dehydrated to but-1-ene. Describe how this experiment can be carried out. [4]

e i Give the structural formula of an alcohol that is an isomer of butan-1-ol. [1]

  ii Describe the observations made when this isomer reacts with a warm alkaline solution of iodine. Explain your answer by referring to the structure of this isomer. [2]

[Total: 17]

TIPS

Once you have studied the chemistry of different functional groups, you may be asked questions about a synthesis involving several steps. It is important that you build up your knowledge of these steps, adding to them as you go along. Changing functional groups is an important part of this process.

Chapter 18

Carbonyl compounds

CHAPTER OUTLINE

In this chapter you will learn how to:

- describe the formation of aldehydes from the oxidation of primary alcohols and the formation of ketones from the oxidation of secondary alcohols

- describe the reduction of aldehydes and ketones, e.g. using $NaBH_4$ or $LiAlH_4$

- describe the reaction of aldehydes and ketones with HCN (hydrogen cyanide) and KCN (potassium cyanide)

- describe the mechanism of the nucleophilic addition reactions of hydrogen cyanide with aldehydes and ketones

- describe the detection of carbonyl compounds by the use of 2,4-dinitrophenylhydrazine (2,4-DNPH) reagent

- distinguish between aldehydes and ketones by testing with Fehling's and Tollens' reagents

- describe the reaction of CH_3CO- compounds with alkaline aqueous iodine to give tri-iodomethane, CHI_3, and a carboxylate ion, $RCOO^-$

- deduce the presence of a $CH_3CH(OH)-$ group in an alcohol from its reaction with alkaline aqueous iodine to form tri-iodomethane

- analyse an infrared spectrum of a simple molecule to identify functional groups.

Exercise 18.1 Carbonyl compounds: Synthesis and reduction

This exercise will familiarise you with the formulae of aldehydes as it revises the practical procedure for making these compounds. You will also revise the use of $LiAlH_4$ and $NaBH_4$ in reducing **carbonyl compounds**.

a   Name these carbonyl compounds.

  i   HCHO

  ii $CH_3CH_2COCH_2CH_2CH_3$

  iii $CH_3CH_2CH_2CHO$

b   Write the structural formulae for:

  i   butan-2-one

  ii   pentanal

  iii pentan-2,4-dione (this has two CO carbonyl groups).

KEY WORDS

carbonyl compound: a compound containing a C=O group joined to one or two alkyl groups or a hydrogen atom.

c Read the paragraph below about the preparation of carbonyl compounds then answer the questions that follow.

To make propanal, propan-1-ol is heated gently with acidified potassium dichromate, $K_2Cr_2O_7$. The acidified dichromate is added a drop at a time to the alcohol and the propanal is distilled off immediately, leaving unreacted propan-1-ol in the flask. The mixture turns green as the orange dichromate ions are reduced to chromium(III) ions. Further heating oxidises the alcohol in the flask to propanoic acid. Propan-2-ol can be oxidised in a similar way but the product need not be distilled off immediately.

i Identify the oxidising agent in these reactions.

ii Write formulae for the dichromate ion and the chromium(III) ion.

iii How do you know from the information in the passage that propanal has a lower boiling point than propan-1-ol?

iv Why is the propanal distilled off straight away and not refluxed?

v What is the name of the organic product formed when propan-2-ol is oxidised?

vi Why does the product of the oxidation of propan-2-ol not need to be distilled off immediately?

d Write equations for the following reactions using structural formulae.

i The reduction of butan-2-one by $LiAlH_4$.

ii The reduction of propanal by $NaBH_4$.

iii The reduction of hexan-2,4-dione by $LiAlH_4$.

e Give the name of each of the products in part **d**.

Exercise 18.2 Distinguishing carbonyl compounds

This exercise will familiarise you with the use of **Tollens' reagent** and **Fehling's solution** to distinguish aldehydes from ketones. It also revises the use of **2,4-dinitrophenylhydrazine (2,4-DNPH)** to identify particular carbonyl compounds.

a Copy and complete these statements.

When propanal is warmed gently with Tollens' reagent the colour changes from

_____ to a _____ mirror. Propanal is oxidised to _____

_____. Silver ions are _____ to silver. When propanal is

warmed gently with Fehling's solution, the colour changes from _____

to _____. Propanal is oxidised to _____. Copper(II) ions are

_____ to _____ ions. When a ketone is heated with Tollens'

reagent _____.

TIP

When naming ketones, remember that the CO group is given the smallest number counting from either end of the molecule.

KEY WORDS

Tollens' reagent: an aqueous solution of silver nitrate in excess aqueous ammonia used to distinguish between aldehydes and ketones. A 'silver mirror' is formed when aldehydes are warmed with the reagent. No change is observed when ketones are warmed with the reagent.

Fehling's solution: an alkaline solution containing copper(II) ions (Cu^{2+}) used to test for the –CHO group to distinguish between aldehydes and ketones. Compounds containing this group give an orange precipitate on warming with Fehling's solution.

2,4-DNPH (2,4-dinitro phenylhydrazine): compound used to form condensation products with carbonyl compounds. The products have characteristic melting points.

Particular aldehydes and ketones can be identified by reacting them with 2,4-DNPH in a condensation reaction. Yellow or orange crystalline precipitates are formed which have specific melting points.

b   Copy and complete these statements.

A solution of 2,4-DNPH is added to a carbonyl compound. An _____

coloured _____ of a dinitrophenylhydrazone is formed. The precipitate

is purified by _____ and the _____ point is measured. Each

dinitrophenylhydrazone derivative of an aldehyde or _____ has a characteristic

melting point which can be compared with known data book values.

c   The reaction between 2,4-DNPH and ethanal, CH_3CHO, is shown.

$$RNH_2 + CH_3CHO \rightarrow RN{=}CHCH_3 + H_2O$$

where R is the rest of 2,4-DNPH molecule.

Explain why this is a condensation reaction.

d   The table gives the melting points of some dinitrophenylhydrazones.

Dinitrophenylhdyrazone	Melting point / °C
propanal	150
butanal	126
hexanal	104
propanone	126
butan-2-one	117
pentan-2-one	144

Table 18.1: Melting points of some dinitrophenylhydrazones.

The melting point of the dinitrophenylhydrazone derivative of an unknown carbonyl compound, X, is 126 °C.

i   How does the table of melting points help in the identification of X?

ii   Describe one other experiment you could do to confirm the identity of X.

Exercise 18.3 Nucleophilic addition in carbonyl compounds

This exercise will help you revise the mechanism of nucleophilic addition of the nitrile ion to carbonyl compounds. It will also help you practise writing the formulae for the organic products of these reactions.

TIPS

Tollens' reagent and Fehling's solution both oxidise aldehydes but not ketones.

You need to know the colour changes that occur when these reagents oxidise reducing agents.

TIPS

Remember that in organic reaction mechanisms a nucleophile is a substance with a lone pair of electrons, which attacks an area that is deficient in electrons.

The direction of the curly arrows is the direction in which the electron pair moves.

a Figure 18.1 shows the stages of the mechanism of the reaction of the nitrile ion with propanal.

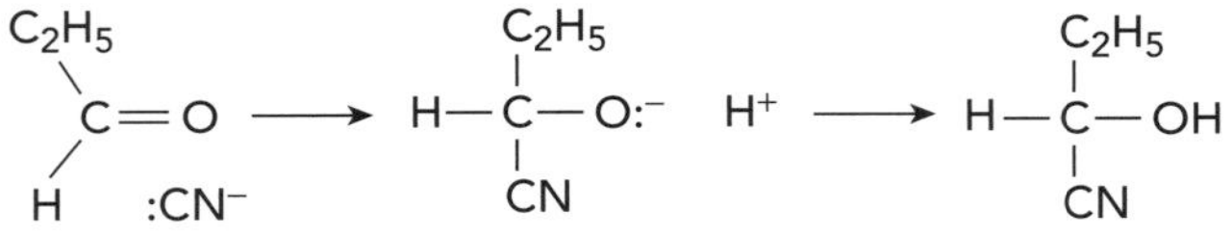

Figure 18.1: Mechanism of a nitrile reacting with propanal.

i Propanal is a polar molecule. Explain why.

ii Copy and complete step A to show:

- The bond polarisation present in propanal, using the symbols δ^+ and δ^-.

- The movement of electron pairs, using curly arrows.

iii What is the nucleophile in this reaction? Explain why.

iv How do chemists describe the organic species in B?

v Suggest the origin of the H^+ ions in B.

vi Describe what happens in the second step, B to C.

b Aldehydes and ketones form 2-**hydroxynitriles** when they undergo **nucleophilic addition** with nitriles. The OH group is always on the C atom next to the CN group.

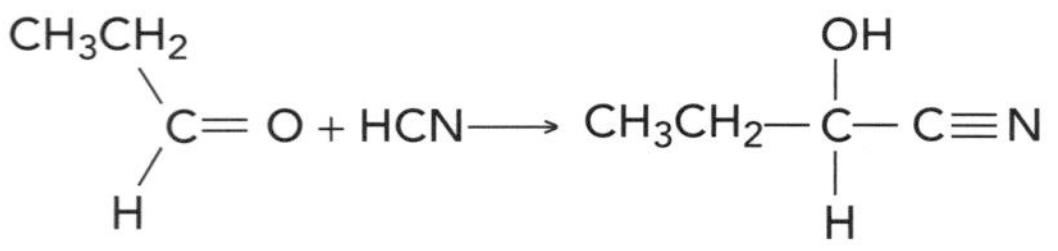

Figure 18.2: Nucleophilic addition of propanal to form 2-hydroxybutanenitrile.

Draw the 2-hydroxynitriles of the following carbonyl compounds:

i propanone

ii ethanal

iii pentan-2-one.

Exercise 18.4 The iodoform test

This exercise will help familiarise you with the use of an alkaline solution of iodine to identify compounds containing the methyl ketone group, CH_3CO- or compounds which can be oxidised by this solution to form a methyl ketone. It also gives you practice at extracting information about the mechanism of the reaction from a flow diagram.

KEY WORDS

hydroxynitrile: an organic compound containing both an –OH and a –CN group.

nucleophilic addition: the mechanism of the reaction in which a nucleophile attacks the carbon atom in a carbonyl group and addition across the C=O bond occurs, e.g. aldehydes or ketones reacting with hydrogen cyanide.

TIPS

When identifying methyl ketones from formulae look for the CH_3CO- group by writing the displayed formula or structural formula.

Remember that alcohols with the $CH_3CH(OH)-$ group also give a positive iodoform test (Chapter 17).

a Which of these compounds gives a yellow precipitate when treated with aqueous alkaline iodine?

i butanone

ii ethanal

iii pentane-2,4-dione

iv methanal

v propan-2-ol

vi pentan-3-one

b The reaction involves two steps:

$$RCOCH_3 \xrightarrow{I_2} [X] \xrightarrow{NaOH \, (aq)} RCOO^-Na^+ + CHI_3$$

i The first step involves the three methyl hydrogen atoms being replaced by iodine.

What type of reaction is this?

ii Give the formula for the intermediate X.

iii What type of reaction is the conversion of X to the products?

iv The common name for CHI_3 is **iodoform**. Give the full chemical name for CHI_3.

v Give the name of $RCOO^-Na^+$ if R is CH_3CH_2-.

c An alkaline solution of iodine can act as a weak oxidising agent.

Explain why some secondary alcohols can give a yellow precipitate when treated with an alkaline solution of iodine.

KEY WORDS

iodoform test: a test for the presence of a CH_3CO- or $CH_3CH(OH)-$ group in a compound. A yellow precipitate is formed on warming these compounds with an alkaline solution of iodine.

Exercise 18.5 Infrared spectroscopy

This exercise gives you practice in understanding the origin of the absorption **peaks** seen in infrared spectra. It also gives practice in the interpretation of infrared spectra.

The bonds in a compound vibrate naturally. When infrared radiation of a particular frequency is absorbed by a particular bond, the bond vibrates more and energy is absorbed. The frequency at which this happens is called the **resonance frequency**.

a Copy and complete this paragraph about the origins of infrared spectra using the following words:

absorb	bending	frequencies	functional	larger	percentage	range
	resonance	wavelength	wavenumber	spectrum		

The bonds in organic compounds vibrate by stretching, _____ and

twisting. They have a natural frequency at which they vibrate. When molecules

_____ infrared radiation that corresponds to these natural _____,

it stimulates _____ vibrations and energy is absorbed. This frequency is

called the _____ frequency. Each type of bond absorbs infrared radiation

at a characteristic _____ of frequencies. We can identify

TIPS

When analysing infrared spectra, identify the **strong peaks** first.

Look out for a broad peak at 3200–3600 cm^{-1} indicating hydrogen-bonded alcohols.

KEY WORDS

peak (in infrared spectroscopy): the downward points in an infrared spectrum. Sometimes the points are widened.

strong peak: the peak goes down a long way on the absorbance scale in the infrared spectrum.

different _____ groups from the absorbance pattern of their infrared

_____. The spectrum shows _____ the absorbance (vertical

axis) and _____ (horizontal axis). Wavenumber is the reciprocal of

the _____.

b   The table shows the wavenumber and intensity of absorption of infrared
     radiation for the bonds in various functional groups.

Bond	Functional group	Wavenumber range of absorption / cm⁻¹	Appearance of 'peak'
C—O	alcohols, esters	1040–1300	strong
C=C	alkenes, aromatic compounds	1500–1680	weak or medium (unless conjugated)
C=O	amides,	1640–1690	strong
	ketones, aldehydes,	1670–1740	strong
	esters	1715–1750	strong
C—H	alkanes, CH₂—H	2850–2950	strong
	alkenes, arenes =C—H	3000–3100	weak
N—H	amines, amides	3300–3500	weak
O—	carboxylic acids,	2500–3000	medium and broad
	H-bonded alcohols,	3200–3600	strong and broad
	non-H-bonded alcohol	3580–3650	strong and **sharp**

Table 18.2: Wavenumber and intensity of wavelength for bonds.

Figures 18.3 and 18.4 show the infrared spectra of ethanol and ethanoic acid.

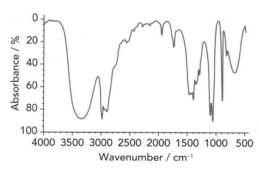
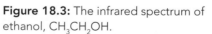

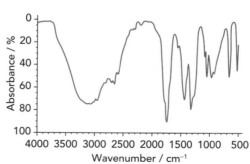

Figure 18.3: The infrared spectrum of ethanol, CH₃CH₂OH.

Figure 18.4: The infrared spectrum of ethanoic acid, CH₃COOH.

Identify the key peaks in each spectrum and the bonds to which each peak
corresponds.

KEY WORD

resonance frequency: the frequency of absorption of radiation which stimulates larger vibrations in bonds to allow the absorption of energy.

KEY WORDS

sharp peak: a narrow pointed peak in an infrared spectrum.

EXAM-STYLE QUESTIONS

1 Butan-1-ol can be oxidised by adding acidified potassium dichromate(VI) and distilling off the organic product immediately.

   a i   Write an equation for this reaction showing the structural formulae of the organic reactant and products. Use [O] to represent the oxygen from the oxidising agent.   **[1]**

      ii   State the name of the product formed.   **[1]**

      iii   State the colour change observed.   **[2]**

      iv   Explain why the product is distilled immediately.   **[1]**

   b i   Describe a test using Tollens' reagent that will enable you to distinguish an aldehyde from a ketone. Give the results of a positive test.   **[3]**

      ii   Give the name of the substances present in Tollens' reagent.   **[1]**

      iii   Write a half-equation to show the metal ion in Tollens' reagent acting as an oxidising agent.   **[1]**

   c Butanone can be reduced using an alkaline solution of $NaBH_4$.

      i   Write an equation for this reaction. Use [H] to represent the hydrogen from the reducing agent.   **[1]**

      ii   State the name of the organic product, **Y**, formed in this reaction.   **[1]**

      iii   Product **Y** is warmed with an alkaline solution of iodine. A yellow precipitate is observed. The product is not a carbonyl compound.
      Give the name and formula of both the yellow precipitate and the other product formed when **Y** is warmed with an alkaline solution of iodine.   **[4]**

   [Total: 16]

2 Propanone reacts with hydrogen cyanide to form an addition product. The hydrogen cyanide is produced in the reaction vessel by adding dilute sulfuric acid to a salt.

   a i   Give the name of a suitable salt that could be used.   **[1]**

      ii   The CN^- ion is a nucleophile. Explain why.   **[1]**

      iii   The first step in the mechanism is the attack of a cyanide ion on the propanone to form an intermediate. Describe this mechanism as fully as you can with the aid of a diagram. Include the polarisation of the propanone and the movement of electron pairs.   **[5]**

      iv   The **intermediate** reacts with a hydrogen ion to form the product. Suggest two possible sources of the hydrogen ions.   **[2]**

      v   Draw the displayed formula of the product.   **[1]**

TIP

You will usually be told when to use [O] to represent the oxidising agent and [H] to represent the reducing agent.

KEY WORD

intermediate: a species, such as a carbocation, which is formed at a particular step of the reaction. Intermediates are stable enough to react with another substance but not stable enough to be a product. They often have a partial positive or negative charge.

CONTINUED

TIP

When matching peaks in an IR spectrum with information in a table you might find that the peaks do not correlate exactly but are on the edge of the wavenumber range.

b The infrared spectrum of propanone is shown in Figure 18.5.

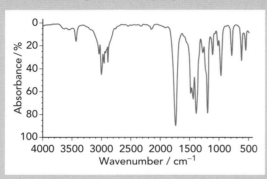

Figure 18.5

Use the table in Exercise 18.5 to identify the key peak in the spectrum which suggests that the compound may be a ketone and the bonds to which this peak corresponds. **[3]**

[Total: 13]

3 a i Write the structural formula for pentan-2-one. **[1]**

   ii Describe a test to distinguish between pentan-2-one and pentan-3-one. Include the results. **[4]**

b Describe how 2,4-dinitrophenylhydrazine (2,4-DNPH) is used to identify aldehydes and ketones. **[4]**

c The reaction of 2,4-DNPH with carbonyl compounds is a condensation reaction.

   Describe what happens during a condensation reaction. **[2]**

d The infrared spectrum of oct-1-ene shows a sharp, strong peak at about 3000 cm^{-1} and a sharp weak peak at around 1600 cm^{-1}.

   i Sketch the infrared spectrum of octane for wavenumbers between 2800 and 4000 cm^{-1}. Label the axes. **[4]**

   ii Use the table in Exercise 18.5 to explain how this information can be used to give information about the bonds present in oct-1-ene. **[3]**

[Total: 18]

TIP

In part **a i** look out for the methyl ketone group, CH_3CO-, in the formula.

Lattice energy

In this chapter you will learn how to:

- define and use the terms enthalpy change of atomisation and lattice energy

- define and use the term first electron affinity (EA_1)

- explain the factors affecting the electron affinities of the elements

- describe and explain the trends in the electron affinities of the Group 16 and Group 17 elements

- construct and use Born–Haber cycles for ionic solids

- carry out calculations involving Born–Haber cycles

- explain the effect of ionic charge and ionic radius on the magnitude (big or small) of the lattice energy

- define and use the terms enthalpy change of hydration and enthalpy change of solution

- construct and use an energy cycle involving enthalpy change of solution, lattice energy and enthalpy changes of hydration

- carry out calculations using an energy cycle involving enthalpy change of solution, lattice energy and enthalpy changes of hydration

- explain the effect of ionic charge and ionic radius on the magnitude (big or small) of the enthalpy change of hydration

- describe and explain qualitatively the trend in the thermal stability of the nitrates and carbonates in Group 2 including the effect of ionic radius on the polarisation of the large anion

- describe and explain qualitatively the variation in solubility and enthalpy change of solution of the hydroxides and sulfates in Group 2 in terms of relative magnitudes of enthalpy change of hydration and the lattice energy.

Exercise 19.1 Enthalpy changes and lattice energy

This exercise will help you revise some terms used in the construction of enthalpy cycles including Born–Haber cycles.

When defining particular enthalpy changes, the key word often gives a clue. For example, **electron affinity (EA)** is related to gaining an electron, **lattice energy** refers to the forces between the ions in the lattice.

The state is also important in defining enthalpy changes. For example, first electron affinity refers to gaseous atoms and gaseous ions.

a Match the terms 1 to 7 with the equations A to G.

1	Third ionisation energy		A	$S^-(g) + e^- \rightarrow S^{2-}(g)$

2	Enthalpy change of atomisation		B	$Mg^{2+}(g) + aq \rightarrow Mg^{2+}(aq)$

3	Second electron affinity		C	$K(s) \rightarrow K(g)$

4	Lattice energy		D	$Li(s) + \frac{1}{2}Cl_2(g) \rightarrow LiCl(s)$

5	Enthalpy change of formation		E	$Na^{2+}(g) \rightarrow Na^{3+}(g) + e^-$

6	**Enthalpy change of solution**		F	$Mg^{2+}(g) + O^{2-}(g) \rightarrow MgO(s)$

7	**Enthalpy change of hydration**		G	$NaCl(s) + aq \rightarrow NaCl(aq)$

b Copy and complete the definition of lattice energy and electron affinity using words from this list.

atoms charge electrons enthalpy gaseous ionic mole one standard

Lattice energy is the _____ change when one _____ of an

_____ compound is formed from its _____ ions under standard

conditions.

First electron affinity is the enthalpy change when one mole of _____

is added to _____ mole of gaseous _____ to form one mole of

gaseous ions with a _____ of 1– under _____ conditions.

electron affinity, EA: the first electron affinity is the enthalpy change when one mole of electrons is added to one mole of gaseous atoms to form one mole of gaseous ions with a single negative charge under standard conditions, e.g. $O(g) + e^- \rightarrow O^-(g)$ EA_1.

lattice energy, $\Delta H^{\ominus}_{latt}$: the energy change when one mole of an ionic compound is formed from its gaseous ions under standard conditions. Strictly speaking, the values given usually refer to the lattice enthalpy rather than the lattice energy but the difference is usually not significant.

enthalpy change of solution, $\Delta H^{\ominus}_{sol}$: the energy absorbed or released when one mole of an ionic solid dissolves in sufficient water to form a very dilute solution.

standard enthalpy change of hydration, $\Delta H^{\ominus}_{hyd}$: the enthalpy change when one mole of gaseous ions dissolve in sufficient water to form a very dilute solution under standard conditions.

c Copy and complete this definition of enthalpy change of atomisation.

The standard enthalpy change of atomisation, $\Delta H_{at}^{\ominus}$, is the enthalpy change

when one _____ of _____ atoms is formed from its _____

under _____ conditions.

d Copy and complete the sentences in part **i** and part **ii** about electron affinity using words from the lists.

i

| first   less   negative |

Electron affinities for non-metal atoms get more _____ across a

period with a maximum at Group 17. In Groups 16 and 17, there is a trend to

_____ negative electron affinities as you go down the group apart from the

_____ member in the group.

ii

| attraction   charge   decreases   electron   energy |
| force   positively   radius |

The value of the first electron affinity depends on the _____ between

the added electron and the _____ charged nucleus. The stronger the

attraction, the greater is the amount of energy released. The greater the nuclear

_____, the greater the attractive force between the nucleus and the outer

electrons. Chlorine has a greater nuclear charge than oxygen and so attracts an

_____ more readily so more _____ is released when a chlorine

atom gains an electron. The further the outer shell electrons are from the nucleus,

the less is the attractive _____ between the nucleus and the outer shell

electrons. Since the atomic _____ increases down Groups 16 and 17, the

electron affinity _____ going from chlorine to bromine to iodine.

e Write equations to represent:

i The second ionisation energy of aluminium, IE_2.

ii The third electron affinity of nitrogen, EA_3.

iii The enthalpy change of formation of magnesium sulfate, $\Delta H_f^{\ominus}$.

iv The lattice energy of potassium oxide, K_2O, $\Delta H_{latt}^{\ominus}$.

Exercise 19.2 Born–Haber cycles

This exercise will give you practice in constructing **Born–Haber cycles** to calculate the lattice energy of an ionic compound. It also provides practice in calculating lattice energy from information provided, and in relating the value of lattice energy to ionic radius.

KEY WORDS

Born–Haber cycle: an enthalpy cycle used to calculate lattice energy.

a Copy and complete the Born–Haber cycle in Figure 19.1 to calculate the lattice energy of calcium bromide.

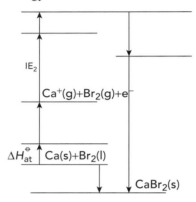

Figure 19.1: Born–Haber cycle for calcium bromide.

TIPS

You need to take into account the number of moles of ions when constructing a Born–Haber cycle.

Take care with the signs of the enthalpy changes!

b Copy and complete the Born–Haber cycle in Figure 19.2 to calculate the lattice energy of sodium sulfide.

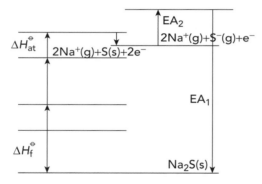

Figure 19.2: Born–Haber cycle for sodium sulfide.

c Calculate the lattice energy of sodium sulfide using the following data:

$\Delta H_f^\ominus [Na_2S] = -364.8 \text{ kJ mol}^{-1}$

$\Delta H_{at}^\ominus [Na] = +107.3 \text{ kJ mol}^{-1}$

$\Delta H_{at}^\ominus [S] = +278.5 \text{ kJ mol}^{-1}$

$IE_1[Na] = +496.0 \text{ kJ mol}^{-1}$

$EA_1[S] = -200.4 \text{ kJ mol}^{-1}$

$EA_2[S] = +640.0 \text{ kJ mol}^{-1}$

d The table shows the theoretically calculated lattice energies of some Group 1 oxides and sulfides.

Oxide	Lattice energy of oxide / kJ mol⁻¹	Sulfide	Lattice energy of sulfide / kJ mol⁻¹
lithium oxide	−2799	lithium sulfide	−2376
sodium oxide	−2481	sodium sulfide	−2134
potassium oxide	−2238	potassium sulfide	−1933
rubidium oxide	−2163	rubidium sulfide	−1904

Table 19.1: Calculated lattice energies of Group 1 oxides and sulfides.

Use the information in the table to describe how lattice energy varies with the radius of the cation and anion.

Exercise 19.3 Enthalpy change of solution

This exercise will familiarise you with calculations involving enthalpy changes of solution and will explain the variation in solubility of the Group 2 sulfates.

a   Copy and complete these sentences defining enthalpy change of hydration and enthalpy change of solution.

Standard enthalpy change of solution is the energy _____ or released

when _____ mole of a _____ dissolves in water to form a very

_____ solution.

Standard enthalpy change of hydration is the enthalpy change when one

_____ of a specified _____ ion dissolves in water to form a very

_____ solution.

TIP

If the anion is very large compared with the cation, the anion has a greater effect on the lattice energy than the cation.

b   Copy and complete the enthalpy cycle to calculate the enthalpy change of solution of magnesium iodide.

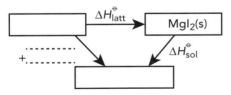

Figure 19.3: Enthalpy cycle.

c   The enthalpy change of solution of magnesium iodide is slightly exothermic. Draw an **energy level diagram** for this enthalpy cycle to show the relationship between $\Delta H_{latt}^{\ominus}$, $\Delta H_{sol}^{\ominus}$ and $\Delta H_{hyd}^{\ominus}$ for the enthalpy cycle you completed in part **b**.

KEY WORDS

energy level diagram (for an enthalpy cycle): an enthalpy cycle arranged to show the various enthalpy changes by arrows going up (endothermic) or down (exothermic).

d Figure 19.4 shows enthalpy cycles that compare the enthalpy change of solution of calcium sulfate and strontium sulfate.

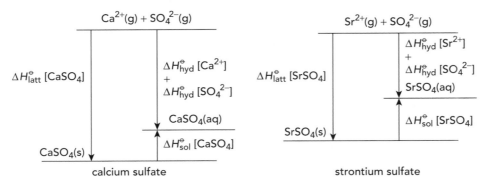

Figure 19.4: Comparing enthalpies of solution.

i How does the value of $\Delta H^{\ominus}_{\text{hyd}}$ vary with the size of the cation?

ii How does the lattice energy vary with the size of the cation?

iii Explain why the percentage change in lattice energy of the sulfates down Group 2 is smaller than the percentage change in the hydration enthalpy.

iv Explain by reference to values of $\Delta H^{\ominus}_{\text{sol}}$, why $SrSO_4$ is less soluble in water than $CaSO_4$.

Exercise 19.4 Thermal stability of Group 2 carbonates and nitrates

This exercise will familiarise you with the concept of **ion polarisation** and how this can be used to explain the difference in thermal stability of the Group 2 carbonates and nitrates.

> **TIPS**
>
> When deducing the **polarising power** of an ion you need to think of ionic radius and ionic charge.
>
> Mg^{2+} and Li^+ ions are similar in size but the polarising power of an Mg^{2+} ion is greater than that of a Li^+ ion because the Mg^{2+} ion has a higher charge density.

a Which of these cations most easily polarises a sulfate ion?

K^+, Mg^{2+}, Na^+, Sr^{2+}

b Which of these anions is most easily polarised by a lithium ion?

Cl^-, F^-, O^{2-}, S^{2-}

c Describe how and explain why a magnesium ion can polarise a nitrate ion.

KEY WORDS

ion polarisation: the distortion of the electron cloud of an anion by a neighbouring cation. The distortion is greatest when the cation is small and highly charged.

polarising power (of a cation): the ability of a cation to attract the electron cloud of an anion and distort it.

d   The relative stability of the Group 2 nitrates to heat is

$$Ba(NO_3)_2 > Sr(NO_3)_2 > Ca(NO_3)_2 > Mg(NO_3)_2$$

most stable ——————————→ least stable

i   Which one of these nitrates has the smallest cation?

ii   Which one of these cations is the best polariser of the nitrate ion?

iii Which one of these compounds is most likely to decompose when heated?

iv   When the O−N bond of the nitrate breaks, what gases are formed?

EXAM-STYLE QUESTIONS

1   a   Define lattice energy. **[2]**

    b   Describe and explain how the size and charge of a cation influences the lattice energy of compounds having the same anion. **[4]**

    c   Draw a simple enthalpy cycle to calculate the lattice energy of potassium iodide. **[3]**

    d   Calculate the lattice energy of potassium iodide using the following data:

$$\Delta H_f^{\ominus}[KI] = -327.9 \text{ kJ mol}^{-1}$$
$$\Delta H_{at}^{\ominus}[K] = +89.20 \text{ kJ mol}^{-1}$$
$$\Delta H_{at}^{\ominus}[\tfrac{1}{2}I_2] = +106.8 \text{ kJ mol}^{-1}$$
$$IE_1[K] = +419.0 \text{ kJ mol}^{-1}$$
$$EA_1[I] = -295.4 \text{ kJ mol}^{-1}$$

Express your answer to 4 significant figures. **[4]**

    e   Explain why the **second electron affinity** of oxygen is endothermic. **[2]**

[Total: 15]

2   When heated, magnesium nitrate undergoes thermal decomposition.

$$Mg(NO_3)_2(s) \rightarrow MgO(s) + 2NO_2(g) + \tfrac{1}{2}O_2(g)$$

    a   Draw an enthalpy cycle diagram for this reaction. **[3]**

    b   Calculate the value of the enthalpy change of decomposition using the following data:

$$\Delta H_f^{\ominus}[Mg(NO_3)_2(s)] = -790.7 \text{ kJ mol}^{-1}$$
$$\Delta H_f^{\ominus}[MgO] = -601.7 \text{ kJ mol}^{-1}$$
$$\Delta H_f^{\ominus}[NO_2] = +33.20 \text{ kJ mol}^{-1}$$

Express your answer to 4 significant figures. **[4]**

    c   The enthalpy change of decomposition of calcium nitrate is 369.7 kJ mol^{-1}.

    The enthalpy change of decomposition of strontium nitrate is 452.6 kJ mol^{-1}.

    Use these values, together with the value you obtained in part **b**, to describe and explain the ease of decomposition of the Group 2 nitrates. **[2]**

TIPS

The main part of this question involves a calculation of lattice energy.

Make sure that you know how to construct an enthalpy cycle for this.

KEY WORDS

second electron affinity, EA$_2$: the enthalpy change when one mole of electrons is added to one mole of gaseous ions with a charge of 1− to form one mole of gaseous ions with a charge of 2− under standard conditions, e.g. $O^-(g) + e^- \rightarrow O^{2-}(g)$ EA$_2$.

CONTINUED

d The trend in ease of decomposition of Group 2 nitrates can be explained in terms of ion polarisation.

    i Give the meaning of the term ion polarisation. **[2]**

    ii State two factors which determine the degree of polarisation of a nitrate ion by a cation. **[2]**

    iii State the relationship between the size of the Group 2 cations and the ease of decomposition of the Group 2 nitrates. **[1]**

[Total: 14]

3 When an ionic solid dissolves in water, the ions separate from each other and become hydrated.

    a Draw a water molecule to show its shape. On your diagram show the value of the H–O–H bond angle and the direction of the dipole. **[2]**

    b **i** Make a sketch to show a sodium ion hydrated by five water molecules. **[1]**

        ii State the name given to the type of bonding between water molecules and sodium ions. **[1]**

    c Use ideas about bonding to explain why sodium bromide is soluble in water. **[3]**

    d **i** Draw an enthalpy cycle to show the relationship between enthalpy change of solution, enthalpy change of hydration and lattice energy. **[3]**

        ii Calculate the value for the enthalpy change of solution of sodium bromide using the following data:

$$\Delta H^{\ominus}_{hyd} [Na^+] = -390 \text{ kJ mol}^{-1}$$

$$\Delta H^{\ominus}_{hyd} [Br^-] = -337 \text{ kJ mol}^{-1}$$

$$\Delta H^{\ominus}_{latt} [NaBr] = -742 \text{ kJ mol}^{-1}$$ **[3]**

        iii Define enthalpy change of solution. **[2]**

    e Barium hydroxide is much more soluble than magnesium hydroxide.

    Explain this difference in solubility by referring to the relative values of enthalpy change of hydration and the lattice energy. **[5]**

[Total: 20]

> **TIP**
>
> Be prepared to answer questions on other areas of the course. Part **a** tests your previous knowledge of the structure of a water molecule.

> **TIP**
>
> Part **c** refers back to ideas of bond forming and bond breaking (see Chapters 4 and 5).

Chapter 20

Electrochemistry

CHAPTER OUTLINE

In this chapter you will learn how to:

- predict the identity of the substance liberated during electrolysis from the state of electrolyte (molten or aqueous), the position of the ions (in the electrolyte) in the redox series (electrode potential) and the concentration of the ions in the electrolyte

- state and apply the relationship, $F = Le$, between the Faraday constant, F, the Avogadro constant, L and the charge on the electron, e

- calculate the quantity of charge passed during electrolysis using $Q = It$

- calculate the mass and/or volume of substance liberated during electrolysis

- describe the determination of a value of the Avogadro constant by an electrolytic method

- define the terms standard electrode (reduction) potential and standard cell potential

- describe the standard hydrogen electrode

- describe methods used to measure the standard electrode potentials of metals or non-metals in contact with their ions in aqueous solution and of ions of the same element in different oxidation states

- calculate a standard cell potential by combining two standard electrode potentials

- use standard cell potential to deduce the polarity of each electrode and the direction of electron flow in the external circuit of a simple cell

- use standard cell potential to predict the feasibility of a reaction

- deduce from standard electrode potential values the relative reactivity of elements, compounds and ions as oxidising agents or reducing agents

- construct redox equations using the relevant half-equations

- predict qualitatively how the value of an electrode potential varies with the concentration of the aqueous ion

- use the Nernst equation to predict how the value of an electrode potential varies with the concentration of the aqueous ions

Exercise 20.1 Electrolysis

This exercise will familiarise you with the components of an **electrolysis** cell. It also revises previous work on electrical conduction in metals and ionic compounds. The redox reactions at the **electrodes** are also considered, giving further practice in writing ionic half-equations.

Electrolysis is carried out in an electrolysis cell. Figure 20.1 shows an electrolysis cell.

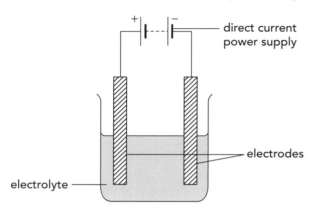

Figure 20.1: An electrolysis cell.

a   Use the diagram and your knowledge of ionic compounds (see Chapter 5) to answer these questions.

   i   Which electrode is the **cathode** in Figure 20.1? Explain your answer.

   ii   Explain why anions move towards the **anode** in electrolysis.

   iii Why does solid magnesium oxide not conduct electricity?

   iv   Suggest two properties of the electrodes that make them suitable for electrolysis.

   v   In which direction does the electric current flow in the wires? Explain your answer.

   vi   Explain why the metal wires conduct electricity.

b   During electrolysis:

   • Cations move to the cathode and gain electrons (reduction), e.g.

      $Cu^{2+} + 2e^- \rightarrow Cu$

   • Anions move to the anode and lose electrons (oxidation), e.g.

      $2Cl^- \rightarrow Cl_2 + 2e^-$

Write similar half-equations for the reactions at the anode and cathode for the following molten compounds. In each case, state whether oxidation or reduction has occurred.

   i   magnesium chloride   ii   zinc oxide   iii   aluminium oxide
   iv   calcium bromide   v   lithium iodide.

KEY WORDS

electrolysis: the decomposition of an ionic compound when molten or in aqueous solution by an electric current.

electrode: a rod or plate of metal or carbon (graphite) which conducts electricity to or from an electrolyte.

cathode: the negative electrode (where reduction reactions occur).

anode: the positive electrode (where oxidation reactions occur).

TIPS

Remember that anions are negatively charged (they go to the anode) and cations are positively charged (they go to the cathode).

c   When aqueous ionic solutions are electrolysed, hydrogen and oxygen may be formed at the electrodes depending on the position of the ions in the reactivity series:

$$Mg^{2+} \quad Al^{3+} \quad H^+ \quad Cu^{2+} \quad Ag^+$$

more likely to be **discharged** →

$$SO_4^{2-} \quad OH^- \quad Cl^- \quad Br^- \quad I^-$$

more likely to be discharged →

Predict the products of the electrolysis of the following aqueous solutions using graphite electrodes. In each case give a reason for your answer in terms of the reactivity series.

i   concentrated aqueous sodium chloride

ii   very dilute aqueous sodium chloride

iii   dilute sulfuric acid

iv   aqueous copper(II) sulfate

v   concentrated hydrochloric acid

vi   aqueous silver nitrate.

KEY WORD

discharge (of ions): the conversion of ions to atoms or molecules at the electrodes during electrolysis by loss or gain of electrons.

Exercise 20.2 Electrolysis calculations

This exercise will familiarise you with calculations to find the mass of substance deposited or volume of gas given off during electrolysis. It also revises how to calculate values for the Avogadro constant and the **Faraday constant**.

a   Determine the charge needed to deposit:

i   0.200 mol silver

ii   5.00 mol aluminium

iii   0.400 mol lead

b   Copy and complete part **i**, then answer questions **ii**, **iii** and **iv**.

i   Calculate the mass of copper deposited at the cathode, when a current of 3.0 A flows for 10 min. $A_r[Cu] = 63.5$, F = 96 500 C mol⁻¹

Step 1: Charge transferred = $3.0 \times 10 \times$ _____ = _____ C

Step 2: Number of **coulombs** to deposit 1 mol Cu = _____ × 96 500 = _____ C

Step 3: Moles Cu deposited = $\dfrac{\text{Step 1}}{\text{Step 2}}$ = _____ mol

Step 4: Mass of copper deposited = _____ × 63.5 = _____ g

ii   Calculate the mass of silver deposited at the cathode when a current of 0.90 A flows for 10 minutes. $A_r[Ag] = 107.9$

iii   Calculate the mass of lead deposited at the cathode when a current of 0.50 A flows for 30 minutes. $A_r[Pb] = 207.2$

iv   Calculate the volume of oxygen produced at r.t.p. when a concentrated aqueous solution of sulfuric acid is electrolysed for 20 minutes at a current of 0.15 A.

KEY WORDS

Faraday constant: the charge (in coulombs) carried by one mole of electrons or one mole of singly charged ions.

coulombs, C: the units of electrical charge. (coulombs = amperes × seconds).

TIPS

Charge (coulombs) = current (amperes) × time (seconds) ($Q = It$)

Remember that in determining the charge needed to deposit 1 mole of zinc, we need 2 moles of electrons (2F) per mole of zinc deposited because the zinc ion is Zn^{2+}.

In part **b i** remember to convert minutes to seconds.

c   We can calculate the Avogadro constant, L, or the value of F using the relationship:

$$L = \frac{\text{charge on mol of electrons } (F)}{\text{charge on a single electron}}$$

When an electric current of 0.07600 A is passed through a solution of silver nitrate for exactly 90 minutes, the anode decreases in mass by 0.4600 g. Use this data together with the charge on the electron (1.6022×10^{-19} C) to calculate the value of the Avogadro constant. Express your answer to 4 significant figures. $A_r[\text{Ag}] = 107.9$

d   Describe how to determine the value of the Faraday constant, F, by an experiment involving the electrolysis of copper(II) sulfate.

Exercise 20.3 Electrochemical cells

This exercise familiarises you with the structure of **electrochemical cells** and the redox reactions occurring at the anode and cathode. It also helps you revise metal displacement reactions in terms of the reactivity series and to understand how the difference in reactivity can be related to the difference in voltages obtained when different combinations of metals and metal ions are used in electrochemical cells.

a   The order of reactivity of some metals is given here:

Mg > Al > Zn > Fe > Co > Sn > Pb > Cu > Ag

most reactive ⟶ least reactive

Write half-equations for the oxidation and reduction reactions taking place when the following react.

i   Cobalt with lead(**II**) ions

ii   Copper(**II**) ions with zinc

iii Aluminium with silver(**I**) ions

iv   Tin(**II**) ions with magnesium

An electrochemical cell is shown in Figure 20.2.

KEY WORDS

electrochemical cell: two half-cells connected by a salt bridge and external circuit allowing the flow of electrons between them.

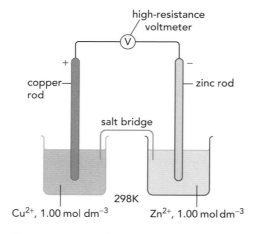

Figure 20.2: An electrochemical cell.

- Electrons flow in the wire from the more reactive metal to the less reactive metal.

- The voltage produced is a measure of the difference in the reactivity of the two metals.

b **i** Write half-equations for the reactions taking place at the copper rod and the zinc rod.

ii Which of these reactions is reduction and which is oxidation? Explain your answer.

iii The zinc rod is the cathode. Explain why.

iv Explain the direction of movement of electrons in the wire.

v What is the purpose of the **salt bridge**?

c We can use the position of metals in the reactivity series to compare the voltages of different combinations of metals and metal ions of concentration 1.0 mol dm^{-3}.

Use the reactivity table and the Figure 20.2 to suggest what would happen to the voltage when:

i The Cu/Cu^{2+} electrode is replaced by an Ag/Ag^+ electrode.

ii The Zn/Zn^{2+} electrode is replaced by an Mg/Mg^{2+} electrode.

iii The Zn/Zn^{2+} electrode is replaced by an Sn/Sn^{2+} electrode.

iv The Cu/Cu^{2+} electrode is replaced by an Fe/Fe^{2+} electrode.

v The Zn/Zn^{2+} electrode is replaced by a Cu/Cu^{2+} electrode.

Exercise 20.4 Using standard electrode potentials

This exercise helps you revise **electrode potentials** and the standard hydrogen electrode. It also familiarises you with how electrode potentials can be used to describe the ease of reduction or oxidation of particular species (molecules, ions or metals).

Make sure that you understand the terms **standard electrode potentials**, half-cell and standard hydrogen electrode.

a Which of these conditions apply to a standard hydrogen electrode?

i hydrogen gas at a pressure of approximately <u>1 kPa</u> / <u>101 kPa</u> / <u>10 atm</u>

ii H^+ ion concentration of <u>0.10 mol dm^{-3}</u> / <u>1.00 mol dm^{-3}</u> / <u>2.00 mol dm^{-3}</u>

iii Electrode is <u>Ag</u> / <u>Pt</u> / <u>Zn</u>

iv Temperature is <u>273 K</u> / <u>298 K</u> / <u>248 K</u>

v The voltage of a standard hydrogen electrode is <u>0 V</u> / <u>1 V</u> / <u>−4 V</u>

b Copy and complete the equation for the reaction of the standard hydrogen electrode.

$$H^+(aq) + \underline{\hspace{2cm}} \rightleftharpoons \underline{\hspace{2cm}}$$

KEY WORDS

salt bridge: an inert material, e.g. filter paper, soaked in an ionic solution, e.g. KNO_3, which is used to make an electrical connection between two **half-cells**.

half-cell: one half of an electrochemical cell which either donates electrons to or receives electrons from an external circuit when connected to another half-cell.

TIP

Another name for standard electrode potential is standard reduction potential.

KEY WORDS

electrode potential, E: the voltage measured for a half-cell compared with another half-cell.

standard electrode potential: the voltage produced when a standard half-cell (ion concentration 1.00 mol dm^{-3} at 298 K) is connected to a standard hydrogen electrode under standard conditions.

c   Copy and complete using words from this list:

| difficult | left | oxidising |
| positive | reactive | reducing |

In the reaction $Fe^{2+}(aq) + 2e^- \rightleftharpoons Fe(s)$ $E^\ominus = -0.44$ V:

The more negative (or less _____) the electrode potential, the more

_____ it is to reduce the ions on the _____ hand side of the

equation. So the metal on the right is a relatively good _____ agent. The

ions on the left hand side are relatively good _____ agents.

TIPS

Standard electrode
potentials refer to a
reduction reaction.
The oxidised form is
on the left, e.g.

$Cu^{2+}(aq) + 2e^- = Cu(s)$

$E^\ominus = +0.34$ V

d   This list gives some electrode potentials. Use these values to answer the questions
     that follow.

$$Cu^{2+}(aq) + 2e^- \rightleftharpoons Cu(s) \quad E^\ominus = +0.34 \text{ V}$$
$$Ni^{2+}(aq) + 2e^- \rightleftharpoons Ni(s) \quad E^\ominus = -0.25 \text{ V}$$
$$Pb^{2+}(aq) + 2e^- \rightleftharpoons Pb(s) \quad E^\ominus = -0.13 \text{ V}$$
$$Sn^{2+}(aq) + 2e^- \rightleftharpoons Sn(s) \quad E^\ominus = -0.14 \text{ V}$$
$$Zn^{2+}(aq) + 2e^- \rightleftharpoons Zn(s) \quad E^\ominus = -0.76 \text{ V}$$

i   Which metal is the best reducing agent?

ii   Which metal ion is the most difficult to reduce?

iii   Which is the least reactive metal?

iv   Which metal ion is easiest to reduce?

TIP

For part **d**, remember
that some the
voltages of some
half-cells are positive
with respect to the
hydrogen electrode
and others are
negative. You must
take the sign into
consideration.

e   We can extend these ideas to half reactions which do not involve metals. The
     species on the left is easier to reduce if the value of $E^\ominus$ is more positive.

This list gives some electrode potentials. Use these values to answer the questions
which follow.

$$NO_3^-(aq) + 10H^+(aq) + 8e^- \rightleftharpoons NH_4^+(aq) + 3H_2O(l) \quad E^\ominus = +0.87 \text{ V}$$

$$\frac{1}{2}I_2(aq) + e^- \rightleftharpoons I^-(aq) \qquad\qquad E^\ominus = +0.54 \text{ V}$$

$$\frac{1}{2}Cl_2(aq) + e^- \rightleftharpoons Cl^-(aq) \qquad\qquad E^\ominus = +1.36 \text{ V}$$

$$\frac{1}{2}Br_2(aq) + e^- \rightleftharpoons Br^-(aq) \qquad\qquad E^\ominus = +1.07 \text{ V}$$

$$Fe^{3+}(aq) + e^- \rightleftharpoons Fe^{2+}(aq) \qquad\qquad E^\ominus = +0.77 \text{ V}$$

$$V^{3+}(aq) + e^- \rightleftharpoons V^{2+}(aq) \qquad\qquad E^\ominus = -0.26 \text{ V}$$

i   Which species on the right-hand side is the easiest to oxidise?

ii   Which species on the left is the best oxidising agent?

iii   Use the $E^\ominus$ values to explain why chlorine can oxidise an aqueous solution of
      iodide ions.

iv   Use the $E^\ominus$ values to explain why aqueous iodine does not oxidise an aqueous
      solution of bromide ions.

Exercise 20.5 Cell potentials

This exercise helps you revise **standard cell potentials**. It also familiarises you with how electrode potentials can be used to describe the ease of reduction or oxidation of particular species and how to determine whether a reaction is likely to take place or not.

An electrochemical cell is a combination of two half-cells. Comparing a Cu / Cu²⁺ half-cell with the hydrogen electrode:

$$Cu^{2+}(aq) + 2e^- \rightleftharpoons Cu(s) \quad E^\ominus = +0.34 \text{ V}$$

$$H^+(aq) + e^- \rightleftharpoons \frac{1}{2}H_2(g) \quad E^\ominus = +0.00 \text{ V}$$

we see that Cu^{2+} ions are easier to reduce than H^+ ions as they have a more positive value of $E^\ominus$. The reaction which occurs is:

$$Cu^{2+}(aq) + H_2(g) \rightleftharpoons Cu(s) + 2H^+(aq)$$

a Look at the following half-equations then answer the questions which follow.

$$Zn^{2+}(aq) + 2e^- \rightleftharpoons Zn(s) \qquad E^\ominus = -0.76 \text{ V}$$

$$H^+(aq) + e^- \rightleftharpoons \frac{1}{2} H_2(g) \qquad E^\ominus = 0.00 \text{ V}$$

   i Which species is easier to reduce and why?

   ii Which ion is most likely to gain electrons?

   iii Write an equation for the reaction which occurs.

b For each of these pairs of half-equations, suggest which species is easier to reduce and write a balanced equation for the reaction which occurs.

   i $\frac{1}{2}Cl_2(aq) + e^- \rightleftharpoons Cl^-(aq)$ $E^\ominus = +1.36 \text{ V}$

       $Fe^{3+}(aq) + e^- \rightleftharpoons Fe^{2+}(aq)$ $E^\ominus = +0.77 \text{ V}$

   ii $MnO_4^-(aq) + 8H^+(aq) + 5e^- \rightleftharpoons Mn^{2+}(aq) + 4H_2O(l)$ $E^\ominus = +1.52 \text{ V}$

       $Fe^{3+}(aq) + e^- \rightleftharpoons Fe^{2+}(aq)$ $E^\ominus = +0.77 \text{ V}$

   iii $Pb^{2+}(aq) + 2e^- \rightleftharpoons Pb(s)$ $E^\ominus = -0.13 \text{ V}$

       $Cr^{3+}(aq) + e^- \rightleftharpoons Cr^{2+}(aq)$ $E^\ominus = -0.41 \text{ V}$

   iv $\frac{1}{2}I_2(aq) + e^- \rightleftharpoons I^-(aq)$ $E^\ominus = +0.54 \text{ V}$

       $\frac{1}{2}Br_2(aq) + e^- \rightleftharpoons Br^-(aq)$ $E^\ominus = +1.07 \text{ V}$

c Deduce the cell potentials from these pairs of half-equations.

   i $\frac{1}{2}Cl_2(aq) + e^- \rightleftharpoons Cl^-(aq)$ $E^\ominus = +1.36 \text{ V}$

       $Ag^+(aq) + e^- \rightleftharpoons Ag(s)$ $E^\ominus = +0.80 \text{ V}$

   ii $Pb^{2+}(aq) + 2e^- \rightleftharpoons Pb(s)$ $E^\ominus = -0.13 \text{ V}$

       $Zn^{2+}(aq) + 2e^- \rightleftharpoons Zn(s)$ $E^\ominus = -0.76 \text{ V}$

   iii $\frac{1}{2}I_2(aq) + e^- \rightleftharpoons I^-(aq)$ $E^\ominus = +0.54 \text{ V}$

       $Ag^+(aq) + e^- \rightleftharpoons Ag(s)$ $E^\ominus = +0.80 \text{ V}$

   iv $Ni^{2+}(aq) + 2e^- \rightleftharpoons Ni(s)$ $E^\ominus = -0.25 \text{ V}$

       $PbO_2(s) + 4H^+(aq) + 2e^- \rightleftharpoons Pb^{2+}(aq) + 2H_2O(l)$ $E^\ominus = +1.47 \text{ V}$

d If the value of $E^{\ominus}_{cell}$ is positive, the reaction is feasible (likely to take place) but if it is negative the reaction is not likely to occur. To see if a reaction is feasible:

- Write the two half-equations with their electrode potentials.

- Reverse the sign of the electrode potential for the oxidation reaction that you want.

- Add the two electrode potentials together.

Example: Will bromine oxidise silver to silver ions?

$Ag^+(aq) + e^- \rightleftharpoons Ag(s)$ $E^{\ominus} = +0.80$ V

So $Ag(s) \rightleftharpoons Ag^+(aq) + e^-$ $E^{\ominus} = -0.80$ V (oxidation reaction wanted)

$\frac{1}{2}Br_2(aq) + e^- \rightleftharpoons Br^-(aq)$ $E^{\ominus} = +1.07$ V

$+1.07 - 0.8 = +0.27$ V so the reaction is feasible.

Use the $E^{\ominus}$ values in Appendix 2 to deduce whether the following reactions are feasible or not.

i Does acidified potassium manganate(VII) react with fluoride ions?

ii Will Ni react with Fe^{3+} ions?

iii Will manganese(II) ions react with iodide ions?

Exercise 20.6 Changing electrode potentials

This exercise familiarises you with how changing the concentration of a reactant in a half-equation can change the value of the electrode potential. It also revises the Nernst equation which shows how concentration and temperature affect the value of electrode potential.

TIPS

Make sure that you know how to apply the Nernst equation in the form

$$E = E^{\ominus} + \frac{0.059}{z} \log_{10} \frac{[\text{oxidised form}]}{[\text{reduced form}]}$$

where z is the number of electrons transferred and the square brackets, [ ], represents the concentration of the **oxidised** and **reduced forms**.

When dealing with $\log_{10}$ remember to press the correct logarithm button on your calculator.

KEY WORDS

oxidised form: in a half equation for a redox reaction, the species with the more positive (or less negative) oxidation number. e.g. Cu^{2+} in $Cu^{2+} + 2e^- \rightleftharpoons Cu$.

reduced form: in a half equation for a redox reaction, the species with the less positive (or more negative) oxidation number.

a We can apply Le Chatelier's principle (Chapter 8) to redox equations. If the concentration of a species on one side of a half-equation is increased, the equilibrium will shift in the direction that opposes the change.

Use Le Chatelier's principle to suggest what happens to the value of the electrode potential, E in the following half reactions.

i Increasing the concentration of Zn^{2+} ions in

$Zn^{2+}(aq) + 2e^- \rightleftharpoons Zn(s)$ $E^{\ominus} = -0.76$ V

ii Diluting the reaction mixture in the equation in part **i**.

iii The concentration of Cr^{2+} ions is 1.5 $mol\,dm^{-3}$ and the concentration of Cr^{3+} ions is 1.0 $mol\,dm^{-3}$ in

$$Cr^{3+}(aq) + e^- \rightleftharpoons Cr^{2+}(aq) \qquad E^\ominus = -0.41 \text{ V}$$

iv In the equation above, the concentration of Cr^{2+} ions is 0.75 $mol\,dm^{-3}$ and the concentration of Cr^{3+} ions is 0.75 $mol\,dm^{-3}$.

b Copy and complete the meaning of the other symbols:

R is the _____ = 8.314 $J\,K^{-1}\,mol^{-1}$

E is the _____ under non-standard conditions

F is the _____ constant in _____ per mole (96 500 _____ mol^{-1})

$\log_{10}$ is the logarithm to _____

c For metal–metal ion equilibria you can apply the shortened form of the Nernst equation.

$$E = E^\ominus + \frac{0.059}{z} \log_{10} [\text{oxidised form}]$$

i Suggest why the reduced form is not shown.

ii Use the Nernst equation to calculate the value of E for

$$Zn^{2+}(aq) + 2e^- \rightleftharpoons Zn(s) \qquad E^\ominus = -0.76 \text{ V}$$

at 25 °C when the concentration of $Zn^{2+}(aq)$ is 2.0 $mol\,dm^{-3}$.

Exercise 20.7 Different types of cell

This exercise introduces you to the reactions taking place in a fuel cell and in a rechargeable cell. The activity gives you further opportunities to deduce half-equations and also gives you practice in extracting information from a diagram.

a Figure 20.3 shows a hydrogen-oxygen **fuel cell**.

In a hydrogen-oxygen fuel cell:

At the negative electrode hydrogen is converted to hydrogen ions.

At the positive electrode oxygen reacts with hydrogen ions to form water.

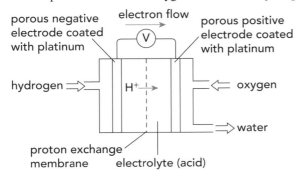

Figure 20.3: A hydrogen-oxygen fuel cell.

KEY WORDS

fuel cell: an electrochemical cell where hydrogen and oxygen undergo redox reactions to produce an electric current.

i   Write an equation for the reaction at the negative electrode.

ii Write an equation for the reaction at the positive electrode.

iii Write an equation for the overall reaction and explain why this reaction is not polluting.

iv What does the direction of electron flow in the diagram tell you about the relative $E^\ominus$ values of the reactions at the positive and negative electrodes?

v   What is the $E^\ominus$ value of the reaction at the negative electrode at r.t.p. if the concentration of H^+ is $1.00\ mol\ dm^{-3}$?

b   A nickel–cadmium cell is rechargeable. The half-equations for the electrode reactions are:

$$Cd(OH)_2 + 2e^- \rightarrow Cd + 2OH^- \qquad\qquad E = -0.81\ V$$
$$NiO_2 + 2H_2O + 2e^- \rightarrow Ni(OH)_2 + 2OH^- \qquad E = +0.49\ V$$

i   Which of these reactions proceeds in a forward direction when electrical energy is being taken from the cell?

ii Predict the cell voltage, assuming that all conditions are standard.

iii Write an equation for the cell reaction that occurs when electrical energy is being taken from the cell.

iv Write an equation for the cell reaction that occurs when the cell is being recharged.

> **TIP**
>
> In part **b iv** remember that this is an equilibrium reaction.

EXAM-STYLE QUESTIONS

1 Aluminium oxide, Al_2O_3, was electrolysed. The volume of oxygen collected at the anode at r.t.p. was $56\ cm^3$.
   a Write the half-equation for the reaction at the anode. **[1]**
   b Calculate the charge in coulombs required to produce $56\ cm^3$ oxygen. $F = 96\ 500\ C\ mol^{-1}$. **[3]**
   c In another experiment, a current of 2.6 A was passed through molten aluminium oxide for 10 minutes. Calculate the mass of aluminium produced. Express your answer to 2 significant figures. A_r values $Al = 27.0$, $O = 16.0$ **[4]**
   d Explain why solid zinc chloride does not conduct electricity. **[1]**
   e A dilute solution of zinc chloride was electrolysed using graphite electrodes.
      i   Give the name of the product at the cathode. Explain your answer. **[2]**
      ii At the anode a mixture of oxygen and chlorine is formed. Explain why. **[2]**

   [Total: 13]

2 The standard electrode potential of a Zn / Zn^{2+} electrode is measured by connecting it to a standard hydrogen electrode via a salt bridge.
   a Define standard electrode potential. **[2]**
   b State the purpose of the salt bridge and suggest what it is made from. **[3]**
   c State the conditions that are necessary to make the Zn / Zn^{2+} electrode **standard**. **[2]**

> **TIP**
>
> Make sure that you know the relevant formulae relating to electrical charge, current and time and how to convert moles to mass.

> **KEY WORD**
>
> **standard:** when applied to electrodes, standard means the specific concentrations, temperature and pressure that apply.

> **TIP**
>
> You need to think about parts **2 b** and **c** in terms of numbers of electrons transferred.

CONTINUED

d Describe the construction of the standard hydrogen electrode. **[3]**

e Write an equation for the overall reaction when the Zn / Zn^{2+} electrode is connected to the standard hydrogen electrode. Include state symbols. **[2]**

f The Zn / Zn^{2+} electrode is connected to an half-cell containing potassium manganate(VII).

$Zn^{2+}(aq) + 2e^- \rightleftharpoons Zn(s)$ $\qquad\qquad\qquad E^{\ominus} = -0.76$ V

$MnO_4^-(aq) + 8H^+(aq) + 5e^- \rightleftharpoons Mn^{2+}(aq) + 4H_2O(l)$ $\qquad E^{\ominus} = +1.52$ V

   i Calculate the value of $E^{\ominus}_{cell}$. **[1]**

   ii **Suggest** how the electrode potential will change if the concentration of the zinc ions is increased but there is no change in the concentrations of the MnO_4^- and H^+ ions. Explain your answer. **[3]**

[Total: 17]

3 A cell is made from the two half-cells represented by the equations:

$Cu^{2+}(aq) + 2e^- \rightleftharpoons Cu(s)$ $\qquad\qquad E^{\ominus} = +0.34$ V

$Fe^{3+}(aq) + e^- \rightleftharpoons Fe^{2+}(aq)$ $\qquad\qquad E^{\ominus} = +0.77$ V

a Draw a labelled diagram to show this cell. On your diagram, among other things, show:

- The negative and the positive electrodes.

- The concentration of each solution. **[6]**

b Deduce the direction of electron flow. Explain why the electrons flow in this direction. **[2]**

c Calculate the value of $E^{\ominus}_{cell}$. **[1]**

d Write a balanced equation for the reaction taking place in the cell. **[2]**

e Use the equation

$$E = E^{\ominus} + \frac{0.059}{z} \log_{10} [\text{oxidised form}]$$

to calculate the value of E for the Cu / Cu^{2+} half-cell at r.t.p. when the concentration of copper ions is 0.15 mol dm^{-3}. Show all your working. **[2]**

f i State the meaning of the term feasible when applied to chemical reactions. **[1]**

   ii A student suggested that the reaction shown is feasible.

$I_2 + Pb^{2+} + 2H_2O \rightarrow 2I^- + PbO_2 + 4H^+$

Explain by referring to the reduction potentials below, whether or not the student is correct.

$\frac{1}{2}I_2 + e^- \rightleftharpoons I^-$ $\qquad\qquad\qquad E^{\ominus} = +0.54$ V

$PbO_2 + 4H^+ + 2e^- \rightleftharpoons Pb^{2+} + 2H_2O$ $\qquad\quad E^{\ominus} = +1.47$ V

In your answer refer to both the relative oxidising ability of the species and the value of $E^{\ominus}_{cell}$. **[5]**

[Total: 19]

TIPS

You must be able to write equations for the whole cell reaction and explain how the electrode potential changes when the concentration changes.

Make sure that you draw diagrams fairly large (about one-quarter of an A4 page) and label them fully. Include as many labels as possible.

TIPS

You should answer part **3 b** in terms of the reducing abilities of the oxidised forms in the half-equations.

In part **3 e** make sure that you use $\log_{10}$ and not ln.

Chapter 21

Further aspects of equilibria

CHAPTER OUTLINE

In this chapter you will learn how to:

- define and use the terms conjugate acid and conjugate base

- define mathematically the terms pH, K_a, pK_a and K_w and use them in calculations

- calculate [H$^+$(aq)] and pH values for strong acids, strong alkalis and weak acids

- define a buffer solution and explain how a buffer solution can be made

- explain how buffer solutions control pH, using chemical equations in these explanations

- describe and explain the uses of buffer solutions, including the role of HCO_3^- in controlling pH in the blood

- calculate the pH of buffer solutions, given appropriate data

- describe and use term solubility product, K_{sp}

- write an expression for K_{sp}

- calculate K_{sp} from concentrations and vice versa

- describe and use the common ion effect to explain the different solubility of a compound in a solution containing a common ion

- perform calculations using K_{sp} values and concentration of a common ion

- state what is meant by the term partition coefficient, K_{pc}

- calculate and use a partition coefficient for a system in which the solute is in the same physical state in the two solvents.

- understand the factors affecting the numerical value of a partition coefficient in terms of the polarities of the solute and the solvents used.

Exercise 21.1 Acids and bases

This exercise revises some of the terms used in acid–base reactions, including the idea of **conjugate acids–base pairs**.

a   Copy and complete these sentences about acids and bases:

    i   A Brønsted–Lowry acid is defined as _____

    ii   A weak acid is incompletely _____ in aqueous _____.

    iii   Ammonia is a _____ base because it is incompletely _____

        when it dissolves in water. Sodium hydroxide is a _____ base because

        _____.

b   Use ideas of collisions between particles to explain why $0.5\ mol\,dm^{-3}$ ethanoic acid reacts slowly with a 1 cm strip of magnesium ribbon but $0.5\ mol\,dm^{-3}$ hydrochloric acid reacts rapidly.

c   In each of the following equations identify the reactant that is the acid and the reactant that is the base.

    i $HNO_3 + H_2O \rightleftharpoons H_3O^+ + NO_3^-$

    ii $NH_3 + H_2O \rightleftharpoons NH_4^+ + OH^-$

    iii $CH_3OH + NH_2^- \rightleftharpoons CH_3O^- + NH_3$

    iv $NH_2OH + H_2O \rightleftharpoons NH_3OH^+ + OH^-$

    v $H_3PO_4 + H_2O \rightleftharpoons H_3O^+ + H_2PO_4^-$

    vi $H_2SO_4 + HIO_3 \rightleftharpoons HSO_4^- + H_2IO_3^+$

d   Identify the two pairs of acids and bases which are conjugate in these equations.

    i $NH_3 + H_2O \rightleftharpoons NH_4^+ + OH^-$

    ii $CH_3COOH + H_2O \rightleftharpoons CH_3COO^- + H_3O^+$

    iii $CH_3NHCH_2NH_3^+ + H_2O \rightleftharpoons CH_3NHCH_2NH_2 + H_3O^+$

    iv $HSiO_3^- + H_2O \rightleftharpoons SiO_3^{2-} + H_3O^+$

    v $HCO_2H + H_2O \rightleftharpoons HCO_2^- + H_3O^+$

    vi $NH_2OH + H_2O \rightleftharpoons NH_3OH^+ + OH^-$

KEY WORDS

conjugate pair (acid–base): an acid–base pair on each side of an acid–base equilibrium equation that are related to each other by the difference of a hydrogen ion, e.g. the acid in the forward reaction and the base in the backward reaction.

TIP

Another way to remember about conjugate acids and bases is acid$_1$ / base$_2$ – acid$_2$ / base$_1$. Remember that there is an acid and base on each side of the equation.

Exercise 21.2 Hydrogen ions in equilibrium expressions

This exercise will familiarise you with some terms used in acid–base equilibria and solubility equilibria. It also gives you practice in writing equilibrium expressions and simple pH calculations.

a   Link the symbols 1–6 on the left with the expressions A–E on the right.

1 $K_w =$	**A** $\dfrac{[H^+(aq)]\,[A^-(aq)]}{[HA(aq)]}$
2 $K_a =$	**B** $-\log\dfrac{[H^+(aq)]^2}{[HA]}$
3 $K_{sp} =$	**C** $[H^+(aq)]\,[OH^-(aq)]$
4 $K_{pc} =$	**D** $-\log[H^+(aq)]$
5 $pK_a =$	**E** $\dfrac{[X(\text{solvent A})]}{[X(\text{solvent B})]}$
6 **pH** $=$	**F** $[C^{y+}(aq)]^a[A^{x-}(aq)]^b$

b   Give the meanings of the symbols:
   i K_w **ii** K_a **iii** K_{sp} **iv** K_{pc}

c   Calculate the pH values of:
   i $0.02\ \text{mol dm}^{-3}$ HCl   **ii** $0.125\ \text{mol dm}^{-3}$ HNO_3 **iii** $6.4 \times 10^{-5}\ \text{mol dm}^{-3}$ HCl

d   Calculate the hydrogen ion concentration of solutions with pH values of:
   i 10.2   **ii** 6.4   **iii** 1.9

e   **i**   Calculate the pH of aqueous potassium hydroxide of concentration $6.40 \times 10^{-3}\ \text{mol dm}^{-3}$.

   ii   Calculate the pH of aqueous barium hydroxide, $Ba(OH)_2$, of concentration $1.50 \times 10^{-4}\ \text{mol dm}^{-3}$.

   iii   Calculate the concentration of hydroxide ions in a solution of sodium hydroxide of pH 12.5.

Exercise 21.3 Solubility product

This exercise will give you practice in calculating solubility product, K_{sp}, and in understanding the importance of the common ion effect.

> **TIP**
>
> Remember that the **common ion effect** decreases the solubility of a dissolved salt. Adding sulfuric acid to a solution of strontium sulfate (common ion, sulfate) may cause strontium sulfate to precipitate.

a Copy and complete the equilibrium expressions for a K_{sp} together with the correct units. The first two have been partly done for you.

Chemical equation	Equilibrium expression	Units
$Fe^{2+}(aq) + 2OH^-(aq) \rightleftharpoons Fe(OH)_2(s)$	$K_{sp} = [\underline{\quad}][OH^-(aq)]^2$	$mol^3\,dm^{-9}$
$Sn^{2+}(aq) + CO_3^{2-}(aq) \rightleftharpoons SnCO_3(s)$	$K_{sp} = [\underline{\quad}][\underline{\quad}]$	$mol^2\,dm^{-6}$
$\underline{\qquad\qquad} \rightleftharpoons Ag_2CrO_4(s)$		
$\underline{\qquad\qquad} \rightleftharpoons Ag_3PO_4(s)$		
$\underline{\qquad\qquad} \rightleftharpoons Cr(OH)_3(s)$		
$\underline{\qquad\qquad} \rightleftharpoons Ag_2S(s)$		

Table 21.1: Equilibrium expressions.

b Calculate the **solubility product** of the following saturated aqueous solutions.
  i Ag_2S (solubility $5.25 \times 10^{-17}\,mol\,dm^{-3}$)
  ii $PbSO_4$ (solubility $1.48 \times 10^{-6}\,mol\,dm^{-3}$)
  iii $Ba(BrO_3)_2$ (solubility $9.86 \times 10^{-5}\,mol\,dm^{-3}$)

c Calculate the solubility of the following compounds in $mol\,dm^{-3}$.
  i $BaSO_4$ ($K_{sp} = 1.0 \times 10^{-10}\,mol^2\,dm^{-6}$)
  ii CdS ($K_{sp} = 8.0 \times 10^{-27}\,mol^2\,dm^{-6}$)

d Will a precipitate be formed by mixing equal volumes of aqueous sodium carbonate of concentration $8.0 \times 10^{-6}\,mol\,dm^{-3}$ with aqueous strontium chloride of concentration $1.0 \times 10^{-4}\,mol\,dm^{-3}$? Show all your working. (K_{sp} of $SrCO_3 = 1.1 \times 10^{-10}\,mol^2\,dm^{-6}$).

e Will a precipitate form when $10\,cm^3$ of $0.050\,mol\,dm^{-3}$ sulfuric acid is mixed with $10\,cm^3$ $5.0 \times 10^{-7}\,mol\,dm^{-3}$ strontium sulfate? (K_{sp} of $SrCO_3 = 1.1 \times 10^{-10}\,mol^2\,dm^{-6}$). Show your working.

> **KEY WORDS**
>
> **common ion effect:** the reduction of the solubility of a dissolved salt by adding a compound that has an ion in common with the dissolved salt, e.g. addition of sodium chloride to a solution of very slightly soluble lead(II) chloride.

> **TIP**
>
> When calculating the solubility product, make sure that you take into account the number of ions present, e.g. in a $0.2\,mol\,dm^{-3}$ solution of $PbCl_2$, there are $0.4\,mol\,dm^{-3}$ of Cl^- ions.

> **KEY WORDS**
>
> **solubility product** K_{sp}: the product of the concentrations of each ion in a saturated solution of a sparingly soluble salt at 298 K, raised to the power of their relative concentrations.

Exercise 21.4 pH calculations

This exercise will give you further practice in calculating pH values from hydrogen ion concentration. It also familiarises you with using these values in calculations involving K_a values for weak acids.

TIPS

In part **a** use the relationship

$$K_a = \frac{[H^+(aq)][A^-(aq)]}{[HA(aq)]}$$

to calculate the **acid dissociation constant, K_a**. We can simplify the top line of the equation to $[H^+(aq)]^2$ if the concentrations of $[H^+(aq)]$ and $[A^-(aq)]$ are equal. You might first have to convert pH to $[H^+(aq)]$.

In part **b** use the relationship

$$K_a = -\log\frac{[H^+(aq)]^2}{[HA]}$$

to calculate pH from K_a.

KEY WORDS

acid dissociation constant, K_a: the equilibrium constant for the dissociation of a weak acid.

a Calculate the values of K_a of:

   i $0.10 \, \text{mol} \, \text{dm}^{-3}$ aqueous ethanoic acid, pH 2.9

   ii $0.002 \, \text{mol} \, \text{dm}^{-3}$ aqueous $HSiO_3^-$, pH 7.29

   iii $0.005 \, \text{mol} \, \text{dm}^{-3}$ aqueous HSO_3^-, pH 4.75

b Calculate the pH of $0.20 \, \text{mol} \, \text{dm}^{-3}$ aqueous methanoic acid ($K_a = 1.5 \times 10^{-5} \, \text{mol dm}^{-3}$) following these steps.

   i Write the equilibrium expression for the reaction.

   ii Rearrange the expression to make $[H^+(aq)]^2$ the subject.

   iii Calculate the value of $[H^+(aq)]^2$ and then $[H^+(aq)]$.

   iv Calculate the pH using $pH = -\log[H^+(aq)]$.

c Calculate:

   i The pH of $0.10 \, \text{mol} \, \text{dm}^{-3}$ aqueous propanoic acid ($K_a = 1.3 \times 10^{-5} \, \text{mol dm}^{-3}$)

   ii The pH of $0.015 \, \text{mol} \, \text{dm}^{-3}$ aqueous nitrous acid ($K_a = 4.7 \times 10^{-4} \, \text{mol dm}^{-3}$)

Exercise 21.5 Buffer solutions

This exercise familiarises you with how buffer solutions keep the pH relatively constant when small amounts of acid or alkali are added. It also gives you practice in calculations involving buffer solutions.

> **TIPS**
>
> We can use the relationship
>
> $$K_a = \frac{[H^+(aq)][A^-(aq)]}{[HA(aq)]}$$
>
> to calculate the pH of a buffer solution. The concentration of the weak acid, HA, and its conjugate base, A⁻, both appear in the equation because extra base (salt) is added.

a   Explain the meaning of the term buffer solution.

b   Copy and complete these sentences about the following buffer solution:

$$C_3H_7COOH \rightleftharpoons C_3H_7COO^- + H^+$$
$$0.2\ mol\,dm^{-3} \quad 0.2\ mol\,dm^{-3}$$

In this buffer solution the conjugate base is _____.

Addition of acid shifts the equilibrium to the _____ because _____ ions from the acid combine with _____ ions from the buffer solution. The concentration of _____ does not fall significantly and the concentration of _____ does not rise significantly because the acid and base (salt) are both in relatively _____ concentrations. The concentration ratio $[C_3H_7COO^-]$ to $[C_3H_7COOH]$ does not change much so the pH _____ (use a suitable phrase to complete).

c   Write a similar description about what happens when a small amount of alkali is added to the buffer solution in part **a**.

d   A solution contains 0.5 mol dm⁻³ propanoic acid, C_2H_5COOH, and 0.4 mol dm⁻³ sodium propanoate. Calculate the pH of this buffer solution. ($K_a = 1.35 \times 10^{-5}$ mol dm⁻³)

e   How many moles of sodium propanoate must be added to 1 dm³ of a solution containing sodium propanoate and 1.00 mol dm⁻³ propanoic acid to make a buffer solution of pH 5.2?

f   Determine the pH of a buffer solution of containing 300 cm³ of 0.50 mol dm⁻³ ethanoic acid and 100 cm³ of 0.80 mol dm⁻³ sodium ethanoate. ($K_a = 1.70 \times 10^{-5}$ mol dm⁻³)

g   Copy and complete these sentences about buffering action of HCO_3^- ions in the blood using words from the list.

Each word may be used once, more than once or not at all.

concentrations	direction	dissolved	excess	hydrogen
hydrogencarbonate	pH	temperature	volumes	

The pH of blood is kept steady by buffer action involving _____

carbon dioxide and _____ ions. If the blood is slightly too acidic, the

concentration of _____ ions is slightly greater than normally present,

the equilibrium shifts in the _____ that removes the _____

hydrogen ions. The concentration of _____ and dissolved carbon dioxide

does not change significantly because they are both present in high enough

_____ to prevent slight _____ changes.

Exercise 21.6 Partition coefficients

This exercise will give you practice in the use of partition coefficients and calculations involving these. It also familiarises you with the significance of partition coefficients in paper chromatography.

KEY WORDS

partition coefficient, K_{pc}: the ratio of the concentrations of a solute in two different immiscible solvents in contact with each other when equilibrium has been established (immiscible solvents are solvents which do not mix).

> **TIPS**
>
> In this exercise remember that K_{pc}, can be expressed as
>
> $$\frac{[X(\text{solvent A})]}{[X(\text{solvent B})]}$$
>
> where X is the concentration of the same dissolved substance in two immiscible solvents A and B when equilibrium has been reached.

a   Some values of **partition coefficients** are shown here.
    In which solvent is each of these solutes more soluble?

   i $\dfrac{[I_2(CCl_4]}{[I_2(aq)]} = 87.3$

   ii $\dfrac{[C_6H_5COOH(aq)]}{[C_6H_5COOH(C_6H_6)]} = 0.01$

   iii $\dfrac{[NH_3(aq)]}{[NH_3(CHCl_3)]} = 23.3$

b   A solution of ammonia in trichloromethane, $CHCl_3$, was shaken with an equal volume of aqueous copper(II) sulfate. Equilibrium was established.

   The equilibrium is $NH_3(CHCl_3) \rightleftharpoons NH_3(CuSO_4(aq))$

   The two layers were run off separately and $5\ cm^3$ of each was taken to determine the concentration of ammonia in each layer. The remaining solutions were then put back into the separating funnel and $5\ cm^3$ of each solvent was added to replace that removed for analysis. This procedure was repeated several times.

   i   Describe how the concentration of ammonia could be determined. Give a suitable indicator which could be used.

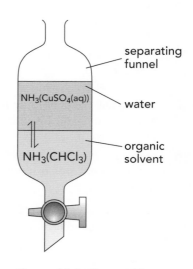

Figure 21.1: The equilibrium $NH_3(CHCl_3) \rightleftharpoons NH_3(CuSO_4(aq))$.

ii Figure 21.2 shows the results of the experiment.

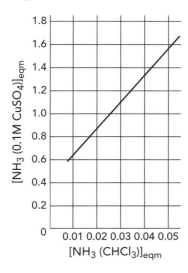

Figure 21.2: The results of the experiment.

Use the information in the graph to calculate the partition coefficient

$$\frac{[NH_3(CuSO_4(aq))]}{[NH_3(CHCl_3)]}$$

c The partition coefficient $\frac{[I_2(CCl_4)]}{[I_2(aq)]}$ is much greater than 1.

Explain why the partition coefficient is much greater than 1 in terms of the **polarity** of the solute and the solvent.

KEY WORD

polarity: the degree to which a molecule is polarised so that one end is slightly $\delta+$ and the other is slightly $\delta-$.

EXAM-STYLE QUESTIONS

1 Carbonated water contains an aqueous solution of carbonic acid.

$$H_2CO_3(aq) + H_2O(l) \rightleftharpoons HCO_3^-(aq) + H_3O^+(aq) \ (K_a = 4.5 \times 10^{-7} \ mol \, dm^{-3})$$

a i Explain why carbonic acid is a Brønsted–Lowry acid. [2]

ii Identify the conjugate pairs in the equation. [2]

b Write a simplified equilibrium expression for this reaction. [1]

c i Calculate the pH of a $0.01 \ mol \, dm^{-3}$ solution of carbonic acid. [4]

ii State two assumptions you made in the construction of your equilibrium expression. **Justify** each of these assumptions. [4]

[Total: 13]

2 A mixture of butanoic acid and sodium **butanoate** acts as a buffer solution.

$$C_3H_7COOH \rightleftharpoons C_3H_7COO^- + H^+$$

a Describe and explain what happens to the pH of this buffer solution when a small amount of alkali is added. [5]

TIP

In part **c ii** you should consider the degree of ionisation of both the acid and the solvent (water).

COMMAND WORD

Justify: support a case with evidence/ argument.

CONTINUED

b Calculate the pH of a solution of butanoic acid which contains 50 cm³ of 0.2 mol dm⁻³ butanoic acid and 150 cm³ of 0.4 mol dm⁻³ sodium butanoate. ($K_a = 1.5 \times 10^{-5}$ mol dm⁻³) **[4]**

c Describe the role of HCO_3^- ions in controlling the pH of the blood. Include a relevant equation in your answer. **[4]**

[Total: 13]

3 Figure 21.3 shows the pH change when 0.20 mol dm⁻³ aqueous sodium hydroxide is added to ethanoic acid.

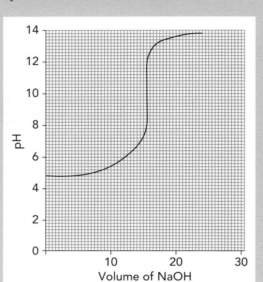

Figure 21.3

a Deduce the ionic equation for this reaction. **[1]**

b Calculate the H⁺ ion concentration in the ethanoic acid at the start of the experiment. **[2]**

c Calculate the H⁺ ion concentration in the aqueous sodium hydroxide at the start of the experiment. ($K_w = 1.00 \times 10^{-14}$ mol dm⁻³) **[2]**

d i Suggest a suitable indicator that could be used. **[1]**

ii Bromophenol blue is yellow at pH 2.8 and blue at pH 4.6. Explain why bromophenol blue would not be used to indicate the end-point of this reaction. **[1]**

e Describe how to use ethanoic acid and sodium ethanoate to make a solution that acts as a buffer at a particular pH value. **[4]**

[Total: 11]

TIP

Some parts of Question 2 involve the rearrangement of equations. Make sure that you know how to do this.

KEY WORD

butanoate: in this context, the negative ion, $C_3H_7CO_2^-$, present in sodium butanoate. The ion is the conjugate base of butanoic acid.

TIPS

In part **3 b** you have to calculate the concentrations after the two solutions have been mixed.

You should revise the action of buffers in the bloodstream before tackling part **c**.

In part **c** use the value of K_w in your calculation and do some rearrangement of the equation.

Part **d** revises material from earlier in the course. Remember that exam questions at A Level can cover a wide area especially the practical exam.

CONTINUED

4   The **solubility product** of aqueous magnesium carbonate, $MgCO_3$, is
1.0×10^{-5} units.

   a   i   Write the equilibrium expression to calculate the solubility product
of magnesium carbonate. Include the correct units.   [2]

   ii   Deduce the solubility of magnesium carbonate.   [3]

   b   The solubility of silver carbonate, Ag_2CO_3, in water is 1.2×10^{-5} mol dm^{-3}.

   i   Write the equilibrium expression to calculate the solubility product
of silver carbonate. Include the correct units.   [2]

   ii   Deduce the solubility product of silver carbonate.   [4]

   c   i   Define the term *common ion effect*.   [2]

   ii   In accurate work where a precipitate is being weighed, a precipitate of
barium sulfate is washed with dilute sulfuric acid rather than with
water. Explain why.   [2]

   d   Equal volumes of 0.01 mol dm^{-3} aqueous calcium chloride and
0.02 mol dm^{-3} aqueous potassium sulfate are mixed. **Demonstrate** by
calculation whether or not a precipitate will be formed.
$(K_{sp} = 2.0 \times 10^{-5}$ mol^2 dm$^{-6})$ [3]

[Total: 18]

TIPS

In parts **4 b** and **d**, take care with the concentrations. The concentrations to be substituted into the equations are not always those given in the question.

In part **c ii** you need to consider the common ion effect.

COMMAND WORD

Demonstrate: show how or give an example.

Chapter 22
Reaction kinetics

CHAPTER OUTLINE

In this chapter you will learn how to:

- define and explain the terms rate equation, order of reaction, overall order of reaction, rate constant, half-life, rate-determining step and intermediate

- construct and use rate equations of the form rate = $k[A]^m[B]^n$ for which m and n are 0, 1 or more

- deduce the order of a reaction from concentration-time graphs or from experimental data relating to the initial rate method or half-life method.

- interpret experimental data in graphical form, including concentration-time and rate-concentration graphs

- calculate initial rates using concentration data

- use the half-life of a first order reaction in calculations

- calculate the numerical value of a rate constant by using initial rates and the rate equation and by using the half-life method

- suggest a multistep reaction mechanism that is consistent with the rate equation and the equation for the overall reaction

- predict the order that would result from a given reaction mechanism and rate-determining step, and deduce a rate equation given a reaction mechanism and rate-determining step for a given reaction

- identify an intermediate or catalyst from a given reaction mechanism

- identify the rate-determining step from a rate equation and a given reaction mechanism

- describe and explain the mode of action of homogeneous and heterogeneous catalysts

- describe qualitatively the effect of temperature change on the rate constant and on rate

Exercise 22.1 Introducing reaction kinetics

This exercise will build on the work you did on rates of reaction in Chapter 9. It familiarises you with the concept of reaction rate and with the various methods used to follow the course of a reaction. It also provides you with an opportunity to develop your skills in determining reaction rates by drawing tangents to points on a curved line graph. The concept of order of reaction is also introduced.

a Convert these rates into $mol\,dm^{-3}\,s^{-1}$.

  i 0.004 mol Br_2 consumed in 30 min in a reaction mixture of volume 200 cm^3.

  ii 80 cm^3 of carbon dioxide released in 2 min from a reaction mixture containing 50 cm^3 of solution.

  iii 3 g of propanol, C_3H_7OH, consumed in 15 min in a reaction mixture of volume 250 cm^3.

> **TIP**
>
> In part **a** remember that at r.t.p. 1 mol of gas occupies 24 dm^3.

b Suggest suitable methods for following the course of these reactions.

  i $(CH_3)_3CBr(aq) + H_2O(l) \rightarrow (CH_3)_3COH(aq) + H^+(aq) + Br^-(aq)$

  ii $CH_3CHO(g) \rightarrow CH_4(g) + CO(g)$

  iii $3Cu(s) + Cr_2O_7^{2-}(aq) + 14H^+(aq) \rightarrow 3Cu^{2+}(aq) + 2Cr^{3+}(aq) + 7H_2O(l)$

  iv $2H_2O_2(aq) \rightarrow 2H_2O(l) + O_2(g)$

  v $C_3H_7Br(aq) + OH^-(aq) \rightarrow C_3H_7OH(aq) + Br^-(aq)$

c Figure 22.1 shows how the concentration of hydrogen peroxide changes with time when it undergoes catalysed decomposition.

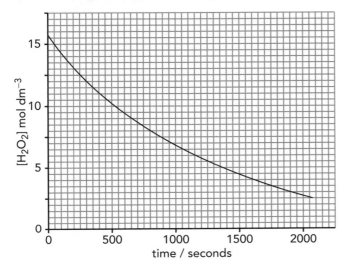

Figure 22.1: How the concentration of hydrogen peroxide changes with time when it undergoes catalysed decomposition.

  i Use a ruler to help you calculate:

  • the initial gradient

  • the gradient at 500 s

  • the gradient at 1000 s.

  ii The gradients you have calculated give the rates of reaction at different concentrations of H_2O_2. Comment on how the rate varies with the concentration.

d We can calculate the **order of reaction** from the results in part **c i**.

  i Define order of reaction.

  ii Draw a graph of the rate of reaction against concentration of hydrogen peroxide.

  iii Determine the order of reaction from the shape of your graph. Explain why you chose this order and evaluate the data.

  iv Explain how to determine the order of the reaction in part **c i** using a half-life method.

  v Deduce the half-life using the method you suggested in part **iv**.

  vi Use the relationship $t_{\frac{1}{2}} = \dfrac{0.693}{k}$ to calculate the value of the **rate constant** for the reaction.

e i State the meaning of the term rate equation.

ii Write the rate equation for the reaction in **c i**.

Exercise 22.2 Rate equations and order of reaction

This exercise will familiarise you with the construction of rate equations and provides practice in determining order of reaction by analysing graphs. It also helps you revise the idea of **half-life** and how this is used to determine order of reaction.

a Copy and complete these sentences about the rate equation.

The rate equation relates the _____ of reaction to the rate of reaction. The

proportionality constant, k, is the _____ _____. Rate equations

take the form:

$$_____ = k[A]^m[B]^n$$

where A and B are the _____ of the reactants that influence the rate of

reaction and m and n are the orders of A and B. Remember that the square

brackets mean _____.

b Copy the graphs in Figure 22.2.

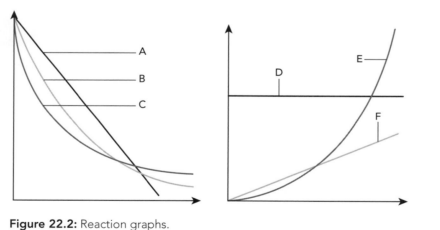

Figure 22.2: Reaction graphs.

i Label the axes using the following terms: concentration of reactants; reaction rate; time

ii Which lines, A to F, represent:

- **zero order reactions**

- **first order reactions**

- **second order reactions?**

KEY WORD

half-life, $t_{\frac{1}{2}}$: the time taken for the amount (or concentration) of the limiting reactant in a reaction to decrease to half its initial value.

KEY WORDS

zero order reaction: reaction in which rate does not depend on concentration.

first order reaction: reaction in which rate is proportional to the concentration of a particular reactant.

second order reaction: reaction in which rate is proportional to the product of two concentration terms, e.g. $[H^+]^2$ or $[H^+][Br^-]$.

c Copy and complete the table to show the rate equation and **overall order of reaction**. The first example has been done for you.

Details of reaction	Rate equation	Overall order of reaction
rate proportional to concentration of I_2 and concentration of H_2	rate = $k[H_2][I_2]$	2nd order
rate proportional to the square of the concentration of NO_2		
rate proportional to concentration of I_2 and the square of the concentration of O_2		
rate proportional to concentration of HI and concentration of H_2O_2		
rate independent of the concentration of any of the reactants		

Table 22.1: Rate equations and overall order of reaction.

d i Copy and complete these phrases about half-lives.

Zero order reaction: Successive half-lives _____ with time.

First order reaction: Successive half-lives are _____ .

Second order reaction: Successive half-lives _____ with time.

ii Use the idea of half-life to explain how the data in the table below shows that A is a first order reaction and B is zero order.

Time / s	0	5	10	15	20	30	40
Concentration A	6.4	4.8	3.2	2.4	1.6	0.8	0.4
Concentration B	6.4	5.8	5.3	4.8	4.2	2.0	0

Table 22.2: Data table.

e i Describe how a temperature rise of 10°C affects the rate of reaction.

ii Describe how a decrease in temperature affects the value of the rate constant.

Exercise 22.3 Deducing order of reaction

> **KEY WORDS**
>
> **overall order of reaction:** the product of the individual orders of reaction of the reactants that appear in the rate equation, e.g. if the rate is first order with respect to A and first order with respect to B, the overall rate equation is $k[A][B]$

> **TIP**
>
> When doing calculations involving half-lives in part **d i** you will only need to consider first order reactions where the half-life is constant.

This exercise will familiarise you with the construction of rate equations and gives you practice in deducing the units of the rate constant, k. It also gives you practice in determining order of reaction by analysing tables of data and from the construction of graphs. It will also familiarise you with the use of half-lives to determine the order of reaction.

> **TIP**
>
> The units for the rate constant, k, are calculated by using the rate equation in the form
>
> $$k = \frac{rate}{[A]^m \, [B]^n}$$
>
> Units of k are found by substituting the relevant units for rate and order in the rate equation
>
> Example: $k = \text{mol dm}^{-3}\,\text{s}^{-1} / \text{mol dm}^{-3} \times \text{mol dm}^{-3} = \text{s}^{-1}/\text{mol dm}^{-3} = \text{dm}^3\,\text{mol}^{-1}\,\text{s}^{-1}$
>
> Note that the rearrangement has the positive index first.

a Copy and complete the table to calculate the order of reaction and units of k.

Rate equation	Overall order of reaction	Units of k
rate = $k[HCOOCH_3][H^+]$		
rate = $k[H_2O_2]$		
rate = $k[NH_3]$		
rate = $k[N_2O]$		
rate = $k[BrO_3^-][Br^-][H^+]^2$		
rate = $k[NO_2]^2$		

Table 22.3: Deducing order of reaction.

b The table shows how the rate of reaction of hydrogen with nitrogen(II) oxide varies with the initial concentrations of hydrogen and nitrogen(II) oxide.

$[H_2]$ / mol dm^{-3}	[NO] / mol dm^{-3}	Rate of reaction / mol dm^{-3} s^{-1}
1.0×10^{-2}	1.25×10^{-2}	2.4×10^{-6}
1.0×10^{-2}	0.63×10^{-2}	0.6×10^{-6}
1.0×10^{-2}	2.50×10^{-2}	9.6×10^{-6}
0.5×10^{-2}	0.63×10^{-2}	0.3×10^{-6}
2.0×10^{-2}	1.25×10^{-2}	4.8×10^{-6}

Table 22.4: Rate of reaction table.

> **TIP**
>
> When deducing order of reaction from tables showing rate and initial concentrations of reactants, look at how the rate changes when the concentration of one of the reactants changes but keeping the concentration of the other reactant(s) constant.

i Deduce the order of reaction with respect to:

- hydrogen

- nitrogen(II) oxide.

ii Construct the rate equation for this reaction.

iii Calculate the value of the rate constant and give the correct units.

Half-lives are deduced by comparing the times when rates are halved, e.g. $100 \text{ mol dm}^{-3}\,\text{s}^{-1} \rightarrow 50 \text{ mol dm}^{-3}\,\text{s}^{-1} \rightarrow 25 \text{ mol dm}^{-3}\,\text{s}^{-1}$

c   Figure 22.3 shows how the rate of enzyme-catalysed decomposition of hydrogen peroxide changes with its concentration. The enzyme is in excess.

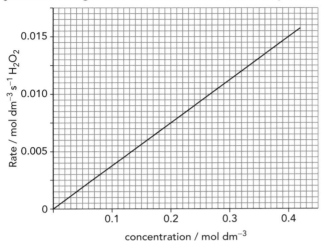

Figure 22.3: How the rate of enzyme-catalysed decomposition of hydrogen peroxide changes with its concentration.

i   Deduce the order of reaction with respect to hydrogen peroxide. Explain your answer.

ii   Calculate the value of the rate constant from the information in the graph.

iii   The reaction is first order with respect to the catalyst. Construct the rate equation for this reaction.

iv   Sketch a graph to show how the concentration of hydrogen peroxide changes with time. Label the axes, but you do not need to add numbers.

d   The data in the table shows the percentage of cyclopropane in the reaction mixture when cyclopropane isomerises into propene.

Time / s	0	15×10^3	36×10^3	56×10^3	84×10^3	110×10^3
% cyclopropane	100	82	62	49	32	23

Table 22.5: Data table.

i   Plot a graph of % cyclopropane against time.

ii   Use your graph to determine relevant half-life values and find the order of reaction.

iii   Deduce the rate constant using the formula $k \times t_{\frac{1}{2}} = 0.693$

iv   Why does it not matter that the values given in the table are quoted as % cyclopropane rather than in $mol\,dm^{-3}$?

Exercise 22.4 Reaction mechanisms

This exercise gives you practice in showing how a proposed reaction mechanism is consistent with the rate equation. It also builds upon the reaction mechanisms that you have come across so far in organic chemistry in Chapters 16 and 18.

> **TIP**
>
> If the concentration of a reagent appears in the rate equation, it is usually also involved in the **rate-determining step**.

> **KEY WORDS**
>
> **rate-determining step:** the slowest step in a reaction mechanism.

a Bromoethane reacts with sodium hydroxide to form ethanol. A proposed mechanism for this reaction is:

$$CH_3CH_2Br + OH^- \rightarrow CH_3CH_2(OH)Br^- \text{ (slow step)}$$

$$CH_3CH_2(OH)Br^- \rightarrow CH_3CH_2OH + Br^- \text{ (fast step)}$$

Experiments show that the reaction is first order with respect to bromoethane and first order with respect to OH^- ions.

i Construct the rate equation for this reaction.

ii Identify the intermediate in this reaction.

iii How is this rate equation consistent with the proposed mechanism?

iv What type of reagent is the OH^- ion? Explain your answer.

b Bromine reacts with an alkaline solution of propanone.

$$CH_3COCH_3 + Br_2 + OH^- \xrightarrow{NaOH} CH_3COCH_2Br + Br^- + H_2O$$

A proposed mechanism for this reaction is:

$$CH_3COCH_3 + OH^- \rightarrow CH_3COCH_2^- + H_2O \text{ (slow step)}$$

$$CH_3COCH_2^- + Br_2 \rightarrow CH_3COCH_2Br + Br^- \text{ (fast step)}$$

i Where have the OH^- ions come from?

ii Suggest the rate equation for this reaction.

iii What type of reagent is the Br_2 in this reaction? Explain your answer.

c Butyl sulfate is hydrolysed by aqueous hydroxide ions.

$$RSO_4^-(aq) + OH^-(aq) \rightarrow ROH(aq) + SO_4^{2-}(aq)$$

(R is $CH_3CH_2CH\cdot CH_3$)

The reaction is first order with respect to butyl sulfate but is independent of the OH^- concentration.

i Write a rate equation for this reaction.

A proposed mechanism for this reaction is:

$$RSO_4^- + H_2O \rightarrow ROH + HSO_4^- \text{ (slow step)}$$

$$HSO_4^- + OH^- \rightarrow H_2O + SO_4^{2-} \text{ (fast step)}$$

ii Water does not appear in the rate equation but does appear in the slow step. Suggest why.

iii How is the rate equation consistent with the proposed mechanism?

Exercise 22.5 Catalysis

This exercise familiarises you with homogeneous and heterogeneous catalysis and revises catalytic mechanisms. It also builds upon the work you have already done about catalytic converters.

a A platinum-rhodium catalyst is used in a catalytic converter to reduce the concentration of CO and NO_x from petrol engine exhausts.

i What is NO_x?

> **TIP**
>
> A catalyst provides an alternative mechanism for the reaction which has lower activation energy than the uncatalysed reaction.

ii   Why is it important that CO and NO_x should not get into the atmosphere?

iii   The sentences below describe how the catalyst works. Put the stages A to G in the correct order.

> **A**   Adsorbed molecules of NO_x and CO which are close together start to form bonds between them.
>
> **B** N_2 and CO_2 diffuse away from the catalyst.
>
> **C** N_2 and CO_2 are formed on the surface of the catalyst.
>
> **D** NO_x and CO diffuse to the catalyst surface.
>
> **E**   This is called **adsorption**.
>
> **F** NO_x and CO form weak bonds with the atoms on the catalyst surface.
>
> **G**   The bonds between the products and the surface atoms are weakened.

iv   Suggest why the adsorption should not be too strong.

v   Suggest why the adsorption should not be too weak.

vi   What is the scientific name for steps **G** and **B** together?

b Fe^{2+} ions catalyse the oxidation of I^- ions by $S_2O_8^{2-}$ ions.

The reaction occurs in two steps:

$$S_2O_8^{2-}(aq) + 2Fe^{2+}(aq) \rightarrow 2SO_4^{2-}(aq) + 2Fe^{3+}(aq)$$

$$2Fe^{3+}(aq) + 2I^-(aq) \rightarrow 2Fe^{2+}(aq) + I_2(aq)$$

i   Construct the overall equation for this reaction.

ii   How can you tell from these two equations that the Fe^{2+} ions are acting as a catalyst?

iii   What type of catalyst is the Fe^{2+} ion?

iv Fe^{3+} ions also catalyse the oxidation of I^- ions by $S_2O_8^{2-}$ ions. Explain why by referring to the equations above.

v   Draw a reaction pathway diagram to show the catalysed and uncatalysed reactions for the oxidation of I^- ions by $S_2O_8^{2-}$ ions. The reaction is exothermic. In your diagram include:

- The reactants and the products.

- The oxidation and reduction of the iron ions as two energy 'humps'.

> **KEY WORD**
>
> **adsorption:** the first stage in heterogeneous catalysis where reactant molecules form bonds with atoms on the catalyst surface.

EXAM-STYLE QUESTIONS

1 Ethanedioate ions react with mercury(**II**) chloride.

$$C_2O_4^{2-}(aq) + 2HgCl_2(aq) \rightarrow 2CO_2(g) + 2Cl^-(aq) + Hg_2Cl_2(s)$$

conductivity 148 units   conductivity 76 units

a Suggest two methods of following the **progress of this reaction**. Explain your answers and suggest any problems involved in the use of these methods. [5]

b The reaction was carried out using different concentrations of ethanoate ions and mercury(**II**) chloride.

$[C_2O_4^{2-}(aq)]$ / mol dm^{-3}	$[HgCl_2(aq)]$ / mol dm^{-3}	Rate of reaction / mol dm^{-3} s^{-1}
0.11	0.0418	4.3×10^{-4}
0.22	0.0418	17.2×10^{-4}
0.11	0.0209	2.1×10^{-4}

Table 22.6

i Determine the order of reaction with respect to each reactant. [2]

ii Construct the rate equation for this reaction. [1]

iii Calculate the value for the rate constant and give the units. [3]

[Total: 11]

2 Methyl ethanoate is hydrolysed by water containing a little hydrochloric acid

$$CH_3COOCH_3(l) + H_2O(l) \rightarrow CH_3COOH(aq) + CH_3OH(aq)$$

The reaction was carried out in a constant temperature water bath.

The table shows how the concentration of methyl ethanoate changes with time.

Time / s	$[CH_3COOCH_3(l)]$ / mol dm^{-3}
0	0.230
180	0.156
360	0.104
540	0.068
720	0.045

Table 22.7

TIP

In part **a** look carefully at the information in the equation to help you and consider factors such as solubility and the state and charge of other substances in the reaction mixture.

KEY WORDS

progress of reaction: the extent to which the reactants are converted to products as the reaction proceeds.

TIPS

Determine is similar to deduce: Make a conclusion form the information that you have.

In part **2 d** make sure that you draw each tangent carefully so that it is at 90° to the curve and extend the tangent to meet the axes of the graph so that an accurate calculation of the gradient can be made.

CONTINUED

a Explain the purpose of the hydrochloric acid. [1]

b Explain why a constant temperature water bath used. [1]

c Plot a graph of concentration of methyl ethanoate against time. [2]

d Draw tangents of the graph at 0 s, 180 s, 360 s and 540 s and calculate the rate of reaction at each of these times. [2]

e Use your answer to part d to deduce the order of the reaction. Give an explanation for your answer. [2]

f Explain why this is not necessarily the overall order of reaction. [2]

[Total: 10]

3 Bromate(V) ions react with bromide ions in acidic solution.

$$BrO_3^-(aq) + 5Br^-(aq) + 6H^+(aq) \rightarrow 3Br_2(aq) + 3H_2O(l)$$

The rate equation for this reaction is

$$\text{rate} = k[BrO_3^-(aq)][Br^-(aq)][H^+(aq)]^2$$

a i State the order of reaction with respect to hydrogen ions. [1]

ii Deduce the overall order of reaction. [1]

b Deduce the units of the rate constant. [1]

c One possible mechanism for this reaction is:

$H^+ + Br^- \rightarrow HBr$ (fast)

$H^+ + BrO_3^- \rightarrow HBrO_3$ (fast)

$HBr + HBrO_3 \rightarrow HBrO + HBrO_2$ (slow)

$HBrO_2 + HBr \rightarrow 2HBrO$ (fast)

$HBrO + HBr \rightarrow Br_2 + H_2O$ (fast)

Explain why this mechanism is **consistent** with the rate equation. [5]

d Hydroxide ions react with 2-bromo-2-methylpropane.

$$(CH_3)_3CBr + OH^- \rightarrow (CH_3)_3COH + Br^-$$

The reaction is first order with respect to $(CH_3)_3CBr$ and zero order with respect to OH^- ions.

i Suggest how the concentration of OH^- ions could be found at various times during the progress of the reaction. [3]

ii Write the rate equation for this reaction. [1]

iii Suggest a mechanism for this reaction which is consistent with this data. Explain why. [5]

[Total: 17]

TIP

For part **2 f** refer back to the equation.

TIP

In part **3 c** you should give your reasons by discussing each of the three reactants in turn. You should consider the substances present in the slow step and how they are formed.

KEY WORD

consistent (mechanism): the mechanism fits with the rate equation (but doesn't prove it).

CONTINUED

4 Nickel catalyses the hydrogenation of ethene.

$$C_2H_4(g) + H_2(g) \xrightarrow{Ni} C_2H_6(g) \quad \Delta H \ -125 \ kJ \, mol^{-1}$$

a Sketch a labelled reaction pathway diagram to show the catalysed and uncatalysed reactions. [3]

b Explain how catalysts increase the rate of reaction. [2]

c Suggest, using ideas of bond making and bond breaking, how nickel catalyses the hydrogenation of ethene. [5]

d Nitrogen(IV) oxide catalyses the oxidation of sulfur dioxide to sulfur trioxide in the atmosphere.

$$SO_2(g) + NO_2(g) \rightarrow SO_3(g) + NO(g)$$

$$NO(g) + \frac{1}{2}O_2 \rightarrow NO_2(g)$$

i Explain why nitrogen(IV) oxide is described as a catalyst in this reaction. [1]

ii Give the name of the type of catalysis in this reaction. Explain your answer. [2]

[Total: 13]

TIPS

In part **a** make sure that you take note of the enthalpy change.

In part **b** there are two marks, so you have to give two points.

In part **c** make sure that you use correct chemical terms.

Part **d** builds on your knowledge of mechanisms. You might find it useful to revise the mechanisms in Chapter 16 before tackling this question.

> Chapter 23

Entropy and Gibbs free energy

CHAPTER OUTLINE

In this chapter you will learn how to:

- define the term entropy as being the number of possible arrangements of the particles and their energy in a given system

- predict and explain the sign of the entropy changes that occur during a change in state, during a temperature change and during a reaction in which there is a change in the number of gaseous molecules

- calculate the entropy change for a reaction using standard entropy values of the reactants and products

- perform calculations using the Gibbs equation $\Delta G^{\ominus} = \Delta H^{\ominus} - T\Delta S^{\ominus}$

- determine if a reaction is feasible by referring to the sign of $\Delta G^{\ominus}$

- predict the effect of temperature change on the feasibility of a reaction when given standard enthalpy and entropy changes

- predict the feasibility of a reaction using the equation $\Delta G^{\ominus} = -nFE^{\ominus}_{cell}$

Exercise 23.1 Entropy in different states

This exercise familiarises you with the concept of **entropy** and helps you understand how entropy values vary according to the state of a substance and the complexity of the substance.

a Copy and complete these sentences using words from the list.

disorder	energy	greater	increases	likelihood	sodium
statistics	spontaneous	stable	surroundings	system	ways

A _____ change is a change that, once started, will carry on until it is

finished. Examples are diffusion, or the reaction of _____ with water.

Spontaneous reactions happen because _____ tell us that there is a greater

_____ of the particles having more ways of arranging their _____

. In a spontaneous reaction, the entropy _____. Entropy is a measure of

randomness or _____. The greater the randomness, the _____ is

> **KEY WORD**
>
> **entropy:** the number of possible arrangements of the particles and their energy in a given system.

> **TIP**
>
> In general solids have low entropy (ordered), liquids have medium entropy (some order) and gases have high entropy (disorder).

the entropy. The total entropy takes into account the _____ (the reactants and products) and the _____ (everything else around the reactants and products). The **system** is more _____ when it is more disordered. The entropy is also greater when there are more _____ of arranging the energy.

b   Identify the system and the surroundings in the following passage:

A student adds some magnesium to some hydrochloric acid in water in a test-tube. She records the temperature rise using a thermometer placed in the acid. The air around the tube also feels warm.

c   Link the substances 1–5 to their entropy values A–E.

1	C(s)		A	$126.0 \, J\,K^{-1}\,mol^{-1}$
2	CaO(s)		B	$213.6 \, J\,K^{-1}\,mol^{-1}$
3	He(g)		C	$69.9 \, J\,K^{-1}\,mol^{-1}$
4	CO_2(g)		D	$39.7 \, J\,K^{-1}\,mol^{-1}$
5	H_2O(l)		E	$2.4 \, J\,K^{-1}\,mol^{-1}$

For each pair, think about the degree of order or disorder in the structure.

d   Explain the difference in entropy in each of the following pairs of substances.

Substance	Entropy / $J\,K^{-1}\,mol^{-1}$	Substance	Entropy / $J\,K^{-1}\,mol^{-1}$
H_2O(l)	69.9	C_2H_5OH(l)	160.7
NaCl(s)	72.1	$NaClO_3$(s)	123.4
Br_2(g)	245.4	Br_2(l)	174.9
HCl(g)	186.8	HBr(g)	198.6
CH_4(g)	186.2	C_3H_8(g)	269.9

Table 23.1: Entropy differences.

Exercise 23.2 Entropy changes

This exercise gives you practice in deciding whether entropy increases or decreases by reference to the state and complexity of the reactants and products. It also familiarises you with calculations involving standard entropy values.

KEY WORDS

spontaneous change: a change which is statistically likely to occur.

system: the reactants and products of a chemical reaction.

TIPS

When answering questions about entropy changes in chemical reactions without knowing entropy values, think about the degree of disorder of the reactants and the products. The state symbols and the complexity of each species give you clues.

The more electrons or the greater the variety / number of atoms in a molecule, the greater is the entropy.

Standard entropy change of a reaction, $\Delta S^\ominus = \Sigma S^\ominus_{products} - \Sigma S^\ominus_{reactants}$.

KEY WORDS

standard entropy change, $\Delta S^\ominus$: the change in entropy when the reactants form products at 298 K and 101 kPa (given by $\Sigma S^\ominus_{products} - \Sigma S^\ominus_{reactants}$)

Chemical reactions are likely to happen if their entropy increases. So if the products are more disordered than the reactants, the reaction is likely to occur: there is an increase in entropy.

a The equation below represents the synthesis of ammonia.

$N_2(g) + 3H_2(g) \rightarrow 2NH_3(g)$

Take a piece of paper and draw two squares (4 cm × 4 cm) side by side.

Put a dot • to represent an N_2 molecule anywhere at random in the left-hand square.

Put 3 circles o to represent 3 H_2 molecules at random in the left-hand square.

Put 2 crosses × to represent 2 NH_3 molecules at random in the right-hand square.

Repeat these processes three times.

- **i** Which square, the left (reactants) or the right (product), has the most disorder?
- **ii** Which square has the most molecules?
- **iii** Is ammonia likely to have a higher or lower entropy than either nitrogen or hydrogen? Explain your answer.
- **iv** Are the reactants likely to have a higher or lower entropy than the products? Explain your answer.
- **v** Is the entropy of this reaction likely to increase or decrease?
- **vi** Will this reaction be spontaneous at r.t.p.? Explain your answer.

b For each of the following reactions, suggest whether the entropy of the reactants or products is greater or whether it is difficult to decide. Explain your answers.

- **i** $2Na(s) + Cl_2(g) \rightarrow 2NaCl(s)$
- **ii** $FeCl_2(aq) + 2NaOH(aq) \rightarrow Fe(OH)_2(s) + 2NaCl(aq)$
- **iii** $2H_2O_2(l) \rightarrow 2H_2O(l) + O_2(g)$
- **iv** $C_2H_4(g) + H_2(g) \rightarrow C_2H_6(g)$
- **v** $2FeSO_4(s) \rightarrow Fe_2O_3(s) + SO_2(g) + SO_3(g)$

c Describe and explain the changes in entropy which occur and the relative size of the entropy changes when:

- **i** ice is heated to form water
- **ii** water is heated to form steam.

d Calculate the standard entropy changes in equations **i** to **v** using the **standard molar entropy** values below (all in $J K^{-1} mol^{-1}$).

$B(s)$	5.9	$Mg(NO_3)_2(s)$	164.0
$B_2O_3(s)$	54.0	$MgO(s)$	26.9
$C(graphite)$	5.7	$NO_2(g)$	240.0
$CO(g)$	197.6	$O_2(g)$	205
$H_2(g)$	130.6	$SiF_4(g)$	282.4
$HF(g)$	173.7	$SiO_2(s)$	41.8
$H_2O(g)$	188.7	$SO_2(g)$	248.1
$H_2O(l)$	69.9	$SO_3(g)$	95.6
$Mg(s)$	32.7		

i $2SO_2(g) + O_2(g) \rightarrow 2SO_3(g)$

ii $H_2O(g) + C(graphite) \rightarrow H_2(g) + CO(g)$

iii $B_2O_3(s) + 3Mg(s) \rightarrow 2B(s) + 3MgO(s)$

iv $SiO_2(s) + 4HF(g) \rightarrow SiF_4(g) + 2H_2O(l)$

v $Mg(NO_3)_2(s) \rightarrow MgO(s) + 2NO_2(g) + \frac{1}{2}O_2(g)$

KEY WORDS

standard molar entropy: the entropy of a mole of a species under standard conditions of 101kPa and 298 K.

TIP

In part **d** don't forget to take the number of moles into account and note the state of water in the reactions!

Exercise 23.3 Gibbs free energy

This exercise familiarises you with the concept of **Gibbs free energy** and its relationship with entropy and enthalpy change of reaction. It gives you further practice in constructing energy cycles and describes how the sign and value of Gibbs free energy informs us of the extent of a reaction.

TIPS

Gibbs free energy change is related to the entropy change of the system by the relationship: $\Delta G^{\ominus} = \Delta H^{\ominus} - T\Delta S$. This is the **Gibbs equation**

In the equation $\Delta G^{\ominus} = \Delta H^{\ominus} - T\Delta S$, $\Delta H^{\ominus}$ in $kJ mol^{-1}$ must be multiplied by 1000 to make the units consistent with those of entropy.

a What do these values of $\Delta G_r^{\ominus}$ tell you about a reaction?

i The value of $\Delta G_r^{\ominus}$ is small and positive.

ii The value of $\Delta G_r^{\ominus}$ is zero.

iii The value of $\Delta G_r^{\ominus}$ is high and positive.

iv The value of $\Delta G_r^{\ominus}$ is small and negative.

b Calculate the Gibbs free energy change of the following reactions at 298 K and state whether or not they are likely to occur (molar entropy values below are all in $J K^{-1} mol^{-1}$).

KEY WORDS

Gibbs free energy: the energy change that takes into account both the entropy change of a reaction and the enthalpy change.

Gibbs equation: the equation relating the Gibbs free energy change, $\Delta G^{\ominus}$, to the enthalpy change of the system, $\Delta H^{\ominus}$ and the entropy change of the system, $\Delta S^{\ominus}$. $\Delta G^{\ominus} = \Delta H^{\ominus} - T\Delta S^{\ominus}$.

$C_2H_5OH(l)$	160.7	$Mg(s)$	32.7
$CO_2(g)$	213.6	$MgO(s)$	26.9
$Fe(s)$	27.3	$O_2(g)$	205
$Fe_2O_3(s)$	87.4	$SrCO_3$	97.1
$H_2O(l)$	69.9	SrO	54.4

  i $C_2H_5OH(l) + 3O_2(g) \rightarrow 2CO_2(g) + 3H_2O(l)$ $\Delta H_r = -1367.3\ kJ\,mol^{-1}$

  ii $SrCO_3(s) \rightarrow SrO(s) + CO_2(g)$ $\Delta H_r = +1418.6\ kJ\,mol^{-1}$

  iii $3Mg(s) + Fe_2O_3(s) \rightarrow 3MgO(s) + 2Fe(s)$ $\Delta H_r = -980.9\ kJ\,mol^{-1}$

c **i**   Copy and complete the Gibbs free energy cycle in Figure 23.1 for the reaction:

       $Fe_2O_3(s) + 3CO(g) \rightarrow 2Fe(s) + 3CO_2(g)$

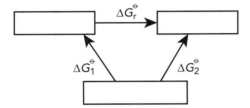

Figure 23.1: Gibbs free energy cycle.

  ii Use the standard free energy of formation values below to calculate the free energy change of the reaction. $\Delta G^\ominus$ [$Fe_2O_3(s)$] $-742.2\ kJ\,mol^{-1}$; $\Delta G^\ominus$ [$CO(g)$] $-137.2\ kJ\,mol^{-1}$; $\Delta G^\ominus$ [$CO_2(g)$] $-394.4\ kJ\,mol^{-1}$

  iii Is the **reaction feasible** at room temperature?

d Calculate the standard free energy change of these reactions.

  i $SiO_2(s) + 4HF(g) \rightarrow SiF_4(g) + 2H_2O(l)$

     Standard free energy of formation values: $\Delta G^\ominus$ [$CO_2(g)$] $-394.4\ kJ\,mol^{-1}$; $\Delta G^\ominus$[$HF(g)$]$-273.2\ kJ\,mol^{-1}$; $\Delta G^\ominus$ [$H_2O(l)$] $-69.9\ kJ\,mol^{-1}$; $\Delta G^\ominus$ [$SiF_4(g)$] $-1572.7\ kJ\,mol^{-1}$; $\Delta G^\ominus$ [$SiO_2(s)$] $-856.7\ kJ\,mol^{-1}$.

  ii $SrCO_3(s) \rightarrow SrO(s) + CO_2(g)$

     Standard free energy of formation values: $\Delta G^\ominus$ [$SrCO_3(s)$] $-1140.4\ kJ\,mol^{-1}$; $\Delta G^\ominus$ [$SrO(s)$] $-561.9\ kJ\,mol^{-1}$.

KEY WORDS

feasible reaction: a reaction that is likely to take place under particular conditions.

Exercise 23.4 Is the reaction feasible?

This exercise familiarises you with the extent to which the entropy change of the system and Gibbs free energy contribute to the feasibility of a reaction. It also revises the effect of change in temperature on the **feasibility** of a reaction.

a Use the Gibbs equation to calculate the value of $\Delta G^\ominus$ of these reactions at 298 K.

  i $ZnO(s) + C(s) \rightarrow Zn(s)\ CO(g)$

  ii $MgO(s) + CO(g) \rightarrow Mg(s) + CO_2(g)$

  iii $CaCO_3(s) \rightarrow CaO(s) + CO_2(g)$

  iv $2SO_2(g) + O_2(g) \rightarrow 2SO_3(l)$

  v $Al_2O_3(s) + 3C(s) \rightarrow 2Al(s) + 3CO(g)$

KEY WORD

feasibility: the likelihood or not of a reaction occurring.

$S^{\ominus}_{system}$ values (in $J\,mol^{-1}\,K^{-1}$):

Al(s)	28.3	Mg(s)	32.7
$Al_2O_3(s)$	50.9	MgO(s)	26.9
C(s)	5.7	$O_2(g)$	102.5
$CaCO_3(s)$	92.9	$SO_2(g)$	248.1
CaO(s)	39.7	$SO_3(l)$	95.6
CO(g)	197.6	Zn(s)	41.6
$CO_2(g)$	213.6	ZnO(s)	43.6

$\Delta H^{\ominus}_f$ values (in $kJ\,mol^{-1}$):

$Al_2O_3(s)$	1675.7	MgO(s)	601.7
$CaCO_3(s)$	1206.9	$SO_2(g)$	296.8
CaO(s)	635.1	$SO_3(l)$	441.0
CO(g)	110.5	ZnO(s)	348.3
$CO_2(g)$	393.5		

b Identify the reactions in part **a** which are feasible at 298 K? Explain why.

c Calculate the temperatures at which the following reactions in part **a** become just feasible.

  i The reaction between ZnO(s) and C(s) (part **i**).

  ii The reaction between $Al_2O_3(s) + 3C(s)$ (part **v**).

d i What assumptions have been made about the values used in the calculations in part **c**.

  ii Use the results from part **c** to suggest why aluminium is extracted by electrolysis and zinc can be extracted by reduction with carbon.

e Refer to the Gibbs equation to suggest whether or not the following reactions are feasible. Explain your answers.

  i the reaction is only slightly endothermic and a solid is being converted to a gas and a liquid at a high temperature.

  ii the reaction is highly exothermic and there is a slight decrease in the entropy of the system at room temperature.

  iii the reaction is highly endothermic and a solid is being converted to a gas and a liquid at a high temperature.

f The feasibility of a reaction can also be deduced by using the relationship between $\Delta G^{\ominus}$ and the standard cell potential, $E^{\ominus}_{cell}$

Determine whether not each of these reactions is feasible by calculating the value of $\Delta G^{\ominus}$.

  - for **i** $Ni^{2+}(aq) + 2e^- \rightleftharpoons Ni(s)$ $E^{\ominus} = -0.25$ V
    $Cd^{2+}(aq) + 2e^- \rightleftharpoons Cd(s)$ $E^{\ominus} = -0.40$ V

  - for part **ii** and **iii**, use the standard electrode potentials in Appendix 2.
    $F = 96\,500\,C\,mol^{-1}$

    i $Cd(s) + Ni^{2+}(aq) \rightarrow Cd^{2+}(aq) + Ni(s)$

    ii $Cu^{2+}(aq) + 2Fe^{2+}(aq) \rightarrow Cu(s) + 2Fe^{3+}(aq)$

    iii $2I^-(aq) + Ag^+(aq) \rightarrow I_2(aq) + Ag(s)$

> **TIPS**
>
> Before answering part **f** make sure that you know how to deduce $E^{\ominus}_{cell}$
>
> Use the relationship $\Delta G^{\ominus} = -nFE^{\ominus}_{cell}$ when answering part **f**.

EXAM-STYLE QUESTIONS

1 a Define the term entropy. [1]

  b Sodium reacts rapidly with water.

$$2Na(s) + 2H_2O(l) \rightarrow 2NaOH(aq) + H_2(g)$$

  Explain in terms of the entropy of the reactants and products why the products are energetically more **stable** than the reactants. [5]

  c The equation for the reaction of copper(II) oxide with carbon monoxide is given.

$$CuO(s) + CO(g) \rightarrow Cu(s) + CO_2(g)$$

  i Calculate the entropy change of the system in this reaction. [2]
  $S^{\ominus}_{system}$ values (in $J\,mol^{-1}\,K^{-1}$): CO(g) 197.6; CO_2(g) 213.6; Cu(s) 33.2; CuO(s) 42.6

  ii Calculate the enthalpy change of the system. [2]
  $\Delta H^{\ominus}_f$ values (in $kJ\,mol^{-1}$): CO(g) –110.5; CO_2(g) –393.5; CuO(s) –157.3

  iii Use the Gibbs equation to calculate the Gibbs free energy of the reaction at 200 °C. [3]

  iv State whether or not the reaction is feasible at 200 °C. Explain your answer. [1]

  v State any assumptions you made about the values of $\Delta H^{\ominus}_r$ and $S^{\ominus}_{system}$ in the calculation in part **iii**. [1]

[Total: 15]

2 a Titanium can be extracted from titanium oxide by heating with carbon.

$$TiO_2(s) + 2C(s) \rightarrow Ti(s) + 2CO(g) \qquad \Delta H^{\ominus}_r = +720\ kJ\,mol^{-1}\ (at\ 298\ K)$$

  i Sketch an energy cycle to calculate the standard Gibbs free energy change of reaction. ($\Delta G^{\ominus}_f$ [TiO_2(s)] –884.5 $kJ\,mol^{-1}$; $\Delta G^{\ominus}_f$ [CO(g)] –137.2 $kJ\,mol^{-1}$) [2]

  ii Calculate a value for the Gibbs free energy change of reaction. Include units. [3]

  iii Determine whether or not the reaction is feasible. Explain your answer. [1]

  b Refer to the Gibbs equation to explain in terms of entropy change and temperature why the reaction occurs at 2000 K but not at room temperature. [3]

  c An equation for the reaction of titanium(III) ions with cobalt is shown.

$$2Ti^{3+}(aq) + Co(s) \rightarrow 2Ti^{2+}(aq) + Co^{2+}(aq)$$

  The standard electrode potentials are:

  $Ti^{3+}(aq) + e^- \rightleftharpoons Ti^{2+}(aq)$ $E^{\ominus} = -0.37$ V

  $Co^{2+}(aq) + 2e^- \rightleftharpoons Co(s)$ $E^{\ominus} = -0.28$ V

  i Calculate the value of $\Delta G^{\ominus}$ for this reaction. [3]

  ii Determine the feasibility and position of equilibrium of this reaction by reference to the value and sign of $E^{\ominus}_{cell}$ and $\Delta G^{\ominus}$. [3]

[Total: 15]

TIPS

The state symbols in the equation should help you answer part **1 b**.

Part **c** requires thought about the signs of the entropy change.

In part **c v** think about the answers you gave to Exercise 23.1 **c**.

KEY WORD

stable (system): a system having a lower energy than another. The greater the entropy, the more stable is the system.

TIPS

In part **2 b** you need to compare each of the two parts of the Gibbs equation.

In part **c** you need to use the equation relating $\Delta G^{\ominus}$ to $E^{\ominus}_{cell}$ (calculate $E^{\ominus}_{cell}$ from standard electrode potentials given).

CONTINUED

3   Rubidium reacts with sulfur to form rubidium sulfide.

$$2Rb(s) + S(s) \rightarrow Rb_2S(s) \qquad \Delta H_r^\ominus = +360.7 \text{ kJ mol}^{-1} \text{ (at 298 K)}$$

a   Calculate the entropy change of the system.   [2]

(values for $S^\ominus$ in $J K^{-1} mol^{-1}$: Rb(s) +76.8; S(s) +32.6; Rb_2S(s) +134.0)

b   1.0 mol of rubidium chloride, RbCl, is dissolved in 1.00 dm^3 of water at 25 °C.

   i   Calculate the entropy change of the system.

   (values for $S^\ominus$ in $J K^{-1} mol^{-1}$: RbCl(s) +95.9; Rb^+(aq) +121.5;
   Cl^-(aq) +56.5)   [2]

   ii   The enthalpy change of solution is + 9.5 kJ mol^{-1}.

   Calculate the Gibbs free energy change for this process.   [3]

   iii   Explain in terms of entropy changes and Gibbs free energy changes,
   why rubidium chloride dissolves in water even though the process is
   endothermic.   [5]

[Total: 12]

TIPS

In **3 b** you need
not worry about
the water that you
are dissolving the
rubidium chloride in.

In **b iii** think about
the two parts on the
right-hand side of the
Gibbs equation as
well as the reasons for
the entropy change.

Transition elements

In this chapter you will learn how to:

- explain what is meant by the term transition element

- describe how transition elements have variable oxidation states, behave as catalysts, form complex ions and form coloured ions

- state the electronic configuration of a first-row transition element and of its ions

- describe and explain the use of $MnO_4^- / C_2O_4^{2-}$, MnO_4^- / Fe^{2+} and Cu^{2+} / I^- as examples of redox systems

- predict, using $E^{\ominus}$ values, the feasibility of redox reactions involving transition element compounds

- define the terms ligand, complex and co-ordination number

- deduce the overall polarity of complexes

- describe and explain the reactions of transition elements with ligands to form complexes and describe the shapes and bond angles of complexes

- describe the types of stereoisomerism (cis/trans and optical isomerism) shown by complexes including those with bidentate and polydentate ligands

- explain ligand exchange in terms of stability constants

- sketch the general shape of atomic d orbitals

- describe the splitting of degenerate d orbitals into two energy levels in octahedral and tetrahedral complexes

- explain the origin of colour in transition element complexes

- describe in qualitative terms the effects of different ligands on the absorption of light and hence the colour of complexes

Exercise 24.1 Properties of transition elements

This exercise will familiarise you with the properties of the **transition elements** as well as the electronic configurations of their atoms and ions in terms of s, p and d orbitals. It will also give you practice in understanding why the compounds of transition element appear coloured.

a Most transition elements have high melting points and high densities.

Give 4 *other* properties of transition elements or their ions that are *not* characteristic of other groups of metals.

b The physical properties of transition elements differ from those of Group 2 elements. The values of some physical properties of iron and calcium are compared here. Which are the values for iron and which are the values for calcium?

melting point 1808 K; 1112 K   density 7.86 g cm^{-3}; 1.54 g cm^{-3}

metallic radius 0.197 nm; 0.126 nm   boiling point 1380 K; 3023 K

ionic radius (X^{2+}) 0.061 nm; 0.100 nm   first ionisation energy 759 kJ mol^{-1}; 590 kJ mol^{-1}

electrical conductivity 2.82×10^7 S m^{-1}; 9.04×10^6 S m^{-1}

c Some electron configurations of some transition elements are given here.

V (Z = 23) $1s^22s^22p^63s^23p^63d^34s^2$

Cr (Z = 24) $1s^22s^22p^63s^23p^63d^54s^1$

Mn (Z = 25) $1s^22s^22p^63s^23p^63d^54s^2$

Fe (Z = 26) $1s^22s^22p^63s^23p^63d^64s^2$

i Deduce the electronic configuration of the next three elements, Co, Ni, Cu.

ii Draw an energy level diagram for Cr with electrons in square boxes like the one in Chapter 2, Exercise 2.4. Show only the 3rd and 4th principal quantum shells.

iii Suggest why Cr does not have the electronic structure $1s^22s^22p^63s^23p^63d^44s^2$.

iv Why are Sc (Z = 21) and Zn (Z = 30) not classed as transition elements?

d Deduce the electron configurations of these ions:

i Fe^{2+} **ii** Cr^{3+} **iii** Co^{2+} **iv** Cu^+

e i The following passage describes why transition element ions are coloured. The phrases 1 to 8 are in the correct order but the ends of the phrases are muddled. Match each beginning 1 to 8 with the endings A to H.

1 The d orbitals in an isolated transition element ion…	**A** …d orbital splitting.
2 In the presence of ligands…	**B** …repel the electrons of the d orbitals.
3 The lone pairs on the ligand…	**C** …energy is absorbed.
4 The repulsion causes…	**D** …to jump to the higher split d level.
5 One set of **non-degenerate orbitals**…	**E** …subtracts light of a particular colour from the spectrum giving the complex a particular colour.
6 When white light shines on the complex ion…	**F** …a complex is formed.

TIP

You will find it helpful to revise electronic configurations (Chapter 3) before doing this exercise.

KEY WORDS

non-degenerate orbitals: groups of atomic orbitals in the same sub-shell that have slightly different amounts of energy (splitting of orbitals).

degenerate orbitals: atomic orbitals in the same energy level in a given sub-shell.

<table>
<tr><td>7</td><td>The energy causes an electron in the lower split d level…</td><td>G</td><td>…is in a slightly higher energy level than the other.</td></tr>
<tr><td>8</td><td>The frequency of the light absorbed…</td><td>H</td><td>…are **degenerate**.</td></tr>
</table>

    ii Suggest, in terms of electronic configurations, why zinc and scandium do not form coloured compounds.

Exercise 24.2 Transition elements and redox reactions

This exercise will give you further practice in writing redox equations and deducing oxidation numbers. It also helps improve your understanding of electrode potentials, $E^\ominus$.

You might find it useful to revise these topics in Chapters 7 and 20 before starting this exercise.

a Complete these half-equations by balancing with electrons:

  i $3Cr^{3+} \rightarrow 3Cr^{2+}$

  ii $VO^{2+} + 2H^+ \rightarrow V^{3+} + H_2O$

  iii $2Ni \rightarrow 2Ni^{2+}$

  iv $Fe^{2+} \rightarrow Fe^{3+}$

  v $MnO_4^- + 8H^+ \rightarrow Mn^{2+} + 4H_2O$

  vi $CrO_4^{2-} + 4H_2O \rightarrow Cr(OH)_3 + 5OH^-$

b Construct full equations for:

  i The reaction of MnO_4^- in acidic conditions with aqueous Fe^{2+} ions.

  ii The reaction of acidified VO^{2+} ions with Ni.

  iii The reaction of Cr^{2+} ions with Ni^{2+} ions.

  iv The reaction of Cu^{2+} ions with I^- ions.

  v The reaction of acidified MnO_4^- ions with $C_2O_4^{2-}$ ions to form Mn^{2+} ions, CO_2 and water.

> **TIP**
>
> In part **b i**, **ii** and **iii** the full equation can be constructed from two half equations by balancing the electrons.

c Dichromate ions and manganate(VII) ions are good oxidising agents. We can use standard electrode potentials to find out whether or not potassium dichromate or potassium manganate(VII) is able to oxidise other species and become reduced.

The electrode potentials of the two half-equations are shown here:

$$Cr_2O_7^{2-}(aq) + 14H^+(aq) + 6e^- \rightarrow 2Cr^{3+}(aq) + 7H_2O(l) \qquad E^\ominus = +1.33 \text{ V}$$
$$Fe^{3+}(aq) + e^- \rightarrow Fe^{2+}(aq) \qquad E^\ominus = +0.77 \text{ V}$$

  i Use $E^\ominus$ values to explain why dichromate ions are acting as oxidising agents in this reaction.

  ii Write a balanced equation for the reaction.

  iii Deduce the oxidation number changes of the Cr and the Fe in this reaction.

iv Potassium dichromate is orange in colour and $Cr^{3+}(aq)$ ions are green. Potassium manganate(VII) is purple. Explain why it is easier to use potassium manganate(VII) to estimate the concentration of $Fe^{2+}(aq)$ ions in solution than to use potassium dichromate.

d Use $E^{\ominus}$ values to deduce which of the reduced forms below will be oxidised by potassium manganate(VII).

$$MnO_4^- + 8H^+ + 5e^- \rightarrow Mn^{2+} + 4H_2O \qquad E^{\ominus} = +1.52 \text{ V}$$
$$Mn^{3+} + e^- \rightarrow Mn^{2+} \qquad E^{\ominus} = +1.49 \text{ V}$$
$$I_2 + 2e^- \rightarrow 2I^- \qquad E^{\ominus} = +0.54 \text{ V}$$
$$Co^{3+} + e^- \rightarrow Co^{2+} \qquad E^{\ominus} = +1.81 \text{ V}$$
$$Cu^{2+} + 2e^- \rightarrow Cu \qquad E^{\ominus} = +0.34 \text{ V}$$

TIP

Before doing the next exercise, you should make sure you know what the terms ligand, complex and co-ordination number mean.

Exercise 24.3 Ligands and complexes

This exercise will familiarise you with some of the terms used in transition element chemistry. It also gives you practice in drawing stereoisomers and deducing the shapes of **complex ions**.

a Copy and complete these sentences by choosing one of the underlined words.

i A molecule or <u>ion</u> / <u>polymer</u> with one or more <u>lone</u> / <u>bonding</u> pairs of electrons available to donate to a transition element ion is called a **ligand** / <u>complex</u>.

ii A <u>complex</u> / <u>simple</u> ion is formed when the ion of a <u>transition</u> / <u>s block</u> element bonds to one or more <u>ligands</u> / <u>electrons</u>.

iii The number of <u>dative covalent</u> / <u>ionic</u> bonds formed by one ligand with a transition element ion in a complex is called the <u>co-ordination</u> / <u>ligand</u> number.

b Two complex ions, A and B, are shown in Figure 24.1.

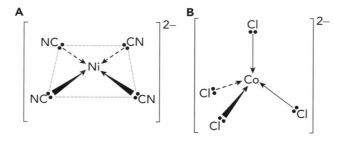

Figure 24.1: Two complex ions.

For each ion:

i Name the ligands.
ii Deduce the **co-ordination numbers**.
iii Describe the shape of the ions.
iv Deduce the oxidation numbers of the transition metals.
v Give the simplest formula for each complex ion.
vi Suggest values for the bond angles in each of these complex ions.

KEY WORDS

complex ion: a central transition metal ion surrounded by ligands, bonded to the central ion by dative (also called co-ordinate) covalent bonds.

co-ordination number: the number of co-ordinate bonds formed by ligands with a transition element ion in a complex.

ligand: a molecule or ion with one or more lone pairs of electrons which form dative covalent bonds to a central transition element atom or ion.

TIP

When describing the shapes of the ions, you can use the same terms as you used for the shapes of molecules in Chapter 4: e.g. planar, octahedral.

c Deduce the oxidation number of the metal ion in each of these complexes.

 i $[Fe(CN)_6]^{4-}$ **iv** $[CrO_3Cl]^-$

 ii $[Ag(NH_3)_2]^+$ **v** $[Co(NH_3)_4Cl_2]^+$

 iii $[Cr(H_2O)_4Cl_2]^+$

d Draw three-dimensional structures of:

 i $[Fe(CN)_6]^{4-}$

 ii $[Ag(NH_3)_2]^+$

 iii $[PtCl_4]^{2-}$

e The structure of an isomer of $[Cr(en)_2Cl_2]$ is shown below, where 'en' stands for $H_2NCH_2CH_2NH_2$.

Figure 24.2: The structure of an isomer of $[Cr(en)_2Cl_2]$.

 i   Would you describe 'en' as being **monodentate**, **bidentate** or **hexadentate**? Explain your answer.

 ii   Draw a three-dimensional diagram of the **optical isomer** (stereoisomer) of the structure shown in Figure 24.2.

 iii $[Cr(en)_2Cl_2]$ also exists as a third form which is not an optical isomer. Draw a three-dimensional diagram of this structure.

f When deciding whether or not a ligand is monodentate, bidentate or hexadentate, start by looking at the position of any lone pairs of electrons.

Are these ions likely to be monodentate, bidentate or hexadentate (polydentate)? Give reasons for your answers.

 i $^-OOCCH_2CH_2COO^-$

 ii $HOCH_2CH_2COO^-$

 iii

   $^-OOCCH_2$ CH_2COO^-

      NCH_2CH_2N

   $^-OOCCH_2$ CH_2COO^-

g The structure of an ion of chromium is shown

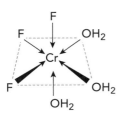

Figure 24.3: The structure of an ion of chromium.

Suggest why this ion is polar.

Exercise 24.4 Ligand exchange

This exercise will familiarise you with the idea of the substitution of one ligand for another in a complex. It also gives you practice in using stability constants to determine whether a particular ligand is able to substitute another in a particular complex.

TIPS

When constructing equilibrium expressions for the substitution of one ligand by another, we follow the same rules as for writing standard equilibrium expressions (see Exercise 21.3).

The units for K_{stab} can be worked out in a similar way: substitute $mol\,dm^{-3}$ for each concentration term and then cancel.

If we use log stability constant, there are no units.

---

a Write equilibrium expressions for the following **ligand exchange** reactions. In each case give the units for the **stability constant**.

  i $[Co(H_2O)_6]^{2+}(aq) + 6NH_3(aq) \rightleftharpoons [Co(NH_3)_6]^{2+}(aq)]$

  ii $[Co(H_2O)_6]^{2+}(aq) + 4Cl^-(aq) \rightleftharpoons [CoCl_4]^{2-}(aq) + 6H_2O(l)]$

  iii $[Cu(H_2O)_6]^{2+}(aq) + (EDTA)^{4-}(aq) \rightleftharpoons [Cu(EDTA)]^{2-}(aq) + 6H_2O(l)]$

b The stability constants for some complexes of Ni are given in the table.

Complex	Colour	Log stability constant
$[Ni(H_2O)_6]^{2+}(aq)$	green	0
$[Ni(NH_3)_6]^{2+}(aq)$	light violet	8.01
$[Ni(EDTA)]^{2+}(aq)$	blue	18.6

Table 24.1: Data table.

KEY WORDS

ligand exchange: in a complex ion, the substitution of one or more ligands by other ligands.

stability constant, K_{stab}: the equilibrium constant for the formation of a complex ion in a solvent from its constituent ions or molecules.

  i Describe what colour change occurs when:

  • concentrated aqueous ammonia is added to $[Ni(H_2O)_6]^{2+}(aq)$

  • water is added to $[Ni(EDTA)]^{2+}(aq)$

  • EDTA is added to $[Ni(NH_3)_6]^{2+}(aq)$

  In each case explain your answer.

  ii Write a balanced equation for the addition of concentrated aqueous ammonia to $[Ni(H_2O)_6]^{2+}(aq)$.

  iii Hexadentate ligands tend to have higher stability constants than bidentate ligands. Bidentate ligands tend to have higher stability constants than monodentate ligands.

  Suggest a value for the stability constant of $[Ni(en)_3]^{2+}(aq)$.

EXAM-STYLE QUESTIONS

1   Platinum is a transition element.

   a   State three differences between the physical properties of platinum
and those of a Group 2 element such as barium.   **[3]**

   b   The electron configuration of the outer shells of platinum is
$5s^25p^65d^96s^1$. Explain how this configuration shows that platinum is
a transition element.   **[1]**

   c   Platinum forms complex ions such as *cis*-platin.

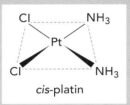

        cis-platin

Figure 24.4

    i   State the type of bonding between the Pt and Cl atoms.   **[1]**

    ii   Give the feature of Cl that is responsible for this bonding.   **[1]**

    iii   Suggest a value for the Cl—Pt—Cl bond angle.
Give a reason for your answer.   **[2]**

    iv   Draw a three-dimensional diagram of the stereoisomer
trans-platin.   **[1]**

                                 [Total: 9]

2   1,2-Diaminoethane, $H_2NCH_2CH_2NH_2$, is a bidentate ligand.

   a   Explain the meaning of a bidentate ligand.   **[3]**

   b   1,2-Diaminoethane (en) and 1,3-diaminopropane (pn) both form
complexes by ligand exchange with $[Cu(H_2O)_6]^{2+}(aq)$ ions.

    i   Write an equation for the reaction of 'en' with $[Cu(H_2O)_6]^{2+}(aq)$
to show the replacement of four of the water molecules with 'en'.   **[2]**

    ii   Deduce the equilibrium expression for the reaction above and
give the units.   **[2]**

    iii   The stability constants for the complexes with 'en' and 'pn' are shown in
the table.

Bidentate ligand	log K_{stab}
en	20.3
pn	17.7

Table 24.2

    State which ligand forms a more stable complex. Explain
your answer.   **[1]**

                                 [Total: 8]

TIPS

In part **1 a** note that
it is the *physical*
properties that are
required.

To answer part **c iii**
you will need to
refer to electron pair
repulsion theory
(see Chapter 4).

TIPS

In part **2 b i** be
careful to substitute
the correct number of
molecules.

In part **b ii** make
sure that each
concentration term is
raised to the correct
power.

CONTINUED

3 a Explain in terms of electron transfer and $E^\ominus$ values why Fe^{3+} ions can be reduced to Fe^{2+} ions by zinc. **[3]**

$$Zn^{2+}(aq) + 2e^- \rightleftharpoons Zn(s) \qquad E^\ominus = -0.76 \text{ V}$$
$$Fe^{3+}(aq) + e^- \rightleftharpoons Fe^{2+}(aq) \qquad E^\ominus = +0.77 \text{ V}$$

b Iron ions react with fluoride ions to form a complex, FeF_6^{3-}.

   i Deduce the oxidation number of Fe in this complex. **[1]**

   ii Suggest the shape of this complex. **[1]**

c i Fe^{3+} ions react with aqueous iodide ions to form iodine and Fe^{2+} ions. Write an equation for this reaction. **[2]**

   ii When sodium fluoride is added before the iodide ions, no iodine is formed. Explain why not. **[3]**

d Ethanedioic acid reacts with acidified potassium manganate(VII).

$$2MnO_4^- + 5H_2C_2O_4 + 6H^+ \rightarrow 2Mn^{2+} + 10CO_2 + 8H_2O$$

A 20.0 cm³ sample of aqueous ethanedioic acid was titrated with 0.0200 mol dm⁻³ acidified potassium manganate(VII). The titration was complete when 18.6 cm³ of potassium manganate(VII) had been added.

   i Describe and explain how the end-point of the titration was determined. **[2]**

   ii Calculate the concentration of the oxalic acid. **[3]**

   [Total: 15]

4 a Deduce the electronic configuration of:

   i a cobalt atom **[1]**

   ii a Co^{3+} ion. **[1]**

b The stability constants for some cobalt complexes are shown in the table.

Complex	log K_{stab}	Colour of complex
$[Co(H_2O)_6]^{2+}(aq)$	0	pink
$[Co(NH_3)_6]^{2+}(aq)$	4.3	green
$[Co(EDTA)]^{2-}(aq)$	16.3	pink

Table 24.3

   i Describe your observations when concentrated aqueous ammonia is added to $[Co(H_2O)_6]^{2+}(aq)$. Explain your answer. **[2]**

   ii Construct an equation for the reaction in part **i**. **[2]**

   iii The ligand EDTA is hexadentate. Explain the meaning of hexadentate. **[2]**

   iv Describe what you will observe if a small volume of ammonia is added to $[Co(EDTA)]^{2+}(aq)$. Explain your answer. **[2]**

c Cobalt forms a tetrahedral complex, $[CoCl_4]^{2-}(aq)$.

Draw the three-dimensional structure of this complex and determine the Cl—Co—Cl bond angle. **[3]**

TIPS

Part **3 a** revises electrode potentials and redox reactions (Chapters 7 and 20).

For part **c ii** you need to use the information in part **b**.

Part **d** is a titration calculation. Make sure that you show all the steps in the calculation.

TIP

In part **4 b i** and **iv** make sure that you give observations using the information in the table.

CONTINUED

d A complex ion of cobalt and chlorine has a tetrahedral structure.
A complex ion of cobalt and water has an octahedral structure.
The complexes have different colours.

The colour arises because of the splitting of degenerate d-orbitals.

  i Explain the meaning of the term degenerate. [1]

  ii Sketch the shape of a d-orbital. [1]

  iii The presence of the ligands causes electron repulsion between
the d-orbitals. The d-orbitals split to form non-degenerate
orbitals. Describe the difference in the splitting pattern for tetrahedral
and octadedral complexes. [2]

  iv Explain why different complexes have different colours. [5]

[Total: 22]

Chapter 25

Benzene and its compounds

CHAPTER OUTLINE

In this chapter you will learn how to:

- interpret, name and use the general, structural and displayed formulae of benzene and simple aryl compounds

- describe and explain the shape of and bond angles in benzene molecules in terms of σ and π-bonds

- describe the reactions of arenes such as benzene and methylbenzene in substitution reactions with chlorine and with bromine

- describe the nitration reactions of arenes such as benzene and methylbenzene

- describe the reactions of arenes in Friedel-Crafts alkylation and acylation reactions

- describe the complete oxidation of the side chain of methylbenzene to give benzoic acid

- describe the hydrogenation of the benzene ring to form a cyclohexane ring

- describe the mechanism of electrophilic substitution in arenes and the effect of delocalisation of electrons in such reactions

- interpret the difference in reactivity between benzene and chlorobenzene

- predict whether halogenation will occur in the side chain or in the benzene ring in arenes depending on the reaction conditions

- apply knowledge relating to the positions of the substituents in the electrophilic substitution of arenes and aryl compounds such as phenols

- describe the reactions (reagents and conditions) by which phenol can be prepared

- describe the reactions of phenol with bases, with sodium and with diazonium salts

- describe the nitration and bromination of the phenol aromatic ring and compare these reactions with benzene

- explain the acidity of phenol and the relative acidities of water, phenol and ethanol

- apply a knowledge of the reactions of phenols to the reactions of other phenolic compounds such as naphthol

Exercise 25.1 Aromatic hydrocarbons

This exercise will familiarise you with the structure of benzene in terms of atomic orbitals. It also revises drawing molecular and displayed formulae for aromatic compounds and how these compounds are named.

TIPS

In order to understand the structure of benzene, you need to know about hybridisation of atomic orbitals and the shapes of atomic orbitals. If you are not sure about these check Chapter 3 and Chapter 14 in the coursebook.

We write the structures of aromatic compounds (**arenes**), showing a circle in the middle to represent the delocalised electrons of the benzene ring. The numbering positions usually run from the top (position 1), clockwise. The substituted groups are named in alphabetic order and the lowest number given to the one with the letter lowest in the alphabet. You will, however, come across other ways of naming. Two examples are given here.

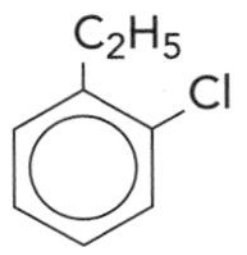

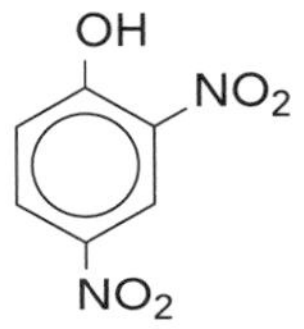

1-chloro-2-ethylbenzene   2,4-dinitrophenol

Figure 25.1: Structures of two aromatic compounds.

KEY WORD

arenes: hydrocarbons containing one or more benzene rings.

a   Copy the passage about bonding in benzene, selecting the correct word from each of the underlined choices.

Each carbon atom in the benzene ring forms sp / sp^2 / sp^3 hybrid orbitals, sharing one pair of electrons with each of the two neighbouring carbon / hydrogen atoms and one pair with a carbon / hydrogen atom. These are pi / sigma bonds. The remaining p / s / d electron from each carbon atom contributes to a pi / sigma bond by sideways / end-on overlap of p / s / d type atomic orbitals. These form two / six rings of delocalised / localised electrons above and below the benzene ring. To allow maximum overlap of electrons, the benzene ring must be planar / zig-zag. The bond angles around each carbon atom are 90° / 109.5° / 120°.

b   State two pieces of experimental evidence that suggest that benzene does not have alternating double and single bonds.

c   Draw structural formulae for these compounds. Show the aromatic ring as a hexagon with a circle in it.

i   4-nitrophenol
iii   (chloro)methylbenzene
v   2,4,6-tribromophenol
ii   1,2-dimethylbenzene
iv   1-methyl-3-nitrobenzene
vi   1-bromo-4-ethylbenzene

d   Draw displayed formulae for:
i   ethylbenzene   ii   2-aminophenol   iii   3-methylbenzoic acid

Exercise 25.2 Halogenation and nitration of benzene

This exercise revises the mechanism of electrophilic substitution of halogen atoms or NO_2 groups into a benzene ring. It also familiarises you with some terms used when discussing reaction mechanisms.

TIP

The electron density in the benzene ring is open to attack by electrophiles because of the presence of delocalised electrons above and below the plane of the ring.

a Figure 25.2 shows the stages involved in the bromination of benzene.

Stage A $Br - Br$ $FeBr_3$ ⟶ Br^+ + _____

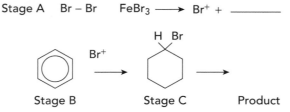

Figure 25.2: Stages involved in the bromination of benzene.

KEY WORD

polarisation: the ability of an ion or molecule to pull electrons in a covalent bond in an adjacent molecule towards it and so cause the adjacent molecule to become polar.

i Copy and complete Stage A to show:

- the **polarisation** of the bromine molecule by $FeBr_3$

- the movement of electron pairs (use a curly arrow)

- the formula of the other ionic product.

ii Explain why $FeBr_3$ is able to polarise a bromine molecule.

iii Copy and complete stages B and C by using curly arrows and adding a suitable symbol to the benzene ring in C.

iv Complete your diagram by drawing the structure of the product.

v Why is this mechanism described as electrophilic? Name the electrophile.

vi Suggest a different halogen carrier that can be used to produce chlorobenzene from a mixture of benzene and chlorine and explain how it attacks the benzene ring.

vii State the names of the organic products formed when the halogen carrier in part **a vi** reacts with a mixture of methylbenzene and chlorine.

b When concentrated nitric and sulfuric acids are mixed NO_2^+ ions are formed.

$$HNO_3 + 2H_2SO_4 \rightarrow NO_2^+ + 2HSO_4^- + H_3O^+$$

i Which is the stronger acid? Explain your answer.

ii Explain why NO_2^+ is an electrophile when it reacts with benzene.

iii Draw the structure of the intermediate formed when NO_2^+ ions react with benzene.

iv Describe how this intermediate forms nitrobenzene.

TIP

In part **b iv** you need to consider whether the nitro-group is 2,4- or 3,5-directing.

Exercise 25.3 Some other reactions of aromatic compounds

This exercise revises the electrophilic mechanism involved in the alkylation and **acylation** of benzene.

It also familiarises you with the reagents used to oxidise or reduce methylbenzene as well as how to introduce a Cl atom into an alkyl side chain attached to an aromatic ring.

a The mechanism of a typical **Friedel-Crafts reaction** is shown in Figure 25.3.

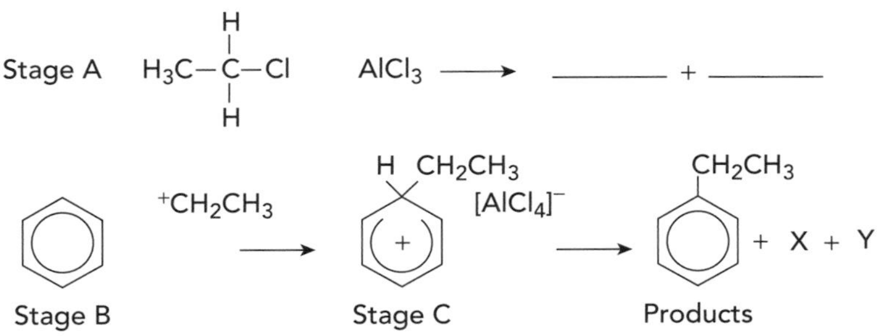

Figure 25.3: The mechanism of a typical Friedel-Crafts reaction.

i Copy and complete Stage A to show:

- the polarisation of the halogenoalkane molecule by $AlCl_3$
- the movement of electron pairs (use a curly arrow)
- the formula of the ionic products.

ii Copy and complete stages B and C by using curly arrows to show the movement of electron pairs.

iii State the name of the organic product.

iv Write the formulae for X and Y.

v Why is this mechanism described as electrophilic? Name the electrophile.

vi What is the formula of the acyl halide used in the synthesis of the ketone, $C_6H_5COC_3H_7$ from benzene using the Friedel–Crafts reaction?

b When chlorine is bubbled through boiling methylbenzene for a few minutes in the presence of light, one or more chlorine atoms may be substituted into the methyl group but not into the benzene ring.

i State the type of reaction and mechanism which take place.

ii Describe the first step in this reaction mechanism.

c i Copy and complete this equation for the oxidation of methylbenzene to form an acid.

$$C_6H_5-CH_3 + \underline{\hspace{2cm}} \rightarrow C_6H_5- \underline{\hspace{2cm}} + \underline{\hspace{2cm}}$$

ii State the name of the organic product.

iii Give the name of a suitable oxidising agent.

iv What conditions are needed for this reaction?

d i Copy and complete the reduction of methylbenzene using excess reducing agent.

$$C_6H_5-CH_3 + \underline{\hspace{2cm}} \xrightarrow{Ni} \underline{\hspace{2cm}}$$

ii State the name of the product.

iii What is the purpose of the Ni?

iv What conditions are needed for this reaction?

TIP

In part **a**, an alkyl group, e.g. C_2H_5, or an **acyl group**, e.g. CH_3CO, is substituted into an aromatic ring.

KEY WORDS

acylation: the process of inserting an acyl group, CH_3CO, into a molecule.

acyl group: a group which contains both an alkyl and a carbonyl group, e.g. CH_3CO-.

Friedel-Crafts reaction: the electrophilic substitution of an alkyl or acyl group into a benzene ring.

TIP

In parts **c** and **d** remember that oxidation can be shown by [O] and reduction by [H] if the equations could prove difficult to write. If hydrogen gas is used for reduction, we can use the symbol H_2.

Exercise 25.4 Phenol and its reactions

This exercise revises the idea that the substitution of a hydrogen atom in the benzene ring by an –OH group causes the ring to become activated. So phenol, C_6H_5OH, is more reactive with electrophilic reagents than is benzene. The exercise also familiarises you with the difference in the charge in the ring between phenol and benzene and how this affects the position of substitution.

a   Suggest reactants and conditions for the preparation of phenol.

b   Copy and complete the table to show the difference in reaction conditions when benzene and phenol react with various electrophiles.

Reaction	Reaction conditions with benzene	Reaction conditions with phenol	Comparison of ease and extent of reaction
bromination			benzene: need excess Br_2 to get 2 Br atoms substituted phenol: 3 Br atoms easily substituted
nitration			
substitution of SO_3H group		heat with H_2SO_4 at 100 °C	phenol: quite difficult to substitute a second SO_3H group
substitution of NO group		$NaNO_2$, H_2SO_4, (electrophile only stable at low temperatures)	

Table 25.1: Difference in reaction conditions.

c   A diagram of phenol is shown in Figure 25.4. Use the information in this diagram and the word list to help you complete the passage.

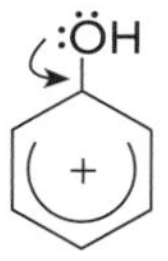

Figure 25.4: Phenol

activating	deficient density	electrophiles	intermediate
oxygen	pair	positive	reduction	substituted

The –OH group in phenol is an ＿＿＿＿＿＿ group. This means that the reaction

with ＿＿＿＿＿ is much more rapid than with benzene. The ＿＿＿＿＿ atom

in the –OH group in phenol has an electron ＿＿＿＿＿ that can be partly donated

to the carbon atom next to it. The ＿＿＿＿＿ formed when an electrophile

is ＿＿＿＿＿ has partial ＿＿＿＿＿ charge in various parts of the ring.

The ＿＿＿＿＿ in the positive charge by the donation of electrons means that

the electron ＿＿＿＿＿ in various parts of the ring increases. This makes the

aryl ring more open to attack by electron ＿＿＿＿＿ electrophiles.

> **TIP**
>
> In part **c**, remember that an intermediate is more stable if the positive charge is reduced.

d Copy and complete these reactions of phenol with sodium, potassium hydroxide and a **diazonium salt**.

   i   ___ C_6H_5OH + ___ Na → _____ + _____

   ii C_6H_5OH + KOH → _____ + _____

   iii $C_6H_5O^-Na^+$ + $C_{10}H_7N^+{\equiv}NCl^-$ → _____ + _____

e Copy these phrases about the acidity of phenol, water and ethanol by selecting the correct word from each of the choices in underlined.

   i   Phenol is a <u>stronger</u> / <u>weaker</u> acid than ethanol. This is shown by its <u>higher</u> / <u>lower</u> K_a value.

   ii   One of the <u>p</u> / <u>s</u> orbitals from the <u>oxygen</u> / <u>hydrogen</u> atom of phenol forms a delocalised system with the p electrons in the aryl ring and this <u>increases</u> / <u>reduces</u> the <u>negative</u> / <u>positive</u> charge on the phenoxide ion. This makes the phenoxide ion <u>less</u> / <u>more</u> stable.

   iii In alcohols and water, there is no <u>delocalisation</u> / <u>electronegativity</u> between the oxygen atoms and the other <u>groups</u> / <u>ions</u> present and so alcohols and water are not acidic.

   iv Phenol is a <u>stronger</u> / <u>weaker</u> acid than ethanoic acid. This is shown by the fact that phenol does not react with <u>sodium carbonate</u> / <u>sodium hydroxide</u>.

Exercise 25.5 Substitution in the aromatic ring

This exercise familiarises you with the idea that the position of substitution varies with the nature of the substituent already present.

a Draw the structures of the products formed in each of these cases.

   i   One Cl atom is substituted into $C_6H_5NH_2$

   ii   Two NO_2 groups are substituted into $C_6H_5-CH_3$

   iii Two Br atoms are substituted into C_6H_5-COOH

   iv One NO_2 group is substituted into C_6H_5Cl

   v   Three Br atoms are substituted into C_6H_5OH

   vi Two Cl atoms are substituted into C_6H_5CN

   vii In the dark, two Cl atoms are substituted into $C_6H_5-C_2H_5$.

b Benzene sulfonic acid has the formula $C_6H_5SO_3H$. It can be synthesised from benzene by refluxing with fuming sulfuric acid. The electrophile is SO_3.

   i   Use ideas about electronegativity and bond polarisation to suggest why SO_3 acts as an electrophile.

   ii   Describe the first step in the reaction of SO_3 with benzene.

   iii The $-SO_3H$ group directs an incoming electrophile in the same way as an NO_2 group. In what position(s) will a Cl atom be substituted into the aryl ring?

c Chlorine atoms can be substituted into an alkyl side chain instead of into the ring. For example C_6H_5–C_2H_5 can be converted to C_6H_5–C_2H_4Cl.

  i State the reagents and conditions needed for this reaction.

  ii State the name of the mechanism in this reaction.

EXAM-STYLE QUESTIONS

1 Methylbenzene can be nitrated using a mixture of nitric acid and sulfuric acid.

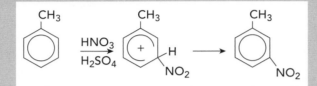

Figure 25.5

a Give the formula of the **nitrating agent**. [1]

b State the type of reaction and its mechanism. [2]

c Explain how the intermediate changes to the product. [4]

d The CH_3– group is an **activating group**. Explain what this means. [3]

e The methyl group in methylbenzene can be chlorinated.

  i State the conditions needed for this reaction. [2]

  ii Describe the mechanism of this reaction. [1]

f Compare the nitration of methylbenzene with the nitration of phenol. Give any differences in the reagents used and name the products formed. [6]

[Total: 19]

2 a Phenol ionises in water to form a weakly acidic solution.

  i Write an equation for the reaction of phenol with water to form phenoxide ions, $C_6H_5O^-$. [2]

  ii The negative charge on the phenoxide ion is spread over the whole ion as one of the lone pairs of electrons on the oxygen atom overlaps with the delocalised electrons in the ring. Explain how this makes phenol more acidic than ethanol. [3]

  iii Write an equation for the reaction of phenol with sodium. [2]

b Phenol reacts with excess bromine water.

  i Name the product of this reaction. [1]

  ii Explain why phenol reacts more readily than benzene with bromine. [3]

c i Give the name of the reagents needed for benzene to react with bromine. [2]

  ii Give the formula of the electrophile that attacks benzene and explain how this acts as an electrophile. [3]

KEY WORDS

nitrating agent: a compound, or combination of compounds, that are responsible for inserting an NO_2 group into another molecule.

activating group: a group attached to a benzene ring which makes the conditions needed for substitution in the ring easier.

TIP

For part **2 a** you will have to use your knowledge about acids and the stability of ions. Although this may be new to you, there is enough information given for you to answer the question.

CONTINUED

d The structure of 1-naphthol is shown in Figure 25.6.

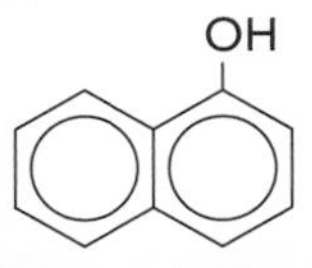

Figure 25.6

1-Naphthol reacts with the diazonium salt $C_6H_5N^+\equiv NCl^-$ to form an azo dye.

i Give the conditions required for this reaction. [2]

ii Suggest the structural formula of the azo dye formed. Show the arene rings as hexagons with circles. [1]

[Total: 19]

TIP

In part **2 d**, remember that the diazonium salt couples at the opposite end of the molecule to the OH group.

3 Benzene can undergo alkylation using the Friedel–Crafts reaction.

a Define the term alkylation. [2]

b State the type of reaction and its mechanism. [2]

c Give the name of the reagents and conditions needed to synthesise compound A from benzene. [3]

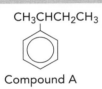

Compound A

Figure 25.7

TIPS

Make sure that you know the conditions and reagents required for the alkylation and reduction.

Refer back to Exercise 25.3 to revise alkylation.

d Deduce the molecular formula of compound A. [1]

e i The Friedel–Crafts reaction can be used to introduce an acyl group into the benzene ring. Write the formula of the organic compound needed to form $C_6H_5COCH_2CH_3$ from benzene. [1]

ii Other than being aromatic, state the name of the class of compounds that $C_6H_5COCH_2CH_3$ belongs to. [1]

f i Ethylbenzene is reduced by hydrogen. State the conditions needed for this reaction. [2]

ii Name the product of this reaction. [1]

[Total: 13]

> Chapter 26

Carboxylic acids and their derivatives

CHAPTER OUTLINE

In this chapter you will learn how to:

- describe and explain the relative acidity of carboxylic acids and of chlorine-substituted ethanoic acids

- describe how some carboxylic acids, such as methanoic acid and ethandioic acid can be further oxidised

- describe the reactions of carboxylic acids in the preparation of acyl chlorides

- describe the hydrolysis of acyl chlorides

- describe the reactions of acyl chlorides with alcohols, phenols, ammonia and primary or secondary amines

- explain the relative ease of hydrolysis of acyl chlorides, alkyl chlorides and aryl chlorides

- describe the condensation (addition-elimination) mechanism for the reactions of acyl chlorides

- recall the reactions by which esters can be produced using ethyl ethanoate and phenyl benzoate as examples

Exercise 26.1 Acidity of carboxylic acids

This exercise revises weak acids and familiarises you with how electron-withdrawing groups or electron-donating groups affect the relative strengths of carboxylic acids and substituted carboxylic acids.

a   Structure A in Figure 26.1 shows the generalised structure of a carboxylic acid.

   The arrows show the **electron-withdrawing effects**. Use this diagram and the word list below to help you copy and complete these sentences about why carboxylic acids are stronger acids than are alcohols.

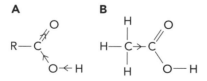

Figure 26.1: The generalised structure of a carboxylic acid.

carbon	charge	delocalisation	hydrogen	ion
stronger	stable	towards	weaken	withdrawing

KEY WORDS

electron-withdrawing effect: the ability of atoms or groups in an organic compound to pull the electrons in bonds towards themselves. The greater the electro-negativity of the atoms, the stronger the electron withdrawing effect.

The electron _____ groups bonded to the _____ atom next to

the –COOH group in carboxylic acids makes the acid _____ . These

groups _____ the O—H bond more than in alcohols, so that a COO⁻

_____ is formed. This is because in carboxylic acids, the electrons in the

C—O bond are drawn _____ the C=O bond and away from the O—H

bond. The electron withdrawing groups increase the _____ of the negative

_____ on the COO⁻ group causing this ion to be more _____. So

the ion is less likely to accept a _____ ion and form a molecule compared

with alcohol, where no such stabilisation occurs.

b Some K_a values are given:
HCOOH 1.6×10^{-4} mol dm⁻³
CH$_3$COOH 1.7×10^{-5} mol dm⁻³
CH$_2$ClCOOH 1.3×10^{-3} mol dm⁻³
Structure B in Figure 26.1 shows ethanoic acid.
Use the information in this diagram and the values of K_a to describe and explain the relative acidities of:

   i CH$_2$ClCOOH and CH$_3$COOH
   ii CH$_3$COOH and HCOOH

c Put these acids in order of their acidity. Explain your answer.
CCl$_3$COOH   CH$_2$ClCOOH   CHCl$_2$COOH

d Put these acids in order of their acidity. Explain your answer.
CH$_3$CH$_2$CHClCOOH   CH$_2$ClCH$_2$CH$_2$COOH   CH$_3$CHClCH$_2$COOH

TIP

You might find a quick revision of the meaning of K_a useful before doing part **b** (see Chapter 21).

Exercise 26.2 Reactions of carboxylic acids

This exercise revises the oxidation of carboxylic acids and the formation of acyl chlorides. Some of this material builds upon what you already know about the formation of carboxylic acids from alcohols (Chapter 17).

a Some reactions of carboxylic acids are given here but the products have been left out. Match the possible products in the list to the reactants. Each product may be used once or more than once.
Products: Ag; CH$_3$COCl; CO$_2$; HCl; HCOOCH$_3$; H$_2$O; H$_3$PO$_3$; Mn^{2+}; POCl$_3$; SO$_2$

   i methanoic acid + methanol + H$_2$SO$_4$ $\xrightarrow{heat}$

   ii methanoic acid + acidified potassium manganate(VII) $\xrightarrow{heat}$

   iii ethanoic acid + sulfur dichloride oxide $\xrightarrow{heat}$

   iv methanoic acid + silver nitrate in ammonia $\xrightarrow{warm}$

   v ethanoic acid + phosphorus(V) chloride $\xrightarrow{\hspace{1cm}}$

TIPS

To get the maximum advantage from part **a** and **b** of this exercise, it is best to revise these topics first to see how much you can remember.

In part **c** think about the key functional groups in the structure of methanoic acid.

vi ethanedioic acid + acidified potassium manganate(VII) $\xrightarrow{\textit{warm}}$

vii ethanoic acid + phosphorus trichloride ⟶

b Copy and complete these equations:

i $HCOOH + [O] \rightarrow$ _____ + _____

ii $C_2H_5COOH + C_3H_7OH \rightarrow$ _____ + _____

iii $CH_3COOH + KOH \rightarrow$ _____ + _____

iv $C_3H_7COCl + CH_3OH \rightarrow$ _____ + _____

v $HOOCCOOH +$ ___ $Na \rightarrow$ _____ + _____

vi $C_2H_5COOH + PCl_5 \rightarrow$ _____ + _____ + _____

vii $CH_3COOH + SOCl_2 \rightarrow$ _____ + _____ + _____

viii $HOOCCOOH + [O] \rightarrow$ _____ + _____

c **i** Draw the displayed formula for methanoic acid.

ii Use this formula to explain why Fehling's solution is reduced by methanoic acid.

iii Write the equation for this reaction using [O] to represent the oxidising agent (Fehling's solution).

iv Write the half-equation for the oxidation of methanoic acid in terms of electron transfer to form H^+ ions.

d Ethanedioic acid reacts with potassium manganate(VII).

i Complete the equation for this reaction.

$$5(COOH)_2 + 2MnO_4^- + \underline{\hspace{2cm}} H^+ \rightarrow$$

$$\underline{\hspace{2cm}} Mn^{2+} + \underline{\hspace{2cm}} + \underline{\hspace{2cm}}$$

ii Figure 26.2 shows how the concentration of potassium manganate(VII) changes as the reaction progresses. The reaction is catalysed by Mn^{2+} ions. How is this consistent with the results from the graph?

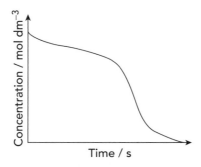

Figure 26.2: Changes in the concentration of potassium manganate(VII).

Exercise 26.3 Acyl chlorides

This exercise revises the reactions of the acyl chlorides, ROCl, and familiarises you with the mechanism of their typical condensation reactions. It also reminds you of the reasons why the rates of hydrolysis of acyl chlorides, halogenoalkanes and aryl chlorides differ.

a **i**   Draw the displayed formula of ethanoyl chloride, CH_3COCl.

    ii   On your structure, show the polarisation as δ^+ and δ^-.

   iii Explain why ethanoyl chloride is very reactive.

   iv Which of these species are nucleophiles that react with ethanoyl chloride?

       Br^+; C_2H_5OH; H_2O; NH_3; NO_2^+; H_3O^+; $(CH_3)_2NH$

b Copy and complete these equations:

    i $C_6H_5COCl + NH_3 \rightarrow$

    ii $C_2H_5COCl + CH_3OH \rightarrow$

   iii $CH_3CH_2CH_2COCl + C_2H_5NH_2 \rightarrow$

   iv $C_6H_5O^-Na^+ + C_6H_5COCl \rightarrow$

    v $CH_3COCl + C_2H_5OH \rightarrow$

   vi $C_6H_5COCl + C_6H_5OH \rightarrow$

  vii $(C_2H_5)_2NH + CH_3COCl \rightarrow$

 viii $CH_3COCl + NH_3 \rightarrow$

c The mechanism of hydrolysis of ethanoyl chloride is shown in Figure 26.3.

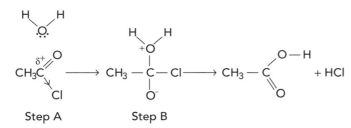

Step A   Step B

Figure 26.3: The mechanism of hydrolysis of ethanoyl chloride.

    i   Explain why water is a polar molecule.

    ii   Copy and complete stage A to show the movement of electron pairs from water and in the C=O group.

   iii Which is the nucleophile in step A?

   iv Describe what happens in step B.

    v   Why is this mechanism described as an addition-elimination reaction?

   vi What is an alternative name for an addition-elimination reaction?

d Explanations for the relative ease of hydrolysis of acyl chlorides, alkyl chlorides and aryl chlorides are described below but the statements have become muddled up. Put these phrases in the correct order for each chloride then write them out.

    A Hydrolysis of an alkyl chloride needs…

    B Aryl chlorides…

    C Hydrolysis of an acyl chloride needs…

D …with the pi electrons in the benzene ring.

E …the p orbitals from the chlorine atoms partly overlap…

F The carbon atom bonded to the chlorine is strongly δ^+…

G …no special conditions.

H … o it needs a stronger nucleophile to attack the carbon atom.

I This causes the C—Cl bond to have enough double bond character…

J …are not easily hydrolysed because…

K …because it is also attached to a strongly electronegative oxygen atom.

L The carbon atom bonded to the chlorine is only weakly δ^+…

M This makes the attack of a nucleophile very rapid.

N …a strong alkali such as sodium hydroxide.

O …to make hydrolysis impossible.

e Ethanoyl chloride reacts with ethanol to form an ester.

$$CH_3COCl + C_2H_5OH \rightarrow CH_3COOC_2H_5 + HCl$$

i State the mechanism and type of reaction which occurs.

ii Give the name of the organic product of the reaction.

iii Show, using displayed formulae, the first stage of the reaction mechanism. On your diagram, show the movement of the electron pairs and the polarisation in the bonds of the ethanoyl chloride.

> **TIP**
>
> In part **e iii** make sure that you draw the displayed formulae large enough to show the curly arrows correctly. The diagram in part **c** should help you with the arrangement of the molecules.

EXAM-STYLE QUESTIONS

1 Ethanoic acid is a weak acid.

a Write equations and give the conditions for the reaction of ethanoic acid with:

   i propan-1-ol   **[3]**

   ii sulfur dichloride oxide, $SOCl_2$.   **[2]**

b The K_a values for three substituted carboxylic acids are given here:

   CH_2FCOOH $K_a = 2.9 \times 10^{-3}\ mol\,dm^{-3}$

   $CH_2ClCOOH$ $K_a = 1.3 \times 10^{-3}\ mol\,dm^{-3}$

   CH_2ICOOH $K_a = 6.8 \times 10^{-4}\ mol\,dm^{-3}$

   i Explain the difference in these values.   **[5]**

   ii Predict the value of K_a for $CH_2BrCOOH$ **[1]**

c Methanoic acid reacts with silver nitrate dissolved in ammonia.

   i Write the equation for this reaction using [O] to represent the oxidising agent.   **[1]**

   ii Give the feature of the methanoic acid molecule that is responsible for this reaction.   **[1]**

                                    [Total: 13]

> **TIP**
>
> Before answering this question make sure that you know about the chemical behaviour of methanoic acid, and have an understanding of K_a values (Chapter 21).

> **TIP**
>
> Part **b** requires a knowledge of the electron-withdrawing effects of substituents.

CONTINUED

2 High yields of an ester can be made in a two-step reaction:

carboxylic acid → acyl chloride → ester

   a **i** State the reagents and conditions would you use to convert the ethanoic acid to ethanoyl chloride using a compound containing phosphorus. **[2]**

      ii Construct a balanced equation for this reaction. **[1]**

   b Butyl ethanoate is then made by adding excess butan-1-ol to the ethanoyl chloride drop by drop in a vessel to which a tube of **drying agent** is attached. Boiling points: butanol 390.3 K; butyl ethanoate 394 K; ethanoic acid 391 K

      i Construct the equation for this reaction. **[1]**

      ii Explain why the reaction must be carried out in a fume cupboard. **[1]**

      iii Explain why the butanol was added slowly. **[1]**

      iv The drying tube prevents water entering the apparatus. Explain why water must be prevented from entering. **[1]**

      v When the reaction is complete, the ester is separated from the rest of the reaction mixture. Suggest how this can be done. **[2]**

   c Calculate the mass of butyl ethanoate obtained from 15 g of ethanoic acid assuming that the percentage yield in each step is 90%. **[3]**

[Total: 12]

3 Butanoic acid and butanol both have an –OH group. Butanoic acid is a weak acid but butanol exhibits no acidity.

   a Explain the difference in acidity of butanoic acid and butanol. **[4]**

   b Butanoyl chloride can be made by the action of sulfur dichloride oxide on butanoic acid.

      i Write an equation for this reaction. **[1]**

      ii State a condition that is required for this reaction. **[1]**

   c Butanoyl chloride can be used to **acylate** benzene. A mixture of aluminium chloride and benzene is placed in a flask and butanoyl chloride is added slowly down the reflux condenser connected to a drying tube. The mixture is refluxed at 50 °C for an hour.

      i When butanoyl chloride is added, white fumes are seen. Suggest the name of these fumes. **[1]**

      ii State the purpose of the aluminium chloride. **[1]**

      iii Give the formula of the ion derived from butanoyl chloride which attacks the benzene molecule, and state the type of mechanism. **[2]**

      iv When the reaction is complete, the contents of the flask are poured into cold water containing sodium carbonate. State the purpose of the sodium carbonate. **[1]**

      v After leaving the mixture, two layers are formed. Suggest why two layers are formed and how you can separate these. **[2]**

      vi Write an equation for the acylation of benzene using butanoyl chloride. **[1]**

TIP

Question 2 is about the formation of an ester by a two-step route involving an acyl chloride. It involves ideas about practical procedures as well as a calculation. Make sure that you know about practical procedures.

KEY WORDS

drying agent: a compound which removes excess water from a substance.

acylate: to substitute a CH_3CO- group into a compound.

TIPS

To answer part **3 a** you should consider electron withdrawing effects and stabilisation of the anion.

TIP

Part **c** involves ideas about practical procedures as well as revisiting some of the material in Chapter 25. Make sure that you have revised Exercise 25.3 before you attempt this question.

CONTINUED

d Ethanoyl chloride is hydrolysed rapidly by water. Chloroethane is hydrolysed slowly by aqueous sodium hydroxide. Chlorobenzene is only hydrolysed with OH^- ions under high pressure at 350 °C.

Explain the differences in these rates of hydrolysis. **[6]**

[Total: 20]

4 a Ethanoyl chloride reacts with ammonia.

$$CH_3COCl + NH_3 \rightarrow CH_3CONH_2 + HCl$$

i Give the name of the organic product of this reaction. **[1]**

ii State the mechanism and type of reaction which occurs. **[2]**

iii Explain why NH_3 is a polar molecule. **[2]**

iv Draw a diagram to show the first stage of the reaction mechanism. On your diagram, show the movement of the electron pairs and the polarisation in the bonds of the ethanoyl chloride. **[4]**

v Figure 26.4 shows the formula of the intermediate formed in this reaction.

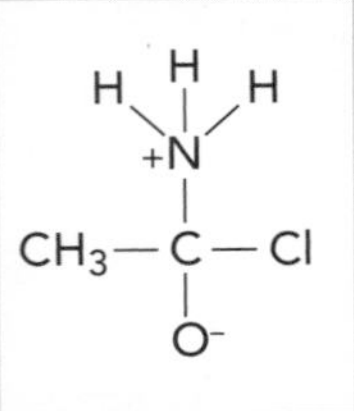

Figure 26.4

Copy this diagram. Use curly arrows to show the movement of electron pairs which takes place in order to form the product. **[3]**

b Ethanoyl chloride is hydrolysed by water.

i State the meaning of the term hydrolysis. **[1]**

ii Draw the structural formula for the organic product formed in this reaction. **[1]**

c Phenyl benzoate is an ester made by reacting benzoyl chloride, C_6H_5COCl, with phenol.

i Draw the displayed formula of phenyl benzoate. **[2]**

ii A few drops of aqueous sodium hydroxide are added to the phenol before the benzyl chloride is added. Suggest a reason why sodium hydroxide is added. **[1]**

[Total: 17]

TIP

Remember that mechanism is electrophilic, nucleophilic, free radical, whereas type of reaction is oxidation, addition and so on.

> Chapter 27

Organic nitrogen compounds

CHAPTER OUTLINE

In this chapter you will learn how to:

- describe the formation of primary and secondary amines (reaction of ammonia with halogenoalkanes / reduction of amides with $LiAlH_4$ / reduction of nitriles with $LiAlH_4$ or H_2 / Ni)

- describe the formation of phenylamine (reduction of nitrobenzene with tin / concentrated HCl)

- describe and explain the basicity of amines and the relative basicity of ammonia, ethylamine and phenylamine

- describe the reaction of phenylamine with aqueous bromine

- describe the reaction of phenylamine and with nitric(III) acid to give a diazonium salt and phenol, followed by coupling with benzenediazonium chloride and phenol to make a dye

- identify the azo group and describe the formation of other azo dyes

- describe the formation of amides from the reaction between amines and acyl chlorides and the hydrolysis of amides by aqueous alkali or acid

- describe the reactions of amides with aqueous acid or alkali and the reduction of the CO group with $LiAlH_4$

- explain why amides are weaker bases than amines

- describe the acid–base properties of amino acids and the formation of zwitterions including the isoelectric point

- describe the formation of amide (peptide) bonds between amino acids to give di-peptides and tri-peptides

- describe electrophoresis and the effect of pH, using peptides and amino acids as examples

Exercise 27.1 Amines

This exercise familiarises you with the structures and reactions of amines. It also revises ideas about comparative basicity of ammonia and amines using the concept of the relative electron-donating abilities of alkyl and aryl groups.

a   Classify these amines as **primary**, secondary or tertiary.

   i $CH_3NHCH_2CH_3$

   ii $CH_3CH_2NH_2$

   iii $(CH_3)_3N$

   iv $C_6H_5NHCH_2CH_2CH_3$

   v $(CH_3)_2NCH_2CH_2CH_3$

b   Name these amines or amine salts.

   i $CH_3CH_2CH_2NH_2$

   ii $C_3H_7NH_3^+Cl^-$

   iii $C_6H_5NH_3^+Cl^-$

   iv $(C_2H_5)_2NH$

   v $(CH_3)_3N$

   vi $CH_3CH_2CH(NH_2)CH_3$

c   Write equations for:

   i   The reaction of hydrochloric acid with methylamine.

   ii   The reaction of sulfuric acid with propylamine.

   iii   The reaction of hydrochloric acid with diethylamine.

d   Explain why ethylamine is more basic than ammonia but phenylamine is less basic than ammonia.

e   Link the reactants in **i–v** with the products and the reaction conditions. Each reaction condition or product may be used once or more than once.

   Products: $CH_3CH_2CH_2NH_2$; $C_6H_5NH_2$; $CH_3CH_2NH_2$; CH_3CN

   Reaction conditions: concentrated hydrochloric acid; cyanide ions; dry ether; excess ammonia; in ethanol; lithium tetrahydridoaluminate; reflux; tin; warm

   i CH_3CH_2Br

   ii CH_3Br

   iii CH_3CH_2CN

   iv CH_3CONH_2

   v $C_6H_5NO_2$

f   Write equations for:

   i   The formation of propylamine from a bromoalkane.

   ii   The formation of butylamine from a nitrile.

   iii   The formation of phenylamine from nitrobenzene.

   iv   The formation of propylamine from an amide.

   v   The formation of a secondary amine from the amide $CH_3CH_2CONHCH_3$

g   State the names of two different reducing agents that can be used to produce amines from nitriles.

TIP

We name secondary or tertiary amines with the same alkyl groups by putting the prefix di- or tri- before the alkyl group, e.g. dimethylamine.

KEY WORDS

primary amines: compounds where one hydrogen atom in ammonia has been substituted by an alkyl group.

TIP

When comparing the basic character of amines, remember that alkyl groups are electron releasing and that a p orbital of the N atom in phenylamine overlaps with delocalised electrons in the benzene ring.

TIP

Amines can be formed from alkyl halides, cyanides or amides. You need to remember the reactants and conditions.

Exercise 27.2 Phenylamine and diazonium salts

This exercise familiarises you with the reactions of phenylamine with acids, bases and with diazonium salts. It also revises the ideas about substitution in aromatic rings.

a Bromine reacts with phenylamine.

- **i** Draw the structure of the product formed.
- **ii** What conditions are needed for this reaction?

b

- **i** Write an equation for the reaction of phenylamine with hydrochloric acid.
- **ii** Write an equation for the reaction of phenylamine hydrochloride with sodium hydroxide.

c Figure 27.1 shows a **diazotisation** reaction to form a diazonium salt and the **coupling reaction** to form an **azo dye**.

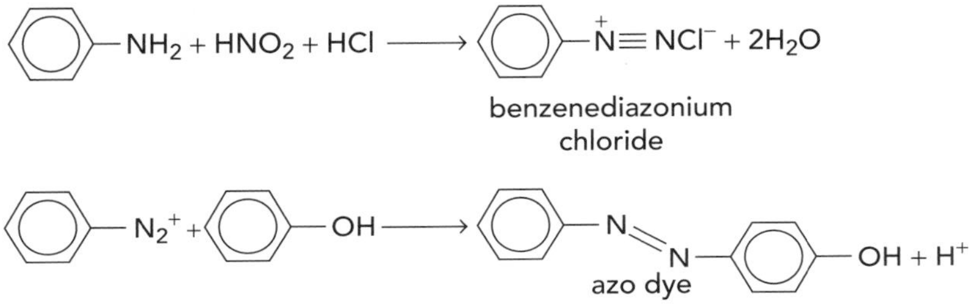

Figure 27.1: A diazotisation reaction.

- **i** Nitric(III) acid is made from $NaNO_2$ and HCl. Give the chemical name of $NaNO_2$ and write an equation for this reaction.
- **ii** Why is diazotisation carried out at 10 °C?
- **iii** Construct an equation to show the decomposition of aqueous benzenediazonium chloride. Nitrogen is one of the products formed.
- **iv** What type of reagent is the benzenediazonium ion when it attacks phenol?
- **v** Draw the structure of the azo dye formed when the reactants in Figure 27.2 are involved in diazotisation and coupling.

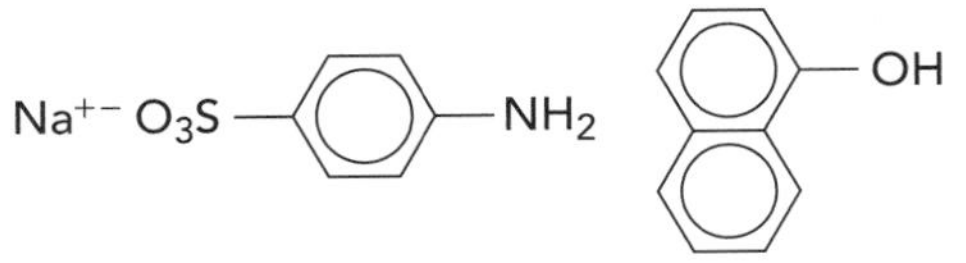

Figure 27.2: Reactants.

TIPS

A more common name for nitric(III) acid is nitrous acid.

When an NH_2 group is attached directly to the benzene ring, it directs the same substitution as an –OH group and it activates the ring.

KEY WORDS

diazotisation: the reaction between phenylamine and nitrous acid (HNO_2) to give a diazonium salt in the first step in preparing an azo dye.

azo dyes: coloured compounds formed on the addition of phenol (or another aryl compound) to a solution containing a diazonium ion. They contain the N≡N group.

coupling reaction: the reaction between a diazonium salt and an alkaline solution of phenol (or similar compound) to make an azo dye.

Exercise 27.3 Amino acids and electrophoresis

This exercise familiarises you with the structure, acid–base characteristics and some reactions of amino acids. It also revises the use of electrophoresis in separating amino acids and **proteins**.

a Write equations for the reaction of glycine, H_2NCH_2COOH, with:

   i   hydrochloric acid

   ii   methanol in the presence of hydrochloric acid

   iii phosphorus pentachloride

   iv lithium tetrahydridoaluminate.

b Write equations to show the reactions of the following **zwitterions** under acidic (H^+) or basic (OH^-) conditions. The symbols in brackets are the side chains of the **amino acid**.

   i $^+H_3NCH(CH_3)COO^-$ under alkaline conditions.

   ii $^+H_3NCH(CH_2COO^-)COO^-$ under acidic conditions.

   iii $^+H_3NCH(CH_2NH_3^+)COO^-$ under alkaline conditions.

   iv $^+H_3NCH(CH_2NH_3^+)COO^-$ under acidic conditions.

c Figure 27.3 shows the separation of proteins using **electrophoresis**. The process is carried out so that the species are negatively charged. Smaller and more highly charged species move the furthest during electrophoresis.

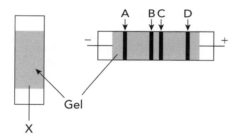

Figure 27.3: Electrophoresis.

   i   X shows a tube of gel for electrophoresis. Suggest how and where the protein is put into the gel.

   ii   The gel contains a buffer solution of high pH. Suggest why this buffer solution is used.

   iii The tube is placed horizontally (Y) and electrophoresis is carried out. Would it matter if the tube were not placed horizontally? Give a reason for your answer.

   iv Can you tell how many proteins have been separated? Explain your answer.

   v   Which protein, A, B, C or D, has the highest charge/mass ratio? Explain your answer.

vi   Proteins are colourless. Suggest how you would know when to stop the electrophoresis.

vii   How would you alter the apparatus in order to carry out the separation of + and − charged amino acids at pH 7?

d   Glycine is an amino acid. Figure 27.4 shows the percentage of charged forms of glycine at different pH values.

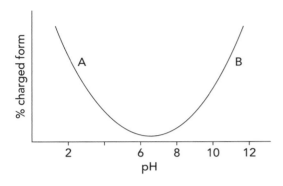

Figure 27.4: % charge plotted against pH

At point A on the graph, glycine is largely in the form $HOOCCH_2NH_3^+$

i   Deduce the ionic form of glycine at point B on the graph.

ii   Deduce from the graph the approximate isoelectric point of glycine.

iii   State the meaning of the term **isoelectric point.**

Exercise 27.4 Amides and peptides

This exercise familiarises you with the structure, acid–base characteristics and some chemical reactions of amides. It also revises the formation of peptides through the formation of **(di)peptide bonds**.

a   Name these amides:

i $CH_3CH_2CH_2CONH_2$

ii $C_2H_5CONHC_2H_5$

iii $CH_3CH_2CON(CH_3)_2$

iv $C_3H_7CONHC_3H_7$

b Copy and complete these sentences about the acid–base characteristics of amides using words from the list.

| donate | electron | hydrogen | lone |
| nitrogen | oxygen | weaker |

The presence of the _____ withdrawing _____ atom in the amide group means that the _____ pair on the _____ atom of the amide is not available to _____ electrons to the electron-deficient _____ ions. This means that amides are _____ bases than amines.

TIP

A tripeptide is formed by the condensation of three amino acids.

c Write equations for:
  i The reaction of $CH_3CH_2CH_2NH_2$ with ethanoyl chloride.
  ii The reaction of CH_3NH_2 with butanoyl chloride.
  iii The reaction of $C_6H_5NH_2$ with ethanoyl chloride.
  iv The acid hydrolysis of CH_3CONH_2 (excess acid).
  v The alkaline hydrolysis of $CH_3CONHCH_2CH_2CH_3$ (excess alkali).
  vi The acid hydrolysis of $CH_3CONHCH_2CH_3$ (excess acid).
  vii The alkaline hydrolysis of CH_3CONH_2 (excess alkali).

d **i** What is meant by the term *condensation reaction*?
  ii Glycine has the structure H_2NCH_2COOH. Lysine is also a 2-aminocarboxylic acid but its side chain is $-CH_2CH_2CH_2CH_2NH_2$. Why are more than two different dipeptides of Gly-Lys possible?
  iii The formula for alanine is $H_2NCH(CH_3)COOH$. Draw the simplest structural formula for a tripeptide of alanine.
  iv The dipeptide glycyl-alanine is hydrolysed by excess hydroxide ions. Write the simplest structural formulae of the two hydrolysis products.

EXAM-STYLE QUESTIONS

1 a Explain why phenylamine is a weaker base than ammonia. **[4]**
  b Propylamine can be made by boiling 1-bromopropane with excess hot ethanolic ammonia.
    i Write the equation for this reaction. **[1]**
    ii Explain why excess ammonia is used. **[2]**
    iii Explain why ethanolic ammonia is used and not aqueous ammonia. **[2]**
    iv Describe the mechanism of the reaction between 1-bromopropane and ethanolic ammonia. **[3]**
  c Suggest how ethylamine can be prepared in a two-step reaction starting with methylamine as the only organic reactant. **[4]**

[Total: 16]

TIPS

In part **1 a** you need to think about the ease with which alkyl groups donate electrons.

Part **c** introduces you to the idea of a two-step synthesis. Look for possible changes in the functional groups.

CONTINUED

TIP

Before you answer
Question 2, make
sure that you know
about optical isomers,
oxidation number
changes, complex
formation and the
theory of paper
chromatography.

2 a Phenylamine is prepared by refluxing nitrobenzene with tin and
concentrated hydrochloric acid.

$$2C_6H_5NO_2 + 3Sn + 14HCl \rightarrow (C_6H_5NH_3^+)_2 \cdot SnCl_6^{2-} + 4H_2O + 2SnCl_4$$

   i Write a simplified equation for this reaction using [H] for the
reducing agent. Show the product in its un-ionised form. **[2]**

   ii State the name of the reducing agent in this reaction. **[1]**

   iii Deduce the change in oxidation number of the tin. **[1]**

   iv Once the reaction is complete, sodium hydroxide is added to the
reaction mixture. Suggest why sodium hydroxide is added to
the reaction mixture. Include an equation in your answer. **[2]**

b The phenyl group is present in the amino acid phenylalanine. The structure
of phenylalanine is shown in Figure 27.5.

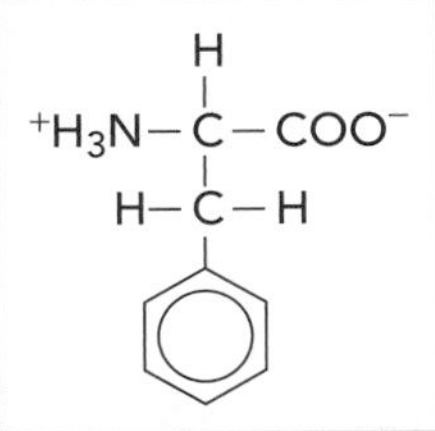

$$^+H_3N-\underset{\underset{\overset{|}{\underset{}{\text{H}}}}{\overset{|}{\underset{|}{\text{C}}}}-COO^-$$

Figure 27.5

   i Draw the two optical isomers of phenylalanine. Represent the side
chain by the letter R. **[3]**

   ii Deduce the overall charge on phenylalanine at pH 12. **[1]**

   iii Aspartic acid has a side chain containing a −COO⁻ group. A mixture
of phenylalanine and aspartic acid can be easily separated by
electrophoresis. Explain why. **[3]**

c When glycine, $^+H_3NCH_2COO^-$, is added to aqueous copper(II) sulfate,
the solution turns a dark blue colour. Explain why. **[2]**

[Total: 15]

3 a i State the names of the reagents and give the conditions needed to
make diazonium salts. **[3]**

   ii Write the formula for the diazonium chloride salt formed from
compound **R**. **[1]**

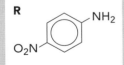

Figure 27.6

TIPS

Question 3 introduces
some unfamiliar
reactions. Look out
for the information
that will help you
answer this question.

Diazonium salts are
used to make azo
dyes in a two-step
process:

diazotisation, then
coupling with a
$C_6H_5O^-$ ion or
similar ion.

CONTINUED

b When an aqueous solution of benzenediazonium chloride is boiled, phenol and nitrogen are formed.

Construct an equation for this reaction. [2]

c Suggest the formula of the organic compound which is formed when a solution of a diazonium salt is warmed with potassium iodide solution. [1]

d The coupling reaction is carried out in alkaline solution. Explain why. [1]

e Explain why a diazonium salt acts as an electrophile in the coupling reaction. [2]

f **i** Explain why azo dyes are very stable. [2]

  ii Give the formula for the azo group. [1]

g Suggest one other property that a good dye must possess. [1]

[Total: 14]

4 a Ethylamine, $C_2H_5NH_2$ is a primary amine.

  i Ethylamine is a stronger base than ammonia. Explain why. [2]

  ii Describe how ethylamine can be prepared from ethanamide. [2]

  iii Construct an equation for the reaction in part **a ii.** [1]

  iv Ethylamine reacts with 1-chloroethane to form a secondary amine, $(C_2H_5)_2NH$. State the conditions required for this reaction. [2]

b Phenylamine, $C_6H_5NH_2$, is an aryl amine.

  i Explain why phenylamine is a weaker base than ammonia. [4]

  ii Phenylamine reacts with ethanoyl chloride. Describe the mechanism and type of reaction that takes place and construct an equation for this reaction. [3]

  iii Bromine can be substituted into the ring of both phenylamine and benzene. Compare the reaction of phenylamine and benzene with bromine, explaining any differences. [7]

[Total: 21]

TIPS

In part **4 a i** use ideas about the inductive effect.

In parts **b i** and **b iii** you need to consider the delocalisation of the aryl ring in phenylamine.

Chapter 28

Polymerisation

CHAPTER OUTLINE

In this chapter you will learn how to:

- describe the characteristics of condensation polymerisation in polyesters and polyamides

- describe how polyesters are formed from a diol and a dicarboxylic acid / dioyl chloride

- describe how polyesters are formed from hydroxycarboxylic acid

- describe how polyamides are formed from a diamine and a dicarboxylic acid / dioyl chloride

- describe how polyamides are formed from amino acids

- deduce repeat units, identify monomer(s) and predict the type of polymerisation reaction which produces a given section of a polymer molecule

- recognise that polyalkenes are chemically inert and non-biodegradable but that polyesters and polyamides are biodegradable by acidic or alkaline hydrolysis

- recognise that some polymers can be degraded by the action of light

Exercise 28.1 The building blocks of polymers

This exercise will familiarise you with the structure and names of some of the monomers used in making polymers as well as identifying monomers which have joined together to form particular polymers.

a   Copy and complete these sentences using words from the list.

> TIP
>
> In part **a** you need to know the functional groups that react with each other.

| condensation   eliminated   monomers   small   two   water |

A _____ reaction is a reaction in which _____ organic molecules

join together and in the process a _____ molecule such as hydrogen

chloride or _____ is _____. Condensation polymers are usually

formed from _____ with two reactive groups in each molecule.

b   The formulae of six molecules **A** to **F** are shown.

   A $HO(CH_2)_6OH$ **B** $H_2N(CH_2)_4NH_2$ **C** $HOOC(C_6H_4)COOH$

   D $HO(CH_2)_6COOH$ **E** $H_2N(CH_2)_4COOH$ **F** $ClOC(CH_2)_4COCl$

   i   Which of these molecules is a diol?

   ii   Which of these molecules is a dicarboxylic acid?

> TIP
>
> In parts **b vi, vii** and **viii** there are two answers for each question.

iii Which of these molecules is a diamide?

iv Which of these molecules is a dioyl chloride?

v State the general name for a molecule like $HO(CH_2)_6COOH$ with OH and COOH functional groups.

vi Which of these molecules react with other molecules identical to itself to form a polymer?

vii Which of these molecules react with other molecules **not** identical to themselves to form **polyamides**?

viii Which of these molecules react with other molecules **not** identical to themselves to form polyesters?

c Draw displayed formulae for the **linkage groups** in:

i polyamides   ii polyesters   iii peptides

d Give the formulae of the monomers that combine to form these polymers using the additional information in square brackets.

i $-OC(CH_2)_6CONH(CH_2)_4NHOC(CH_2)_6CONH(CH_2)_4NH-$

[2 different monomers; water is eliminated]

ii $-O(CH_2)_6OOC(C_6H_4)COO(CH_2)_6OOC(C_6H_4)CO-$

[2 different monomers; hydrogen chloride is eliminated]

iii $-HN(CH_2)_4CONH(CH_2)_4CONH(CH_2)_4CO-$

[a single monomer; water is eliminated]

Exercise 28.2 Drawing polymer structures

This exercise will familiarise you with the structure of condensation polymers and the difference in the **biodegradability** of polyalkanes, polyesters and polyamides.

a Draw the structures of the polymers formed from these monomers. Show one repeat unit with brackets and *n*.

i
$$HO-\underset{\underset{CH_3}{|}}{\overset{\overset{H}{|}}{C}}-COOH$$

ii
$$\underset{H}{\overset{H}{>}}N-\underset{\underset{H}{|}}{\overset{\overset{H}{|}}{C}}-C\overset{\overset{O}{\nearrow}}{\underset{O-H}{\searrow}}$$

iii $ClOC(CH_2)_6COCl + HO\,(CH_2)_4\,OH$

iv
$$\overset{O}{\underset{H-O}{\overset{\diagup}{\diagdown}}}C-\bigcirc-C\overset{\overset{O}{\diagup}}{\underset{O-H}{\diagdown}} + H_2N-\bigcirc-NH_2$$

v $C_6H_5CH=CH_2$

b For each of the polymers you have drawn, state, where appropriate, the name of the small molecule eliminated, and class the polymers as either polyalkenes, polyamides or **polyesters**.

c Draw the partial structure for polymer **v**. Show at least four repeat units.

d Draw the structures of the monomer(s) which form these polymers.

i

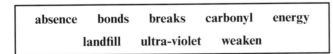

ii

$$-O-\underset{\underset{CH_3}{|}}{CH}-\underset{\underset{O}{\parallel}}{C}-O-\underset{\underset{CH_3}{|}}{CH}-\underset{\underset{O}{\parallel}}{C}-O-\underset{\underset{CH_3}{|}}{CH}-\underset{\underset{O}{\parallel}}{C}-$$

iii

$$-\underset{\underset{H}{|}}{N}-\underset{\underset{O}{\parallel}}{C}-\bigcirc-\underset{\underset{O}{\parallel}}{C}-\underset{\underset{H}{|}}{N}-\bigcirc-\underset{\underset{H}{|}}{N}-\underset{\underset{O}{\parallel}}{C}-\bigcirc-\underset{\underset{H}{|}}{N}-$$

iv

$$\left[\begin{array}{cc} \underset{\underset{H}{|}}{\overset{\overset{Cl}{|}}{C}} & \underset{\underset{H}{|}}{\overset{\overset{H}{|}}{C}} \end{array}\right]_n$$

> **TIP**
>
> To deduce the structure of the monomer(s) of a condensation polymer, first draw the repeat unit. Then add the atoms at both ends that were lost in forming the molecule that was eliminated.

e **i** Which of the polymers A, B, C or D is biodegradable?

  A $-NHCH_2CH_2NHOC(CH_2)_6CO-$

  B $-CH_2CH(CH_3)CH_2CH(CH_3)-$

  C $-O(CH_2)_6COO(CH_2)_6CO-$

  D $-CH_2CH_2CH_2CH_2-$

ii Write the formula for the hydrolysis products of those polymers in part **e i** which are capable of being hydrolysed with excess acid.

iii Suggest why the hydrolysis of these polymers occurs when they are:

  • in the soil

  • in landfill sites.

iv Suggest why polymer in part **d ii** is not harmful to the environment.

v Some polymers decompose in the presence of light.

  Copy and complete this passage about light degradable polymers using words from the list.

> | absence | bonds | breaks | carbonyl | energy |
> |---------|-------|--------|----------|--------|
> | | landfill | ultra-violet | weaken | |

Some polymers have _____ groups in their chains which absorb

_____ from _____ radiation. The radiation causes _____

near the carbonyl group to _____ . The polymer then _____ into

smaller fragments. These fragments are easier to decompose but may still stay

in the ground for a long time. If they are buried in _____ sites, they

may not break down because of the _____ of light.

Exercise 28.3 Relating structures to properties

This exercise will familiarise you with how the nature of the side chains and the presence of crystalline areas in polymers affects their properties. It also introduces you to how silicon-based adhesives work by forming cross links between polymer chains. You will be expected to be able to answer questions on unfamiliar compounds when given sufficient information.

> **TIPS**
>
> Anything that limits the movement of polymer chains makes the polymer stronger and less flexible.
>
> Factors which influence the **flexibility** of the polymer chains include the presence of polar groups and the presence or absence of bulky side chains.

> **KEY WORD**
>
> **flexibility:** ease of bending when a force is applied.

a   Comment on the comparative flexibility of each of the following polymers. Explain your answer.

- poly(chloroethene) $\leftarrow CH_2-CH(Cl)\rightarrow_n$
- poly(phenylethene) $\leftarrow CH_2-CH(C_6H_5)\rightarrow_n$
- poly(propene) $\leftarrow CH_2-CH(CH_3)\rightarrow_n$

b   A plasticiser is a non-volatile liquid that is absorbed into the polymer. Suggest how plasticisers work.

c   Poly(tetrafluoroethene), $\leftarrow CF_2-CF_2\rightarrow_n$ is used as a non-stick coating for cooking pans. Suggest why by referring to its structure.

d   Terylene and nylon are both condensation polymers. Terylene has ester links and nylon has amide links.

   i   Assuming that the rest of the molecule is the same, describe the intermolecular forces between terylene chains and nylon chains and suggest which are stronger.

   ii   Some types of terylene have a benzene ring between the amide groups. What effect will this have on the terylene chains?

e   Read the paragraph then answer the questions that follow.

When some polymers are cooled, some of the chains arrange themselves in rows. The polymer is said to be crystalline. The polymer is then relatively harder. If the chains are randomly arranged, they can still move relatively easily over each other and the polymer is less hard and less **brittle** than crystalline polymers.

   i   Describe the difference between the crystalline regions and non-crystalline regions of the polymer.

   ii   Explain in terms of intermolecular forces why highly crystalline poly(ethene) has a higher melting range than non-crystalline poly(ethene).

   iii   How will crystalline and non-crystalline poly(ethene) differ in their elasticity and tensile strength? Explain your answer.

> **KEY WORD**
>
> **brittle:** breaks easily when a force is applied.

f Read the paragraph, then answer the questions which follow.

Silicon-based **adhesives** do not rely on organic solvents to dissolve polymers. They depend on the formation of a network of **cross-linked** Si–O–Si bridges between the polymer chains to form a network of strong bonds which can stick two surfaces together.

The phrases A to I describe how non-solvent-based adhesives based on silicon work. Put these phrases in the correct order.

A   ...forms cross links containing...

B   ...contain SiOCH$_3$ groups.

C   ...the water hydrolyses the SiOCH$_3$ groups and...

D   Many of these siloxane cross links form...

E   ...to make a network of strong covalent bonds.

F   ...when the adhesive is setting, ...

G   ...–Si–O–Si– bonds.

H   In the presence of moisture in the air...

I   Silicon-based adhesives have polymer chains which...

> **KEY WORDS**
>
> **adhesives:** substances which stick things together.
>
> **cross-linked (polymers):** polymer chains with covalent bonds linking the chains together.

Exercise 28.4 Natural and synthetic polymers

This exercise revises the structure of some natural and synthetic polymers and reviews the types of intermolecular forces present in **polypeptides**.

> **KEY WORD**
>
> **polypeptide:** a polymer of many amino acids.

a The partial structures of polyamide **X** and polyester **Y** are shown in Figure 28.1.

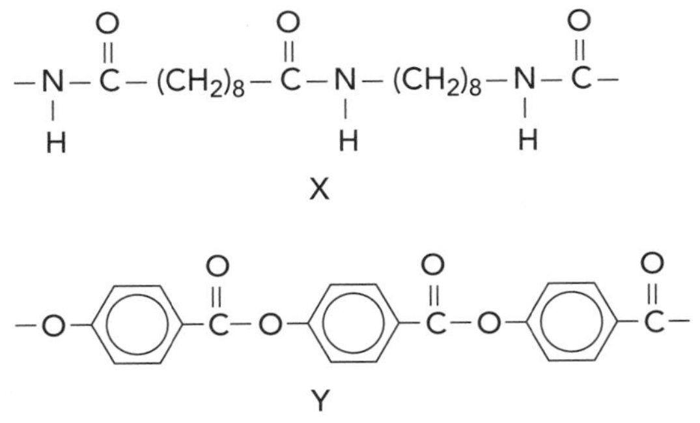

Figure 28.1: Partial structures of polyamide X and polyester Y.

Suggest structures for the monomers which are used to produce these polymers.

b The polymers X and Y can both be broken down by acid or alkaline hydrolysis.

i   Describe how to carry out acid hydrolysis in the laboratory.

ii   Give the formula of the products of alkaline hydrolysis of polymer Y.

iii   Both polymer X and polymer Y are biodegradable. Explain why they are biodegradable.

iv   Both polymer X and polymer Y can still cause environmental problems if left in landfill. Explain why.

c Some plastics including addition polymers such as poly(propene), undergo *photodegradation*.

- i Suggest what is meant by the term photodegradation.
- ii Photodegradation takes place by a free radical mechanism. Give the 3 stages in a free radical mechanism.
- iii When poly(propene) undergoes photodegradation, the free radicals react with oxygen and parts of the chain are converted to C=O groups. Suggest what effect this has on the polymer structure.
- iv Suggest why photodegradation does very little to help with the problem of plastic waste.

d **Amino acid residues** in a polypeptide have side chains which form intermolecular forces with other amino acid residues. Some side chains are shown here. Match the type of bonding to the pairs of side chains that could be involved.

Each side chain can be used more than once.

Type of bonding:	Side chains:
i hydrogen bonding	$-CH(CH_3)_2$
ii ionic bonds	$-CH_2OH$
iii instantaneous dipole-induced dipole forces	$-(CH_2)_4NH_3^+$ / $-(CH_2)_4NH_2$
	$-CH_2COO^-$ / $-CH_2COOH$
	$-CH_3$

e

- i A polypeptide containing serine and aspartic acid is hydrolysed with excess hydrochloric acid. The side chain of serine is $-CH_2OH$. The side chain of aspartic acid is $-CH_2COOH$. Draw the structures of the hydrolysis products showing all atoms and bonds.
- ii A polypeptide containing only glycine, H_2NCH_2COOH, is hydrolysed with excess sodium hydroxide. Draw the structural formula of the hydrolysis product.

TIP

In part **c** degrade means to break down. In part **c iii** think about the type of bonding that usually exists in a polymer chain that has few side groups.

KEY WORDS

amino acid residue: the individual units of the amino acids that make up a polypeptide or protein.

EXAM-STYLE QUESTIONS

1 a X and Y react to form a polymer.

X is $H_2N(CH_2)_6NH_2$; Y is $ClOC(CH_2)_4COCl$

- i **State** the type of polymerisation that occurs. [1]
- ii **Give** the general name of the polymer produced. [1]
- iii Give the name of the molecule eliminated. [1]
- iv Draw one **repeat unit** of the polymer. Use square brackets and *n*. [2]

b Another polymer has the partial structure shown in Figure 28.2.

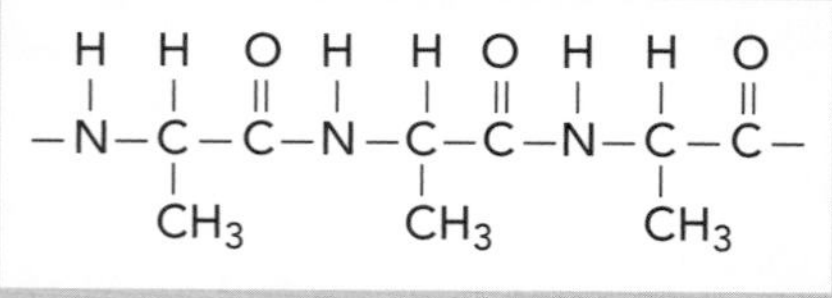

Figure 28.2

Deduce the number of repeat units shown in this partial structure. [1]

CONTINUED

c Synthetic rubber can be made from the monomer with this structure.

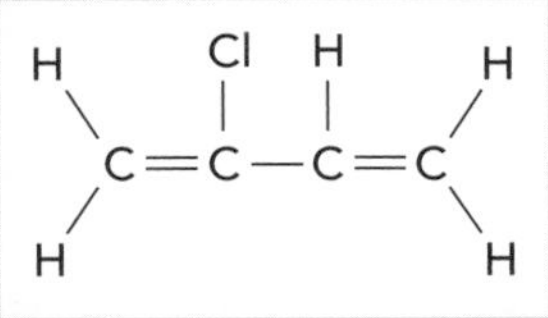

Figure 28.3

i Draw the formula for one unit of the polymer which is formed given that the two $H_2C=C$ bonds are broken when the monomers link together. **[2]**

ii The polymer is too elastic to be useful for car tyres. Suggest in general terms how the properties of the polymer could be altered to make it more resistant to wear. Explain your answer. **[2]**

d i A polymer with the structure $-CH=CH-CH=CH-CH=CH-$ conducts electricity.

Suggest why it conducts electricity. **[2]**

ii Draw the displayed formula of a monomer that might be used to make this polymer. **[1]**

iii State one advantage of this polymer as an electrical conductor over that of a metal. **[1]**

[Total: 14]

2 a The structures of two compounds, **P** and **Q** are shown here.

P $HO(CH_2)_6COOH$ **Q** $H_2N(C_6H_4)OH$

i State the general name for a molecule with an OH and a COOH functional group. **[1]**

ii Explain why a polymer can be formed from compound **P** only. **[1]**

iii Explain why a **co-polymer** containing equal numbers of repeat units of **P** and **Q** cannot be formed. **[4]**

b The structure of a tripeptide is shown here.

$H_2N(CH_2)_3CONH(CH_2)_3CONH(CH_2)_3COOH$

i State what is meant by the term tripeptide. **[1]**

ii When the tripeptide is formed, water is eliminated.

State the meaning of the term eliminated. **[1]**

iii Deduce the formula of the monomer used to make this tripeptide. **[1]**

iv The monomer reacts with excess ethanoyl chloride. Deduce the formula of the organic product of this reaction. **[1]**

c i Polypeptides can be hydrolysed to amino acids by acid. Give the name of the acid and conditions used in this reaction. **[2]**

ii After hydrolysis excess ammonia is usually added to the reaction mixture. Explain why. **[1]**

TIP

For part **1 c** you need to use the information provided in the question and count the number of bonds around each carbon atom.

In part **d i** a giant covalent structure which conducts electricity may give you a clue.

KEY WORD

co-polymer: a polymer which is synthesised from more than one monomer.

TIP

In part **b iv** and part **d** make sure that you take note of the functional groups present.

TIP

Epoxy **resins** are used as adhesives. When monomer X reacts with monomer Y, a polymer is formed.

CONTINUED

  d The structural formula of serine is $H_2NCH(CH_2OH)COOH$.

    Explain why more than one type of dipeptide of serine can be made. In each case give the name of the linkage group. [3]

                                                            [Total: 16]

3 The structures of two monomers, X and Y, are shown. They combine to form polymer Z.

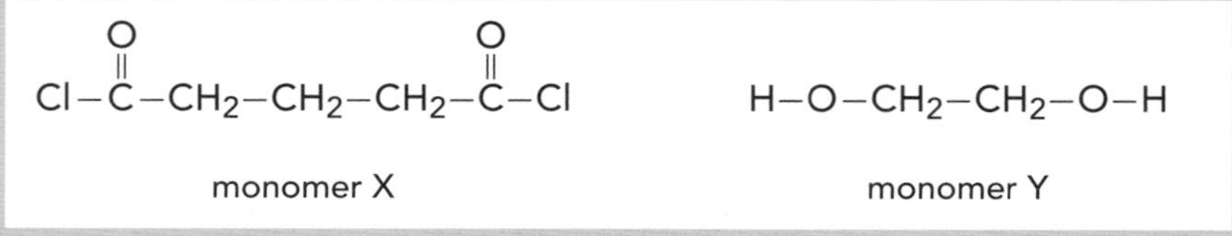

monomer X   monomer Y

Figure 28.4

  a Copy monomer X and monomer Y and circle the bonds which break in each monomer when polymer Z is formed. [2]

  b State the name of the small molecule which is eliminated when polymer Z is formed from monomer X and monomer Y. [1]

  c Draw the structure of polymer Z. [2]

  d **i** In the absence of light, $CH_2{=}CH{-}CH_3$ polymerises to form an addition polymer. State the name of this polymer. [1]

     ii This polymer is not easily decomposed when put into a landfill site but the polymer with the structure in Figure 28.5 readily decomposes in the soil.

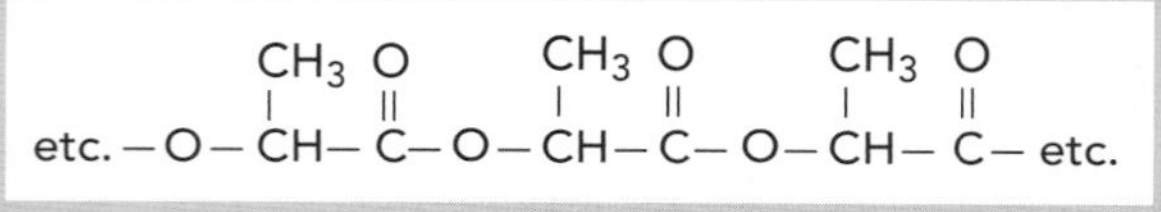

Figure 28.5

    Explain this difference. [4]

                                                          [Total: 10]

TIPS

In part **b** you have to consider the general properties of substances which modify the properties of polymers by crosslinking.

In parts **c i** and **c ii** you have to use your knowledge of hydrocarbons from Chapter 15.

Organic synthesis

In this chapter you will learn how to:

- explain the meaning of the terms enantiomers, chiral centre, polarised light, optically active isomers, racemic mixtures

- give reasons why the synthetic preparation of drug molecules often requires the production of a single optical isomer (better therapeutic activity, fewer side effects)

- identify functional groups (in compounds with several functional groups) using reactions in the syllabus

- predict the properties and reactions of organic molecules

- analyse a synthetic route in terms of the type of reaction, reagents used for each step and possible by-products

Exercise 29.1 Optical isomers and racemic mixtures

This exercise revises optical isomers and develops the concept that, in developing drug molecules, only one of the optical isomers of a pair is useful. It also introduces you to some extension work about the concept of resolution of a mixture of optical isomers.

a   Copy and complete these sentences about optical isomers using words from the list.

| chiral | four | left | mirror optical opposite | plane |
| polarimeter | rotates | structural | superimposable | |

When two compounds have the same _____ formula but one is not

_____ on the other, they are described as _____ isomers. Optical

isomers have _____ different groups attached to a central atom. This

central atom is called a _____ centre. One of these two isomers is a

_____ image of the other. Optical isomers differ in their behaviour to

_____ polarised light. One of the optical isomers _____ the plane

of the polarised light in one direction when viewed in a _____ (e.g. to the

right or +). The other optical isomer, which is its mirror image, rotates it in the

_____ direction (e.g. to the _____ or −).

> **TIP**
>
> Before starting this exercise, make sure that you know how to draw optical isomers (Chapters 14 and 24). Optical isomers are often distinguished by + and − (which relates to the direction they rotate plane polarised light), or D and L (which relates to the absolute position of some of the atoms in space).

b Pair the words **A** to **F** on the left with the descriptions **1** to **6** on the right.

A Enantiomers	1 The image does not fit exactly over another
B Plane polarised	2 A compound containing a central atom with four different groups attached
C **Racemic mixture**	3 A pair of optical isomers
D Chiral centre	4 An equimolar mixture of both forms of an optical isomer
E Non-**superimposable**	5 Instrument used to measure the rotation of plane polarised light
F **Polarimeter**	6 Light which vibrates only in one plane

c Drugs extracted directly from plant material are usually active in their effects but when modified or made by chemical synthesis in the laboratory may only show half this activity unless treated further. Explain why.

d The drug thalidomide exists as two stereoisomers, one is an effective drug but the other causes mutations. Give two reasons why the use of a single optical isomer is beneficial.

e i State the meaning of the term enantiomers.

ii The structure of an amino acid is shown in Figure 29.1.

Draw a diagram of the optical isomer of this amino acid.

iii A mixture of 40% of one of the optical isomers and 60% of the other optical isomer is made. Suggest why this mixture rotates **plane polarised light**.

iv State the name given to a mixture of optical isomers which does not rotate plane polarised light.

f A particular optical isomer can be separated from a 50 : 50 mixture of optical isomers by a process called resolution. Resolution is the separation of optically active isomers (enantiomers) from a mixture of isomers.

A mixture of optical isomers of an acid (±)Acid can be separated by making it into a mixture of two soluble salts by reaction with an optically active base (–)Base.

i Copy and complete the equation to show the two salts formed.

(±)Acid + (–)Base → ____________ + ____________

ii The salts can be separated by fractional crystallisation because one of the salts is less soluble in a particular solvent than the other.

Suggest how you might carry out this process.

iii Suggest how you could get the resolved isomers back into the acid form.

iv A mixture of optical isomers of a base needs to be resolved into separate isomers. Suggest how this could be done. Write an equation similar to the one in **d i** to describe this resolution.

KEY WORDS

racemic mixture: a mixture containing equal amounts of a pair of enantiomers.

superimposable (images): all parts of one image can be placed exactly in the same place as all parts of another

polarimeter: an instrument used to measure the rotation of plane polarised light by a sample. (The sample is placed between 2 pieces of polaroid and rotated until the light-dark boundary is seen.)

plane polarised light: light which vibrates only in one plane (imagine a waveform drawn on a piece of paper)

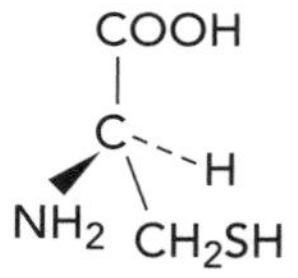

Figure 29.1: The structure of an amino acid.

TIP

Part **f** is extension work but it is useful for revising general chemical ideas.

Exercise 29.2 Forming C–C bonds

This exercise revises the methods of increasing the number of carbon atoms in a compound.

a   What reagents and conditions are needed to convert benzene to ethylbenzene?

b   Write an equation for the reaction of 2-chloropropane with benzene.

c   Benzene can also be acylated.

   i   What is the meaning of the term acylation?

   ii   What conditions are required for acylation?

   iii   Write an equation for the reaction of propanoyl chloride with benzene.

   iv   Why are alkylation and acylation important in terms of synthesising new chemicals?

d   The Friedel–Crafts reaction can also be used to add alkenes and substitute alcohols.

   i   Write an equation to show the Friedel–Crafts reaction of ethene with benzene (no small molecule is given off).

   ii   Write an equation to show the Friedel–Crafts reaction of ethanol with benzene (a small molecule is given off).

e   What conditions are needed to convert bromoethane to ethanenitrile?

f   Write an equation for the reaction of 1-bromopropane with nitrile (cyanide) ions.

g   **i**   What reagents and conditions are needed to convert benzonitrile, C_6H_5CN, to phenylmethylamine, $C_6H_5CH_2NH_2$?

   ii   Write an equation for this reaction, showing the reducing agent as [H].

h   Compound Z can be synthesised in three stages starting from ethanoic acid.

   i   Give the formula of the salt X formed when ammonia reacts with ethanoic acid.

   ii   When X is heated, water is lost. Write the formula for the compound Y formed.

   iii   Phosphorus(V) oxide is a good dehydrating agent. It dehydrates Y to Z. Identify Z by name and formula.

> **TIP**
>
> Make sure that you are familiar with the Friedel–Crafts reaction (see Chapter 25) before you start this activity.

> **TIP**
>
> Part **h** introduces you to an unfamiliar reaction. You should be able to answer this question from your prior knowledge.

Exercise 29.3 Changing functional groups

This exercise familiarises you with the general concepts of a multistage synthesis. It also revises the idea of replacing one functional group by another.

> **TIPS**
>
> In order to synthesise the **target molecule**, it is often useful to work backwards until you get to a suitable starting material:
>
> target molecule → intermediate compound → intermediate compound → starting material

> **KEY WORDS**
>
> **target molecule:** in organic synthesis, the molecule that you want to make

a Suggest the advantages of having as few steps as possible from the starting material to the target molecule.

b Suggest why the starting materials should be relatively simple molecules.

c Suggest suitable sources of starting materials.

d Copy and complete the following **synthesis**, stating the conditions and additional reagents needed for each step.

$$CH_3CH_2OH \rightarrow \text{intermediate compound} \rightarrow CH_3CH_2CN$$

e **i** What is the important point about the following synthesis?

$$CH_3COOH \rightarrow CH_3CH_2OH \rightarrow \text{intermediate} \rightarrow CH_3CH_2CN \rightarrow CH_3CH_2COOH$$

   ii Give the name and type of reagent you would use to convert CH_3COOH to CH_3CH_2OH.

f You need to convert butan-1-ol to 1,2-dibromobutane in two steps.

   i Write the structural formula of the target molecule.

   ii What type of reaction do you need to put two Br atoms on adjacent carbon atoms?

   iii What intermediate compound do you need to make 1,2-dibromobutane?

   iv How can you make this compound from butan-1-ol?

   v Write down the two-step route.

g You need to convert propan-1-ol to butanoic acid in three steps.

   i Are there the same number of carbon atoms in the target molecule as in the starting material?

   ii Based on you answer to **i**, what type of intermediate do you need?

   iii How can you make this intermediate from a compound, X, which is not an alcohol, i.e. it is another intermediate?

   iv Suggest how you can you make X from propan-1-ol.

   v Write down the three-step route stating the conditions and reagents needed in each step.

> ### KEY WORD
>
> **(organic) synthesis:** the series of steps taken to produce an organic product by changing functional groups or lengthening or shortening the carbon chain

> ### TIP
>
> In parts **f** and **g** you should be familiar with all the types of organic reactions you have met during the course and know the conditions and additional reagents required. Make sure that you know which chapters to refer to if you are not sure of the conditions.

Exercise 29.4 Mapping synthetic routes

This exercise familiarises you with the range of organic reactions and how you can convert one functional group to another. It also gives you practice in predicting the properties and reactions of an unfamiliar organic molecule.

> ### TIPS
>
> For this exercise you need to refer back to the organic reactions in Chapters 15 to 18 and 25 to 27.
>
> Maps like Figures 29.2 and 29.3 are useful for telling us how to make a target material from a particular starting material.
>
> When revising organic reactions, you will find it useful to construct 'mind maps' like the ones below to get an overview of the reactions that you have learned.

a i Copy and complete the map of synthetic routes A, Figure 29.2, by adding the structural formulae in brackets starting with ethene.

ii Draw arrows to show the direction of each reaction.

iii Add the conditions above or to the side of each arrow.

iv Copy and complete the map of synthetic routes B, Figure 29.3, by adding the structural formulae in brackets starting with ethanol.

v Draw arrows to show the direction of each reaction.

vi Add the conditions above or to the side of each arrow.

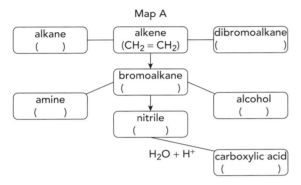

Figure 29.2: Map A.

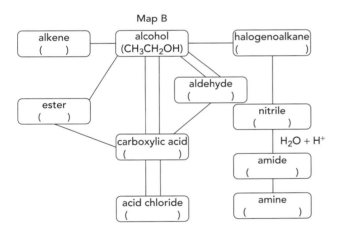

Figure 29.3: Map B.

b The structure of estrone is shown in Figure 29.4.

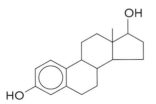

Figure 29.4: The structure of estrone.

Predict the properties and reactions of this molecule.

EXAM-STYLE QUESTIONS

1 a Methylbenzene is treated with chlorine gas in the presence of sunlight.

    i State the type of reaction and the type of mechanism that takes place. **[2]**

    ii Write the structural formula of the product, M, when methylbenzene is in excess. **[1]**

  b M can be converted to compound N which has the formula $C_6H_5CH_2NH_2$.

    Describe the reagents and conditions needed for this reaction. **[3]**

  c A mixture of compound N and hydrogen is passed over a nickel catalyst at 150 °C. Draw the displayed formula for the product of this reaction. **[2]**

  d The structures of 4-nitromethylbenzene and benzocaine are shown in Figure 29.5.

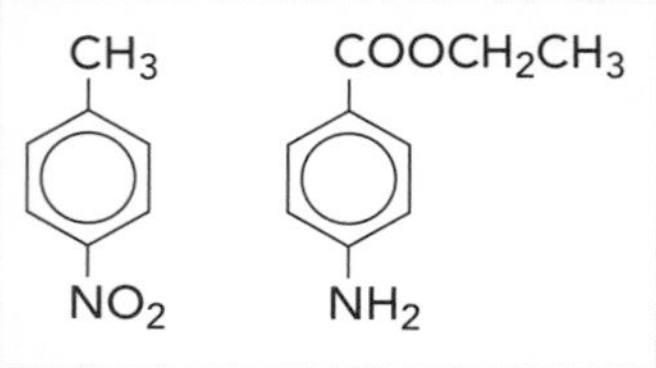

Figure 29.5

Benzocaine can be formed from 4-nitromethylbenzene in a three-step reaction. The first step involves the oxidation of the methyl group and the third involves a reaction involving this oxidised group.

Describe the steps in the synthesis of benzocaine from 4-nitromethylbenzene. For each step give the reaction conditions and additional reagents required. **[7]**

[Total: 15]

2 a Butan-2-ol, $CH_3CH(OH)CH_2CH_3$, exists as two optical isomers (+ butan-2-ol and – butan-2-ol). A mixture of these isomers is esterified with benzene-1,2-dicarboxylic acid. The product of this reaction is shown incompletely in Figure 29.6.

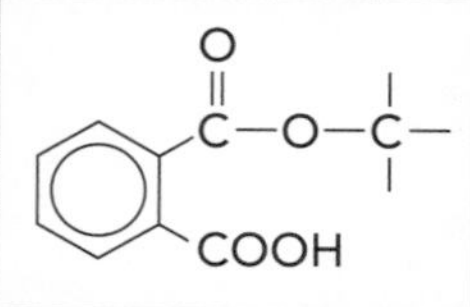

Figure 29.6

TIP

Notice the key word sunlight in part **a i**.

TIP

In part **d** you are given minimum information. You have to look at the different groups in the benzene ring and use your knowledge of the conversion of one functional group to another to help you. The final stage involves an esterification.

TIP

In part **2 a**, remember that there are two ways of showing the difference between optical isomers (+ and – or D- and L-).

CONTINUED

    i   Copy and complete the formula. Show the **chiral centre** with a star (*) [2]

    ii State the name given to an equimolar mixture of the optical isomers + butan-2-ol and – butan-2-ol. [1]

    iii Define the term plane polarised light. [1]

    iv State the effect of plane polarised light on the two optical isomers of butan-2-ol of the same concentration when placed in a polarimeter cell. [2]

b Propan-1-ol, $CH_3CH_2CH_2OH$, is reacted with hydrogen bromide.

    i   Name the organic product, P, formed in this reaction. [1]

    ii Give the structural formula of the product formed when P reacts with ammonia. [1]

    iii Give the structural formula of another substance that would be formed when excess P reacts with excess ammonia. [1]

c Suggest how you could convert P into an amine with the formula $CH_3CH_2CH_2CH_2NH_2$. [4]

[Total: 13]

TIPS

In part **b** make sure that you know your organic reactions including those of alcohols.

In part **c** count the number of carbon atoms carefully.

3 Two possible ways of synthesising aspirin (compound D) from phenol are shown in Figure 29.7:

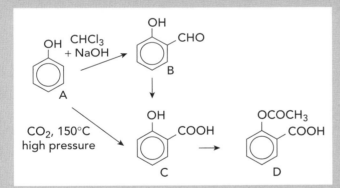

Figure 29.7

a State the name of compound A. [1]

b Give a test for the CHO group in compound B and state the result if the test is positive. [2]

c State the reagent and conditions needed for carrying out the reaction B → C. [2]

d State the reagents and conditions needed for carrying out the reaction C → D. [2]

e Deduce which method of synthesising aspirin (A → B → C → D or A → C → D) is more **economical**. Explain why. [2]

TIP

For parts **3 c** and **d** you need to know about reactions involving oxidation and esterification

KEY WORD

economical: saving money (or energy or time)

CONTINUED

f   Aspirin can be made more soluble in water by reaction with aqueous sodium hydroxide. Explain why this makes aspirin more soluble. [2]

g   Describe how to substitute a CH_3 group into the aromatic ring of compound A. State the position in the ring of the substitution. Give a reason for your answer. [4]

h   Compound C reacts with sodium hydroxide and can be esterified.

Predict four **other** chemical reactions of compound C. In each case, state which group in the molecule reacts. [4]

[Total: 19]

TIP

In part **g** you need to consider the nature of the groups attached to the aryl ring. In part h you need to refer the Friedel–Crafts reaction.

Analytical chemistry

Exercise 30.1 Chromatography

This exercise will familiarise you with four types of chromatography and also gives you practice with calculations involving chromatograms.

TIPS

Adsorption and partition chromatography both depend on partitioning the parts (components) of the mixture between a **stationary phase** and a **mobile phase** (see Chapter 21).

In paper chromatography R_f **values** are used to calculate the relative rate of movement of compounds compared with the rate of movement of the solvent front. In gas-liquid chromatography we use the **retention time**.

KEY WORDS

stationary phase: the immobile phase in chromatography that the mobile phase passes over or through. Examples are the surface of the thin-layer particles in TLC (thin-layer chromatography) or the non-volatile liquid absorbed onto the column in GLC.

a **i** Copy and complete the table to include the stationary phase and mobile phase which are listed beneath the table.

type of chromatography	stationary phase	mobile phase
paper chromatography		
gas-liquid chromatography **(GLC)**		
thin-layer chromatography **(TLC)**		
high-performance liquid chromatography (HPLC)		

Table 30.1: Types of chromatography.

Silica/aluminium support

Organic liquid or mixture of solvents, sometimes aqueous

Non-volatile liquid absorbed on support

Water absorbed onto cellulose

Polar liquid, e.g. methanol

Gas such as N_2, H_2 or He

Liquid (long-chain alkane) absorbed on support

Organic solvent

ii Copy and complete these sentences about thin-layer chromatography (TLC) using words from the list.

attraction	**dissolve**	**heptane**	**mixture**
phase	**slower**	**stationary**	

TLC can be used to separate different types of plant pigments (colourings). A ________ of plant pigments is placed on the solid ________ phase of the TLC sheet. A solvent such as ________ is used as the mobile ________. As the solvent runs up the sheet, the pigments separate. This is because pigments with more polar molecules have a greater ________ for the polar solid used as a stationary phase. The more polar the molecules are, the ________ they travel up the sheet. This allows separation from molecules that are less polar and ________ more easily in heptane.

KEY WORDS

mobile phase: the solvent used in chromatography, which moves along the paper, thin layer of aluminium oxide, or column containing liquid supported on a solid.

R_f value (retention factor): in paper chromatography (or TLC), the ratio of the distance travelled by a specific component to the distance travelled by the solvent front.

KEY WORDS

retention time: the time taken for a compound to travel through a chromatography column in GLC.

GLC (gas-liquid chromatography): chromatography in which the stationary phase is a liquid and the mobile phase is a gas.

TLC (thin-layer chromatography): a type of chromatography in which the stationary phase is a solid such as alumina which adsorbs the solute molecules to different extents.

b   Copy and complete the following passage about gas-liquid chromatography using words from the list.

> **carrier   components   equilibrium   further**
> **hydrocarbon   less   retention   stationary   times**

The mixture to be separated is injected into the _____ gas and the time noted.

The gas flows through a long tube containing a long-chain _____ supported

on silica (_____ phase). As the gas moves through the tube, _____,

which are _____ soluble in the stationary phase, move _____, while

those that are more soluble are in _____ with the stationary phase for longer.

The compounds leave the tube at different _____. The time taken between

injection and detection is called the _____ time.

c   **i**   An amino acid has an R_f value of 0.42. The solvent front moves 30 cm from the base line of the chromatogram. How far is the amino acid from the base line of the chromatogram?

    ii   How can we identify the amino acid from the position of the amino acid on the chromatogram?

    iii What are the advantages of TLC over paper chromatography?

d   The percentage composition of a particular component in a mixture can be deduced from a gas chromatogram.

$$\% \text{ component X} = \frac{\text{area under the peak of X}}{\text{sum of the areas under all components}}$$

$$\text{Area of a triangle} = \frac{1}{2} \times \text{base} \times \text{height}$$

What assumptions must be made for this method to work?

e   Calculate the percentage of pentan-2-one in the mixture shown in Figure 30.1.

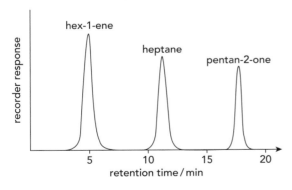

Figure 30.1: How much pentan-2-one?

Exercise 30.2 Proton NMR spectroscopy

This exercise will give you practice in understanding and interpreting the results of proton NMR spectroscopy and how the splitting of the main signals in high-resolution NMR spectroscopy gives information about the number of ^1H atoms there are on an adjacent carbon atom in an unknown molecule.

TIPS

NMR spectroscopy tells you about the environment in which a ^1H atom (proton) exists and how many ^1H atoms are in these particular environments.

The area under each peak in an NMR spectrum gives you the number of 1H atoms responsible for the chemical shift. This is given by labels 1H, 2H, etc. on NMR spectra.

In high-resolution NMR spectra, some of the peaks show a splitting pattern. The number of splits in a peak = $n + 1$, where n is the number of 1H atoms on the carbon atom next to that peak.

---

a Put these statements about **NMR** in the correct order (start with A).

    A When placed in a strong magnetic field…

    B …'flip' from being lined up with the magnetic field (lower energy) to…

    C The size of the energy gap varies with the environment in which the ^1H nuclei are placed and so…

    D When the correct frequency of radiation is absorbed, the nuclei…

    E 1H nuclei behave like tiny magnets and line…

    F …to different radio frequencies emitted when the proton returns to the lower energy level.

    G …being lined up against the magnetic field (higher energy).

    H …themselves up with or against the field.

    I …different frequencies give different NMR peaks corresponding…

b In CH_3COOCH_3 there are two different environments for H atoms, CH_3C- and $-OCH_3$.

How many different environments for hydrogen atoms are there in the following compounds? In each case show clearly what these different environments are.

    i $CH_3CH_2NH_2$ **ii** $(CH_3)_2CHCH_2$ **iii** $CH_3COOCH_2CH_3$

c **i** Tetramethylsilane (**TMS**), $(CH_3)_4Si$, is used as a reference standard in NMR spectroscopy. Suggest why.

    ii The extent to which a peak in the NMR spectrum differs from the TMS peak is represented by the symbol δ. What is the name given to this symbol?

KEY WORDS

NMR: an abbreviation for 'nuclear magnetic resonance', a type of spectroscopy used to determine the identity and structure of organic compounds.

TMS: an abbreviation for tetramethylsilane, $Si(CH_3)_4$, the standard compound used in NMR spectroscopy, providing the peak to measure chemical shifts relative to its given value of zero.

d   Use the values of **chemical shift** below to identify the groups present in the NMR spectra A and B in Figure 30.2. Identify these molecules.

KEY WORDS
chemical shift: the resonant frequency of a nucleus relative to a standard (usually TMS).

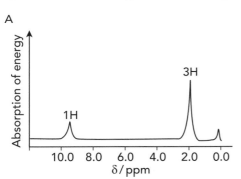 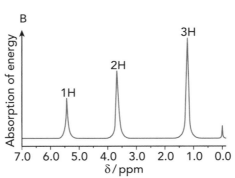

Figure 30.2: Spectra **A** and **B**.

Values of δ
R–OH 1.0–5.5
R–CH₃ 0.7–1.6
R–CHO (aliphatic aldehyde) 9.0–10.0
R–CHO (aromatic aldehyde) 11.0–12.0
R–COCH₃ (carbonyl bonded to CH₃) 2.3
R–O–CH₂–R 4.0

e   **i**   Figure 30.3 shows the high-resolution NMR spectrum of ethanol. Explain the **splitting pattern** in each of the peaks.

KEY WORDS
splitting pattern: the series of peaks that main signals are divided into in high resolution NMR.

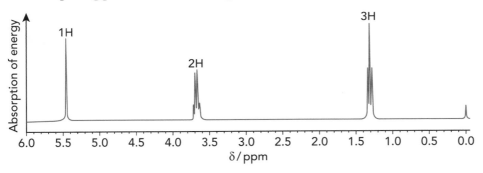

Figure 30.3: High-resolution NMR spectrum of ethanol.

ii   Copy and complete this table about splitting patterns.

Splitting pattern	1 peak (singlet)	2 peaks	3 peaks	
Relative intensities of splitting pattern			1 : 2 : 1	

Table 30.2: Splitting patterns.

iii   In a CH₃– group there are four combinations in which three 'proton magnets' 'north-south' (NS) can be arranged. Deduce these four arrangements. Use this to explain why a CHO group next to a CH₃ group is split into four peaks.

f   Copy and complete these sentences about the use of deuterated solvents using words from the list.

deuterated	interfere	reduces
solvent	standard	triplet

The NMR spectra for most compounds are recorded for the compound dissolved

in a _____. The solvent used in an NMR spectrum causes signals (peaks)

which can _____ with the interpretation of the spectrum. The use of

_____ solvents such as CDCl₃ _____ the interference because it

gives a signal which corresponds to _____ peaks at 79 ppm. Modern NMR

spectrometers can take account of this signal so that a _____ such as

tetramethylsilane is not necessary.

Exercise 30.3 ¹H and ¹³C NMR spectroscopy

This exercise familiarises you with the use of proton NMR spectroscopy by introducing the use of deuterium to identify O–H and N–H protons. It will also familiarise you with the use of **carbon-13 NMR spectroscopy**.

KEY WORDS

carbon-13 NMR spectroscopy: a technique for identifying the types of groups adjacent to specific ¹³C atoms.

TIPS

The –OH proton exchanges very rapidly with protons from any water present. This causes only a single –OH signal in the high-resolution NMR spectrum.

The addition of deuterium oxide, D₂O (²H₂O), makes the –OH peak disappear.

Carbon-13 NMR spectroscopy works in a similar way to proton NMR spectroscopy. Look for particular chemical shifts to identify the different environments of the carbon atoms.

Take care in interpreting carbon-13 spectra: the heights of the lines are not always proportional to the number of equivalent carbon atoms present.

a   What other functional groups have this rapid proton exchange?
b   Why is it difficult to distinguish protons from different environments such as –OH, –NH–, R₃CH and R–CH₂–R?

c   Write an equation for the exchange of protons in D_2O with protons in:

    i   −OH   **ii**   one of the protons in −NH−

d   **i**   Why do the −OH and −NH− peaks disappear in the presence of D_2O?

    ii   How does this help in checking if these groups are present in a compound?

e   How many different environments for carbon atoms are there in the following compounds? In each case show clearly what these different environments are.

    i $CH_3CH_2CH_3$ **ii** $(CH_3)_3CH$ **iii** $CH_3COCH_2CH_2NH_2$

f   Use the values of chemical shift here to identify possible groups present in the carbon-13 NMR spectra A and B in Figures 30.4 and 30.5 and explain why these spectra are consistent with A being propanone and B being ethanol.

A

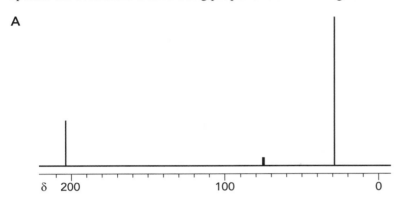

Figure 30.4: Spectrum A.

B

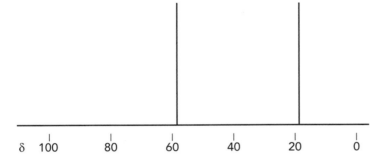

Figure 30.5: Spectrum B.

Values of δ

$CH_3–C, –CH–$	0–50
$–CH_2–OH$	50–70
$R–CHO, R–CO–R$	190–220

g   **i**   Predict the number of peaks in a ^{13}C NMR spectrum for ethyl ethanoate, $CH_3COOCH_2CH_3$. Explain your answer.

    ii   The actual ^{13}C NMR spectrum shows an additional peak at 79 ppm. This is not due to the ethyl ethanoate. Account for this peak.

> **TIP**
>
> In part **g**, think about the number of different environments the carbon atoms are in.

EXAM-STYLE QUESTIONS

1 The mass spectrum of phenylethanone, $C_6H_5COCH_3$, shows peaks at *m/e* values of 15, 28, 77 and 105.

   a Suggest the structure of the ions which form this fragmentation pattern.   **[4]**

   b The infrared spectrum of phenylethanone is shown in Figure 30.6.

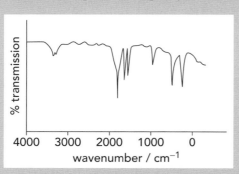

Figure 30.6

Use the information here to show how this spectrum is consistent with the structure of phenylethene.

Wavenumber for groups in cm^{-1}:

alkanes	2850–2950 (medium peaks)
alkyl/aryl ketone	1680–1750
arene	1450–1650
arene	3000–3030 (several weak peaks)
arene ring with 5 carbons	700–750 (several strong peaks)
alkyl/aryl ketone	1680–1750 (strong peaks) **[3]**

   c Predict the high-resolution NMR spectrum of ethanal, CH_3CHO, to show the splitting pattern. The low resolution spectrum is shown below to help you (Figure 30.7).

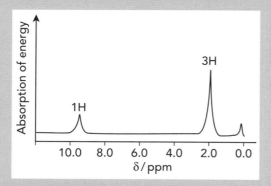

Figure 30.7

Explain your answer.   **[5]**

    [Total: 12]

TIPS

Be prepared to make deductions about the structure of a compound using any of the analytical methods you have learned about. In this question, mass spectra and infrared spectroscopy (Chapters 3 and 18) is used for confirmatory evidence.

TIP

In part **c** think about the number of ways of arranging the 'nuclear magnets'.

CONTINUED

2   Ibuprofen and caffeine are both drugs.

Ibuprofen can be identified from its R_f value obtained using thin-layer chromatography.

a   Define R_f [1]

b   State the meaning of these terms used in thin-layer chromatography.

   i   Stationary phase   [1]

   ii   Mobile phase   [1]

c   Describe how thin-layer chromatography is carried out.   [3]

d   The result of the thin-layer chromatography of a mixture of ibuprofen and compounds R and S is shown in Figure 30.8.

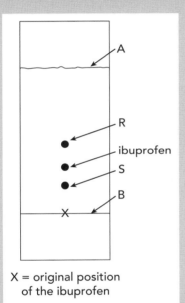

X = original position of the ibuprofen

Figure 30.8

   i   State the names of A and B on the diagram.   [1]

   ii   Calculate the R_f value of ibuprofen.   [1]

   iii Ibuprofen, R and S are polar molecules. Suggest why using a non-polar solvent may not separate the mixture of ibuprofen R and S.   [4]

TIP

In part **a** make sure that you give a definition and not another phrase for the abbreviation.

CONTINUED

TIP

In part **e** remember that you have to compare the areas of the triangles.

e A gas chromatogram of a mixture of caffeine and theobromine is shown in Figure 30.9.

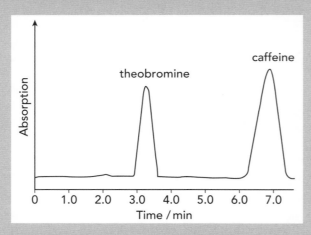

Figure 30.9

Calculate the percentage of caffeine in this mixture. **[3]**

[Total: 15]

3 Vanilla pods contain many different compounds. One of these is vanillin. The NMR spectrum and structure of vanillin are shown in Figure 30.10.

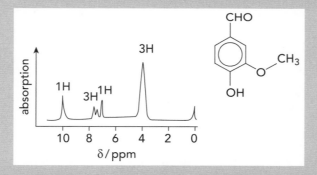

Figure 30.10

Some chemical shifts are given here:

$R–CH_3 = 0.9$; $R–CH_2–R = 1.3$; $–CO–CH_3 = 2.3$; $–O–CH_3 = 3.8$; $–O–H = 4.7$; $C_6H_5–H = 7.5$; CHO (aromatic aldehyde) = 10.0; $–COOH = 11.0$; phenolic $–O–H = 4.5$ to 10.0

a Explain how the NMR spectrum is consistent with the structure of vanillin. **[4]**

b Vanillin can be separated from other compounds in vanilla seeds (many of which are relatively volatile) by gas-liquid chromatography. Explain how this method is able to separate compounds. **[6]**

[Total: 10]

TIPS

In part **a** you have to match the chemical shifts given to the peaks in the NMR spectrum.

In part **b** you have to write in general terms about the phases in GLC and relate this to the different types of compounds that might be present.

> # Chapter P1 and P2
Practical skills

Exercise P.1 Tables and graphs

This exercise will familiarise you with drawing a table and plotting graphs.

TIPS

When drawing graphs, we plot the **independent variable** along the horizontal axis and the **dependent variable** on the vertical axis.

When drawing tables, the independent variable usually goes in the first column.

KEY WORDS

independent variable: the variable under investigation for which we choose different values.

dependent variable: the variable we measure to judge the effect of changing the independent variable.

Sodium thiosulfate reacts with dilute hydrochloric acid to produce a fine yellow precipitate of sulfur. The rate of reaction can be followed by measuring the time taken for a cross on a piece of paper placed under the reaction mixture to be blocked from view by the precipitate.

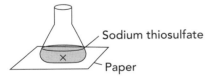

Figure P.1: Clouding in sodium thiosulfate solution.

50 cm³ of aqueous sodium thiosulfate was placed in a flask and 10 cm³ of 0.1 mol dm³ hydrochloric acid added. The flask was warmed to a specific temperature and then placed over the cross. The temperature was recorded at the start and when the cross had just disappeared. The time taken for the cross to disappear was recorded. The reaction was repeated at different temperatures using the same volume and concentration of sodium thiosulfate.

a   Why should the flasks used in each experiment have the same dimensions?

b   The results of the first 6 experiments are shown here.

- **Experiment 1:** temperature at start 26 °C; temperature when cross disappears 22 °C; time 130 s

- **Experiment 2:** temperature at start 36 °C; temperature when cross disappears 32 °C; time 70 s

- **Experiment 3:** temperature at start 43 °C; temperature when cross disappears 35 °C; time 55 s

- **Experiment 4:** temperature at start 46 °C; temperature when cross disappears 40 °C; time 37 s

- **Experiment 5:** temperature at start 51 °C; temperature when cross disappears 47 °C; time 33 s

- **Experiment 6:** The time taken for the cross to disappear was 26 s.

The diagrams show part of the thermometer used to measure the temperature.

i   Deduce the temperature change for **Experiment 6**.

ii   Why does the temperature decrease?

iii   Calculate the average temperature in each experiment.

iv   What assumptions have you made about this average?

c   Draw up a table to show these results.

d   i   On a piece of graph paper, plot the points for the time taken for the cross to disappear against the average temperature.

ii   Identify the **anomalous result**.

iii   Draw the best curve through the points.

iv   From your graph, deduce the time for the cross to disappear if the experiment were repeated at 70 °C. State the problems that arise from this extrapolation.

e   i   State which experiment had the highest rate of reaction. Explain your answer.

ii   Plot a graph of $\dfrac{1}{\text{time}}$ against average temperature excluding the anomalous point.

f   **Evaluate** this experimental method.

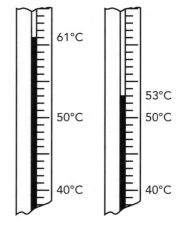

Figure P.2: Change in temperature.

KEY WORDS

anomalous result: a result that does not follow the pattern shown by the rest of the data.

COMMAND WORD

Evaluate: judge or calculate the quality, importance, amount, or value of something.

Exercise P.2 Qualitative analysis

This exercise will familiarise you with some tests for specific ions and gases.

> **TIPS**
>
> You usually acidify solutions of silver nitrate or barium chloride used as test reagents. Make sure you choose the correct acid so that an unwanted precipitate does not form.
>
> Knowing how to draw up or complete tables of results of quantitative tests is an important skill. You need to know your test reagents and the expected result of a positive test for specific ions in order to complete this. Think about what is not present as well as what is present.

KEY WORDS

qualitative tests: specific chemical tests used to determine the type of compounds, elements or ions present in a sample, e.g. silver nitrate test for halide ions.

We can test for specific anions and cations in solution by carrying out **qualitative tests**. Some of these involve the use of sodium hydroxide or silver nitrate.

a   Match the ions or gases (1–6 on the left) to the reagents which give a positive test for them (A–F on the right).

1 $Cu^{2+}(aq)$	**A** add hydrochloric acid and test with limewater
2 $Br^-(aq)$	**B** aqueous barium chloride
3 $SO_4^{2-}(aq)$	**C** aqueous sodium hydroxide
4 $NO_3^-(aq)$	**D** damp red litmus paper
5 $CO_3^{2-}(aq)$	**E** heat with aluminium foil and aqueous sodium hydroxide
6 $NH_3(g)$	**F** aqueous silver nitrate

b   Give the positive results you would expect for the ions or gases 1–6 in part **a**.

If it is difficult to distinguish between some ions using sodium hydroxide, you might have to conduct **confirmatory tests** on separate samples. In order to distinguish between halides you might have to see whether or not the precipitate dissolves in ammonia.

c   Explain why you need to carry out confirmatory tests to distinguish between these pairs of aqueous ions. Describe how you can use these tests to distinguish between these ions.

   i   zinc and magnesium

   ii   zinc and aluminium

   iii   iron(II) and chromium(III)

KEY WORDS

confirmatory test: a different test to ensure that the result from a qualitative analysis experiment is correct.

    iv   bromide and chloride

    v   nitrate and nitrite

    vi very dilute aqueous solutions of iron(II) and iron(III) ions

d **i**   Which of these acids could you use to acidify barium chloride when being used as a test reagent? Explain your answer for each acid.

      Acids: hydrochloric; nitric; sulfuric

  ii Which of these acids could you use to acidify silver nitrate when being used as a test reagent? Explain your answer for each acid.

      Acids: hydrobromic; nitric; sulfuric

e **i**   Write suitable answers for boxes A to G to identify the compound present.

Experiment	Observation	Inference
1. appearance	colourless crystals	
2. heat solid gently in a test-tube	**A**	salt contains water of crystallisation
3. solid warmed with dilute hydrochloric acid	no gas evolved	**B**
4. dilute nitric acid and barium nitrate added to solution of the solid	white precipitate	**C**
5. small volume of sodium hydroxide added to solution of the solid	white precipitate	**D**
6. excess sodium hydroxide added	white precipitate dissolves	**E**
7. small volume of aqueous ammonia added	**F**	could be aluminium, magnesium or zinc
8. aqueous ammonia added in excess	white precipitate dissolves	**G**

Table P.1: Identifying compounds.

  ii Give the name of the compound.

Exercise P.3 Planning and analysing

This exercise will familiarise you with the idea of planning an experiment, analysing the result and evaluating the experimental method.

TIPS

When you select measuring apparatus for accurate experiments, the glassware should be selected so that it gives the most accurate reading possible. As long as there are no other errors, the accuracy of the results you get depends on the least accurate measuring implement.

Remember that hydrogen has a very low relative molecular mass.

Hydrochloric acid reacts with iron to form iron(II) chloride and hydrogen.

a   It is possible to follow the course of this reaction by either measuring the volume of hydrogen gas given off using a gas syringe or by measuring the loss of mass of hydrogen.

  i   Draw labelled diagrams of the apparatus you would use for each method.

  ii   Give advantages and disadvantages for each method.

b   A student wants to investigate the rate of corrosion of iron at different pH values. Suggest how you would carry out this experiment. Include the following:

  •   Reference to the **accuracy** of the measurements of the equipment you select.

  •   Reference to the **control variables**, the dependent variable and the independent variable.

c   Some results are given for different pH values.

| pH | Volume of hydrogen in $cm^3\ hr^{-1}$ | | | | |
	Run 1	Run 2	Run 3	Run 4	Mean
4.0	0.70	1.08	1.45	1.64	
5.0	0.34	0.60	0.51	0.45	
5.5	0.28	0.33	0.31	0.29	
6.0	0.10	0.14	0.20	0.15	

Table P.2: Volume of hydrochloric acid.

  i   Calculate the **mean** volume of hydrogen for each pH.

  ii   At which pH are the readings most **precise**? Explain your answer.

KEY WORDS

accuracy (of measurement): how close a measurement is to its true value.

control variables: variables (other than the dependent and independent variables) that must be kept the same during an experiment.

mean: the average of the numbers taken from the data in a number of identical experiments.

precision (of measurements): measurements where sets of repeat readings are grouped closely together (even though they might not be close to the true value).

EXAM-STYLE QUESTIONS

TIP

This question is about a practical procedure for finding relative molecular mass that is new to you. The way to tackle this question is to think of it as a variation of an experiment you have seen in Chapter 5.

1 An old method of determining the relative molecular mass of a **volatile** liquid is to use a Dumas bulb (a thin-walled glass bulb). The empty bulb is weighed and a small amount of a volatile liquid is introduced. The bulb is then immersed in a water bath which is at a temperature about 10 °C higher than the boiling point of the liquid. When no more drops of liquid can be seen, the bulb is kept in the water bath for another minute. The bulb is then removed and dipped into a beaker of cold water. The bulb is then removed, sealed and allowed to return to room temperature. It is then reweighed.

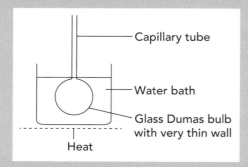

Figure P.3

KEY WORD

volatile: easily turned into vapour when the temperature is increased. Volatile liquids have low boiling points.

a Suggest how you could introduce the volatile liquid into the bulb. [1]

b Suggest how the bulb could be kept in position. [2]

c Suggest why it is necessary to immerse as much of the flask as possible in the water bath. [1]

d Explain why the temperature of the water bath is kept constant. [1]

e Suggest why the bulb was kept in the flask for another minute after no more liquid was seen? [1]

f If the liquid has a very low boiling point there may be considerable evaporation during the cooling period. Suggest how this problem can be overcome. [1]

g During the second weighing, the pressure of the air in the bulb is not the same as the atmospheric pressure. Suggest why it is different. [1]

h The results are:

• mass of empty bulb = 95.30 g

• mass of bulb at end of experiment = 96.05 g

• volume of bulb = 250 cm³

• temperature of water bath = 77 °C

• atmospheric pressure = 101 000 Pa

• $R = 8.31 \, \text{J K}^{-1} \text{mol}^{-1}$

Calculate the mass in g, the temperature in K and the volume in m³ [3]

CONTINUED

i Use the equation $M_r = \dfrac{mRT}{pV}$ to calculate a value for M_r. [2]

j The value of M_r can also be found using a gas syringe. The plunger of the gas syringe was set at zero and the volume of gas was recorded after 1 minute.

    i Figure P.4 shows part of the gas syringe. State the volume of gas shown on the gas syringe. [1]

Figure P.4

    ii Suggest two inaccuracies in reading the volume of the gas in the syringe. [2]

[Total: 16]

2 When a fizzy drink bottle is left open, carbon dioxide escapes from the **carbonated water**. A scientist suggests that this is a first order process. Describe an experiment you could do to prove whether or not this is correct. In your answer include:

- Details of apparatus

- The measurements you would make

- How you would process your results

- Sources of error

- How you would deduce the order of reaction

[Total: 14]

TIP

The idea of carbon dioxide escaping should give you the clue to how to carry out the experiment.

KEY WORDS

carbonated water: water with carbon dioxide dissolved in it.

CONTINUED

TIPS

Although this practical procedure will be unfamiliar to you, you should be able to do this question by thinking of it as a variation of a typical acid–base titration but without using an indicator.

The end-point in this titration is the point of minimum conductivity.

3 Hydrogen ions conduct electricity better than hydroxide, sodium or chloride ions. We can measure change in electrical conductivity using a conductivity electrode connected to a meter. We can use this apparatus to determine the concentration of a dilute solution of hydrochloric acid by titrating with a more concentrated solution of sodium hydroxide.

Dilute hydrochloric acid of unknown concentration was titrated with $1.00\ mol\ dm^{-3}$ sodium hydroxide using the apparatus in Figure P.5.

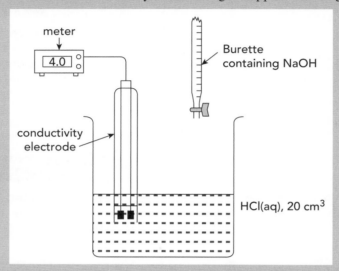

meter

Burette containing NaOH

conductivity electrode

$HCl(aq)$, 20 cm^3

Figure P.5

a Suggest how you would carry out this titration.   [5]

b Suggest any sources of error might arise from this method.   [2]

c The results of this titration are shown in the table.

Volume of NaOH / cm^3	0	1.0	2.0	2.5	3.6	4.5	5.0	7.0
Conductivity / $\Omega^{-1}\ m^{-1}$	3.75	3.10	2.70	2.05	1.30	1.20	1.40	2.25

Table P.3

Plot a graph of the volume of the conductivity against the volume of sodium hydroxide.   [2]

d State which result is anomalous.   [1]

e Draw two straight lines to calculate the end-point of the titration.   [3]

f Suggest why it is more difficult to see when the end-point is approaching in this type of titration than in an acid–base titration.   [1]

g Describe how to improve the accuracy of your results.   [1]

h Use the end-point from your graph to calculate the concentration of the hydrochloric acid.   [2]

[Total: 17]

Appendix 1

The Periodic Table of the Elements

Key

| atomic number |
| atomic symbol |
| name |
| relative atomic mass |

Group																	
1	2											13	14	15	16	17	18
							1 H hydrogen 1.0										2 He helium 4.0
3 Li lithium 6.9	4 Be beryllium 9.0											5 B boron 10.8	6 C carbon 12.0	7 N nitrogen 14.0	8 O oxygen 16.0	9 F fluorine 19.0	10 Ne neon 20.2
11 Na sodium 23.0	12 Mg magnesium 24.3	3	4	5	6	7	8	9	10	11	12	13 Al aluminium 27.0	14 Si silicon 28.1	15 P phosphorus 31.0	16 S sulfur 32.1	17 Cl chlorine 35.5	18 Ar argon 39.9
19 K potassium 39.1	20 Ca calcium 40.1	21 Sc scandium 45.0	22 Ti titanium 47.9	23 V vanadium 50.9	24 Cr chromium 52.0	25 Mn manganese 54.9	26 Fe iron 55.8	27 Co cobalt 58.9	28 Ni nickel 58.7	29 Cu copper 63.5	30 Zn zinc 65.4	31 Ga gallium 69.7	32 Ge germanium 72.6	33 As arsenic 74.9	34 Se selenium 79.0	35 Br bromine 79.9	36 Kr krypton 83.8
37 Rb rubidium 85.5	38 Sr strontium 87.6	39 Y yttrium 88.9	40 Zr zirconium 91.2	41 Nb niobium 92.9	42 Mo molybdenum 95.9	43 Tc technetium –	44 Ru ruthenium 101.1	45 Rh rhodium 102.9	46 Pd palladium 106.4	47 Ag silver 107.9	48 Cd cadmium 112.4	49 In indium 114.8	50 Sn tin 118.7	51 Sb antimony 121.8	52 Te tellurium 127.6	53 I iodine 126.9	54 Xe xenon 131.3
55 Cs caesium 132.9	56 Ba barium 137.3	57–71 lanthanoids	72 Hf hafnium 178.5	73 Ta tantalum 180.9	74 W tungsten 183.8	75 Re rhenium 186.2	76 Os osmium 190.2	77 Ir iridium 192.2	78 Pt platinum 195.1	79 Au gold 197.0	80 Hg mercury 200.6	81 Tl thallium 204.4	82 Pb lead 207.2	83 Bi bismuth 209.0	84 Po polonium –	85 At astatine –	86 Rn radon –
87 Fr francium –	88 Ra radium –	89–103 actinoids	104 Rf rutherfordium –	105 Db dubnium –	106 Sg seaborgium –	107 Bh bohrium –	108 Hs hassium –	109 Mt meitnerium –	110 Ds darmstadtium –	111 Rg roentgenium –	112 Cn copernicium –	113 Nh nihonium –	114 Fl flerovium –	115 Mc moscovium –	116 Lv livermorium –	117 Ts tennessine –	118 Og oganesson –

| lanthanoids | 57
La
lanthanum
138.9 | 58
Ce
cerium
140.1 | 59
Pr
praseodymium
140.9 | 60
Nd
neodymium
144.4 | 61
Pm
promethium
– | 62
Sm
samarium
150.4 | 63
Eu
europium
152.0 | 64
Gd
gadolinium
157.3 | 65
Tb
terbium
158.9 | 66
Dy
dysprosium
162.5 | 67
Ho
holmium
164.9 | 68
Er
erbium
167.3 | 69
Tm
thulium
168.9 | 70
Yb
ytterbium
173.1 | 71
Lu
lutetium
175.0 |
| actinoids | 89
Ac
actinium
– | 90
Th
thorium
232.0 | 91
Pa
protactinium
231.0 | 92
U
uranium
238.0 | 93
Np
neptunium
– | 94
Pu
plutonium
– | 95
Am
americium
– | 96
Cm
curium
– | 97
Bk
berkelium
– | 98
Cf
californium
– | 99
Es
einsteinium
– | 100
Fm
fermium
– | 101
Md
mendelevium
– | 102
No
nobelium
– | 103
Lr
lawrencium
– |

> Appendix 2

Selected standard electrode potentials

Electrode reaction	$E^{\ominus}/V$	Electrode reaction	$E^{\ominus}/V$
$Ag^+ + e^- \rightleftharpoons Ag$	+0.80	$Mn^{2+} + 2e^- \rightleftharpoons Mn$	−1.18
$Br_2 + 2e^- \rightleftharpoons 2Br^-$	+1.07	$MnO_4^- + 8H^+ + 5e^- \rightleftharpoons Mn^{2+} + 4H_2O$	+1.52
$Ca^{2+} + 2e^- \rightleftharpoons Ca$	−2.87	$Ni^{2+} + 2e^- \rightleftharpoons Ni$	−0.25
$Cl_2 + 2e^- \rightleftharpoons 2Cl^-$	+1.36	$NO_3^- + 2H^+ + e^- \rightleftharpoons NO_2 + H_2O$	+0.81
$ClO^- + H_2O + 2e^- \rightleftharpoons Cl^- + 2OH^-$	+0.89	$NO_3^- + 10H^+ + 8e^- \rightleftharpoons NH_4^+ + 3H_2O$	+0.87
$Cr^{2+} + 2e^- \rightleftharpoons Cr$	−0.91	$O_2 + 4H^+ + 4e^- \rightleftharpoons 2H_2O$	+1.23
$Cr^{3+} + 3e^- \rightleftharpoons Cr$	−0.74	$O_2 + 2H_2O + 4e^- \rightleftharpoons 4OH^-$	+0.40
$Cr_2O_7^{2-} + 14H^+ + 6e^- \rightleftharpoons 2Cr^{3+} + 7H_2O$	+1.33	$Pb^{2+} + 2e^- \rightleftharpoons Pb$	−0.13
$Cu^+ + e^- \rightleftharpoons Cu$	+0.52	$PbO_2 + 4H^+ + 2e^- \rightleftharpoons Pb^{2+} + 2H_2O$	+1.47
$Cu^{2+} + e^- \rightleftharpoons Cu^+$	+0.15	$Sn^{2+} + 2e^- \rightleftharpoons Sn$	−0.14
$Cu^{2+} + 2e^- \rightleftharpoons Cu$	+0.34	$Sn^{4+} + 2e^- \rightleftharpoons Sn^{2+}$	+0.15
$F_2 + 2e^- \rightleftharpoons 2F^-$	+2.87	$SO_4^{2-} + 4H^+ + 2e^- \rightleftharpoons SO_2 + 2H_2O$	+0.17
$Fe^{2+} + 2e^- \rightleftharpoons Fe$	−0.44	$S_2O_8^{2-} + 2e^- \rightleftharpoons 2SO_4^{2-}$	+2.01
$Fe^{3+} + e^- \rightleftharpoons Fe^{2+}$	+0.77	$S_4O_6^{2-} + 2e^- \rightleftharpoons 2S_2O_3^{2-}$	+0.09
$Fe^{3+} + 3e^- \rightleftharpoons Fe$	−0.04	$V^{2+} + 2e^- \rightleftharpoons V$	−1.20
$2H^+ + 2e^- \rightleftharpoons H_2$	0.00	$V^{3+} + e^- \rightleftharpoons V^{2+}$	−0.26
$2H_2O + 2e^- \rightleftharpoons H_2 + 2OH^-$	−0.83	$VO^{2+} + 2H^+ + e^- \rightleftharpoons V^{3+} + H_2O$	+0.34
$H_2O_2 + 2H^+ + 2e^- \rightleftharpoons 2H_2O$	+1.77	$VO_2^+ + 2H^+ + e^- \rightleftharpoons VO^{2+} + H_2O$	+1.00
$I_2 + 2e^- \rightleftharpoons 2I^-$	+0.54	$VO_3^- + 4H^+ + e^- \rightleftharpoons VO^{2+} + 2H_2O$	+1.00
$K^+ + e^- \rightleftharpoons K$	−2.92	$Zn^{2+} + 2e^- \rightleftharpoons Zn$	−0.76
$Mg^{2+} + 2e^- \rightleftharpoons Mg$	−2.38		

> Appendix 3

Qualitative analysis notes

1 Reactions of aqueous cations

Cation	Reaction with	
	NaOH(aq)	NH$_3$(aq)
aluminium, Al^{3+}(aq)	white precipitate soluble in excess	white precipitate insoluble in excess
ammonium, NH$_4^+$(aq)	no precipitate NH$_3$ produced on heating	–
barium, Ba^{2+}(aq)	faint white precipitate is nearly always observed unless reagents are pure	no precipitate
calcium, Ca^{2+}(aq)	white precipitate with high [Ca^{2+}(aq)]	no precipitate
chromium(III), Cr^{3+}(aq)	grey-green precipitate soluble in excess	grey-green precipitate insoluble in excess
copper(II), Cu^{2+}(aq)	pale blue precipitate insoluble in excess	pale blue precipitate soluble in excess giving dark blue solution
iron(II), Fe^{2+}(aq)	green precipitate turning brown on contact with air insoluble in excess	green precipitate turning brown on contact with air insoluble in excess
iron(III), Fe^{3+}(aq)	red-brown precipitate insoluble in excess	red-brown precipitate insoluble in excess
magnesium, Mg^{2+}(aq)	white precipitate insoluble in excess	white precipitate insoluble in excess
manganese(II), Mn^{2+}(aq)	off-white precipitate rapidly turning brown on contact with air insoluble in excess	off-white precipitate rapidly turning brown on contact with air insoluble in excess
zinc, Zn^{2+}(aq)	white precipitate soluble in excess	white precipitate soluble in excess

2 Reactions of anions

Ion	Reaction
carbonate, $CO_3^{2-}(aq)$	CO_2 liberated by dilute acids
chloride, $Cl^-(aq)$	gives white precipitate with $Ag^+(aq)$ (soluble in $NH_3(aq)$)
bromide, $Br^-(aq)$	gives cream precipitate with $Ag^+(aq)$ (partially soluble in $NH_3(aq)$)
iodide, $I^-(aq)$	gives yellow precipitate with $Ag^+(aq)$ (insoluble in $NH_3(aq)$)
nitrate, $NO_3^-(aq)$	NH_3 liberated on heating with $OH^-(aq)$ and Al foil
nitrite, $NO_2^-(aq)$	NH_3 liberated on heating with $OH^-(aq)$ and Al foil; NO liberated by dilute acids (colourless NO → (pale) brown NO_2 in air)
sulfate, $SO_4^{2-}(aq)$	gives white precipitate with $Ba^{2+}(aq)$ (insoluble in excess dilute strong acids)
sulfite, $SO_3^{2-}(aq)$	SO_2 liberated on warming with dilute acids; gives white precipitate with $Ba^{2+}(aq)$ (soluble in excess dilute strong acids)
thiosulfate, $S_2O_3^{2-}(aq)$	gives white ppt. slowly with H^+

3 Tests for gases

Gas	Test and test result
ammonia, NH_3	turns damp red litmus paper blue
carbon dioxide, CO_2	gives a white precipitate with limewater (precipitate dissolves with excess CO_2)
hydrogen, H_2	'pops' with a lighted splint
oxygen, O_2	relights a glowing splint

4 Tests for elements

Element	Test and test result
iodine, I_2	gives blue-black colour on addition of starch solution

> Glossary

Command Words

Below are the Cambridge International syllabus definitions for Commands words which may be used in exams. The information in this section is taken from the Cambridge International syllabus for examination from 2022. You should always refer to the appropriate syllabus document for the year of your examination to confirm the details and for more information. The syllabus document is available on the Cambridge International website at www.cambridgeinternational.org. Cambridge International copyright material in this publication is reproduced under licence and remains the intellectual property of Cambridge Assessment International Education.

Analyse: examine in detail to show meaning, identify elements and the relationship between them

Calculate: work out from given facts, figures or information

Compare: identify/comment on similarities and/or differences

Consider: review and respond to given information

Contrast: identify/comment on differences

Deduce: conclude from available information

Define: give precise meaning

Demonstrate: show how or give an example

Describe: state the points of a topic / give characteristics and main features

Determine: establish an answer using the information available

Discuss: write about issue(s) or topic(s) in depth in a structured way

Evaluate: judge or calculate the quality, importance, amount, or value of something

Examine: investigate closely, in detail

Explain: set out purposes or reasons / make the relationships between things evident / provide why and/or how and support with relevant evidence

Give: produce an answer from a given source or recall/memory

Identify: name/select/recognise

Justify: support a case with evidence/argument

Predict: suggest what may happen based on available information

Show (that): provide structural evidence that leads to a given result

Sketch: make a simple drawing showing the key features

State: express in clear terms

Suggest: apply knowledge and understanding to situations where there are a range of valid responses in order to make proposals / put forward considerations

Key Words

2,4-DNPH (2,4-dinitrophenylhydrazine): compound used to form condensation products with carbonyl compounds. The products have characteristic melting points

Accuracy (of measurement): how close a measurement is to its true value

Acid: a proton (H^+ ion) donor (Brønsted-Lowry definition)

Acid-base indicator: a compound that has two different ranges of colours depending on the pH of the solution in which it is placed. It changes colour over a narrow range of pH values

Acid dissociation constant, K_a: the equilibrium constant for the dissociation of a weak acid

Acid rain: rain with an acidity of below about pH 5.5 due to the reactions in the atmosphere involving acidic oxides

Activation energy, E_A: the minimum energy that colliding particles must possess to break bonds to start a chemical reaction

Activating group: a group attached to a benzene ring which makes the conditions needed for substitution in the ring easier

Acylate: to substitute a CH_3CO- group into a compound

Acylation: the process of inserting an acyl group, CH_3CO, into a molecule

Acyl group: a group which contains both an alkyl and a carbonyl group, e.g. CH_3CO-

Addition polymerisation: the reaction of many monomers containing at least one double C=C bond to form the long-chain polymers as the only product

Addition reaction: an organic reaction in which two (or more) molecules combine to give a single product

Adhesives: substances which stick things together

Adsorption: the first stage in heterogeneous catalysis where reactant molecules form bonds with atoms on the catalyst surface

Alcohols: organic chain compounds containing the –OH group. (Ring compounds with an OH connected directly to the ring are called phenols)

Aldehydes: organic compounds containing the —C=O group

Alkanes: saturated hydrocarbons with the general formula C_nH_{2n+2}

Alkenes: unsaturated hydrocarbons with C=C double bonds and the general formula C_nH_{2n}

Alkyl group: a group having one fewer hydrogen atom than the corresponding alkane

Allotrope: different crystalline or molecular forms of the same element

Amino acid residue: the individual units of the amino acids that make up a polypeptide or protein

Amines: compounds with an $-NH_2$ functional group

Amino acids: compounds containing a carboxylic acid group and an amine group

Amphoteric oxide: an oxide which reacts with both acids and alkalis

Anhydrous salt: a salt which does not contain water of crystallisation

Anode: the positive electrode (where oxidation reactions occur)

Anomalous result: a result that does not follow the pattern shown by the rest of the data

Arenes: hydrocarbons containing one or more benzene rings

Atomic orbitals: regions of space outside the nucleus that can be occupied by a maximum of two electrons. Orbitals are named s, p, d and f. They have different shapes.

Atomic radius: the covalent atomic radius is half the distance between the nuclei of two covalently bonded atoms of the same type. This is not the only type of atomic radius but it gives us the best data when comparing the elements across a period

Attacking reagent: an atom or compound which is an electrophile or a nucleophile

Average bond energy: the average energy needed to break a specific covalent bond averaged from a variety of molecules in the gaseous state, e.g. the average O—H bond energy in ethanol, water and other compounds

Avogadro constant, L: the number of specified particles (atoms, ions, molecules or electrons) in a mole of those particles. Its numerical value is 6.02×10^{23}

Azo dyes: coloured compounds formed on the addition of phenol (or another aryl compound) to a solution containing a diazonium ion

Base: a proton (H^+ ion) acceptor (Brønsted–Lowry definition)

Basic oxide: an oxide which reacts only with an acid to form a salt and water. They are generally metal oxides

Bidentate ligand: a ligand that forms two co-ordinate (or dative) bonds to the central transition metal ion in a complex

Biodegradable: can be decomposed by natural means, e.g by bacteria / fungi

Boltzmann distribution: a graph showing the number of molecules with a particular kinetic energy plotted against the kinetic energy. The exact shape of the curve varies with temperature. The curve shows that only a very small proportion of the molecules have very high energies.

Bond energy: the energy required to break one mole of a particular covalent bond in the gaseous state. The units of bond energy are kilojoules per mole, $kJ\ mol^{-1}$

Bond length: the distance between the nuclei of two covalently bonded atoms

Bond polarisation: occurs in a covalent bond in which the bonding electrons are attracted more to one atom than the other leading to a dipole in the bond, e.g. $C^{\delta+}—Cl^{\delta-}$

Born-Haber cycle: an enthalpy cycle used to calculate lattice energy

Brittle: breaks easily when a force is applied

Brønsted-Lowry theory: acids are defined as hydrogen ions donors and bases as hydrogen ion acceptors

Buckminsterfullerene: a simple molecular structure of carbon, with formula C_{60}. The molecule has the shape of a football (soccer ball). The carbon atoms are arranged at the corners of 20 hexagons and 12 pentagons

The bonds where two hexagons join are shorter than the bonds between the hexagons and the pentagons.

Butanoate: in this context, the negative ion, $C_3H_7CO_2^-$, present in sodium butanoate. The ion is the conjugate base of butanoic acid

Carbocation: an alkyl group with a single positive charge on one of its carbon atoms. It is formed in reaction mechanisms

Carbon-13 NMR spectroscopy: a technique for identifying the types of groups adjacent to specific ^{13}C atoms

Carbonated water: water with carbon dioxide dissolved in it

Carbonyl compound: a compound containing a C=O group joined to one or two alkyl groups or a hydrogen atom

Carboxylic acids: organic compounds which have a $-CO_2H$ functional group and a general formula $C_nH_{2n+1}CO_2H$

Carcinogenic: cancer forming

Catalyst: a substance that increases the rate of a chemical reaction but is chemically unchanged at the end of the reaction. It provides a different mechanism of reaction which has a lower activation energy

Catalytic converter: a piece of equipment put on the exhaust of cars with petrol engines to remove oxides of nitrogen and carbon monoxide produced in the engine

Catalytic oxidation: an oxidation reaction whose rate of reaction is increased by a catalyst

Cathode: the negative electrode (where reduction reactions occur)

CFCs (chlorofluorocarbons): halogenoalkanes which have chlorine and fluorine atoms in their structures e.g. $CH_2FCH_2CCl_3$

Chain reaction: a reaction which continues by similar propagation steps. The propagation steps in the free radical substitution of hydrogen atoms in alkanes by chlorine is an example

Chemical shift: the resonant frequency of a nucleus relative to a standard (usually TMS)

Chiral centre: a carbon atom with the four different atoms or groups of atoms attached. This allows optical isomers to exist

Chloroalkanes: halogenoalkanes in which chlorine is the halogen

***cis/trans* isomerism:** a type of geometric isomerism where two different substituent groups joined to the carbon atoms on each side of a double bond are arranged either on the same side of the double bond (*cis*-isomer) or on opposite sides (*trans*-isomer)

Closed system: a system in which matter is not lost or gained, e.g. gases in a closed jar

Collision theory: in order for particles to react when they collide, they must have sufficient energy and collide in the correct orientation

Combustion: burning (usually burning a substance in oxygen gas or air)

Common ion effect: the reduction of the solubility of a dissolved salt by adding a compound that has an ion in common with the dissolved salt, e.g. addition of sodium chloride to a solution of very slightly soluble lead(II) chloride

Complex ion: a central transition metal ion surrounded by ligands, bonded to the central ion by dative (also called co-ordinate) covalent bonds

Compound: a substance containing atoms from two or more different elements which are chemically bonded (joined) together

Condensation: a reaction in which two organic molecules join together and in the process eliminate a small molecule, such as water or hydrogen chloride

Conditions: when referring to chemical reactions, things other than specific chemicals used in the reaction, e.g. temperature, pressure, pH

Confirmatory test: a different test to ensure that the result from a qualitative analysis experiment is correct

Conjugate pair (acid-base): an acid-base pair on each side of an acid–base equilibrium equation that are related to each other by the difference of a hydrogen ion, e.g. the acid in the forward reaction and the base in the backward reaction

Consistent (mechanism): the mechanism fits with the rate equation (but doesn't prove it)

Contact process: the process used to produce sulfuric acid. It specifically refers to the reaction $2SO_2(g) + O_2(g) \rightleftharpoons 2SO_3(g)$, using a V_2O_5 catalyst

Control variables: variables (other than the dependent and independent variables) that must be kept the same during an experiment

Coupling reaction: the reaction between a diazonium salt and an alkaline solution of phenol (or similar compound) to make an azo dye

Co-ordination number: the number of co-ordinate bonds formed by ligands with a transition element ion in a complex

Co-ordinate bond: the sharing of a pair of electrons between two atoms where both the electrons in the bond come from the same atom. Also called a dative covalent bond

Co-polymer: a polymer which is synthesised from more than one monomer

Coulombs, c: the units of electrical charge. (coulombs = amperes $\times$ seconds)

Covalent bond: the electrostatic attraction between the nuclei of two atoms and a shared pair of electrons

Cracking: the process in which large, less useful hydrocarbon molecules are broken down into smaller, more useful molecules in an oil refinery

Cross-linked (polymers): polymer chains with covalent bonds linking the chains together

D-block element: the elements in groups 3 to 12, where the d-orbitals are gradually being filled

Degenerate orbitals: atomic orbitals in the same energy level in a given sub-shell

Dehydration: a reaction in which water is removed from a larger molecule

Delocalised electrons: electrons that are not associated with any particular atom. In metals, the delocalised electrons move throughout the metallic structure between the metal ions when a voltage is applied. In the molecule benzene, the delocalised electrons have a more limited movement

Dependent variable: the variable we measure to judge the effect of changing the independent variable

Diazotisation: the reaction between phenylamine and nitrous acid (HNO_2) to give a diazonium salt in the first step in preparing an azo dye

Diazonium salt: a salt with a cation which has the formula $RN^+\equiv N$. In stable diazonium salts R is an aryl ring

Dipeptide: a compound formed from the condensation reaction between two amino acids. The $-COOH$ group of one amino acid reacts with the $-NH_2$ group of another amino acid

Discharge (of ions): the conversion of ions to atoms or molecules at the electrodes during electrolysis by loss or gain of electrons

Displayed formula: a 2D representation of an organic molecule, showing *all* its atoms (by their symbols) and their bonds (by short single, double or triple lines between the symbols)

Disproportionation: the simultaneous oxidation and reduction of the same species in a chemical reaction

Dissociation: the break-up of molecules into ions

Dot-and-cross diagram: a diagram showing the arrangement of the outer-shell electrons in an ionic or covalent element or compound. The electrons are shown as dots or crosses to show their origin

Drying agent: a compound which removes excess water from a substance

Dynamic equilibrium: reactants are being converted to products at the same rate as products are being converted back to reactants

Economical: saving money (or energy or time)

Effective collisions: collisions of particles which lead to bond breaking and a chemical reaction

Electrical conductivity: the ease with which an electric current can pass through a substance. The higher the value, the greater the conductivity

Electrochemical cell: two half-cells connected by a salt bridge and external circuit allowing the flow of electrons between them

Electrode: a rod or plate of metal or carbon (graphite) which conducts electricity to or from an electrolyte

Electrode potential, *E*: the voltage measured for a half-cell compared with another half-cell

Electrolysis: the decomposition of an ionic compound when molten or in aqueous solution by an electric current

Electron: negatively charged particle found in orbitals outside the nucleus of an atom. It has negligible mass compared with a proton

Electron affinity: the first electron affinity is the enthalpy change when one mole of electrons is added to one mole of gaseous atoms to form one mole of gaseous ions with a $1-$ charge under standard conditions, e.g. $O(g) + e^- \rightarrow O^-(g)$ EA_1

Electrophoresis: the separation of ions placed in an electric field between a positive and a negative electrode

Electronegativity: the power of a particular atom that is covalently bonded to another atom to attract the bonding electron pair towards itself

Electronic configuration: a way of representing the arrangement of the electrons in atoms showing the principal quantum shells, the sub-shells and the number of electrons present, e.g. $1s^2\,2s^2\,2p^3$. The electrons may also be shown in boxes

Electrons in boxes notation: shows each orbital s, p_x, p_y, p_z, etc. as a box. The boxes are arranged vertically in sets of increasing energy levels e.g.$1s$ = 1 box, $2p$ = 3 boxes higher up

Electron transfer: in terms of redox reactions - loss of electrons by one species (oxidation) and gain of electrons by another species (reduction)

Electron-withdrawing effect: the ability of atoms or groups in an organic compound to pull the electrons in bonds towards themselves. The greater the electronegativity of the atoms, the stronger the electron withdrawing effect

Electrophile: a species in organic chemistry that can act as an electron pair acceptor

Electrophilic: a reaction where the mechanism involves an electrophile accepting a pair of electrons

Elimination: a reaction in which a small molecule is removed from an organic molecule

Empirical formula: the simplest whole number ratio of the elements present in one molecule or formula unit of the compound.

End-point (of a titration): the point in a titration where the reaction is just complete in terms of the stoichiometry

Endothermic reaction: heat energy is absorbed during a reaction. The value of ΔH is positive

Energy cycle: a diagram showing alternative routes between reactants and products that allows the determination of one energy change from other energy changes using Hess's Law

Energy level diagram (for an enthalpy cycle): an enthalpy cycle arranged to show the various enthalpy changes by arrows going up (endothermic) or down (exothermic)

Energy levels: each electron in an atom has its particular average amount of energy. The further away the electron is from the nucleus, the more energy it has. Each principal energy level (symbol n) corresponds to an electron shell at a certain distance from the nucleus. Energy levels are split up into sub-levels which are given the names s, p, d, etc.

Enhanced greenhouse effect: increase in the average temperature of the atmosphere as a consequence of the increase in greenhouse gases produced by human activity

Enthalpy change, ΔH: the heat energy transferred during a chemical reaction

Enthalpy change of solution, $\Delta H^{\ominus}_{sol}$: the energy absorbed or released when one mole of an ionic solid dissolves in sufficient water to form a very dilute solution

Enthalpy cycle diagram: a diagram showing alternative routes between reactants and products that allows the determination of one enthalpy change from other known enthalpy changes by using Hess's Law

Entropy: the number of possible arrangements of the particles and their energy in a given system

Equilibrium constant: a constant which is calculated from the equilibrium expression for the reaction. It can be in terms of concentrations, K_c or partial pressures, K_p

Equilibrium expression: a simple relationship that links K_c to the equilibrium concentrations, or K_p to the equilibrium partial pressures, of reactants and products and the stoichiometric equation

Esterification: a reaction of a carboxylic or acyl chloride with an alcohol (or phenol) to produce an ester and a small molecule (water or a salt such as NaCl)

Ethanolic: dissolved in ethanol. This is sometimes written as 'alcoholic' when the alcohol is not specified

Eutrophication: an environmental problem caused by fertilisers leaching from fields into rivers and lakes

Excess (reactant): a reactant that has more moles than needed to react with a given amount of another reactant. There will be some left unused when the reaction is complete

Expanded octet: atoms such as P and S can accommodate more than eight electrons in their outer shell

Exothermic reaction: heat energy is released during a reaction. The value of ΔH is negative

Faraday constant: the charge (in coulombs) carried by one mole of electrons or one mole of singly charged ions

Feasibility: the likelihood or not of a reaction occurring

Feasible reaction: a reaction that is likely to take place under particular conditions

Fehling's solution: an alkaline solution containing copper(II) ions (Cu^{2+}) used to test for the $-CHO$ group to distinguish between aldehydes and ketones. Compounds containing this group give an orange precipitate on warming with Fehling's solution

First ionisation energy, IE_1: the energy needed to remove 1 mole of electrons from 1 mole of atoms of an element in the gaseous state to form 1 mole of gaseous ions

First order reaction: reaction in which rate is proportional to the concentration of a particular reactant

Flexibility: ease of bending when a force is applied

Fluorohalogenoalkanes: general term for halogenoalkanes containing fluorine and sometimes oxygen (and occasionally chlorine) which are used in anaesthetics. Note that fluoroalkanes contain only fluorine atoms as substituents of hydrogen

Fragmentation: the breaking up of a covalent compound during mass spectrometry into smaller positively charged species, e.g. CH_3^+

Free radical: a species with one (or sometimes more than one) unpaired electron

Frequency: the number of events happening in a particular time e.g. number of waves per second / number of collisions per second

Frequency of collisions: the number of collisions per unit time, e.g. number of collisions per second

Friedel-Crafts reaction: the electrophilic substitution of an alkyl or acyl group into a benzene ring

Fuel cell: an electrochemical cell where hydrogen and oxygen undergo redox reactions to produce an electric current

Functional group: an atom or group of atoms in an organic molecule that determines its characteristic chemical reactions

General formula: a formula that represents a homologous series of compounds using letters and numbers; e.g. the general formula for the alkanes is C_nH_{2n+2}

Geometric isomers: molecules or ions with the same molecular formula and same bonds between their atoms but which cannot be superimposed on each other, due to some lack of rotation around their bonds; these are also known as *cis/trans* isomers

Giant ionic structure: structures having a three-dimensional network (lattice) of ionic bonds

Giant metallic structure: structures having a three-dimensional network of positive ions attracted to a sea of delocalised electrons between the ions (metallic bond)

Giant molecular structure / giant covalent structure: structures having a three-dimensional network of covalent bonds throughout the whole structure

Gibbs equation: the equation relating the Gibbs free energy change, $\Delta G^\ominus$, to the enthalpy change of the system, $\Delta H^\ominus$ and the entropy change of the system, $\Delta S^\ominus$. $\Delta G^\ominus = \Delta H^\ominus - T\Delta S^\ominus$

Gibbs free energy: the energy change that takes into account both the entropy change of a reaction and the enthalpy change

GLC (gas-liquid chromatography): chromatography in which the stationary phase is a liquid and the mobile phase is a gas

Global warming: the warming of the atmosphere caused by greenhouse gases trapping infrared radiation

reflected from the surface of the Earth. Enhanced global warming is the increased global warming due to the increase in greenhouse gases caused by human activity

Haber process: the process used to produce ammonia. It specifically refers to the reaction $N_2(g) + 3H_2(g) \rightleftharpoons 2NH_3(g)$, using a catalyst of iron

Half-cell: one half of an electrochemical cell which either donates electrons to or receives electrons from an external circuit when connected to another half-cell

Half-equation: an equation which shows either oxidation or reduction only. These are sometimes called ion–electron equations, because you need to balance the equation by including the correct number of electrons. Example: $Al^{3+} + 3e^- \rightarrow Al$

Half-life, $t_{\frac{1}{2}}$: the time taken for the amount (or concentration) of the limiting reactant in a reaction to decrease to half its initial value

Halide: a compound containing an anion with a single negative charge formed by the addition of an electron to a halogen atom

Halogenate: to substitute one or more halogen atoms in a compound or add one or more halogen atoms to a compound

Halogenoalkane: an organic molecule where one of more hydrogen atoms in an alkane has been replaced by one or more halogen atoms

Halogens: the Group 17 elements

Hess's Law: the enthalpy change in a chemical reaction is independent of the route by which the chemical reaction takes place as long as the initial and final conditions and states of reactants and products are the same for each route

Heterogeneous catalysis: the type of catalysis in which the catalyst is in a different phase to the reactants. For example, iron in the Haber process

Heterolytic fission: the breaking of a covalent bond in which one atom takes both electrons from the bond, forming a negative ion, and leaving behind a positive ion

Hexadentate ligand: a ligand forming six co-ordinate bonds with a transition element ion in a complex

Homogeneous catalysis: the type of catalysis in which the catalyst and reactants are in the same phase. For example, sulfuric acid catalysing the formation of an ester from an alcohol and carboxylic acid

Homologous series: a group of organic compounds having the same functional group, the same general formula and similar chemical properties

Homolytic fission: the breaking of a covalent bond in which each atom takes one electron from the bond to form free radicals

Hybridisation: the formation of a covalent bond by mixing different types of atomic orbitals. They are given the symbols sp, sp^2, sp^3, etc.

Hydrated salt: a salt which contains water of crystallisation

Hydrocarbon: a compound made up of carbon and hydrogen only

Hydrogen bonding: the strongest type of intermolecular force but weaker than covalent bonds. It is a strong type of pd-pd force.

Hydrolysed: undergoes hydrolysis

Hydrolysis: the breakdown of a compound by water. Hydrolysis is also used to describe the breakdown of a substance by dilute acids or alkali

Hydroxynitrile: an organic compound containing both an $-OH$ and a $-CN$ group

Ideal gas: a gas whose volume varies in proportion to the temperature and in inverse proportion to the pressure. Noble gases such as helium and neon approach ideal behaviour because of their low intermolecular forces

Independent variable: the variable under investigation for which we choose different values

Inductive effect: the uneven sharing of electrons along a covalent bond. Electron-donating species, such as an alkyl group, are said to have a positive inductive effect, whereas electron-withdrawing species, such as an oxygen atom, have a negative inductive effect

Infrared spectroscopy: a technique for identifying compounds based on the change in vibrations of particular atoms when infrared radiation of specific frequencies is absorbed

Initial rate (of reaction): the rate of reaction at the start of the experiment calculated from a tangent drawn to the curve at time zero

Initiation: the first step in the mechanism of free radical substitution of alkanes by halogens. It involves the breaking of the halogen–halogen bond using energy from ultra-violet light from the Sun

Instantaneous dipole-induce dipole forces (id-id forces): the weakest intermolecular attractive force. It results from temporary instantaneous dipoles induced in both polar and non-polar molecules. These forces are also called London dispersion forces

'In situ': latin words meaning 'in that place'. If we make a gas 'in situ', it means that we add the chemicals needed to make the gas to the test-tube of reactants. Adding zinc and acid to a reaction mixture gives off hydrogen, which can be used to reduce something else

Intermediate: a species, such as a carbocation, which is formed at a particular step of the reaction. Intermediates are stable enough to react with another substance but not stable enough to be a product. They often have a partial positive or negative charge

Iodoform test: a test for the presence of a CH_3CO- or $CH_3CH(OH)-$ group in a compound. A yellow precipitate is formed on warming these compounds with an alkaline solution of iodine

Ion: a substance formed when an atom or molecule gains or loses one or more electrons

Ionic bond: the electrostatic attraction between oppositely charged ions (cations and anons)

Ionic equation: a balanced equation showing only those ions, atoms or molecules taking part in the reaction. Spectator ions are not shown. Ionic equations are often written for reactions involving a change in oxidation state

Ionic product of water, K_w: the equilibrium constant for the ionisation of water. $K_w = [H^+][OH^-]$

Ion polarisation: the distortion of the electron cloud of an anion by a neighbouring cation. The distortion is greatest when the cation is small and highly charged.

Isotope: atoms of the same element with different mass numbers. They have the same number of protons but a different number of neutrons. Note that the word 'atom' is essential in this definition

Isotopic abundance: the proportion of each isotope contained in a sample of the element

Isoelectric point: the pH value at which there is no overall charge on a particular amino acid in its aqueous solution

K_c (equilibrium constant in terms of concentrations): constant calculated from the equilibrium expression using concentrations in mol dm^{-3}

Ketones: organic compounds with a C=O group in the middle of the carbon chain

K_p (equilibrium constant in terms of partial pressures): constant calculated from the equilibrium expression using partial pressures in kPa or atmospheres (atm)

Lattice: a regularly repeating arrangement of atoms, molecules or ions in three dimensions throughout the whole crystal structure

Lattice energy, $\Delta H^{\ominus}_{latt}$: the energy change when one mole of an ionic compound is formed from its gaseous ions under standard conditions. Strictly speaking, the values given usually refer to the lattice enthalpy rather than the lattice energy but the difference is usually not significant

Le Chatelier's principle: if one or more factors that affect a dynamic equilibrium is changed, the position of equilibrium moves to minimise this change

Ligand: a molecule or ion with one or more lone pairs of electrons which form dative covalent bonds to a central transition element atom or ion

Ligand exchange: in a complex ion, the substitution of one or more ligands by other ligands

Linkage group: the group of atoms formed when the functional groups of the monomers react e.g. the amide group in polyamides or the ester group in polyesters

Lithium tetrahydridoaluminate: the full chemical name for lithium aluminium tetrahydride, $LiAlH_4$. It is usually acceptable just to write $LiAlH_4$ if you cannot remember the name

London dispersion forces: another name for instantaneous dipole-induced dipole forces

Lone pairs (of electrons): pairs of electrons in the outer shell of an atom not involved in bonding

$M+1$ peak: the peak seen 1 unit to the right of the molecular ion peak due to the presence of the C-13 isotope

$M+2$ peak: the peak seen 2 units to the right of the molecular ion peak due to the presence of the Cl-37 or Br-81 isotope

Mass spectrometer: an instrument for finding the relative abundance of isotopes in an element or to help to identify organic compounds

Mass spectrum: the chart obtained from the mass spectrometer showing the I of the isotopic abundance on the y-axis and the mass / charge ratio of the particle on the x-axis

Mean: the average of the numbers taken from the data in a number of identical experiments

Mechanism of reaction: the individual steps in the reaction, showing the movement of electron pairs or production and movement of free radicals

Metallic radius: half the distance between the nuclei of two adjacent metal ions in a metallic structure

Mobile phase: the solvent used in chromatography, which moves along the paper, thin layer of aluminium oxide, or column containing liquid supported on a solid

Molar mass: the mass of a mole of substance in grams

Molecular formula: the formula that shows the number and type of each atom in a molecule, e.g. the molecular formula for ethanol is C_2H_6O

Molecular ion: the ion that is formed by the loss of an electron from the original complete molecule during mass spectrometry. This gives us the relative molecular mass of an unknown compound

Mole: the amount of substance which contains 6.02×10^{23} specified particles (atoms, molecules, ions or electrons)

Monodentate ligand: a ligand forming one co-ordinate bond with a transition element ion in a complex

Monomers: small molecules that react together to make long chain molecules (polymers)

Neutralisation: the reaction of an acid with an alkali to form a salt and water

Neutron: uncharged particle in the nucleus of an atom, with the same relative mass as a proton

Nitrating agent: a compound, or combination of compounds, that are responsible for inserting an NO_2 group into another molecule

Nitriles: organic compounds containing the CN functional group e.g. C_2H_5CN (propanenitrile)

NMR: an abbreviation for 'nuclear magnetic resonance', a type of spectroscopy used to determine the identity and structure of organic compounds

Non-degenerate orbitals: groups of atomic orbitals in the same sub-shell that have slightly different amounts of energy (splitting of orbitals)

Non-polar molecule: a molecule where the centres of positive and negative charge coincide

Nucleophile: species that can act as a donor of a pair of electrons

Nucleophilic addition: the mechanism of the reaction in which a nucleophile attacks the carbon atom in a carbonyl group and addition across the C=O bond occurs, e.g. aldehydes or ketones reacting with hydrogen cyanide

Nucleophilic substitution: the mechanism of the organic reaction in which a nucleophile attacks a carbon atom carrying a partial positive charge ($\delta+$). This results in the replacement of an atom carrying a partial negative charge ($\delta-$) by the nucleophile

Nucleus: the dense core at the centre of an atom containing neutrons (except the ^1H isotope) and protons

Observations: what you see happening (also includes what you hear, feel and smell)

Optical isomers: stereoisomers that exist as two non-superimposable mirror images

Order of reaction: the power to which the concentration of a reactant is raised in the rate equation. If a rate is directly proportional to concentration, it is first order – if the rate is directly proportional to the square of the concentration, it is second order

(Organic) synthesis: the series of steps taken to produce an organic product by changing functional groups or lengthening or shortening the carbon chain

Overall order (of reaction): the product of the individual orders of reaction of the reactants that appear in the rate equation, e.g. if the rate is first order with respect to A and first order with respect to B, the overall rate equation is k [A][B]

Oxidation: the loss of electrons from an atom, ion or molecule

Oxidation number (oxidation state): a number given to an atom or ion in a compound to show how oxidised or reduced it is

Oxidation number change: the increase or decrease in the oxidation number of a given atom in an equation, e.g. in $Fe + 2HCl \rightarrow FeCl_2 + H_2$ the oxidation number change of the Fe is $0 \rightarrow + 2 = + 2$

Oxidised form: in a half equation for a redox reaction, the species with the more positive (or less negative) oxidation number. e.g. Cu^{2+} in $Cu^{2+} + 2e^- \rightleftharpoons Cu$

Oxidising agent: a substance which brings about oxidation by removing electrons from another atom or ion

Partial pressure: pressure that a single gas contributes to the overall pressure in a mixture of gases. It is the proportion of the pressure exerted by a single gas in a mixture

Partition coefficient, K_{pc}: the ratio of the concentrations of a solute in two different immiscible solvents in contact with each other when equilibrium has been established (immiscible solvents are solvents which do not mix)

Peak (in infrared spectroscopy): the downward points in an infrared spectrum. Sometimes the points are widened

Peptide bond: the $-CONH-$ link (amide link) between amino acid residues in a peptide or protein

Percentage yield:

$$= \frac{\text{actual yield}}{\text{predicted yield}} \times 100$$

Periodicity: the repeating patterns in the physical and chemical properties of the elements across the periods of the Periodic Table

Permanent dipole-permanent dipole forces (pd-pd forces): attractive intermolecular forces which result from permanent dipoles in molecules

Photochemical smog: poisonous fog at low level caused by volatile organic compounds from car exhausts reacting with nitrogen oxides in the presence of sunlight

pH: the negative logarithm to the base 10 of the H^+ ion concentration

pH-titration curve: a curve of pH plotted against the volume of acid added to a base or base added to an acid. The exact shape of the curve depends on the strength of the acid and base

pi bond (π-bond): a covalent bond formed by 'sideways' overlap of p and p or p and d atomic orbitals

pK_a: $-\log_{10} K_a$ (where K_a is the acid dissociation constant)

Plane polarised light: light which vibrates only in one plane (imagine a waveform drawn on a piece of paper)

Polarimeter: an instrument used to measure the rotation of plane polarised light by a sample. (The sample is placed between 2 pieces of polaroid and rotated until the light-dark boundary is seen)

Polarisation: the ability of an ion or molecule to pull electrons in a covalent bond in an adjacent molecule towards it and so cause the adjacent molecule to become polar

Polarising power (of a cation): the ability of a cation to attract the electron cloud of an anion and distort it

Polarity: the degree to which a molecule is polarised so that one end is slightly $\delta+$ and the other is slightly $\delta-$

Polar (molecule): a molecule where the centres of positive and negative charge do not coincide, resulting in a dipole ($\delta+ \longleftrightarrow \delta-$) being formed

Polyamides: polymers made in the condensation polymerisation reaction between a diamine and a dicarboxylic acid (or a dioyl chloride) or between amino acids

Polyester: polymer whose monomers are bonded to each other via the ester link, COO

Polymer: a long-chain molecule made up of many repeating units derived from the monomers

Polypeptide: a polymer of many amino acids

Position isomers: isomers where the carbon chain or the functional group(s) are arranged in a different place. e.g. $CH_3CH_2CH_2CH_3$ and $CH_3CH(CH_3)CH_3$

Position of equilibrium: the relative amounts of products and reactants present in an equilibrium mixture

Precision (of measurements): measurements where sets of repeat readings are grouped closely together (even though they might not be close to the true value)

Primary amines: compounds where one hydrogen atom in ammonia has been substituted by an alkyl group

Primary alcohol: an alcohol in which the carbon atom bonded to the $-OH$ group is attached to one other carbon atom (or alkyl group)

Primary bromoalkane: a bromoalkane in which the carbon atom bonded to the $-Br$ group is attached to only one other carbon atom

Primary halogenoalkane: a halogenoalkane where the halogen atom is attached directly to a carbon atom which is attached to only one other carbon atom

Principal quantum shells: the main energy levels in the atoms where electrons have particular amounts of energy. The first quantum shell can hold a maximum of 2 electrons, the second 8 and the third 18

Progress of reaction: the extent to which the reactants are converted to products as the reaction proceeds

Propagation: the second step in a free-radical mechanism in which the radicals formed can then attack reactant molecules generating more free radicals, and so on

Propanal: an aldehyde with three carbon atoms

Protein: a condensation polymer formed from amino acids

Proton: positively charged particle in the nucleus of an atom

Qualitative tests: specific chemical tests used to determine the type of compounds, elements or ions present in a sample e.g. silver nitrate test for halide ions

Racemic mixture: a mixture containing equal amounts of a pair of enantiomers

Range (of indicator): the pH values between the pH at which an indicator starts to change colour and the pH at which the colour change is complete

Rate constant: the proportionality constant, k, in a rate equation

Rate-determining step: the slowest step in a reaction mechanism

Rate of reaction: the change in the amount or concentration of a particular reactant or product per unit time

Reaction pathway diagram: a diagram showing the relative enthalpies of the reactants (on the left) and the products (on the right) and the enthalpy change as an arrow. It may also include the activation energy.

Reduced form: in a half equation for a redox reaction, the species with the less positive (or more negative) oxidation number

Reducing agent: a substance which brings about reduction by donating (giving) electrons to another atom or ion

Reduction: the gain of electrons by an atom, ion or molecule

Reduction potential: another name for electrode potential

Refluxing: heating a flask connected to a condenser in the vertical position to minimise the loss of volatile chemical from the flask

Relative atomic mass, A_r: the weighted average mass of atoms in a given sample of an element compared to the value of the unified atomic mass unit

Relative electrical conductivity: the electrical conductivity of a substance compared with other substances e.g. good, poor, fairly good

Relative formula mass: the weighted average mass of one formula unit compared to the value of the unified atomic mass unit

Relative isotopic mass: the mass of a particular atom of an isotope compared to the value of the unified atomic mass unit

Relative molecular mass, M_r: the weighted average mass of a molecule in a given sample of that molecule compared to the value of the unified atomic mass unit

Repeat unit: the smallest group of atoms that when linked successively make up the whole polymer chain (apart from the two end units)

Resin: a solid or high viscosity liquid, either synthetic or obtained from plants, which can be made into polymers

Resonance frequency: the frequency of absorption of radiation which stimulates larger vibrations in bonds to allow the absorption of energy

Retention time: the time taken for a compound to travel through a chromatography column in GLC

Reversible reaction: a reaction in which products can be changed back to reactants by reversing the conditions

Roman numerals: numbers (I, II, III, IV etc.) used to indicate the oxidation state of the least electronegative element in a compound

R_f value (retention factor): in paper chromatography (or TLC), the ratio of the distance travelled by a specific component to the distance travelled by the solvent front

r.t.p.: room temperature and pressure (1 atmosphere / 101 kPa and 20 °C)

Salt: a substance formed when an acid reacts with a metal, an alkali, a metal oxide or a carbonate

Salt bridge: an inert material, e.g. filter paper, soaked in an ionic solution, e.g. KNO_3, which is used to make an electrical connection between two half-cells

Saturated hydrocarbons: compound of hydrogen and carbon only in which the carbon–carbon bonds are all single covalent bonds, resulting in the maximum number of hydrogen atoms in the molecule

Saturated solution: a solution which can dissolve no more solute at a particular temperature (in the presence of undissolved solute)

Secondary alcohol: an alcohol in which the carbon atom bonded to the −OH group is attached to two other carbon atoms (or alkyl groups)

Secondary amine: an amine formed when two of the hydrogen atoms in ammonia have been substituted by two alkyl groups

Secondary halogenoalkane: a halogenoalkane where the halogen atom is attached directly to a carbon atom which is attached to two other carbon atoms

Second electron affinity, EA_2: the enthalpy change when one mole of electrons is added to 1 mole of gaseous 1− ions to form one mole of gaseous 2− ions under standard conditions, $O^-(g) + e^- \rightarrow O^{2-}(g)$ EA_2

Second order reaction: rate is proportional to the product of two concentration terms, e.g. $[H^+]^2$ or $[H^+][Br^-]$

Sharp peak: a narrow pointed peak in an infrared spectrum

Shielding: the ability of inner shell electrons to reduce the effect of the nuclear charge on outer shell electrons

Sigma bond (σ-bond): a single covalent bond formed by the 'end-on' overlap of atomic orbitals

Simple molecular structure: molecules which are composed of atoms covalently bonded within the molecule but have weak intermolecular forces of attraction between the molecules. Crystalline solids can form lattices

Skeletal formula: a simplified displayed formula with all C and H atoms and C−H bonds removed

S_N1 mechanism: the steps in a nucleophilic substitution reaction in which the rate of the reaction (which is determined by the slow step in the mechanism) involves only the organic reactant, e.g. in the hydrolysis of a *tertiary* halogenoalkane

S_N2 mechanism: the steps in a nucleophilic substitution reaction in which the rate of the reaction (which is determined by the slow step in the mechanism) involves two reacting species, e.g. in the hydrolysis of a *primary* halogenoalkane

Solubility product, K_{sp}: the product of the concentrations of each ion in a saturated solution of a sparingly soluble salt at 298 K, raised to the power of their relative concentrations

Species: a particular atom, ion, molecule or electron

Specific heat capacity, c: the energy needed to raise the temperature of 1 g of a substance by 1°C (by 1 K)

Spectator ions: ions present in a reaction mixture which do not take part in the reaction

Spin-pair repulsion: a pair of electrons in the same orbital repel each other because they have the same charge. Pairing the spinning electrons so they spin in opposite directions reduces the repulsion. The repulsion is more than that of single electrons in separate orbitals. That is why the electrons in the p and d orbitals go into separate orbitals before being paired up

Splitting pattern: the series of peaks that main signals are divided into in high resolution NMR

Spontaneous change: a change which is statistically likely to occur

Stability constant, K_{stab}: the equilibrium constant for the formation of a complex ion in a solvent from its constituent ions or molecules

Stable (system): a system having a lower energy than another. The greater the entropy, the more stable is the system

Standard: when applied to electrodes, standard means the specific concentrations, temperature and pressure that apply

Standard conditions: a pressure of 101 kPa and temperature of 298 K, shown by $^\ominus$

Standard cell potential: the difference in electrode potential when two standard half-cells are connected

Standard electrode potential: the voltage produced when a standard half-cell (ion concentration 1.00 mol dm^{-3} at 298 K) is connected to a standard hydrogen electrode under standard conditions

Standard enthalpy change of combustion, $\Delta H_c^\ominus$: the enthalpy change when one mole of substance is burnt in excess oxygen under standard conditions

Standard enthalpy change of decomposition, $\Delta H_f^\ominus$: the enthalpy change when one mole of a substance is decomposed into products under standard conditions

Standard enthalpy change of formation, $\Delta H_f^\ominus$: the enthalpy change when one mole of compound is formed from its elements under standard conditions

Standard enthalpy change of hydration, $\Delta H_{hyd}^\ominus$: the enthalpy change when one mole of gaseous ions dissolves in sufficient water to form a very dilute solution under standard conditions

Standard enthalpy change of neutralisation, $\Delta H^{\ominus}_{neut}$: the enthalpy change when one mole of water is formed by the reaction of an acid with an alkali under standard conditions

Standard entropy change, $\Delta S^{\ominus}$: the change in entropy when the reactants form products at 298 K and 101 kPa (given by $\Sigma S^{\ominus}_{products} - \Sigma S^{\ominus}_{reactants}$)

Standard molar entropy: the entropy of a mole of a species under standard conditions of 101 kPa and 298 K

State symbol: in a chemical equation a symbol (sign) placed after each reactant and product in a chemical equation to indicate whether they are solid (s), liquid (l), gas (g) or in aqueous solution (aq)

States of matter: the three states of matter are solids, liquids and gases

Stationary phase: the immobile phase in chromatography that the mobile phase passes over or through. Examples are the surface of the thin-layer particles in TLC (thin-layer chromatography) or the non-volatile liquid absorbed onto the column in GLC.

Stereochemical formula: the formula showing the exact arrangement of atoms in space. A bond coming towards you is shown by a wedge of increasing size. A bond going away from you is shown by a dashed line

Stereoisomers: compounds whose molecules have the same atoms bonded to each other in the same way but with a different arrangement of atoms in space so that the molecules cannot be superimposed on each other. (Superimposed means that however you turn the isomer, the atoms are never in exactly the same place – like your hands.)

Stoichiometry: the mole ratios of reactants and products shown in a balanced equation

Strong acids and bases: acid and bases which dissociate completely in solution

Strong peak: the peak goes down a long way on the absorbance scale in the infrared spectrum

Structural formula: the formula that shows how many, and the symbols of, atoms bonded to each carbon atom in an organic molecule e.g. $CH_3CH(OH)$, $CH_2{=}CH_2$

Structural isomers: compounds with the same molecular formula but different structural formulae

Sub-shells (subsidiary quantum shells): regions of the principal quantum shells where electrons exist in defined areas associated with particular amounts of energy. They are named s, p, d, etc.

Substitution: a reaction that involves the replacement of one atom, or group of atoms, by another

Successive ionisation energies: the energy required in each step to remove the first electron, then the second, then the third, and so on from a gaseous atom or ion, e.g. IE_1, IE_2, IE_3. Note: you should be able to write equations for each of these steps

Superimposable (images): all parts of one image can be placed exactly in the same place as all parts of another

Surroundings: anything other than the reactants and products in a chemical reaction, e.g. solvent, reaction vessel

System: the reactants and products of a chemical reaction

Systematic names: the names given by the International Union of Pure and Applied Chemistry to name chemical compounds

Target molecule: in organic synthesis, the molecule that you want to make

Termination: the final steps in a free-radical mechanism in which two free radicals react together to form a product molecule

Tertiary alcohol: an alcohol in which the carbon atom bonded to the $-OH$ group is attached to three other carbon atoms (or alkyl groups)

Tertiary bromoalkane: a bromoalkane in which the carbon atom bonded to the $-Br$ group is attached to three other carbon atoms

Tertiary halogenoalkane: a halogenoalkane where the halogen atom is attached to a carbon atom which is attached directly to three other carbon atoms

Thermal decomposition: the breakdown of a compound by heat into two or more different substances

Titration: a method for finding the amount of substance in a solution by reaction with a known amount of another substance. An indicator is used to show when the substances have reacted exactly (in the correct stoichiometric amounts)

TLC (thin-layer chromatography): a type of chromatography in which the stationary phase is a solid such as alumina which adsorbs the solute molecules to different extents

TMS: an abbreviation for tetramethylsilane, $Si(CH_3)_4$, the standard compound used in NMR spectroscopy, providing the peak to measure chemical shifts relative to its given value of zero

Tollens' reagent: an aqueous solution of silver nitrate in excess aqueous ammonia used to distinguish between aldehydes and ketones. A 'silver mirror' is formed when aldehydes are warmed with the reagent. No change is observed when ketones are warmed with the reagent

Transition element: a d-block element that forms one or more stable ions with incomplete d-orbitals

Unified atomic mass unit: one twelfth of the mass of a carbon-12 atom

Unsaturated hydrocarbons: compounds of hydrogen and carbon only whose molecules contain carbon-to-carbon double bonds (or triple bonds)

Van der Waals' forces: weak forces of attraction between molecules involving either instantaneous (id-id) or permanent dipole-permanent dipole forces (pd-pd) (including hydrogen bonding). The expression covers all types of intermolecular forces

Valence shell electron pair repulsion (VSEPR) theory: two lone pairs of electrons repel each other more than a lone pair and a bonding pair. Two bonding pairs of electrons repel each other even less

VOCs (volatile organic compounds): organic compounds (often hydrocarbons) with low boiling points which are produced in car engines or manufacturing sources. They react with nitrogen oxides and ozone to form photochemical smog

Volatile: easily turned into vapour when the temperature is increased. Volatile liquids have low boiling points

Volatility: the ease with which a substance evaporates. A volatile substance will evaporate at a low temperature

Weak acids and bases: acid and bases which dissociate partially (incompletely) in solution

Zero order reaction: reaction in which rate does not depend on concentration

Zwitterion: a molecule with two or more functional groups, one or more with a positive charge and one or more with a negative charge